SOCIAL RELATIONS IN LATER PREHISTORY

Social Relations in Later Prehistory

Wessex in the First Millennium BC

NIALL SHARPLES

OXFORD

UNIVERSITY PRESS

OXFORD
UNIVERSITY PRESS

Great Clarendon Street, Oxford OX2 6DP

Oxford University Press is a department of the University of Oxford.
It furthers the University's objective of excellence in research, scholarship,
and education by publishing worldwide in

Oxford New York

Auckland Cape Town Dar es Salaam Hong Kong Karachi
Kuala Lumpur Madrid Melbourne Mexico City Nairobi
New Delhi Shanghai Taipei Toronto

With offices in

Argentina Austria Brazil Chile Czech Republic France Greece
Guatemala Hungary Italy Japan Poland Portugal Singapore
South Korea Switzerland Thailand Turkey Ukraine Vietnam

Oxford is a registered trade mark of Oxford University Press
in the UK and in certain other countries

Published in the United States
by Oxford University Press Inc., New York

British Library Cataloguing in Publication Data

Data available

Library of Congress Cataloging in Publication Data

Data available

Typeset by SPI Publisher Services, Pondicherry, India
Printed in Great Britain
on acid-free paper by
MPG Book Group

ISBN 978–0–19–957771–2 (Hbk.)

3 5 7 9 10 8 6 4 2

Contents

List of Figures

List of Tables

Acknowledgements

The lengthy gestation of this book means that many people have influenced me and need to be thanked; it also means that I am quite likely to forget individuals who have made me rethink my position. I will start off with some general thanks and work towards the more specific. My interest in the Iron Age was encouraged by Leslie Alcock, whose questioning intelligence has in many ways influenced the way I approach archaeology. These early interests were further stimulated by Mike Parker Pearson, who provided early access to theory as well as a range of ideas about later prehistory. I met him on my first trip to the region, when I dug at South Lodge in Cranborne Chase, and he came to help with the excavations at Maiden Castle and has made detailed comments on the contents of this book. Richard Hingley has similarly helped reconfigure my ideas on later prehistory in a more theoretical manner, and I have always enjoyed his idiosyncratic approach to archaeology, and his influence should be readily apparent throughout this text. In recent years I have been lucky to teach a number of exceptional students. Kate Waddington and Olly Davis have been subjected to my rather strange ideas on the first millennium for some time now, and I have benefited immeasurably from their own quite different perspectives on the period.

The full text has been read by Richard Bradley, Mary Davis, Colin Haselgrove, Alasdair Whittle, and Kate Waddington, and one anonymous reader for Oxford University Press; their comments and criticism have been immensely useful. Dave Field and Mark Bowden were kind enough to comment on Chapter 2. The early work on Chapter 3 benefited from being delivered and published as a short paper at the Durham conference, and comments by Chris Gosden and corrections by Ruth Davis were particularly helpful. Chapter 4 benefited from comments by Mike Parker Pearson, Richard Hingley, and Richard Harrison, and in its initial formation was heavily influenced by conversations with Jo Brück and Fokke Gerritsen. Chapter 5 benefited from comments by J. D. Hill, Dani Hoffmann, Jacqui McKinley, and Richard Madgwick.

The illustrations could not have been produced without the help of Ian Dennis and Kate Waddington. Professor B. W. Cunliffe has granted permission for the reproduction of material used in Figures 3.15, 3.16, 3.24, 4.7, and 5.8. Professor M. G. Fulford and the Society for the Promotion of Roman Studies have granted permission for the use of material used in Figures 3.17, 3.23, and 3.25. Professor W. Hanson has granted permission for the use of material in Figure 4.6. Professor D. W. Harding and The Hawkes Archive,

Institute of Archaeology, University of Oxford have given permission for the reproduction of the images used in Figure 4.9. The British Museum has granted permission to use Figure 3.18. The Dorset Natural History and Archaeological Society at the Dorset County Museum has granted permission for the reproduction of the images used in Figure 5.11. English Heritage has granted permission for the reproduction of material used in Figures 2.4, 2.6, 2.17, 3.13, 3.16, 3.17, and 5.6. The Hayling Island Excavation project has granted permission for the use of Figure 3.21. Oxford Archaeology has granted permission for the use of material in Figures 2.26, 3.4, and 4.13. The Prehistoric Society has granted permission for the use of material in Figure 4.12. The Society of Antiquaries of London has granted permission to reproduce the photographs used for Figures 3.7 and 5.19. Wessex Archaeology has granted permission for the reproduction of material used in Figures 3.11, 3.12, 5.1, and 5.15. akg-images London has granted permission for the use of Figure 5.2. Crown copyright material is reproduced under Class Licence number C2006000011 with the permission of OPSI and the Queen's printer for Scotland.

Finally, I would again like to thank Mary Davis, who has been forced to read more about later prehistory than anyone ever should be. She has provided tremendous support and much needed help and advice throughout the writing process.

1

Introduction

This book covers the first millennium BC in central southern Britain, or Wessex, a period and an area of considerable importance in understanding the evolution of human society in north-west Europe. Wessex is one of the most intensively studied areas in European prehistory and has a rich and varied archaeological record that provides a finely textured view of a past society that is just beyond the reach of the historical sources.

This book was begun a long time ago and has emerged due to a number of different stimuli. My first significant involvement with Wessex was as a result of my employment as Director of the English Heritage excavations at Maiden Castle in Dorset.[1] During this period I lived in Dorset and became very familiar with the archaeology of this county and the neighbouring county of Wiltshire. The excavations were written up promptly (Sharples 1991a, 1991c) and I was also able to produce a couple of short papers (Sharples 1990b, 1991b) on related issues. These papers were part of a series of publications that came to define a new archaeological understanding of the first millennium BC. They provide a context for the creation of this book that is worth exploring.

In the middle of the 1980s, understanding of the Iron Age of Wessex was dominated by the views of Professor Cunliffe, which were widely disseminated in a range of publications, but most comprehensively in his book *Iron Age Communities in Britain* (Cunliffe 1991, 2005). He presented a picture of Iron Age society where dominant elites lived within hillforts and each hillfort controlled a clearly defined territory. These permanently occupied settlements acted as central places that absorbed cereals and animal products from dependent communities in the surrounding landscape and exchanged these

---

[1] I was not born or brought up in the region. I first visited the area in 1977, when I was a student doing archaeology at Glasgow University. I returned in 1979 to dig with John Barrett and Richard Bradley on Cranborne Chase and was offered the job of Director of the Maiden Castle excavations in 1985. I spent four years living in Dorchester and became very attached to the landscape and the archaeology of that county. I will always be attracted to the region because of this work, and the area competes in my affection with the islands of Atlantic Scotland.

basic foodstuffs for materials not available in the region. The communities in hillforts controlled contact with neighbouring territories and were closely tied to ports, through which Continental trade was channelled. As the Iron Age progressed, the territories become larger and the hillforts become fewer until distinct tribal units ruled by kings become recognizable in the Late Iron Age.

This model was attacked as soon as it was proposed,[2] but it was only in the late 1980s and 1990s that it was subject to a detailed and sustained level of critique that could not be ignored. A large number of archaeologists examined a wide range of aspects that seemed to be problematic: the most important papers were by Bowden and McOmish (1987), Hill (1989, 1993, 1995a, 1995b, 1996), Hingley (1984, 1990a, 1990b), Marchant (1989), Sharples (1990b, 1991b), and Stopford (1987). Hill has been one of the most vociferous in his criticism of the established model. In his first paper he effectively challenged the concept of a pan-European Celtic society that can be understood only by detailed reading of classical and medieval Irish texts (Hill 1989). He argued that there were significant differences between the societies presented in these texts and the society visible in Iron Age Wessex. Furthermore, he argued that the privileging of historical sources was unjustified and that anthropological analogies would be more informative. He also emphasized the importance of 'difference'; the Iron Age should not be regarded as a familiar, simplified version of the recent rural societies of Western Europe.

Hill was also very important in focusing attention on the nature of deposition in the period (Hill 1995b). His analysis of the material found in the pits and enclosure ditches of settlements, such as Winnall Down and Gussage All Saints, demonstrated that what had been assumed to be rubbish was in fact carefully selected and placed material that provided an important insight into Iron Age belief systems. Locations inside and outside the settlements were categorized by the material that was buried, and a careful structure was applied to the manner of deposition and the depositional association of each artefact category. This again emphasized that Iron Age society could not simply be read as a system functioning to provide food and shelter in the most efficient manner.

The bulk of critical attention has, however, been concerned with the mechanics of the Cunliffe model and in particular the function and status of hillforts. Bowden and McOmish (1987) and Hingley (1984) convincingly demonstrated that the argument that hillfort boundaries simply acted to

---

[2] The most obvious critical response to the overall approach was a review volume edited by John Collis (1977a) and the reviews of the Danebury excavation report by Haselgrove (1986).

defend/protect the higher status groups, living inside their ramparts, was a naive and inadequate explanation. Hingley argued that the emphasis should be on how communities attempted to define their boundaries and on whether settlement was organized in a dispersed or agglomerated basis. The act of enclosure can then be argued to project the nature of social relationships within and between communities. Bowden and McOmish demonstrated that the ramparts and ditches around many hillforts were so complicated as to undermine any defensive function. They suggested that a ritual function was a more appropriate interpretation of many of these hillfort enclosures.

Both Stopford (1987) and Marchant (1989) have shown that the belief that hillforts had high status occupants and distinctive economic functions was misleading. Cunliffe had argued quite specifically that hillforts had a specialized role in the production of textiles (Cunliffe 1983: 145, 1984a: 32) and this argument was shown to be quite erroneous. The site in Wessex with the best evidence for textile production is Winnall Down, an otherwise relatively impoverished small enclosure (Fasham 1985). It is similarly clear that metalworking, another supposedly high status activity, was not taking place on hillforts with any great frequency. Gussage All Saints, another small enclosure, has the best evidence for prestige metalworking in southern Britain (Foster 1980; Wainwright 1979a). Stopford (1987) also suggested that hillforts may be seasonally occupied with activities concentrating on the processing and storage of grain in the autumn.

My own contribution to this debate was twofold. As a result of my experience excavating Maiden Castle, I argued that the hillforts of Wessex were not a single phenomenon (Sharples 1991b). There were many different types of monument that progressed through a variety of forms; and at Maiden Castle the occupation was effectively organized into four separate and quite distinct periods. I also challenged the accepted economic explanation of continental trade and the significance of sites such as Hengistbury Head (Sharples 1990b). Trade must be understood in the context of the development of communities on this side of the Channel. It is not sensible to assume that the importation of Gaulish and Roman material culture was simply the result of Roman policy.

In the period following these critiques there was a series of papers that attempted to provide alternative models for the understanding of the Iron Age. Fitzpatrick (1994), Hingley (1990a), Parker Pearson (1996) and Oswald (1997) have placed particular emphasis on the house as a metaphor for society (see Chapter 3 for a fuller discussion). Hill (1995b) and Hingley (1990b) have examined artefact deposition and how this can illuminate belief systems, and Hingley (1997) was also concerned with the symbolic nature of metalworking. These new perspectives often used a very simplistic form of structural Marxism as the fundamental theoretical underpinning for the analysis. None of them was particularly concerned with explaining cultural change, and there is often an assumption in much of the writing that the behaviour observed remained the same from the origin of the Iron Age (if not before) through to changes indicated by the influence of Rome at the end of the Iron Age.

Essentially their critique was a post-processual attack on the processual framework, and this is one way of characterizing this book. The critique replicates similar critiques that originated in Cambridge (Hodder 1982) and which had dominated the study of early prehistory (Neolithic and Early Bronze Age) during the 1980s.[3] At that time it seemed likely that a new synthetic account of later prehistory would soon appear but, for a number of reasons, this did not happen.[4]

In the early 1990s I was working in Scotland and my involvement in this debate was minimal. However, in 1995 I was appointed as a lecturer at Cardiff University with a specialist interest in later prehistory; I regained a direct interest in the later prehistory of southern England, and a much more focused interest in the later Bronze Age. Lectures had to be written, book lists had to be organized and a considerable amount of reading was required. The importance of Cunliffe's magisterial synthesis of the Iron Age became more and more apparent. It provided a ready source of detailed evidence that was otherwise unavailable in an organized and synthesized fashion. Whilst this increased my respect for the prodigious effort involved, it also undermined my attempts to present an alternative perspective on the period. The dispersed nature of the critical literature and its frequently limited scope and skimpy detail left many students distinctly under-whelmed. Teaching was improved by the publication of *Reconstructing Iron Age Societies* (Gwilt and Haselgrove 1997), but this was not the comprehensive review of the Iron Age that could be presented as an alternative to *Iron Age Communities*.

In the academic year 1998–9 I was fortunate to be given a year off teaching, which allowed me to take stock of the vast amount of later prehistoric texts

[3] I had a peripheral role in the reorientation of Neolithic studies and knew some of the Cambridge protagonists quite well so I was not unaware of these developments when I wrote the Maiden Castle volume. However, my primary interest, prior to my involvement with the Maiden Castle project, was the Neolithic period, and I was happier writing about this in a more theoretically aware fashion when I came to writing the report.

[4] In contrast, the post-processual analysis of Neolithic society has resulted in a number of broad synthetic accounts of British prehistory, most noticeably by J. Thomas (1999) and Edmonds (1999), both of which are dominated by the archaeology of southern England.

that I had been rather energetically reading over the last four years. In the latter part of this sabbatical I decided that I was as well qualified to write a book on the Iron Age as anyone else, and that as many of the other principal candidates appeared to be losing interest in the project, it was probably as much my responsibility as anyone else's. Nevertheless, the task was clearly not going to be achieved in the near future. In the time remaining in this sabbatical I started work but only got as far as writing drafts for two chapters and thinking about a third.

My first concern was the importance of Iron Age houses,[5] and I was stimulated by an invitation to speak at a conference organized by the Prehistoric Society in London. The conference was on the transition from the Late Bronze Age to the Early Iron Age; I had been asked to speak about hillforts but none of the speakers talked about houses, which seemed an important topic.[6] During this period I also did a lot of writing on the subject of gift exchange in both the Iron Age and the Bronze Age. This research was used in a paper I delivered at a conference in Dublin and then again in the Earlier Iron Age conference in Durham, which was subsequently published (Sharples in Haselgrove and Pope 2007). These two papers effectively form the core of Chapters 3 and 4, though a considerable amount of rewriting has taken place and much additional information has been added to make them fit the parameters of this volume.

I began to think about the nature of individuality (Chapter 5) during this sabbatical, but it was not until I was invited back to Ireland (Cork and Dublin this time) that I began to get a grip on the issues involved. However, most of the detailed analysis of burials presented in this chapter was created during the academic year 2006–7 when I was fortunate to receive a Leverhulme award for a second sabbatical. These ideas were further developed by a Cambridge seminar in the winter of 2006. The second sabbatical allowed me to do the bulk of the work on the text of this volume and by the end of 2007 a complete draft of the principal chapters was sent to Oxford University Press, who were interested in my proposal. Needless to say, it has still taken some time for the book to be completed as changes had to be made, illustrations commissioned and introductions and conclusions written.

---

[5] My interest in roundhouses had been stimulated by work on the Iron Age of Atlantic Scotland where the significance of monumental roundhouses is a central problem (Sharples 2004, 2006).

[6] The paper was well received and in the discussion I was introduced to Jo Brück, who was then just finishing her important paper on Bronze Age houses (Brück 1999), which duplicated much of what I had to say and absolved me from the necessity of rushing into print.

A PERIOD IN TIME

The primary focus of this book is the transformations that occurred within Britain in the first millennium BC. This period is marked by the major technological change from bronze to iron, and I will demonstrate that this technological change coincides with, and indeed is fundamentally connected to, a major transformation of society. The principal archaeological change at this time is the transformation from a dispersed society of individual houses, scattered across a landscape of fields, to large densely occupied permanent settlements that are contained by substantial boundaries—hillforts. Hillforts are the first permanent settlements not occupied by single families, but instead by communities, whose kinship is likely to be tenuous at best (see below). Large gatherings of people in earlier periods were probably seasonal and reflected either religious festivals, or work programmes designed to undertake a specific task.

The desire to come together as a large community was the result of significant external pressures. However, living in large communities required the individuals involved to learn how to react to routine encounters with people whose relationships were not structured by the deference built up from known kinship affiliations. Daily interactions require complex negotiation and the creation of learning contexts to create roles, and form attitudes, that allow the day-to-day intermingling of people who know very little about each other. These processes are very important in providing a framework for the development of the complex tribal societies that emerged prior to the Roman conquest. A key factor in the development of these societies is the development of leaders who had the support of individuals within communities that were only loosely connected by ties of kinship.

In the Early Iron Age these relationships were organized through the monumental construction of boundaries that both created and defined the community, but in the final two centuries of the first millennium BC, the specialist production of elaborate metalwork and the development of ceramic industries become increasingly important. These industries were to be of considerable importance in the development of the Roman province of Britannia, but they precede the direct influence of Rome. The increasing importance of the distribution of raw materials and objects coincides with the development of coinage, and in the last century hundreds of thousands of coins were probably circulating in southern England.

This book consciously avoids an extensive examination of the historical sources for first millennium BC Britain for a number of reasons. First, the limited and quite specific sources that reference Britain directly are likely to be relevant only to a short period of the first century BC and the first century AD. The important changes that are visible in the archaeological record suggest this period is quite different from the previous centuries, and even within this period there are dramatic changes between the middle of the first century BC, when the first direct contact with the Roman empire occurs, and the Roman invasion in AD 43 (Mattingly 2006). Second, many of the sources used to characterize the prehistoric societies of the first millennium are generic sources that derive from supposedly related 'Celtic' societies that are either spatially separate from the British mainland by some distance,[7] or derive from chronologically much later societies in adjacent areas of the British Isles, such as Ireland and Scotland.[8] In both situations the archaeological record for the society is quite different from that which characterizes the prehistoric societies of southern Britain. These societies may be linguistically related but it is clear that there are important differences in the structure of social relations, in particular the importance placed on community and the relative role of individuals. As this book sets out to explore precisely these aspects of difference, it seems counterproductive to emphasize these sources.

Until recently the narrative of British prehistory has been structured around three fundamental transformations in the technology of artefact production: stone, bronze, and iron. It has, however, been recognized that the first period was divided by some fundamental differences; first between our early ancestral hominids, in the early and middle Palaeolithic, and fully developed humans in the upper Palaeolithic, and then between societies organized around hunting and gathering, in the Mesolithic, and the later societies organized around the exploitation of domestic plants and animals, of the Neolithic. These clearly indicated that within a technological stage there were complex changes that may indeed be more significant than the basic and easily visible change in the materials used to produce tools. This is true also for our understanding of the later prehistory of the British Isles. For example, it has become clear that one of the primary transformations of the archaeological record occurred between the Early Bronze Age and the Middle Bronze Age (around 1500 BC). At this point in time the inhabitants of the British Isles become markedly less concerned with the construction and maintenance of

---

[7] Some of the most important sources on the Celts come from the descriptions by Livy and Polybius of the Celtic invasion of the Italian peninsula. This had a traumatic effect on Rome and coloured their view of the Celts from that point onwards (Rankin 1987).

[8] The most recent attempt to reassess the relevance of the Irish sources came out just as this book was being completed (Karl 2008), and though this article is a relatively sophisticated analysis of the Irish sources it adopts an interpretation of the Wessex Iron Age, by J. D. Hill, which I hope to demonstrate is misleading and simplistic.

religious monuments (stone circles and alignments, henge monuments, and burial monuments) and commenced the construction of monuments that appear to have had a more prosaic role in the lives of people (field boundaries and houses). These changes coincided with major changes in the use of material culture. There is an increase in the importance of metal technologies to create objects such as tools, weapons, and ornaments that were actively used to define status and gender distinctions. As metal technologies became more widely available the complex stone and ceramic technologies of the Early Bronze Age declined dramatically and much of the elaborate ornamentation that was visible in these media disappears to be replaced by functional but comparatively crude pots and primitive stone tools.

These important changes have been interpreted as a fundamental transformation of British society from one structured around ancestors—where an individual's daily life involved moving long distances across landscapes following herds, attending communal gatherings (religious festivals) organized around important solar events, and conducting elaborate ritual ceremonies that commemorate the dead—to a society settled in permanent houses, in a landscape controlled by boundaries, and where ritual was embedded into the daily, weekly and yearly cycles of an agricultural regime that was increasingly dominated by crop production. In the later period people lived as individual households separated from their neighbours, but they worked together as communities linked by kinship relations and connected to other communities by the exchange of gifts (primarily metalwork). Some people now came together in building projects that subdivided and organized the landscape. This transformation has been summarized as a move from a ritual landscape to a domestic landscape, though this is a vast oversimplification of the changes taking place (Barrett 1994a).

This book will not deal in detail with that major transformation of British society; instead, it will focus on how the domestic societies that were created in the second millennium BC developed before the Roman conquest. However, some aspects of this early transformation will be discussed, such as the development of field systems and houses, as it is otherwise difficult to understand the later developments. Nor will there be any detailed analysis of the Roman conquest of Britain, since this again is peripheral to the major focus of interpretation and would involve a considerable extension of the book to deal with adequately. Nevertheless, it is important to question the effect the Romans had on British society in the first century BC / AD. Often the tendency has been to interpret these societies in terms of what they become; the importance of Roman influence and preliminary colonization is to my mind over-emphasized by many authors.

WHY WESSEX?

There has frequently been a concern amongst British archaeologists that the Iron Age of Wessex has an all pervasive and deleterious impact on studies of the rest of Britain. This was most forcefully expressed by Bill Bevan (1999a) in his introduction to the book *Northern Exposure*. He was concerned to demonstrate that there was a tendency to frame discussion of later prehistory throughout Britain in terms of the 'descriptions and images borne out of the archaeological study of Wessex, south-east England and the Thames Valley' (Bevan 1999a: 1). There was 'a Wessex dominated conceptualization of later prehistory in Britain where interpretations of many northern and western regions are based upon taxonomic comparisons with dated Iron Age sites in the south of Britain' (Bevan 1999a: 2).

I do not dispute the reality of this statement. Wessex has dominated the literature of later prehistory and to an even greater extent the archaeology of early prehistory, and I have previously argued (Sharples 1996) that the application of a Wessex-centred model of prehistory was seriously detrimental to the development of Scottish archaeology. To some people the dominance of Wessex has led to contempt for the region, and on numerous occasions when I mentioned I was working on a book on the later prehistory of Wessex they have responded with derogatory comments about the area being too well known to provide anything new to say, and asked why I would want to work on this area when there was so much more to be written about elsewhere. The latter point has some truth in it; there are many areas of Britain that have not been studied in great detail and where exciting new syntheses are crying out to be written. Unfortunately, I have never worked in these areas and to understand them would require not only intensive study but a long period of occupation, which I feel is the only way to understand the landscape and the archaeology of a region.

The first point has much less validity, and I was often amazed by the eminence and intelligence of the people who made this suggestion. For most of the twentieth century Wessex was the centre of archaeological interest in Britain; most excavations synonymous with later prehistoric Britain took place in this region and the monuments found here are renowned throughout Europe. Most of the famous archaeologists who worked on British prehistory worked in the region. Several were brought up there and had an emotional attachment to the landscape that is apparent in their work; Pitt Rivers owned the Rushmore Estates in Cranborne Chase, Piggott was brought up in Petersfield on the Hampshire–Sussex border, Hawkes went to school at

Winchester, Cunliffe and Bradley were schoolboy enthusiasts in West Sussex, Collis was a Winchester schoolchild (though of the town not the school). All these people surveyed monuments, excavated sites, worked on the material record and developed their understanding of archaeology in this region, and this has coloured their view of the rest of Britain. However, before we condemn this as a conspiracy perhaps we should try to understand what it is about Wessex that encouraged the emerging discipline of archaeology.

One of the most important features of the archaeological record of Wessex is that it is very visible and well defined. In contrast to most of southern Britain this is a rural area, which at the beginning of the twentieth century had not been extensively cultivated. Much of the region is relatively high ground and the severity of the winter climate and the poor quality of the soils on the chalk downlands discouraged cereal cultivation. As a consequence most of the landscape was given over to sheep grazing, probably since the end of the Roman period. This is perhaps the single most important point that made the prehistoric archaeology of the region so important in the early twentieth century. A landscape existed that was a palimpsest of Neolithic, Bronze Age and Iron Age monuments, which in most other areas of southern Britain had been destroyed and were almost impossible to identify. Furthermore, the archaeological record was characterized by a range of monuments of impressive size and enigmatic character that were exceptional in a British context. There are few sites to compare in grandeur with Maiden Castle, Stonehenge or Avebury. The prevalence and quality of these monuments encouraged explanation and interpretation that was much more detailed than that possible in other regions. Most of the lowlands of southern Britain had been extensively ploughed in the medieval period and the limited patches of upland, such as Dartmoor and the Welsh borders, were not comparable to the more benign landscapes of Wessex. They do not have the longevity and density of occupation that this region has. The potential of the archaeological record of eastern England, for example, was completely misunderstood for most of the twentieth century because it had been systematically destroyed by Roman, medieval and post-medieval agriculture. In 1959 it was still commonly believed that the river valleys were forested swamps that were essentially unoccupied (Hawkes, C. F. C. 1959). It was only the systematic application of aerial photography in the latter half of the century that revealed the presence of complex prehistoric landscapes, as complex if not more so, than those visible in Wessex. Extensive excavation of these landscapes had to wait until the end of the century and the introduction of developer-funded work in advance of housing developments, road schemes and gravel quarries. There is currently much more archaeological work in the eastern river valleys as a result of these developments than in rural Wessex.

The archaeology of Wessex also has several other characteristics that encourage interest and provide added value. The chalk soils, whilst harsh and relatively infertile, are very good at preserving certain categories of archaeological finds, most notably animal and human bone.[9] Bone was used to produce a range of artefacts during later prehistory, and these are clearly an important medium for personal and cultural expression during this period. The burial record of the inhabitants is also well preserved and provides a crucial record of human behaviour and ultimately the ideology of the inhabitants of the area. Finally, the presence of large animal bone assemblages provides not only detailed evidence for the farming economy but also crucial information on the ritual practice and ideology of the inhabitants. Bone only survives in calcareous environments, which normally reflects an underlying geology of chalk or limestone. These landscapes have a very restricted distribution and almost all mainland Scotland and most of northern England have very poor preservation of bone, which severely limits archaeological understanding of these regions.

An important feature of the archaeological record of Wessex is the presence of large assemblages of pottery. It is a strange and so far unexplained feature of the first millennium BC, that only the south and east of England, and the Atlantic Fringe, manufacture and use ceramics on a regular basis (Cunliffe 2005: fig. 5.11). Up until the Early Bronze Age all of Britain had ceramic industries that were producing pots of the highest quality, and the assemblage of Beaker pots from north-east Scotland is as good as anywhere in the country. But for some reason during the Middle Bronze Age pot use declines sharply throughout the country, and it only continues as an important craft activity during the Late Bronze Age and Iron Age in the south and east. It would appear that the north and west relied on organic materials such as wood, leather, and baskets for containers, but unfortunately the recovery of these is restricted to waterlogged conditions, which are very rare. Wessex is doubly fortunate in having a rich ceramic record, which underwent significant change during the first millennium BC. These changes enabled antiquaries and early archaeologists to subdivide the archaeological record into periods, and to explore chronological change at a level that was not possible for most of Britain, and which is still not possible for many regions (Haselgrove *et al.* 2001).

The archaeology of any region is unique and provides its own individual contribution to our understanding of Britain. No region should be prioritized above another, because the narrative for each region is different, and it is the

---

[9] Bone is normally well preserved on the chalk but the surrounding gravels and the clay with flint overlying the chalk generally have very poor preservation of bone.

difference that creates the archaeological record. This is particularly the case in later prehistory. However, it is clear that the variety and complexity of the archaeology of Wessex proved attractive to earlier archaeologists and provided the individuals working in this region with the intellectual and archaeological resources to present a holistic view of British prehistory. For most of the twentieth century the goal was not to emphasize difference, but to generalize. This directly reflected the limited amount of information that was available. The necessity was to create a chronological structure that would enable future generations to examine difference, and in this they were successful.

This history of exploration also favours a contemporary examination of the archaeology of Wessex because it provides a resource that many other regions lack. The availability of large amounts of information that results from the long history of excavation, survey, and collection obviously creates an immensely valuable resource. Ideas and arguments of considerable significance to the development of prehistory have been developed using the evidence from this region, and this encourages people to engage with controversy at a very basic level.

2

The Landscape Context

The archaeological landscape of Wessex is one of the best known in Europe. There are very few students of archaeology who have not been taken to see sites such as Stonehenge, Avebury, Maiden Castle, and Danebury. Most archaeology departments insist that an in-depth knowledge of the region is essential for the training of an archaeologist, and as a student at Glasgow in the 1970s, one of the most distant departments from the region, it was considered a prerequisite for me to visit Wessex. I was loaded on to a coach and after a long journey I arrived at Devizes, where we stayed for a week of site and museum visits. I remember very little of what we saw, certainly the sites named above, but I do remember that I was tremendously excited by certain road signs. As we drove across the landscape I was confronted by names that were exotically familiar: All Cannings Cross, Gussage All Saints, Tollard Royal, and Overton Down. These names were exotic, particularly for a northerner brought up on names like Milngavie and Auchenshuggle, but very familiar since they cropped up frequently in the lectures and text books that were a feature of my course. It should be stressed that this course was untouched by the new ideas of statistical and behavioural studies that were so popular in other universities. My lectures were dominated by site and sequence and at this time, the late seventies, the sites that were available to us were the sites of Wessex that had been excavated and published by the great excavators of the previous generation.[1]

Today I am regularly involved in two trips to the region for the under-graduates studying archaeology at Cardiff University. The first trip involves a visit to the hillforts of Maiden Castle and South Cadbury and the chalk figure at Cerne Abbas. These visits are very site focused and involve standing around listening to me giving a lecture on the context of hillforts—when they were built, what they were for, their distribution and the specific sequence of the

---

[1] I was introduced to the study of hillforts by the first year lectures of my Professor at Glasgow, Leslie Alcock. He had undertaken extensive excavations at South Cadbury (Alcock 1972) and was then still actively involved in the post-excavation analysis of the site. He had worked for Sir Mortimer Wheeler and had taught Geoff Wainwright, so he routinely referenced the excavations at Maiden Castle and Gussage All Saints.

particular site we are visiting. This approach is perfectly legitimate and provides a useful tool for informing students about the important monument types that dominate the study of British prehistory. However, it divorces the monument from the context of its creation and creates the perception that Wessex is an open air museum in which classic monuments are distributed on a verdant green backdrop to illustrate typological developments that characterize periods, and structure our understanding of prehistory.

The second trip involves a long walk around the landscape of Overton and Fyfield Down and is primarily concerned with an examination of a spectacular 'Celtic' field system with associated Roman and Iron Age settlements. It also involves an encounter with a number of barrows and polisoirs[2] of early prehistoric date, and an experimental earthwork of comparatively recent date. This trip is a stimulating introduction to the Wessex landscape that involves a lot of walking and not much lecturing. It allows one to come to terms with the distinction between place and space—between the desire of people to create special points in the landscape that provide a focus for particular types of activity, such as burial or settlement, and the requirement to inhabit a space used for cultivation and grazing animals, as a resource for raw materials, and a route for travelling through. Both space and place can be transcribed by visible and invisible boundaries that are more or less permeable.

This landscape also demonstrates the contested nature of the countryside. Archaeologists, botanists, geologists, farmers, and horse trainers are all actively competing to use the land. They all require a particular type of land management that sometimes restricts the freedom of others. Fyfield and Overton Down are now part of the Avebury World Heritage Site, but they are also Sites of Special Scientific Importance and contain many scheduled ancient monuments.

In later prehistory these issues of contestation, territoriality, and history are all clearly visible. Many of the principal monument types of Wessex are present: field systems, linear boundaries and enclosures, and there is even a distant hillfort to consider. It is clear as you move through this landscape that its historical character must have been important. The arrangement of the Early Bronze Age round barrows influenced the development of settlements and field systems in the Middle Bronze Age, and were used to align boundaries in the Late Bronze Age. These boundaries in turn seem to have attracted later Iron Age settlements, and the layout of the Middle Bronze Age field system was very important in structuring a later Roman field system (Fowler and Blackwell 1998: 50). We also have to consider the significance of the special places that lie just to the west. What did the later prehistoric inhabitants

---

[2] These are naturally occurring sarsen boulders that were used for polishing stone axes in the Neolithic.

of Overton and Fyfield Down think of the ancient monuments of Avebury and Silbury Hill? It is impossible to believe that they simply ignored them, but the evidence from the archaeological excavations at Avebury suggests there was very little physical modification to the monuments or the landscape. Did they avoid this sacred area?

WESSEX DELINEATED

The defining feature of the Wessex landscape is the chalk downland, and this is what most archaeologists think of when they consider the region. However, it must be emphasized that this is but one aspect of a landscape of considerable diversity that ranges from the high uplands of north Wiltshire to the low sheltered coastal plain of Hampshire. The geology is dominated by chalk, but tertiary sands and gravels cover large areas, particularly along the south coast, and the clay vales and limestone deposits that surround the chalk are important parts of the landscape of Dorset and Wiltshire (Figure 2.1).

In recent years the administrators of the countryside have striven to define the essential characteristics of the different landscapes of England in order to preserve this character for future generations (Countryside Commission 1996). These studies have sought a synthesis that brings together the geology, natural history, drainage patterns, topography, and human settlement characteristics, and to identify distinct regions that maintain a similarity of character. Some of these characterization studies have been particularly detailed, whereas others provide a more general overview of the principal features of the landscape, and can be used to provide a brief introduction to variability in the landscape of Wessex.

Figure 2.2 shows the Joint Character Areas used by Natural England to divide Wessex into 15 different areas (Countryside Commission and English Nature 1996). These areas give some idea of the diversity of the landscapes present in the region but they can be grouped into: five downland areas (116, 125, 130, 132, 134); the tertiary clays, sands and gravels of the south coast (126, 128, 131, 135); the tertiary clays, sands and gravels of the Thames Basin (129); the Dorset coast (136, 137, 138); and two small regionally distinctive areas (127, 133).

The character and topography of the chalk downlands show some similarities across the region:

- Steep escarpments distinguish the edge of the chalk, particularly where it overlies the greensand, and are especially prominent on the north side of the South Downs, the north and west sides of the Berkshire and Marlborough Downs and the northern edge of the Dorset coastal plain.

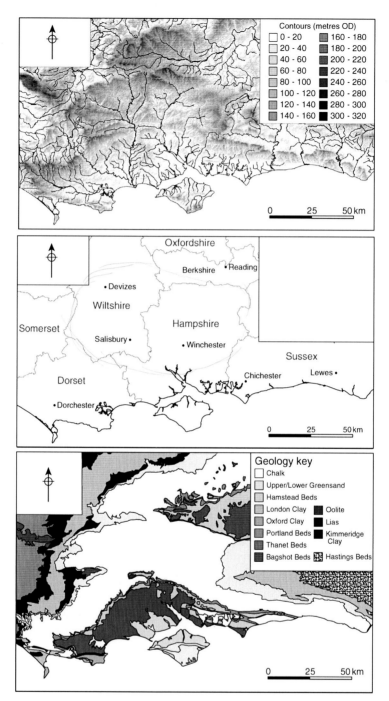

Figure 2.1 A map of the study area showing topography and rivers, county boundaries and principal towns, and the principal geological divisions.

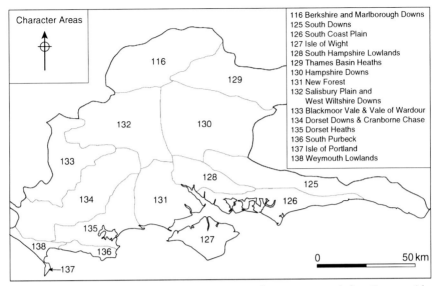

Character Areas

116 Berkshire and Marlborough Downs
125 South Downs
126 South Coast Plain
127 Isle of Wight
128 South Hampshire Lowlands
129 Thames Basin Heaths
130 Hampshire Downs
131 New Forest
132 Salisbury Plain and
      West Wiltshire Downs
133 Blackmoor Vale & Vale of Wardour
134 Dorset Downs & Cranborne Chase
135 Dorset Heaths
136 South Purbeck
137 Isle of Portland
138 Weymouth Lowlands

0   50 km

Figure 2.2 A map of Wessex showing the Joint Character Areas (after Countryside Commission and English Nature 1996).

- The downlands are relatively dry landscapes but are traversed by significant steep-sided coombs (valleys), which indicate the presence of watercourses in earlier periods and which will still produce spring water after a particularly wet winter.
- The main rivers generally follow the dip slope of the underlying geology and flow towards the Hampshire Basin, from west to east in Dorset and from north to south in Wiltshire, Hampshire, and Sussex. The exception is the River Kennet, which flows east into the Thames and cuts off the northern part of the region.
- The higher areas of the chalk are often capped with tertiary deposits of clay-with-flints. These can be extensive in areas such as the South Dorset Ridgeway, Cranborne Chase, Savernake Forest, and North Hampshire, but are generally thinner towards the west.

Historically, the vegetation of the chalk downland is characterized by species-rich grassland, which developed as a result of the extensive use of downlands for grazing sheep. In the latter part of the twentieth century there was an extremely destructive phase of arable agricultural expansion onto the downland.[3] This was brought about by the introduction of agricultural

---

[3] There was also a less damaging phase of entrepreneurial farming in the nineteenth century, which encroached on the downlands (Field pers. comm.).

subsidies that were designed to make Europe self-sufficient in basic foodstuffs, and the use of fertilizers that enhanced the productivity of the nutrient-poor downland soils.

The clay-with-flint uplands and the river valleys have quite different characteristics. Clay-with-flints is generally difficult to cultivate and these deposits are often covered in woodland, including some important historic forests. The river valleys are in places covered by alluvium, which has been deposited over the millennia since the introduction of agriculture. The valleys are the location for most of the historic villages whose origins probably lie in the Saxon period (McOmish *et al.* 2002: 109). From the late seventeenth century these were often heavily managed landscapes with complex water meadows designed to maximize the production of good grass for grazing sheep (McOmish *et al.* 2002: 133).

The coastal plain varies in character as one moves from Sussex to Dorset. The eastern part of the area is basically a low-lying and restricted coastal plain, and in Sussex two distinct terraces, at 10–15 m OD and 30–40 m OD, are present. There are isolated low hills and chalk ridges, the most prominent of which is Portsdown, which overlooks Portsmouth, and this landscape includes some very good arable land. To the west the tertiary sand and gravels are much more extensive and form two distinct landscapes: the raised plateau of the New Forest and the Dorset Heaths that surround Poole Harbour. Both landscapes are characterized by poor, infertile acid soils that are covered with heather, gorse, and bracken moorland. In places ancient woodlands survive, particularly in the New Forest; much of the Dorset Heaths have new plantations.

The coastline in Dorset and east Hampshire is characterized by significant and extensive inlets—Chichester, Langstone, Portsmouth, Christchurch, Poole Harbour, and the Fleet at Weymouth—and these have important mudflats and salt marshes. In west Hampshire and Sussex the coastline is quite different, with shingle and sand bars sometimes forming low cliffs and significant promontories, such as Selsey Bill. Many rivers traverse the coastal lowlands, including the Avon, the Test, the Meon, and the Adur, and the alluvial filled valleys are fertile strips compared with the acid heathlands in the west and the seasonally waterlogged clays in the east.

Only a limited area of the Thames Basin heathlands is included in the present study area: the lower Kennet valley. This is a geologically complex area comprising clays, sands and gravels in a sequence from the Bagshot Beds, through the London Clay to the Reading Beds. These deposits are covered by Pleistocene gravel terraces, which in places have a covering of loess and, in the valley bottom, alluvium. The most agriculturally favourable deposits are the lower terrace gravels, which are generally lighter and better drained soils than the plateau gravels at the edge of the valley, and are less likely to flood than the valley floor deposits (Lobb and Rose 1996: 7). The nutrient-poor acidic soils of the plateau gravels are characterized by heathland and woodland.

The Dorset coastal plain is geologically complex and dominated by distinctive chalk and limestone ridges separated by clay vales and outcrops of shales. South Purbeck is separated from the Dorset Heaths by a chalk ridge, a dramatic topographic feature that led to this area being known as the Isle of Purbeck. The Isle of Portland is a limestone plateau surrounded by spectacular sea cliffs and only connected to the mainland by the unstable deposits of Chesil Beach. This is a spectacularly long beach bar made up of a graded series of flint and limestone pebbles, much of which is separated from the mainland by a tidal inlet known as the Fleet. The landscape of the Weymouth Lowlands includes rich agricultural land but a more important resource was the stone, limestone, chert and shale, which has been exploited since the Bronze Age.

On the west side of Dorset and Wiltshire are the Blackmoor Vale and the Vales of Wardour and Pewsey.[4] These are damp low-lying clay lands with intermittent low limestone hills. The headwaters of the Stour rise in the Blackmoor Vale and the Avon rises in the Vale of Pewsey. Both rivers then follow relatively steep-sided valleys that cut through the chalk downlands and drain into Christchurch Harbour. The Vales were generally used as cattle pasture lands in the recent past and the evidence for early settlement is sporadic and concentrated on the limestone hills.

All of these different regions have their own idiosyncratic characters and could be further sub-divided into easily distinguishable landscapes with their own distinctive historic character (Fairclough 1999; Fairclough *et al.* 1999).

Historic Boundaries

The archaeological understanding of the separate regions of Wessex is also very distinctive and it has to be emphasized that, until the establishment of the Trust for Wessex Archaeology, there was no structure that encompassed the region I am calling Wessex. Archaeological activity was strongly influenced by the distribution of county archaeological societies that originated in the Victorian period and, in recent years, by the County Council Archaeological Services. Until the 1960s almost all the activity in the region was sponsored or organized through the county societies, leading to uneven

---

[4] The Vale of Pewsey was not defined as a separate Joint Character Area by Natural England but included in the Marlborough Downs; for our purposes it will be dealt with as a separate area.

coverage. Most of the excavations were undertaken by local members and the finds and archives were stored in museums run by these societies. Even excavations led by the most famous academic archaeologists were integrated into the county societies: Wheeler relied on Colonel Drew, the Curator of Dorchester Museum, for the organization of the Maiden Castle excavation (Wheeler 1943), and the Hampshire Field Club sponsored the excavations of Quarley Hill and Bury Hill (Hawkes, C. F. C. 1939, 1940).

In the 1960s and 1970s, increasing development, particularly in the town centres, outstripped the ability of societies and museum curators, who then placed pressure on government to recognize and respond to the archaeological damage being caused. The practice of field archaeology effectively became controlled by national government and more focused on rescue archaeology. Some of the fieldwork was undertaken by the Department of the Environment's Central Excavation Unit, but it was very soon apparent that a network of regional units would be necessary to undertake the volume of work that was required in the study area, and this resulted in the setting up of the Trust for Wessex Archaeology. The continued pace of development, and the realization that a more detailed monitoring of this was required, resulted in the establishment of archaeologists in the local government planning departments. These archaeologists are based in county or district councils. The most important development in recent years has been a shift in funding of archaeological fieldwork from central government to the developers responsible for the destruction of the archaeology. This has led to the creation of a free market for archaeological fieldwork and the undermining of Wessex Archaeology's monopoly on rescue archaeology in the region. The recent changes have meant that the principal influence over archaeological work in any region lies within the county or district councils. The curators in these organizations have effective control over the nature of the archaeological work required and monitor the quality of the work undertaken.

This history means that, despite the relatively homogeneous nature of the archaeology in much of the region, there are considerable differences in the manner in which the archaeology has been examined and interpreted in the different counties, and there are further locally significant differences within each county.[5] I have no intention of undertaking an analysis of these developments but it is important to emphasize that many writers on the Iron Age of Wessex (including myself) tend to be very familiar with the area in which they undertake their fieldwork, but have a much more superficial

---

[5] The Bournemouth/Poole conurbation, for example, has always been slightly separate from Dorset and Hampshire and has its own local archaeological society and museum, and in recent years the Council has employed its own archaeologists.

understanding of other areas. The conflict between detailed local knowledge and more superficial regional knowledge creates a number of different discursive responses:

1. Authors can emphasize the area they are working in and simply assume it is representative of the region.
2. Authors can emphasize the area they are working in and assume it is atypical and different from the rest of the region.
3. Authors can discuss the region as a totality, blurring the distinctions and differences between areas but subjectively prioritizing the region they work in.

In this book I will deliberately try to surmount these problems by detailed discussions of specific landscapes scattered throughout the region. This cannot be a complete picture as certain areas have been much more intensively studied than others and it is necessary to prioritize the more informative recent surveys, as these are invaluable for my interpretation. Most of the discussion will centre on the chalk downlands, and there are good reasons why this has to be so, but there are good reasons too why we must also consider the other areas. It is clear that in the first millennium BC the bulk of the population of Wessex was living on the chalk, but it is only through comparison of these areas with the different archaeological record of the topographically and ecologically adjacent regions that we can highlight the unique features of the chalk landscapes.

ENVIRONMENT OF THE CHALK DOWNS

The environmental history of the chalk downlands has been reconstructed largely through molluscan analysis, as pollen-producing peat deposits are restricted to river valleys that have environmental histories quite different from those of the downlands. Mollusc samples have been recovered from several different later prehistoric contexts, but those most commonly analysed are ditch fills, buried soil horizons, and pit fills (Evans, J. G. 1972). All these contexts have taphonomic complexities: the pits and ditches may provide localized environmental data, whereas the soil horizons may aggregate very complex historical developments. However, the overall patterns for later prehistory are so consistent that these problems appear to be of little significance.

Several regional summaries have been undertaken in areas that have been the subject of intensive campaigns of excavation, and general patterns are clearly demonstrated by the results from the Dorchester bypass (Allen in

Smith, R. J. C. *et al.* 1997), Stonehenge Environs (Allen, Entwhistle, and Richards in Richards, J. 1990), and Salisbury Plain (Entwhistle in Bradley *et al.* 1994; Allen and Entwhistle in Fulford *et al.* 2006). The environmental evidence from all these sites suggests that woodland clearance was already more or less complete by the Early Bronze Age. During the later Bronze Age, widespread cultivation also encouraged erosion and the accumulation of colluvium and gravel fans in the dry valleys, and aeolian erosion is also visible in several areas. In the Iron Age, arable activity continued, but many sites appear to have been used for pasture. The only later prehistoric sites to produce distinctive woodland assemblages were two Late Bronze Age linear earthworks on Salisbury Plain (Entwhistle in Bradley *et al.* 1994: 120). These deposits were confined to the summit of hills capped with clay-with-flints, and the woodland appears to have been cleared in the Late Bronze Age.

Molluscan analysis has been undertaken at many hillforts including Segsbury (Ingrem and Robinson in Lock *et al.* 2005), Uffington (Robinson in Miles *et al.* 2003), Danebury (Evans and Hewitt in Cunliffe and Poole 1991; Evans in Cunliffe 1984a), and Maiden Castle (Evans in Sharples 1991a), and the enclosure of Easton Lane (Allen in Fasham *et al.* 1989). The results are consistent with the general surveys discussed above. Most of these enclosures were constructed on grassland, though there is evidence for cultivation at Segsbury, and open downland conditions prevailed throughout their occupation. The exception was Danebury where there was limited woodland regeneration in the first century BC, by which time the hillfort was effectively abandoned.

An important feature of the Wessex chalklands is the river valleys; these have the potential to provide a considerable amount of evidence for the environment of both the river valleys themselves and the adjacent downlands. Very little detailed analysis of these environments has been undertaken but there are important studies of the Kennet valley near Avebury (Evans, J. G. *et al.* 1993), the Anton, Test, and Wallop around Danebury (Williams, D. and Evans, J. G. 2000) and the Frome at Maiden Castle (Evans and Rouse in Sharples 1991a).

The sequence around Avebury provides evidence for sustained periods of water-borne deposition of sediments that probably occurred seasonally and allowed grassland to be re-established every year (Evans, J. G. *et al.* 1993: 188). This commenced in the Beaker period and continued until the Early Iron Age and coincides with extensive forest clearance and cultivation of the surrounding downlands. In the later Bronze Age the edge of the valley was dry enough to allow for the deposition of isolated burials and the creation of a sarsen-defined field system. However, settlement activity was restricted to a burnt mound: a monument type closely associated with wet places. There was no evidence for Iron Age activity in the valley bottom (Evans, J. G. *et al.* 1993: 190). The sequences around Danebury are not as thoroughly explored or as well dated but alluvial deposits of later prehistoric date cover the valley bottoms in the lower reaches of the Wallop and the Test, and it is suggested that in the Test 'swamps may have persisted right up to the post-medieval period' (Williams, D. and Evans, J. G. 2000: 42).

The evidence from a variety of sources suggests that the later prehistoric landscape of the chalk comprised open downland that was densely settled and under various intensive regimes of cultivation; woodland probably survived only on deposits of clay-with-flints. These deposits are relatively common throughout the area and are the dominant feature of some areas of higher ground. The valleys appear to be distinctively different landscapes. They were seasonally flooded and though the upper reaches could be relatively dry, and provide good grazing for part of the year, the lower reaches were probably swamps that provided important wetland resources.

LANDSCAPES WITH HISTORY

One of the most important features of the landscape is its historicity. Wessex is covered with monuments that stand out in a striking fashion, difficult to ignore. As archaeologists we traverse the landscape observing and interpreting the effects of past human activities. We create stories (such as those in this book) that help us to understand these interventions in the landscape. These interventions clearly affect how we behave and how we in turn intervene in the landscape. The stories written about the landscape have a metaphorical significance: they provide moral tales for our own society, they highlight the significance of certain monuments, and they provide locations that can be a focus for contemporary communities (Bender 1998).

These monuments practically affect how we choose to use landscapes. There is a contemporary consensus that we should try to preserve as many of these past interventions as possible. However, this is an area of contention; how can the continued occupation of the landscape be reconciled with preservation when that occupation requires that the landscape be productive? Some may regard the requirements placed on its exploitation to be a dese-cration of that landscape. The resolution of disputes over how we prioritize the protection and exploitation of the landscape demonstrates the contem-porary distribution of power in our society, and has changed significantly within my own lifetime. Environmental protection now has a legislative strength that would have been unthinkable 30 years ago, indicating a clear shift in power away from the agricultural lobby that was dominant for most of the twentieth century. Relations with the landscape could have been as complex for societies occupying Wessex in the first millennium BC as they are for us today. Indeed they may have been more so in a society where individuals believed in a landscape inhabited by gods, ancestors, and spirits, who had to be appeased, consulted and/or avoided.

By the beginning of the first millennium BC Wessex had been occupied for thousands of years. It is unlikely that there was a location that had not been transformed by human occupation, that was not within a couple of hours' walk from a place of inhabitation, and that was not subject to regular visits by someone. It is likely that narratives would have been created that explained the different features that were visible or, more accurately, explained the character of the landscape as it appeared to the inhabitants. These narratives would have been all-embracing and not just restricted to the most dramatic monuments. The fields of sarsens that characterize the Valley of the Stones, in Dorset and Wiltshire, would have required a narrative explanation similar to those used to describe the sarsen trilithons of Stonehenge and the standing stones of Avebury. There may also have been little difference between the narratives that explained what contemporary scholars would understand as natural features and those that we now know to be human creations (Bradley 2000).

It would be difficult, indeed it may be impossible, for contemporary archaeologists to understand what these narratives were, but it is important that we consider how they may have affected a first millennium BC understanding of the landscape and how conceptions altered during that period. In certain circumstances the archaeological record can document how people transformed ancient monuments in the that millennium. These interventions have encouraged archaeologists (for example, Hingley 1999) to speculate on the appropriation or desecration of monuments, but we must also consider the absence of evidence for intervention. What does the lack of a first millennium intervention mean? Does abandonment indicate a lack of interest in an ancient monument or does it indicate reverence or, perhaps more importantly, fear of the spirits that resided within it? These considerations are not simply yes/no alternatives; they need to be considered in relation to the nature of the monument—how it would have appeared in the first millennium, how it was located in relation to contemporary settlement, and how the landscape around it was being used.

A good example of the difficulty of interpreting the historical importance of a monument is the difference between the significance of the Neolithic causewayed enclosure at Maiden Castle and Stonehenge. The Neolithic enclosure at Maiden Castle at first appears to have been of considerable significance to the Iron Age inhabitants as the Early Iron Age hillfort was constructed directly on top of it (Wheeler 1943; Sharples 1991a). The rampart of the hillfort overlay the inner ditch of the causewayed enclosure and most of the outer ditch of the enclosure was completely removed by the ditch of the hillfort. The front face of the rampart appears to be aligned on a slight bank that lay between the two enclosure ditches. However, a detailed consideration of the historical sequence suggests that the relationship between the cause-wayed enclosure and the hillfort was not as important as first appears. The enclosure ditches were almost completely infilled in the Neolithic and the small bank that was used to align the rampart may have been a feature of a period of cultivation of the hilltop in the Early Bronze Age.[6] There then followed a long period in the later Bronze Age when the hill was used as a grazing resource, though probably at some time during this period linear earthworks were constructed across the hilltop and these may have been oriented on the causewayed enclosure. In this period, of about a thousand years, there is little indication that the hill had any special significance to the inhabitants of south Dorset. There are a couple of round barrows on the hill, but far fewer than appear on the Ridgeway to the south or on the low-lying plain to the north. The Early Iron Age construction of the hillfort appears therefore to be related to the later Bronze Age boundaries rather than to the earlier Neolithic monument.

A recent survey of all the causewayed enclosures in England found that only eight hillforts were built on a causewayed enclosure (Oswald *et al.* 2001: 139). This is about 10% of the causewayed enclosures known (Healy pers. comm.) and an insignificant proportion of the number of hillforts built. The Trundle in Sussex is another hillfort that overlies a causewayed enclosure (Figure 2.3). It has been argued that the distinctive angular shape of the hillfort reflects the shape of the earlier enclosure, but angularity has recently been observed at a number of hillforts unconnected with causewayed enclosures (Payne *et al.* 2006); the inner ditch of the causewayed enclosure is not very angular and part of the outer circuit extends beyond the hillfort boundary. It is therefore difficult to accept the claim that the earlier causewayed enclosure had a sig-nificant influence on the later hillfort (RCHME 1995). At Hambledon Hill, Dorset, a large causewayed enclosure lies immediately adjacent to a hillfort (Figure 2.3). The causewayed enclosure sits on the central plateau of a hill with three spurs, and the hillfort is on the longest narrowest spur to the north. It is

---

[6] Mike Hamilton (pers. comm.) has argued that the Beaker material found in the ditch of the enclosure, and other causewayed enclosure ditches, reflects settlement activity and not a symbolic reuse of the earlier monument. It represents a phase of agricultural expansion in the Early Bronze Age that left an imprint all over the Wessex landscape (Allen, M. J. 2005).

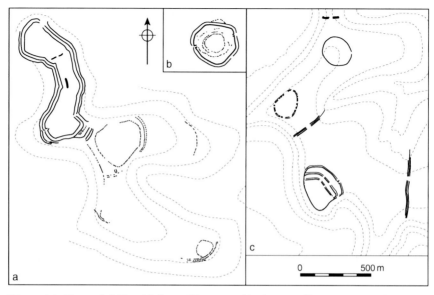

Figure 2.3 Plans of a) Hambledon Hill, Dorset; b) The Trundle, Sussex; c) Whitesheet Hill, Dorset, showing the relationship between Neolithic causewayed enclosures and Iron Age hillforts. In the area around Whitesheet Hill there are also several cross-dykes and a simple undated enclosure (after Mercer and Healy 2008: fig. 1.4; RCHME 1995: figs. 5 and 6; and Rawlings *et al.* 2004: fig. 2).

likely that all the spurs had outworks of Neolithic date and that the hillfort is probably built on an earlier Neolithic outwork (RCHME 1996; Mercer and Healy 2008). Nevertheless, it seems that the topographic requirements of the hillfort overrode any desire that the builders might have had to be associated with the main causewayed enclosure. The principal locational preference appears to be to occupy the spur with the most spectacular views. A similar situation arose at Whitesheet Hill, Dorset, where a hillfort was constructed on the same plateau as, but in quite a different location from, a causewayed enclosure (Figure 2.3). It seems that the landscape requirements of hillforts were subtly different from those of Neolithic enclosures. Hillforts were generally located on the summit of hills with spectacular all-round visibility whereas Neolithic enclosures are often tilted to one side of a hilltop, enabling visual access to the interior from a particular direction (Oswald *et al.* 2001: 99).

The situation at Stonehenge is quite different. This would have been an impressive monument in the Iron Age, highly visible and unlike any other monument in the surrounding landscape (RCHME 1979). I find it difficult to believe that this monument did not play an important role in the mythical narratives of the people occupying the surrounding area. However, archaeological evidence for Iron Age activity at Stonehenge is almost completely absent. The extensive excavations at Stonehenge have recovered only a small scatter of later prehistoric pottery and one bone tool (Gardiner in Cleal *et al.* 1995: 332–43) and there are no obvious features or structures that would indicate veneration or religious activity in the first millennium BC. In this case it seems likely that the significance of the monument was recognized by avoidance and a deliberate desire to leave it unsullied by later prehistoric activity. This situation can be paralleled at Avebury, a monument that has sarsen standing stones of comparable megalithic proportions to Stonehenge. Extensive excavations in and around this monument (Smith, I. F. 1965; Pollard and Reynolds 2002) have so far failed to document any later prehistoric activity within the great henge.[7]

In contrast, work at the comparable large earthwork enclosures at Durrington Walls, near Stonehenge (Wainwright and Longworth 1971), and Mount Pleasant, Dorset (Wainwright 1979b), has revealed significant amounts of evidence for activity in the first millennium BC. At Mount Pleasant, a small enclosure inside the large enclosure was reoccupied in the first century BC and the evidence indicates that a house was constructed and grain storage pits were excavated. It was argued that the activity indicated the existence of a settlement, with no religious or social status, and there was no evidence for unusual deposits or structural peculiarities. Recent geophysical work at Durrington Walls indicates an extensive spread of Iron Age pits in the northern half of the enclosure (David and Payne 1997: fig. 11) and recent excavations have exposed several pits and a large roundhouse at the centre of the main enclosure and burials in the entrance (Parker Pearson pers. comm.). The date of the internal settlement is unknown but an external settlement dates to the Late Iron Age (Wainwright *et al.* 1971; Stone *et al.* 1954). The original interpretation of the material outside the enclosure was that it was unexceptional and simply represented normal settlement activity occurring next to a monument which had lost any religious significance that it had in the Late Neolithic.

The difference between the sanctity of Avebury and Stonehenge and the apparently prosaic use of the henges at Durrington Walls and Mount Pleasant, and the causewayed enclosures, may be because the former had a substantial number of upright sarsens whereas the latter appear as earthworks, a variation in the topography of the land, rather than an intrusion upon it. Megalithic

---

[7] It might be argued that the earlier excavation by Keiller were so focused on the Neolithic that he discarded the evidence for later activity but recent re-examination of the Keiller collections (Pollard and Reynolds 2002) has failed to locate any Iron Age pottery despite the presence of large quantities of Saxon and later medieval pottery.

monuments were consciously avoided presumably because they still contained powerful magic.[8] Earthworks, in contrast, may well have been acknowledged as significant, but they were capable of being actively incorporated into the community's reconfiguration of the landscape.

The monuments mentioned so far are exceptional places in the landscape of Wessex and it might be more informative to consider some more commonplace monuments. Barrows (round and long) are found in large numbers across the chalk downlands and possibly provide a more accurate picture of the routine interactions with the past. There is good evidence that these monuments were respected in the early first millennium BC. There are many occasions where barrows have been used to align linear earthworks and the association between linear earthworks and barrows in the area around Tilshead on Salisbury Plain is particularly clear (Figure 2.4; McOmish *et al.* 2002). This relationship may be because both monuments had a territorial function. The long barrows appear to be located on false crests that make them visible from the valleys and not from the adjacent areas of uplands (McOmish *et al.* 2002: 22), and many of the linear earthworks are laid out to enclose these valleys, which appear to form basic territorial units. The relationship of long barrows and linear earthworks could therefore be caused by the concurrent location of the two monuments. However, the respect shown by the deviation of the linear ditch around Tilshead 2, and the deviation to incorporate Kill Barrow, suggests that the barrows retained or acquired a significance that provided legitimation for the role of the linear earthwork.

In contrast to Salisbury Plain, long barrows in east Hampshire and Sussex are not generally related to the linear earthworks, and in Dorset, or more specifically Cranborne Chase, long barrows are instead incorporated into settlement complexes. One of the most dramatically sited long barrows in Dorset is that at the centre of the spur around which the hillfort of Hambledon Hill is constructed (Figure 2.5; RCHME 1996). This barrow had been built on the narrowest part of the spur, immediately behind the Early Iron Age rampart, and it restricts the area available for settlement to a confined strip on the slopes of the east side. The desire to maintain the long barrow, as a monument in the centre of the hillfort, was clearly extremely strong given its excellent preservation and the density of settlement in the hillfort. A comparable example of the importance of a linear monument in a later prehistoric monument is the bank barrow at Maiden Castle. Geophysical survey of the hillfort (Sharples 1991a: fig. 30) clearly indicates the mound was not used for settlement in the later hillfort. However, there is plenty of evidence for dense

---

[8] These stones may have been considered as tangible ancestors if Parker Pearson and Ramilisonina (1998) have correctly interpreted the evidence.

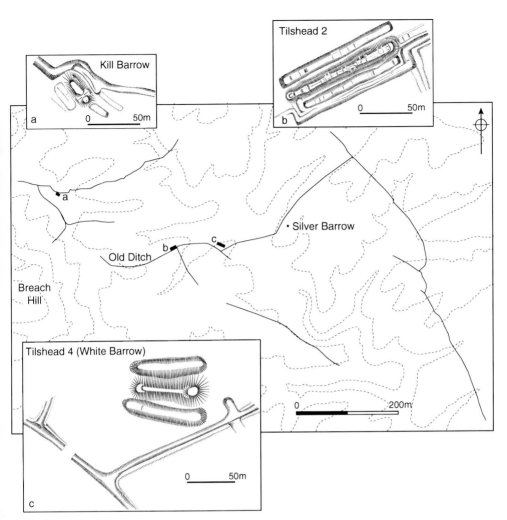

Figure 2.4 A plan of the barrows and linear earthworks around Tilshead on Salisbury Plain (McOmish *et al.* 2002: figs. 2.5, 2.10, and 2.12; © English Heritage, NMR). In the centre the linear earthwork known as Old Ditch emerges from a spur on Breach Hill and becomes aligned on the long axis of an exceptionally large long barrow, Tilshead 2 (Old Ditch). When it reaches the west end of the barrow it detours to the south, avoiding both the barrow mound and ditch. At the east end it returns to its original alignment and is met by a subsidiary linear earthwork, running perpendicular to Old Ditch. Old Ditch then runs across a coombe to the south of Tilshead 4 (the White Barrow), where it is abutted by another linear earthwork. This linear traverses the valley of the Till and is oriented on Silver Barrow, a large round barrow that may be Neolithic in date (McOmish *et al.* 2002: 31). The linear earthwork avoids close contact with Silver Barrow by deviating around the north side of the hill below the summit. An irregular linear earthwork, to the north of this complex, was closely associated with Kill Barrow, running up to and around this small long barrow, and also deviated around a small open settlement (McOmish *et al.* 2002: fig. 3.15).

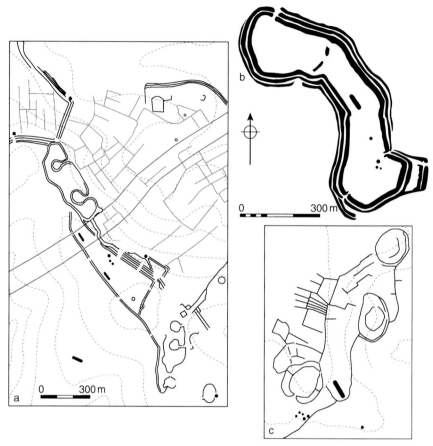

Figure 2.5 The relationship between long barrows and Iron Age enclosures in Dorset.
a) the banjo enclosures, linear earthworks, field systems and barrows on Gussage Hill;
b) the hillfort and long barrow on Hambledon Hill; c) the enclosures, boundary
systems and long barrow at Pimperne (after Bowen 1990: area plan 2; RCHME 1996:
fig. 17; Bowen 1990: fig. 47).

settlement in ditches on either side and it may be that the low mound acted as
a road, which was definitely not the function of the barrow at Hambledon.[9]

It is not only the hillforts in this area that incorporate long barrows: a
substantial long barrow at Pimperne (Bowen 1990: fig. 47) lies immediately
adjacent to a settlement enclosure known as Pimperne 18 (Figure 2.5). This

---

[9] The Late Bronze Age settlement at Winterbourne Stoke (Richards, J. 1990: 209) is also a good
indication of the importance of earlier barrow cemeteries. A small settlement consisting of at least
two buildings was built at the south-west end of one of the most impressive linear cemeteries in

enclosure lies close to two other enclosures and all three were surrounded by a ditch that also enclosed the long barrow. The important complex of banjo enclosures and linear boundaries on Gussage Hill incorporates two very well-preserved long barrows (Figure 2.5).[10] These lie between two paired Iron Age enclosures in a triangle of land delineated by a triple linear boundary to the east and a single linear to the west.[11]

Important relationships also exist between round barrows and linear boundaries. Linear boundaries are often aligned on round barrows but deviate from the alignment to avoid damaging the monument and its immediate environs. This was noted at Silver Barrow (see Figure 2.4) and another good example is Hemp Knoll (Robertson-Mackay 1980: fig. 2) where a linear earthwork, running from Oldbury hillfort to the escarpment above Pewsey, terminates less than 0.5 m from the barrow ditch. At Portway in Hampshire a cemetery of six round barrows was used as a marker for a linear boundary that deliberately changes direction to run between two barrows and across the ditch of a smaller barrow (Cook and Dacre 1985: fig. 3).

The large number of barrow cemeteries in the area around Stonehenge demonstrates another significant feature of the relationship between barrows and linear boundaries. It is clear that some substantial barrow cemeteries were defined by linear boundaries, which create a sacred space separated off from the rest of the landscape. A good example of this is Snail Down (Field and Corney in Thomas, N. 2005: 10–13) where a substantial Early Bronze Age cemetery was enclosed on three sides by linear boundaries. On the west side is a spinal linear boundary that runs down from Sidbury Hill, and running perpendicular to this are two subsidiary linears that enclose the round barrow cemetery. The continuation of these boundaries to the east of the cemetery is unclear—the northern boundary may turn to the north but the southern boundary appears to run down into the valley of the Bourne.

---

the Stonehenge landscape. The buildings are immediately adjacent to a substantial long barrow, which would have provided an impressive backdrop to these houses. A linear boundary on the west side of this cemetery appears to define an enclosure outside the excavated area.

[10] The Gussage Hill complex has been discussed in a number of publications concerned with Iron Age settlement patterns and it is therefore surprising to note that the plans published to accompany these discussions often fail to show the long barrows (i.e. Corney 1989: fig. 6; Barrett, Bradley, and Green 1991: fig. 6.3). This is despite the fact that the long barrows are the most substantial feature of the earthwork complex in the Iron Age.

[11] The Dorset Cursus runs through the complex on Gussage Hill but it has only a minor effect on the layout of the settlement complex. The banjos and enclosures probably represent restructuring of the landscape in the Middle to Late Iron Age. It is clear that the cursus played a more important role in the first half of the first millennium; the west end of the cursus was continued by a triple linear of presumed later prehistoric date and the early field systems are also laid out in alignment with the cursus.

The respect shown for the Snail Down cemetery when the linear boundaries were constructed contrasts with that shown when the field systems were being created in the Middle Bronze Age. The Snail Down field system, which is defined by low banks, was laid out within the barrow cemetery and cultivation encroached upon and damaged the barrows (Field and Corney in Thomas, N. 2005: 12). The construction of the linear boundaries around this cemetery appears to have protected them from later cultivation.

It is also noticeable that a linear running north-west to south-east between the Rivers Till and Avon, south of Stonehenge, splits to enclose the Wilsford Barrow group and stays split around the Lake Barrow group. Another group of linears to the north of these appears to define the Normanton Barrow group and possibly a large area around Stonehenge, where there is remarkably little evidence for later prehistoric activity.

Round barrows are much more frequently enclosed by hillforts than long barrows, and these can include quite substantial barrow cemeteries. Hambledon Hill has five round barrows inside the hillfort (RCHME 1996: 32) with only one on the plateau where the causewayed enclosure was located. Most of these barrows were damaged by post-medieval ploughing so it is difficult to know if they were respected in the Iron Age. The hillfort at Old Winchester Hill in Hampshire (Williams-Freeman 1915: 391; RCHME 1994), which is in a similar spur location to Hambledon, encloses a linear cemetery of three substantial barrows (Figure 2.6). Immediately adjacent to the west entrance of the hillfort is another cluster of six or seven barrows and two more barrows lie outside the east entrance.[12] The barrows inside appear to be well preserved, which suggests they were respected by the Iron Age occupants. However, there was no desire by the builders of the hillfort to enclose all the barrows, even though a relatively small expansion of the hillfort was all that was required. This suggests that the presence of the barrows did not dictate the selection of this hill for enclosure. Nevertheless, the builders were happy to use the barrows to emphasize access to the enclosure.

The relationship between round barrows and smaller settlement enclosures is different. The author has not identified any small settlement that encloses a round barrow.[13] There are also occasions where it is clear that an enclosure has been carefully laid out to avoid incorporating adjacent barrows. A good example is Bishopstone, Sussex (Bell 1977), where the northern enclosure

[12] It is also possible that the counterscarp bank on the south side of the hillfort was built on top of at least three barrows (RCHME 1994).

[13] An apparently unmarked burial of Early Bronze Age date was found inside an enclosure at Overton Down, Wiltshire (Fowler, P. J. 2000: 82) but it is unlikely that the enclosure was located in relationship to this burial.

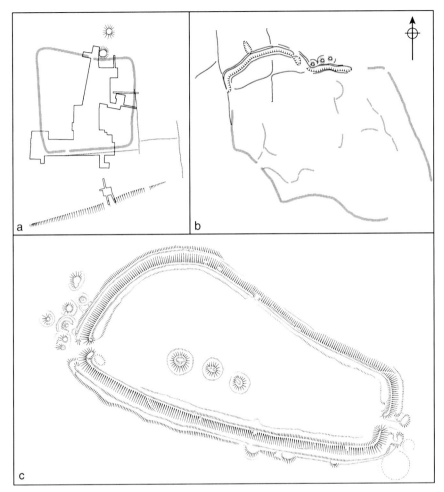

Figure 2.6 The relationship between Iron Age enclosures and Early Bronze Age round barrows at a) Bishopstone, Sussex and b) Marleycombe, Wiltshire; and the hillfort and round barrows at c) Old Winchester Hill, Hampshire (after Bell 1977; RCHME 1999 and RCHME 1994: fig. 1; Old Winchester © Crown copyright, NMR).

ditch deviates to the south to avoid the barrows on the summit of the spur (Figure 2.6). Another unexcavated enclosure on Marleycombe Hill, overlooking the Ebble valley in Wiltshire, again shows a substantial deviation of the northern boundary to avoid enclosing a small cemetery of three barrows (Figure 2.6; RCHME 1999).

The different response to the existence of round barrows by the builders of hillforts and smaller enclosures suggests the barrows were a significant feature of the landscape. The monuments almost certainly retained some mystical significance and were therefore to be avoided for mundane domestic activities. However, the power immanent in these monuments could be ignored by other groups, or perhaps the same group, gathered together as a collective. These groups may even have been capable of controlling and directing the power of these monuments to their advantage.

I have already noted the construction of one of the Sussex hillforts, the Trundle, on top of a causewayed enclosure, but a more unusual feature of this county is the location of the hillforts of Cissbury and the enclosure at Harrow Hill on top of Neolithic flint mines (Figure 2.7; Barber *et al.* 1999). At Cissbury a large part of the eastern half of the hillfort overlies mine shafts, which still survive as substantial hollows on the surface of the hill. The hillfort follows the contours of the hill and excludes a large portion of the mining complex, which extends along a spur from the south-east corner of the fort. Harrow Hill is a much smaller rectangular enclosure, which again only partly overlies the mining complex.[14] Both these enclosures are on very prominent hills, and it has been argued that the Cissbury complex was sited to be visible from the coastal plain whereas the Harrow Hill complex was sited not to be visible from the coastal plain (Barber *et al.* 1999: 55). It seems likely that the principal reason for the location of the hillforts was the spectacular visibility of the hilltops, but the flint mines would undoubtedly have provided a historical or legendary character to these locations that would enhance the status of the inhabitants and probably modify the nature of the internal occupation. However, several equally important mining complexes in Sussex remain undefined in the Iron Age and none of the Wiltshire mines appears to have been enclosed or modified in later prehistory.

This examination of the reuse of Neolithic and Bronze Age monuments in later prehistory has revealed a pattern that is neither chronologically nor spatially consistent. However, there are general conclusions that can be made. It would appear that with the exception of some of the most spectacular megalithic monuments, such as Stonehenge, most monuments were complex components of the everyday domestic landscape of occupation and, given the density of monuments present in Wessex, it is difficult to see how any other response would be possible. This does not mean that monuments were not respected. Apart from a brief period in the Middle Bronze Age, when field systems seem to have encroached on some monuments, it is clear that barrows were carefully protected and the arrangement of some

---

[14] It is debatable if this enclosure should be labelled a hillfort and excavations revealed an unusual bone assemblage that might indicate this site had a ritual aspect of greater significance than most Iron Age enclosures (Manning 1995).

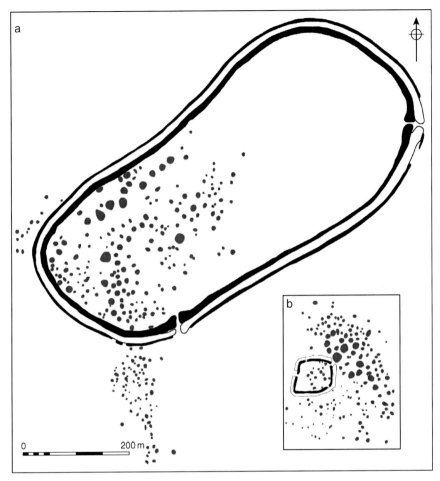

Figure 2.7 The relationship between flint mines and hillforts at a) Cissbury and b) Harrow Hill (after Donachie and Field 1994; Barber *et al.* 1999: fig. 4.2).

linears appears to be deliberately designed to enclose and protect certain barrow cemeteries. There seems to be no documented case of a barrow excavation in the Iron Age and no occasion where Iron Age ritual deposition or burial involved the disturbance of either a barrow, long or round, or a stone monument. Even in Dorset, where long barrows were frequently incorporated into settlements, there is very little sign of disturbance.

The respect for barrows and stone monuments contrasts with the disturbance of causewayed enclosures and mines. These may have been incidental incorporations in the construction of hillforts, but we have no way of knowing what impact this incorporation would have had on the occupants. The presence of ancient ditches and large subterranean shafts would have been obvious to the Iron Age construction teams. The physical nature of these features may have been less important than their contents. Digging through the ditch of the Neolithic enclosure at Maiden Castle would have resulted in the recovery of large quantities of potsherds, animal bones, stone axes, flint tools, and human remains.[15] All of these would be recognized by the Iron Age excavators and it may be they provided a model for some of the ritual activity visible in the Iron Age.

ESTABLISHING A SEQUENCE

Discussion of the historical context of the Wessex landscape has mentioned some of the principal monument types, field systems, linear ditches/boundaries, and enclosures that characterize the human occupation of the landscape in later prehistory. In simplistic terms these represent a chronological succession of human interventions that transform the downland landscapes from the second half of the second millennium through to the end of the first millennium BC. It is necessary to say something about the nature of these archaeological phenomena before we consider their purpose and what they can tell us about the human societies that occupied this region. It must be emphasized that their role is fundamentally concerned with human relationships: they all involved the creation of boundaries that separated and enclosed, and it is these human acts of separation and enclosure that require consideration.

Imposing a Grid

One of the most important features that distinguishes the landscapes of early prehistoric and later prehistoric Wessex is the field system. These are found all over the chalk downland of Wessex and are comparable to similar systems found on Dartmoor (Fleming 1988), in the Thames Valley (Yates 2001), on the edge of the Fens (Evans, C. and Knight 2000; Pryor 1980, 1984, 1992b) and elsewhere in southern Britain (Yates 2007). Dating field systems is difficult as artefact deposition in undisturbed contexts is always going to be

---

[15] Objects of early prehistoric date, and stone axes in particular, have been found in contexts that clearly indicate deliberate burial in the Iron Age.

rare when soils are routinely disturbed as part of the agricultural process. Nevertheless, there is a consensus on the general date for the creation of the extensive systems of Wessex, which is based on a number of detailed case studies.

On the South Downs the Middle Bronze Age settlement at Blackpatch is situated within a contemporary field system defined by very shallow lynchets (Figure 2.8; Drewett 1982: 352). In central Hampshire, the extensive excavations at Winnall Down revealed a ditched field system, with associated houses, that was dated to the Middle Bronze Age (Figure 2.8; Fasham *et al.* 1989: 49). In south Dorset, work at Rowden on the South Dorset Ridgeway has provided convincing evidence for the presence of a lynchet-defined field system of Middle Bronze Age date (Figure 2.8; Woodward, P. J. 1991). This was also the case at South Lodge in Cranborne Chase where a field system, demarcated by shallow lynchets, was associated with an unenclosed settlement and barrow cemetery identified with Deverel Rimbury pottery (Barrett *et al.* 1991: 181–3).[16]

Salisbury Plain provides the most detailed field survey evidence for the extent and character of these field systems and will be discussed in detail below. However, in several locations the Middle Bronze Age date for a system of small fields with low banks can be demonstrated. This is most clear at Snail Down, where a field system defined by low banks was constructed up to the edge of the Early Bronze Age barrow cemetery and then truncated by a Late Bronze Age linear ditch (Thomas, N. 2005: 62). In north Wiltshire work on the Marlborough Downs (Fowler, P. J. 2000: 86) has convincingly demonstrated a Middle Bronze Age date for the inception of the field systems.[17] The only area where conclusive evidence for an extensive Middle Bronze Age system has proved difficult to locate is on the Berkshire Downs, but this is probably because of the intensity of later Roman activity.[18]

---

[16] An earlier phase of cultivation preceded the construction of one of the barrows but this is not securely dated and the extent of the cultivation is unknown. The settlement was later enclosed, in the Middle Bronze Age, and this act of enclosure appears to coincide with the cessation of cultivation.

[17] On Fyfield and Overton Down these early field systems were overwhelmed by the later Roman field system, but this appears to be much less of an intrusion in the area examined by Gingell (1992).

[18] Bowden, Ford, and Mees (1993) excavated many lynchets of the Berkshire system and found none that was earlier than the Roman period. However, they noted that in the Nutwood area the East Ditch linear earthwork has a distinctive kink, which implies an earlier field system and that there are occasional lynchets cut by this field system (Bowden *et al.* 1993: 124). Similarly Lock, Gosden, and Daly (2005: 137) acknowledge that the large quantities of crop remains found in the Ridgeway hillforts imply fields existed in the surrounding landscape. The evidence suggests that though a system of Bronze Age fields existed on the Berkshire Downs it has been erased by later Roman field systems and that the overall patterning of fields relates to this later phase of activity.

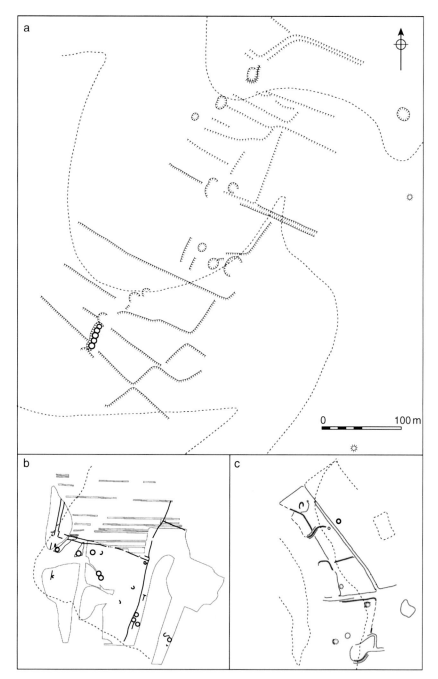

Figure 2.8 The relationship between the Middle Bronze Age field systems and houses at a) Blackpatch, Sussex; b) Winnall Down, Hampshire; c) Rowden, Dorset (after Drewett 1982: fig. 3; Fasham 1985: fig. 64; Woodward 1991: fig. 21).

There is therefore general agreement that field systems were originally laid out at the beginning of the Middle Bronze Age. It must be emphasized that this is specifically referring to the creation of a grid of equivalent and bounded fields. Fields may have existed much earlier, and there is evidence for ard cultivation beneath the Neolithic long barrow at South Street (Ashbee *et al.* 1979). Beaker sherds are commonly found in colluvial soils infilling coombes in the South Downs (Allen, M. J. 2005), which indicates an increasing destabilization of the downlands that must be related to extensive cultivation and woodland clearance in the Early Bronze Age. It seems likely, therefore, that the change taking place at the beginning of the Middle Bronze Age was not concerned with the introduction of new agricultural techniques but the systematic division of the landscape.

The field systems of the Salisbury Plain are perhaps the best-preserved field systems of central southern England. Extensive areas of lynchets survive as upstanding monuments and clearly defined an extensive area of fields that was laid out on a common orientation across the topography (such systems are commonly referred to as coaxial systems). Unfortunately, despite the detailed examination and mapping of the systems on Salisbury Plain (McOmish *et al.* 2002: illus. i.1),[19] there are still difficulties in understanding the extent of cultivation in the prehistoric period. Areas without field systems may indicate destruction by medieval ploughing and it is clear that Roman systems are extensive and have obscured the underlying prehistoric fields. Nevertheless, it is likely that prehistoric field systems did not completely cover the Plain. McOmish, Field, and Brown (2002: 54) suggest that:

- there are clustered groups of fields that cover areas of between 1–15 km^2,
- the earlier fields are characterized by low flattened banks (i.e. Snail Down), rather than lynchets,
- these define small square fields, roughly 25 m^2 to 35 m^2 (e.g. at Lidbury),
- the system was laid out on a consistent axis, oriented north-east to south-west (*c.*26–30°N).[20]

One of the best examples of an early field system is on Orcheston Down on Salisbury Plain (Figure 2.9; McOmish *et al.* 2002: 18–20). The fields in this area can be split into two systems. The southern system is oriented on a

---

[19] This can be extended by the work undertaken around Stonehenge (Richards, J. 1990: fig. 160) and the recent plotting of crop marks by the National Mapping Programme (Winton pers. comm.).

[20] The latter argument is not presented in detail and the supporting illustration (McOmish *et al.* 2002: fig. 3.4) suggests that other possibilities exist.

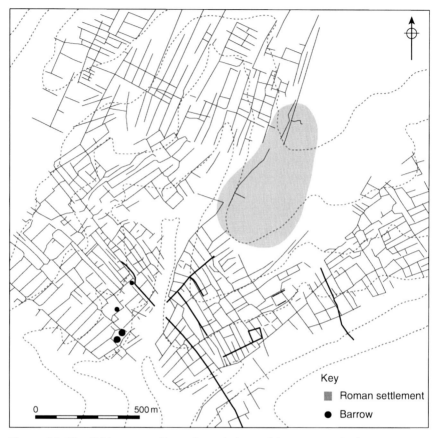

Figure 2.9 The field systems, linear boundaries and barrows on Orcheston Down, Wiltshire (after McOmish *et al.* 2002: fig. 1.17).

north-west to south-east axis and consists of a core element of small square fields, though some of these have been elongated at a later date. The northern system is oriented on the more typical north-east to south-west orientation and seems to have been laid out as large elongated fields. This system is large, extending across the high downlands as far as the linear boundary known as the Old Nursery Ditch. Unfortunately, the junction between the two field systems is obscured by later cultivation, so the relationship between them is unclear. The southern system includes a small barrow cemetery that was encroached upon by cultivation but it was not seriously damaged. A major linear boundary cut across the fields and was clearly oriented on one of the larger barrows, which it then carefully skirted around. This linear completely disappears before it leaves the field system, which suggests that some of the fields were reused after the linear was constructed. The northern system is closely associated with the Roman settlement at Church Pits and there is no published evidence to indicate an early date for these fields. It is argued that Orcheston Down is two separate but contemporary systems, but this seems unlikely, as the size and shape of the fields in each system appear to be significantly different. It seems more likely that the northern system represents a Roman (or possibly Late Iron Age) creation located on the edge of a Bronze Age system that was modified in the Roman period.

The Wessex field systems are normally discussed as coaxial field systems and are integrated into general discussions of other coaxial systems on the Fen edge, Thames Valley, and Dartmoor (Yates 2007). Coaxial systems are defined as having a common axis of orientation and represent a systematic division of the landscape into rectangular blocks (Bradley 1978). They are contrasted with aggregate systems (small patches of which exist in the Wessex region; Palmer 1984: 70) where the fields are irregular and represent organic growth from a focal point that can be adjusted to follow the irregularities of the landscape. The coaxial systems are assumed to represent a planned reorganization of the agricultural landscapes of the region that represents an attempt to maximize the output of the land and to divide it in an equitable fashion between competing groups (see Yates 2007: 120–2 for a detailed discussion of these issues). It is often explained as a response to the growth in population leading to an increasingly densely occupied landscape where boundary disputes and issues of ownership and rights to resources were becoming issues of conflict.

This functionalist framework can be questioned for a number of reasons. The belief that the coaxial field systems helped to maximize the agricultural production of the landscape seems to be an attempt to compare these with the enclosures of the seventeenth and eighteenth centuries AD, which for the landowners concerned were similarly thought to represent an agricultural improvement of the medieval open field systems. The ability to rotate crops and control the movement of animals increased food production and enabled the expansion of the urban centres of the Industrial Revolution. However, this is a dubious analogy as there is no evidence that the Bronze Age field systems were used in such a sophisticated way, and the crops required for rotation did not exist in the Bronze Age; nor is there any evidence for a massive increase in cereal production at this time. For example the settlements of Blackpatch (Drewett 1982) and South Lodge (Barrett *et al.* 1991) produced very small quantities of carbonized plant remains, there are no substantial grain storage structures (pits or four-posters) and the lynchets present at both sites were small and do not suggest a prolonged period of cultivation. The absence of evidence for intensive usage is also observed in other areas with coaxial systems. On Dartmoor most of the fields defined by stone boundaries do not appear to have been cultivated,[21] since lynchet formation is restricted to areas immediately adjacent to houses (Fleming 1988). In the Fen edge the absence of evidence for crop production and the distinctive morphology of the field system led Pryor (1996) to argue that the Fengate fields were designed for intensive sheep management. However, this argument is not convincing because the animal bone assemblage is dominated by cattle and not sheep, and it certainly would not explain the development of coaxial systems in other regions, such as Wessex, where the system is not defined by boundaries that could restrict the movement of primitive breeds of sheep.

The argument for population pressure is also less than convincing. The evidence from Salisbury Plain suggests that blocks of downland up to 15 km² were partitioned up into regular fields. These limited blocks of systematically divided fields are similar to the arrangement suggested by Gingell for the Marlborough Downs, where he identified 'blocks of approximately 20 ha in extent' (Gingell 1992: 155). These blocks do not fill the downlands and it is only later in the Roman period that very extensive systems appear to be created and Salisbury Plain became fully occupied. Again, comparison with other areas is appropriate. On Dartmoor the extensive field systems appear to have been inhabited by small settlement clusters that had the potential for substantial population expansion.

It seems more sensible to view the creation of field systems as having a social role that was concerned with the relationship between people and land. They could be seen as an attempt by the inhabitants to reclassify the landscape. Effectively they imposed a grid on to land occupied on a day-to-day basis that distinguishes it from ungridded land that is exploited on a more irregular basis. It is a system that differentiates controlled land from uncontrolled land. It may be significant that the construction of these field systems occurred in a landscape that was undifferentiated by natural vegetation. It is likely that, by the Middle Bronze Age, there was very little wilderness left on the chalk downlands. Any trees that had survived the Neolithic and Early Bronze Age clearance were restricted to small pockets, probably where deposits of clay-with-flints covered the chalk. These pockets of woodland would have been carefully controlled and represented a resource managed to produce timber for the construction of tools, houses, and enclosures.

---

[21] Dartmoor has one of the best-preserved prehistoric landscapes in southern Britain. Intensive agriculture appears to have ceased in the Late Bronze Age and there was only limited agricultural activity in the medieval period. The underlying geology is granite, and this was used to construct field boundaries, houses, and enclosures, which are consequently substantial monuments much more visible than the monuments on the chalk.

Uncontrolled woodland (wilderness) was quite different and occurred only, if it occurred at all, on the periphery of the downlands in the greensand vales to the west and the Weald to the east. Perhaps the creation of these field systems was part of an existential crisis, a psychological need to create differentiation in the homogeneous landscape of grass (Evans, J. G. 2005). Differentiating the landscape would enable the categorization of seasonal movements between controlled arable, controlled pasture, and uncontrolled pasture as well as daily movements within the controlled landscapes. It would also be possible to restrict, or proscribe, freedom of movement between and within landscapes. People moving from place to place would no longer be able to choose their own route but had to follow paths that linked approved access points. This could be used not only to differentiate the insider from the outsider but also to prescribe the freedoms of some within the community on the basis of age and gender.

The creation of these extensive field systems appears to be a short-lived phenomenon that was abandoned by or during the Late Bronze Age. There is no evidence for the creation of new field systems anywhere in Wessex during the Iron Age (Bradley 2007). Even the maintenance and use of the existing systems appears to be problematic. This is most clearly visible in the extensive excavations at Easton Lane (Fasham *et al.* 1989). The field system laid out in the Middle Bronze Age was at least partially defined by ditches. These were gradually abandoned and allowed to fill up during the later Middle Iron Age when no ditched boundaries appear to have survived, and when the Late Iron Age enclosure system was constructed, it was built on a slightly different axis. This pattern of gradual abandonment of the physical boundaries of the Middle Bronze Age field systems appears to be visible across the region and Later Middle to Late Iron Age enclosures are often documented as ignoring previous alignments (i.e. Gussage Hill). However, it must be emphasized that the evidence for crop production in the Iron Age suggests a gradual inten-sification of cultivation during the first millennium BC. This clearly indicates that field systems cannot be considered a proxy indicator for the importance of arable agriculture.

Creating Territorial Boundaries

One of the principal differences between the field systems in Wessex and the roughly contemporary systems on Dartmoor is the presence of substantial boundaries as an integral part of the Dartmoor system. These boundaries are used to divide the landscape into larger territories that are subsequently divided into fields (Dartmoor fields are also much larger than the Salisbury

Plain fields). Fleming (1988: 37) divided these boundaries, on the basis of their relationship to the topography, into watershed reaves, contour reaves, and parallel reaves (which cut across the grain of the land). The boundaries were used to divide river valley based territories 'into three categories of land; each territory had a parallel reave system, a river valley or low-lying grazing system, and access to the higher moors' (Fleming 1988: 44). In Wessex the field systems laid out in the Bronze Age appear to be just one element of the system discussed above, equivalent to the parallel reaves. The creation of larger landscape divisions was a later modification of the system associated with the construction of linear boundaries that are equivalent to the contour and watershed reaves in Dartmoor.

Explaining the difference between these two areas is problematic. It may reflect a slightly different chronology. The decision to create coaxial field systems may have originated in Wessex at the end of the Early Bronze Age and been adopted slightly later in the Bronze Age in Dartmoor. The chronological difference may have encouraged the development of a more complex division of the landscape, but this may also have been inspired by the more extreme topographic variability of the Dartmoor landscape. A desire to clarify the division of the Wessex landscape then appears to have required the introduction of a system of linear boundaries, which may well have been influenced by the Dartmoor boundary systems. Unfortunately, this hypothesis cannot be assessed, as our understanding of the chronology of these landscape boundaries is not sufficiently precise.

Wessex linear boundaries can be shown to cut across existing field systems in a number of places. Notable examples are Orcheston Down (McOmish *et al.* 2002: illus 1.18), Snail Down (Field and Corney in Thomas, N. 2005: 12), Down Barn, Cholderton (Palmer 1984: 112), Windy Dido (Cunliffe and Poole 2000f: 41) and Danebury, New Buildings (Cunliffe and Poole 2000c: 103). The excavations undertaken on Salisbury Plain indicate that most of the linear boundaries were laid out in the Late Bronze Age and are associated with the use of plain Post Deverel Rimbury pottery (Bradley *et al.* 1994: 58). However, once constructed these linear boundaries underwent considerable modification. Detailed analysis of the system around Quarley Hill (Hawkes, C. F. C. 1939; Cunliffe 2000: fig. 4.16) demonstrates a sequence of change and reconstruction, which would have been of major significance to the local community. These changes largely occurred prior to the construction of the hillfort, in the Early Iron Age, and suggest complex changes could be made over relatively short periods of time. There is also good evidence for later Iron Age modifications and additions to the ditch systems. Radiocarbon dated deposits of human and animal skulls were found in the Salisbury Plain ditches, and Bradley *et al.* (1994: 67) suggest a change from irregular flat-bottomed ditches to regular V-shaped ditches in the Iron Age.[22]

The linear boundaries on the Berkshire Downs, Cranborne Chase, Salisbury Plain, and west Hampshire have all been examined in detail and are depicted and described in Figures 2.10–2.13. The desire in all of these areas seems to have been to create large territories that were based on valleys. Some of these territories are then subdivided into smaller units that are arranged perpendicular to the axis of the landscape to provide access to the different resource zones of river valley and chalk downland. Some river territories, such as that around the Wallop and the Nine Mile River, appear strangely devoid of field systems and subsidiary boundaries, and these areas may have been set apart for grazing or woodland. The systems are seldom complete or clearly defined, and boundaries could be defined by human constructions, linear ditches and banks, and natural formations, such as escarpments, rivers, and possibly woods. It is also clear that boundaries were often unfinished and the line of the boundary could be changed, resulting in an overlapping that would seem to make little sense. The overall patterns seem consistent with the structures suggested by Fleming (1988) for Dartmoor. Large areas were set aside for pasture whereas others became the focus of arable activity. Areas such as the Wallop and the Bourne valleys could be equivalent to the high moors on Dartmoor.

Cross-Ridge Dykes

There are certain regions of chalk downland that do not seem to have been divided by long linear boundaries, most notably the Sussex Downs and the Ebble–Nadder ridge in south Wiltshire. These regions are instead characterized by short stretches of ditch and bank that are known as cross-ridge or spur dykes. The former cut across pronounced ridges whereas the latter generally cut off spurs projecting from the ridges. These short lengths of

---

[22] Cunliffe (2000: 159) has recently argued that, in some situations, linear boundaries were laid out as an integral part of a field system. His evidence is based on the relationship between the linears and field systems at Woolbury and Quarley Hill. In both areas large rectangular fields are laid out transverse to substantial linear earthworks. However, in neither of these situations was it demonstrated by excavation that the linear boundary was a primary feature of the field system. It is possible that the linear boundary was laid out to conform to, and overlie, the existing field system. Just such a relationship is visible at Windy Dido (Cunliffe and Poole 2000f: fig. 7.2) where a linear boundary follows the long axis of the established fields for some distance before turning to cut across the field system. This possibility was also recognized as an explanation for the relationship between the linear ditch and field system at Totterdown in north Wiltshire (Fowler, P. J. 2000: 71), though Fowler dismissed the idea for no obvious reason. I would argue that the contemporaneity of field systems and linear boundaries remains unproven in Wessex.

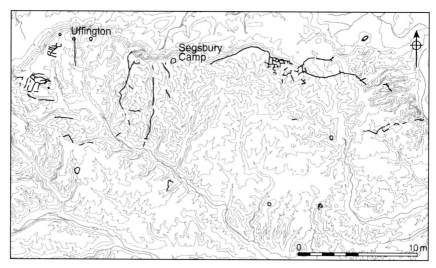

Figure 2.10 The Berkshire linear ditch system (after Gosden and Lock 2007: fig. 4.2; Richards 1978: fig. 21). The northern boundary of this system, Grims Ditch, starts on the high ground to the west of the Thames valley and was built along the northern edge of the chalk escarpment. It meanders up and down the slope of the escarpment in an erratic fashion which is difficult to explain. The escarpment boundary ends abruptly to the east of Segsbury hillfort and the western part of the escarpment has no linear earthwork to enhance its boundary status. Instead linear boundaries, which can be over 1.3 km long, are positioned on the watersheds between the valleys that run into the Lambourn valley, a tributary of the Kennet. The nature of the valley system means that two groups are present. An eastern group, that runs north–south along spurs that separate the tributaries of the Lambourn, and a western group, that runs east–west between the Aldbourne and Lambourn valleys.

boundary have been the subject of considerable controversy over the years; many authors have argued that they are not boundaries but routeways used for moving cattle between river valleys, or coombes (e.g. Curwen 1951; Tilley 2004). However, the arguments for this interpretation are not convincing. It is clear that some boundaries have been used as tracks but this is a secondary aspect of the ditches' history and is comparable to the later Roman use of linear boundaries (McOmish *et al.* 2002; Fowler, P. J. 2000).[23]

Detailed examination of the cross-ridge dykes on the Ebble–Nadder ridge (Figure 2.14) indicated that that they were territorial boundaries (Fowler, P. J. 1964) and this interpretation seems applicable to the Sussex examples.

---

[23] There are several occasions when linear boundaries were reused as trackways in the Roman settlements on Salisbury Plain (Knock Down East: McOmish *et al.* 2002: 95: fig. 4.11).

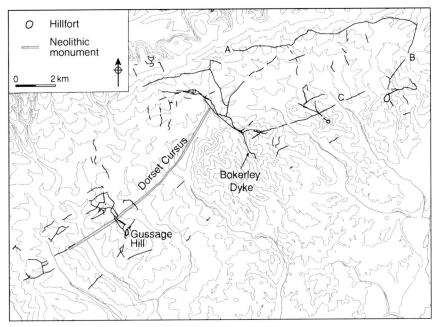

Figure 2.11 The linear boundaries of Cranborne Chase (after Bowen 1990: fig. 3). This can be divided into two halves by the major north-south linear boundary, Bokerley Dyke, which in its final form is Late Roman, or immediately post-Roman in date. The eastern part of the system is relatively well defined with linear ditches providing boundaries to the north, south, east and west (Bokerley Dyke). All of these boundaries are constructed in sympathy with the natural topography. The northern boundary (A) runs parallel to but south of the northern escarpment of the Chase; the eastern boundary (B) runs parallel to the Avon valley; the southern boundary (C) cuts across the head of several valleys running south to the river Allen and coincides with the geological boundary of the chalk. Within the area defined by these boundaries are several truncated or incomplete linear ditches that subdivide the enclosed area into blocks of land around the heads of the valleys.

The continuation of this system to the west of Bokerley Dyke is problematic. Discontinuous linear boundaries cut across the valleys to define the south-east edge of the system and some ditches run along the watersheds, notably through Gussage Hill, and these may indicate the subdivision of the larger unit. The northern boundary may have been woodland as the chalk at this point is covered by a large deposit of clay-with-flints that would discourage settlement.

The main distinction between these systems and the larger linear systems is the absence of the principal 'spinal' linear boundary. This may be because the spinal element of the Sussex and Ebble–Nadder ridge boundary systems is represented by the topography. Both regions are characterized by a steep

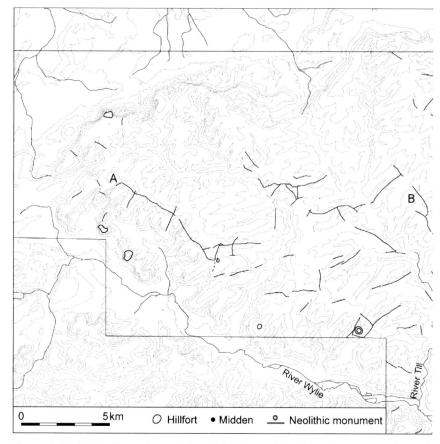

Figure 2.12(a) The linear boundaries of Salisbury Plain (based on McOmish *et al.* 2002: fig. i.1; and data from the National Mapping Programme). Salisbury Plain is characterized by very lengthy linear boundaries and these have been divided into spinal linears, which are 'placed in very prominent positions, often following contours along a false crest, or positioned along watersheds or flanking valley escarpments' (McOmish *et al.* 2002: 57), and subsidiary linears which run off the spinal boundaries, often along subsidiary spurs or across valleys, to define territories.

A good example on the western edge of the plain is Old Ditch West (A), which runs along the high ground that separates the Wylie valley from the Imber/Chitterne valley in the centre of the plain. It cuts across the top of coombes running south, and subsidiary linears run down the spurs to define small territories arranged at right angles to the Wylie valley. The east end of Old Ditch West turns east to run along a spur towards the Chitterne Brook.

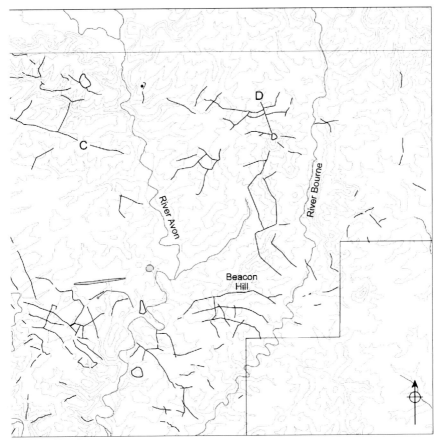

Figure 2.12(b) Another important spinal linear (B) runs along the east side of the Till and separates the valley from a substantial area of high downland. This linear terminates at Winterborne Stoke, where it runs into a complex arrangement of linears that divides the land between the Till and the Avon valleys immediately to the south of Stonehenge.

On the north side of the plain the principal spinal linear, Old Nursery Ditch (C), runs along a ridge of high ground between two valleys that run west to east into the Avon. The land to the north of this boundary is divided by several subsidiary boundaries that cut across the valley.

The situation on the east side of the plain appears more complicated (Bradley *et al.* 1994). The Sidbury linear (D) is part of a complex north-south boundary that runs along the high ground on the west side of the Bourne valley. The spinal element of the boundary appears to be much more closely integrated with the subsidiary elements and the result is a discontinuous linear boundary. This is particularly clear on Beacon Hill where the spinal linear becomes a subsidiary linear that traverses the valley. In places the spinal element of this boundary comprises at least two major linear ditches that must represent some form of re-alignment of the territory.

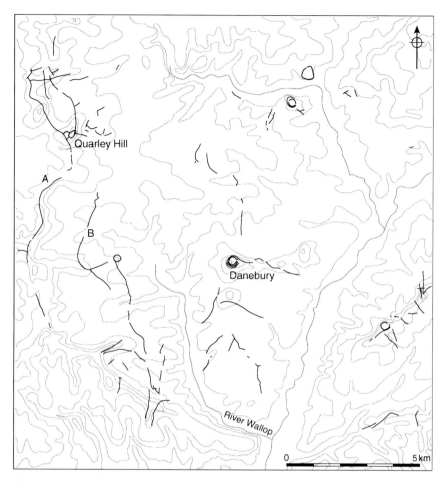

Figure 2.13 The linear boundaries of west Hampshire (after Palmer 1984: map 1). The Quarley Linear (A) can be followed some considerable distance to the south of the hillfort, on the high ground that defines the west side of the Bourne valley (see Figure 2.12). Further east another linear (B), running roughly north–south, appears to define the west edge of the area of land that surrounds the valley of the Wallop. The eastern edge of the territory is defined by a discontinuous boundary running north–south through the hillfort of Danebury, though this boundary is difficult to define as there are field systems in this area that confuse the picture. The area to the east of this boundary is roughly divided by subsidiary linears running east–west and one of these linears runs up to the entrance of the hillfort at Danebury.

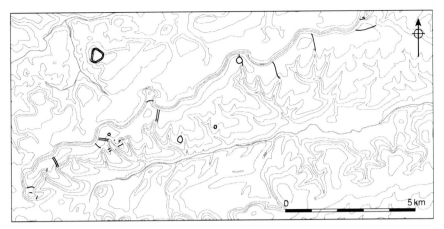

Figure 2.14 The enclosures and linear earthworks, spur and cross dykes, of the chalk ridge between the valleys of the Ebble and the Nadder (after Fowler 1964: fig. 1).

northern escarpment that would have acted as a natural boundary that did not require human definition.[24] The cross dykes also tend to run into steep-sided coombes, which can be interpreted as natural continuations of the boundary.

Spur dykes appear to serve quite a different role. Most of the examples on the Ebble–Nadder ridge were placed on spurs that provide access routes up the escarpment onto the ridge from the valley of the Nadder. They are therefore short physical representations of a natural boundary, the escarpment, where it is breached by entrances. The use of short stretches of boundary to restrict access to parts of the landscape developed during the Late Bronze Age. Several hilltops appear to be delineated by short stretches of linear earthwork that cut across spurs or run along the edge of escarpments; examples include Cold Kitchen Hill (Cunliffe 1971), Butser Hill (Piggott, S. 1930), Swallowcliffe Down (Fowler, P. J. 1964) and Tan Hill (Kirkham 2005).[25] These enclosed hilltops are very similar in location to the earliest enclosures (see below) and good examples are Tan Hill and Martinsell on the northern escarpment of the Vale of Pewsey. The earthworks define a large flat-topped plateau which has extensive views across the vale and across the downlands to the north. Both are associated with substantial linear boundaries that are part of a system dividing the Pewsey Downs, and Martinsell marks the eastern end

[24] The principal Berkshire linear was abandoned when the escarpment overlooking the Vale of the White Horse became a prominent feature of the landscape.

[25] Small enclosures also appear to have been created around ancient monuments, such as long barrows and barrow cemeteries.

of that system. The location, the size of the area enclosed, and the general absence of settlement activity inside (Payne *et al.* 2006) all differentiate these enclosures from the later hillforts.

Middens in the Vale of Pewsey

The southern boundary of the Berkshire and Marlborough Downs includes the Vale of Pewsey, a distinctive area, which is very different geologically, ecologically, and archaeologically from the rest of this region. The dome of a chalk syncline has been eroded away to expose the underlying, and softer, greensand deposits, which have in turn been eroded, leaving two steep chalk scarps on the north and south sides. The west side drops sharply to the damper clay vales around the headwaters of the Bristol Avon. The vale itself is drained by the Salisbury Avon, which cuts through the chalk escarpment on the south side. The vale is characterized by heavy clay soils and these tend to make this a relatively damp landscape, which was difficult to cultivate in prehistory.

There is no published archaeological analysis of the vale but work in progress (Paul Tubb pers. comm.) indicates that later prehistoric settlements were not permanently established in the centre of the vale but instead were concentrated around the edge, on the chalk at the base, and at the top, of the escarpments. These areas were extensively exploited in the Late Bronze Age/ Early Iron Age transition period, and a large number of settlements producing pottery of this date have been identified. A small number of these settlements are exceptionally large mounds, rich in occupation debris, and these are known as midden sites. The principal excavated examples are All Cannings Cross (Cunnington 1923) and Stanton St Bernard (Tullett 2008) at the base of the escarpment on the north side of the vale; East Chisenbury (McOmish 1996) on the downlands just to the south of the vale and Potterne (Lawson 2000) on an isolated outcrop of fertile land on the western edge of the vale. Sites comparable to the Pewsey middens are very rare. The most well documented is Runnymede Bridge on the River Thames (Needham and Spence 1997a, 1997b) but there are also comparable sites at Wallingford, also on the Thames (Cromarty *et al.* 2006) and Whitchurch in Warwickshire (Waddington and Sharples 2007; Waddington 2009).[26]

These middens appear to be located close to routeways into and out of the vale, and their size and complexity suggests they represent localities where

---

[26] Also contemporary with these middens are a number of artefact-rich sites in the Isle of Purbeck: see page 81.

large numbers of people gathered together to socialize at certain times of the year.[27] The basic midden matrix appears to comprise of large quantities of dung, which would indicate that considerable numbers of animals were gathered together. The quantities of animal bones and ceramics discarded in the midden suggest that feasting was one of the principal activities undertaken. Perhaps the unoccupied vale represented neutral ground used for seasonal grazing and the feasts were regular summer events when the animals were moved here away from the cereal fields of the chalk downland.

Focusing on Location and Place: Definitions

Enclosures are a characteristic feature of the Wessex landscape in the Iron Age and they range in size from small enclosures defined by a shallow ditch, which are assumed to represent the homes of a single family, to hillforts with boundaries comprising several substantial banks and ditches that enclosed large numbers of houses, and were clearly the bases for large communities. After the initial appearance of enclosures in the Middle Bronze Age,[28] there seems to be a period at the beginning of the first millennium BC when most settlements were unenclosed. Several small settlements are known on the chalk: Coburg Road in Dorset (Figure 2.15; Smith, R. J. C. *et al.* 1992), Dunch Hill on Salisbury Plain (Andrews 2006), Burderop Down on the Marlborough Downs (Gingell 1992), Winnall Down and Twyford Down in Hampshire (Figure 2.15; Fasham 1985; Walker and Farwell 2000). Some scholars have claimed that hillforts appeared in the Late Bronze Age but

[27] The recent publication of the Salisbury Plain Training Area claims that the midden at East Chisenbury is closely associated with six linear ditches and a pit alignment (McOmish *et al.* 2002: 58) but only one linear boundary is positioned close to the site in their plots of linear boundaries (McOmish *et al.* 2002: figs. i.1, 3.1). The nature of the associated enclosure (McOmish *et al.* 2002: fig. 3.8) also seems problematic without any excavation.

[28] Enclosures were a feature of the Middle Bronze Age settlement of Wessex and excavated examples include the distinctive rectangular enclosures of South Lodge, Martin Down in Cranborne Chase (Barrett *et al.* 1991) and the more irregular forms at Boscombe Down East (Stone 1936) and Thorney Down (Stone 1937) on Porton Down. Unexcavated examples were identified at Dunch Hill and Milston Down on Salisbury Plain (McOmish *et al.* 2002: fig. 3.20), and in the Marlborough Downs (Piggott, C. M. 1942). Several sites are known to have boundaries that do not completely enclose the settlement (Angle Ditch and Down Farm in Cranborne Chase: Barrett *et al.* 1991). At South Lodge the ditched enclosure seems to have been created at the end of the settlement's life and the ditch was backfilled almost immediately after it was excavated. Enclosures of this form are largely restricted to the west, and in Sussex a different form of settlement surrounded by palisades and low banks is known at sites such as Blackpatch (Drewett 1982) and Itford Hill (Burstow and Holleyman 1957). Unenclosed settlements are also quite common throughout Wessex and well-known examples include Easton Lane in Hampshire (Fasham *et al.* 1989) and Rowden in Dorset (Woodward, P. J. 1991).

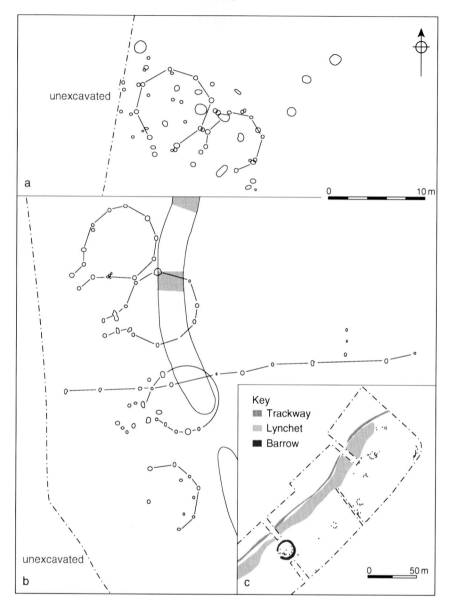

Figure 2.15 Unenclosed settlements of the Late Bronze Age at a) Coburg Road, Dorset; b) Winnall Down, Hampshire; c) Twyford Down, Hampshire (after Smith *et al.* 1992: fig. 3; Fasham 1985: fig. 7; Walker and Farwell 2000: fig. 10).

Needham's detailed assessment of the evidence suggests that this is generally not the case (Needham 2007: 55),[29] though there are early enclosures that are sometimes referred to as hillforts. Balksbury (Wainwright 1969; Wainwright and Davies 1995) has radiocarbon dates that indicate it was constructed at the beginning of the Late Bronze Age/Early Iron Age transition period (Ellis, C. J. and Rawlings 2001). This is a large, sparsely occupied, hilltop enclosure comparable to other potentially early enclosures at Martinsell, Walbury (Payne *et al.* 2006) and Harting Beacon (Bedwin 1978, 1979). The enclosure at Rams Hill on the Berkshire Downs (Needham and Ambers 1994) has also been dated to the beginning of the Late Bronze Age but this seems to be atypical.

The characteristically simple curvilinear enclosure appears to date at its earliest to the Late Bronze Age/Early Iron Age transition, *c.*800–600 BC (Needham 2007: fig. 1).[30] Well-dated early enclosures have been identified at Overton Down, OD X/XI (Figure 2.16; Fowler, P. J. 2000), Old Down Farm (Figure 2.16; Davies 1981) and Houghton Down (Figure 2.16; Cunliffe and Poole 2000g). These small enclosures become very common in the Early Iron Age and examples include Winnall Down (Figure 2.16; Fasham 1985), Gussage All Saints (Figure 2.16; Wainwright 1979a) and Little Woodbury (Figure 2.16; Bersu 1940). Hillforts appear to be a feature of the Early Iron Age and the construction of substantially bounded, and permanently occupied enclosures at Danebury (Cunliffe 1995) and Maiden Castle (Sharples 1991a) date to this period.

Enclosures continued to be a feature of the settlement record of the Middle Iron Age but the number of small enclosures declined and some hillforts were expanded and enhanced by the construction of increasingly substantial boundaries and complex entrances ('developed hillforts'; Cunliffe in Cunliffe and Miles 1984). The best dated sequences are from Danebury (Cunliffe 1995) and Maiden Castle (Sharples 1991a) but comparable complex hillforts include Hambledon Hill (RCHME 1996) and Yarnbury (Cunnington 1933; RCHME 1999). Most of the simple curvilinear enclosures of Early–Middle

---

[29] Hillforts argued to date to the Late Bronze Age/Early Iron Age transition include Liddington (Hirst and Rahtz 1996) and Poundbury (Green, C. S. 1987), but these have not been extensively excavated and the presence of early pre-enclosure activity may confuse the chronology.

[30] This phase is referred to as the Earliest Iron Age by Cunliffe (1991) and Needham (2007) as they believe that social traditions of Iron Age form appear at this time and that the social importance of bronze, the Llyn Fawr tradition, is declining. Whilst I agree with both these views I also believe that bronze retains a social importance that it does not have in the succeeding Iron Age and that Iron Age traditions are not fully established. I therefore wish to highlight the transitional nature of the period by alluding to the presence of both Bronze Age and Iron Age social strategies.

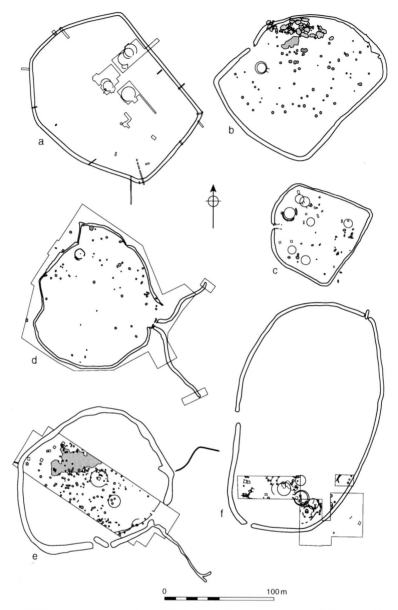

Figure 2.16 A comparative plan of Early Iron Age enclosures at a) Overton Down, Wiltshire; b) Old Down Farm, Hampshire; c) Winnall Down, Hampshire; d) Gussage All Saints, Dorset; e) Little Woodbury, Wiltshire; f) Houghton Down, Hampshire (after Fowler unpublished; Davies 1981; Fasham 1985; Wainwright 1979a; Bersu 1940; Cunliffe and Poole 2000g).

Iron Age type were abandoned before the Late Iron Age, when small rectangular, often multiple, enclosures became common. The sequence is clear at Winnall Down (Fasham 1985) and Gussage All Saints (Wainwright 1979a). However, a morphologically distinct type of enclosure, the banjo, appeared during the Middle Iron Age, namely, Micheldever Wood (Fasham 1987), and banjo enclosures continued to be constructed into the Late Iron Age, as at Nettlebank Copse (Cunliffe and Poole 2000f).

Unenclosed settlements are identifiable throughout the Iron Age though they do not seem to be as common as enclosures. An Early Iron Age settlement was excavated in front of the hillfort at Battlesbury (Ellis, C. J. and Powell 2008) and, for most of the Iron Age, the settlement at Winnall Down was unenclosed (Fasham 1985).

In most considerations of the enclosures of the Iron Age a distinction is made between simple enclosures and hillforts. The simple enclosures are normally considered to be smaller and located in low-lying positions adjacent to agricultural land, whereas hillforts are considered to be larger, to have boundaries of substantial size, and to be located on or near prominent hilltops (Palmer 1984: 9). Enclosures and hillforts are also believed to have significantly different functions. The enclosures are thought to be simple farmsteads occupied by 'households' who owned and farmed the adjacent fields (Hill 1995a: 51; Thomas, R. 1998: 9). In contrast, hillforts are regarded as 'centres for communal rituals and festivals' (Hill 1995a: 55) or 'central places in complex redistribution networks' (Cunliffe 1991: 356). However, despite the extensive debate on the morphological and functional variability of hillforts (Hill 1995a, 1996) there has been little detailed consideration of the variability of small enclosures or the differences that distinguish small hillforts from large enclosures. A detailed examination of the morphology of the small enclosures of Wessex has twice been attempted (Palmer 1984; Bowen 1990).[31]

Palmer (1984) undertook a survey of the landscape around Danebury and isolated four different types of later prehistoric settlement that could be broken down into several sub-classes (Table 2.1).

The Cranborne Chase (Bowen 1990) survey divided enclosures (Figure 2.17) into ten categories (Table 2.2). There was only one hillfort in the study area and this was not identified as a separate category of enclosure.[32]

[31] The recent volume on the archaeology of Salisbury Plain (McOmish *et al.* 2002) does not provide a detailed examination of the character of the later prehistoric enclosures. There is no catalogue, and no attempt to make a systematic classification of form or discuss their size range. The date range for these enclosures in the 'Middle to Late Iron Age' (McOmish *et al.* 2002: 81) is misleading as some of the enclosures were created in the Early Iron Age (Fulford *et al.* 2006).

[32] Bowen (1990) argued that Bokerley Dyke acted as a boundary that separated two tribes who preferred different enclosure forms. However, a re-examination of the Wiltshire SMR indicates the differences are less significant than Bowen suggests.

Table 2.1 The classification of enclosures in the Danebury Environs survey (Palmer 1984)

Hillforts	Hillforts	8
	Possible hillforts	2
	Wide-ditched enclosures	13
Simple enclosures	Curvilinear enclosures	32
	D-shaped enclosures	51
	Rectilinear enclosures	34
Complex enclosures	Cluster complexes	25 + 1?
	Superimposed complexes	8
	Compounds	3 + 5?
Unenclosed settlements		13 + 3?

It is apparent from the classification that the overall pattern of enclosures in the Danebury Environs and the Cranborne Chase surveys are quite different. Significant differences include the large number of banjo enclosures in Cranborne Chase and the large number of complex enclosures in the Danebury Environs. These issues will be discussed later in this chapter but first I will consider the difference between hillforts and enclosures.

Analysis of enclosures indicates that morphology is not the main criterion for separating out hillforts from other enclosures. There are large enclosures that do not have substantial boundaries or a prominent location (e.g. Pimperne 17, Knock Wood), there are relatively small enclosures with complex multiple boundaries that are not on hilltops (e.g. Farnham a14) and there are enclosures with substantial boundaries (Suddern Farm, Upper Copse) that are not classed as hillforts. However, in a general sense size is important, and in the Danebury Environs study there is a clear cut-off between the enclosures below 2.6 ha and those above 3.7 ha (Palmer 1984: fig. 4). Almost all the large enclosures are accepted as hillforts. The size of the boundary is more difficult to assess, especially when examining the crop mark evidence, but some of the multiple boundaries at sites such as Suddern Farm and Farnham a14 may well indicate Late Iron Age developments.

These differences in scale are not sufficient to indicate a significant functional or social distinction between simple enclosures and hillforts. Furthermore, it is clear that there is a great deal of variability in the category of 'simple enclosures' that undermines the suggestion that these represent 'single households' (Hill 1995a: 51). Most of the excavated enclosures are small and one of the smallest, Winnall Down I, contains at least four houses (Fasham 1985: 130) and has been interpreted as containing two separate households (Parker

Figure 2.17 A simplified plan of the enclosures of Cranborne Chase (after Bowen 1990, fig. 46 a–k; © Crown copyright, NMR). The enclosure in the bottom left is Gussage All Saints and the large triple-ditched enclosure above this is Whitsbury, the only hillfort in the illustration.

Pearson 1996: 124). Cunliffe (2000: 170) argues that large enclosures, such as Houghton Down, were nucleated settlements occupied by several households. A larger enclosure or hillfort could simply indicate the desire to enclose more people, and the size and complexity of the enclosure boundary may reflect merely the available labour resources and the length of occupation.

Table 2.2 The classification of enclosures in Cranborne Chase (Bowen 1990, with amendments)[33]

Rectangular and trapezoidal	25
Small polygons	7
Tombstone or D-shaped	21
Parallel-sided and double round-ended	4
Ovoid	23
Sub-circular	17
Banjo	12
Spectacles	2
Concentric	7
Large polygons	2

It would therefore be possible to argue that small enclosures and hillforts essentially served the same purpose and simply reflect the desire to provide a boundary that defined the community. However, there does seem to be a difference in the landscape location taken by enclosures and hillforts that might indicate there was a significant difference in the roles of these two types of site. The name 'hillfort' presumes that these enclosures are situated on hills, and whilst this is the situation for many areas of Wessex (e.g. central Hampshire), there are Wessex hillforts that are not situated on obvious or prominent hilltops. For example, many of the Wessex hillforts are placed on the edge of the chalk escarpment and these are often not distinctive hills (e.g. Bratton Camp). What all the hillforts share is a position that maximizes medium- to long-distance views from the enclosure. Even the escarpment hillforts have been carefully located to maximize their views in all directions and are seldom overlooked by high ground.

The all-round visibility of hillforts contrasts dramatically with the locations chosen for the construction of small enclosures. These enclosures are often placed in positions that have potentially extensive views; they are close to the summits of many areas of high ground, and often on spurs that project from high ground. Yet they are invariably located on a slope on one side of the spur and visibility is restricted to a limited area of the landscape, normally the valley in which the enclosure is located.

Most of the well-known excavated enclosures demonstrate this locational preference. The enclosure at Winnall Down (Fasham 1985) sits at the end of a spur that drops steeply down to the valley of the Itchen. It would have had

---

[33] These categories and the number of enclosures identified have been modified by a reanalysis of the data in the Wiltshire SMR, which incorporates the enclosures of Wiltshire up to the rivers Ebble and Avon.

good views along the dry valley to the south and into the valley of the Itchen but not towards the valley immediately to the north. In contrast, the adjacent enclosure of Winnall Down II (Davis 2007) was positioned with a view into the valley on the north side of the coombe but had no views towards the southern valley. Had either enclosure been positioned a little to the south, or north, then both would have had views into both valleys. Similarly, the Overton Down enclosure (Fowler, P. J. 2000) was located on a south-facing slope which provides good views into Pickledean valley but no visual access to the Valley of the Stones to the north. The enclosure on Swallowcliffe Down (Clay 1925) lies on the Ebble–Nadder ridge but has been positioned on the south side of the ridge and there is no visual access into the Nadder valley from the enclosure. There are good views to the south and a small extension around the south-facing entrance may have been designed to enhance the views into a coombe that cuts into the ridge from the Ebble valley at this point. The location is very different from the location of the nearby hillfort at Chiselbury, which sits in the centre of the ridge and has good all-round visibility. Gussage All Saints is located on a spur to the south of the Gussage Brook and again it is asymmetrically located on the north side of the spur to look along the valley of the Gussage Brook with the entrance facing down the valley to the confluence with the River Allen.

The difference between a hillfort and an enclosure is therefore closely related to their visual dominance of the landscape as well as their monumentality. The all-round visibility from a hilltop location suggests a central relationship with the surrounding landscape and the people that occupied this area as they carried out their daily activities. The desire of the inhabitants to see the hillfort as they worked in the fields might be important and provide a sense of belonging and security, or clarity of relationships (Bloch 1995a: 66). An analogous effect might be that of the panopticon (Foucault 1977). The inhabitants of the hillfort were placed in a visually prominent location which allowed them to survey the surrounding countryside. From these vantage points they could oversee and control the planting of crops, the movement of animals, the exploitation of resources, and, potentially, the construction of dependent settlements.[34] The contrast with the location of simple enclosures is dramatic. Their visual sphere encompasses only the locality, which reflected the concern of the inhabitants with monitoring the land that they cultivated and grazed. Their locations below the highest point of the local terrain might well have been a deliberate attempt to evade supervision from the nearby

---

[34] This visibility has been interpreted as related to the defensive requirements of the fort but it may be significant that hillforts frequently do not have good visual access to their immediate surroundings, which would create tactical problems (Bowden and McOmish 1987).

hillfort but it might also acknowledge the importance of the hillfort (Bloch 1995a: 70).

Focusing on Location and Place: Distributions

Having argued that there is a significant distinction between hillforts and simple enclosures, it is now important to look briefly at how both these enclosure types are distributed in Wessex. Hill has suggested that 'Wessex was characterized by a densely utilised landscape of small dispersed enclosed settlements . . . and large enclosures—traditionally called hillforts' (Hill 1995a: 45). The assumption is that both hillforts and enclosures are evenly distributed across the landscape. However, several authors have noted that the distribution of hillforts is not uniform (Corney in Payne *et al.* 2006: 133; Hill 1995a: 50). For example, there are no hillforts in the central area of Salisbury Plain, between Casterley Camp and Bratton Camp, or on the central Dorset Downs, north of Eggardon and Poundbury, and some areas of downland have only a few small hillforts, such as Cranborne Chase and East Hampshire.

It would also be very misleading to assume that small enclosures were evenly distributed across the downlands of Wessex. In Figure 2.18 the known enclosures and topography of four different areas, 5 km², of Wessex are illustrated. Area a, Overton and Fyfield Downs, lies to the east of the Neolithic henge at Avebury (marked on the map for reference) and was intensively studied by Peter Fowler (2000); area b, Rockbourne Downs, is the northern part of Cranborne Chase, and was studied by Bowen (1990); area c lies between the Rivers Avon and the Bourne, just north of Salisbury, and has been examined as part of the English Heritage National Mapping Programme; area d is the area to the east of the hillfort of Danebury (which is marked) and was intensively examined by Cunliffe (2000). All these areas are well studied and there seem to be few methodological reasons why we should not assume the sites identified in each area reflect the pattern of later prehistoric settlement. However, these maps clearly show major differences in the density of small enclosure settlement which ranges from about 23 to the north of Salisbury to 2 on Fyfield and Overton Downs. These differences are more enhanced in other areas and only one small enclosure of Iron Age date, Bishopstone, has been located in the whole of the county of Sussex (Hamilton 2003; Hamilton and Gregory 2000).

An obvious feature of the distribution of the enclosures to the north of Salisbury, and on Cranborne Chase, is the presence of two or more enclosures on the same hilltop. Many of the excavated small enclosures have adjacent

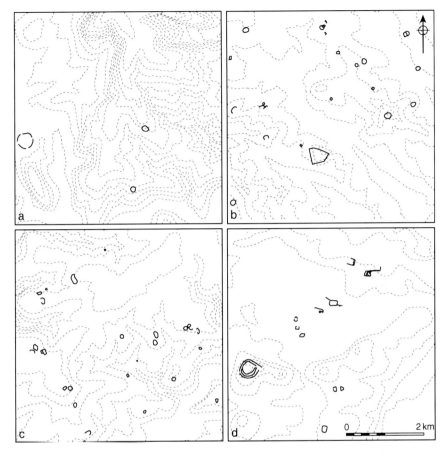

Figure 2.18 The distribution of small enclosures in four areas of 5 km² in Wessex: a) the area centred on Overton Down, showing the great henge at Avebury; b) an area of Cranborne Chase, showing the late Roman polygonal enclosure at Rockbourne; c) an area to the north east of Salisbury; d) an area to the east of Danebury hillfort (after Fowler 2000; Bowen 1990; National Mapping Programme; and Cunliffe 2000).

partners: Little Woodbury is paired with Great Woodbury (Bersu 1940: fig. 1) and there are two enclosures at Pimperne (Harding, D. W. *et al.* 1993), Winnall Down (Davis 2007) and Gussage All Saints (Bowen in Wainwright 1979a: fig. 111). The presence of these linked enclosures and the overall density of enclosures in some areas do not support the argument that enclosures represent autonomous households (Hill 1995a: 51; Thomas, R. 1998: 9), as there would have to have been close cooperation between the households in these enclosures, particularly as they appear to have been farming the same fields (Davis 2007).

Several authors (Bowen 1990; Fasham 1987) have also noted the uneven distribution of banjo enclosures. These morphologically distinctive enclosures are fairly common in Cranborne Chase (Bowen 1990) and in central Hampshire (Fasham 1987), areas where other enclosures are well known. However, they are unknown in the area to the north of Salisbury, despite the high densities of simple enclosures known in this area. There is also a cluster in Berkshire (Winton 2004) where simple enclosures are almost unknown. Fasham (1987: 63) notes a close relationship between the enclosures in central Hampshire and areas of clay-with-flint and suggests they might indicate the adoption of a different agricultural regime. These observations appear to be confirmed by work in other areas of Wessex. The Berkshire enclosures appear to be preferentially located to exploit both heavy and light soils (seven are on light soils, six on heavy soils; Winton 2004: 21) and the distinctive group of paired enclosures on the Great Ridge, between the Nadder and the Wylie, also appear to be on heavy clay soils (Corney 1989). However, the banjo enclosures on Cranborne Chase seem to be located on open downland.

It seems therefore that there may be an explanation for the uneven distribution of banjo enclosures that is based on the expansion of settlement on to previously under-exploited parts of the landscape. This would fit into a model of increasing agricultural complexity in the Late Iron Age. However, this does not explain the uneven distribution of simple enclosures in the Early Iron Age. Unfortunately the distribution of these enclosures is too imperfectly understood to be easily explained. In contrast, the distribution of hillforts has been well studied and we are able to talk with confidence about these relationships.

Hillforts have a clear locational preference for two very distinctive areas of the Wessex landscape, chalk escarpments and river valleys (Corney in Payne *et al.* 2006: 133). The importance of the escarpment is clearly demonstrated by the situation in north Wessex; almost all the enclosures in the Marlborough and Berkshire Downs are located on the escarpment which defines the northern edge of the downlands, and along the southern escarpment, which overlooks the Vale of Pewsey (Figure 2.19).[35] These hillforts are evenly spaced, apart from a cluster of three at Uffington, and a gap between Barbury and

[35] These include, from east to west, Segsbury, Rams Hill, Uffington Castle, Hardwell Camp, Liddington Castle, Barbury Castle, Oldbury, and Olivers Castle above Devizes. Along the north side of the Vale of Pewsey are Rybury, Giants Graves (which some would not accept as a hillfort), and Martinsell Hill.

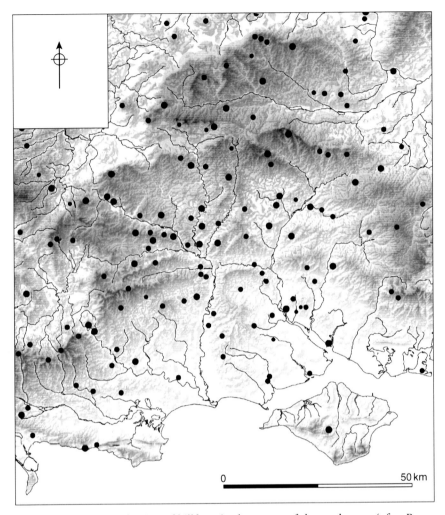

Figure 2.19 The distribution of hillforts in the centre of the study area (after Payne *et al.* 2006: fig. 1.17).

Oldbury that encompasses the area around Avebury. Hillforts are also arranged along the north Hampshire escarpment overlooking the Kennet;[36] along the northern escarpment of central Dorset[37] and along the northern escarpment of the Sussex Downs,[38] though these are not as evenly spaced as the north Wiltshire group.

[36] Chisbury, Walbury Camp, Beacon Hill, Ladle Hill and, arguably, Winklebury.
[37] Rawlsbury and Nettlecombe Tout.
[38] Torberry, Harting Beacon, Chactonbury Ring, Devils Dyke, Wolstonbury, and Ditchling Beacon.

Several river valleys appear to be the foci for hillfort construction (Corney in Payne *et al.* 2006: 134) and this is a particular feature of the Avon[39] and its tributaries, the Wylie[40] and the Bourne,[41] as they cut through the Wiltshire Downs. In Dorset the Stour is the principal river and was the focus for several hillforts.[42] However, some important rivers that one might have expected to be a focus for settlement do not have associated hillforts. The Frome in Dorset is only closely associated with a single hillfort, Poundbury, and the dominant hillfort in the region, Maiden Castle, sits adjacent to the small tributary of the South Winter-bourne some distance from the Frome. In Sussex and Hampshire, east of the Bourne and Avon valleys, river valleys seem not to be preferred locations. Danebury is located well away from the Test and several suitable hills lie between the hillfort and the river. St Catherine's Hill is located above the Itchen, but there are no other comparable hillforts beside this river.

The lack of a close association with natural boundaries in central Hampshire seems to be replaced by a concern with man-made boundaries. Quarley Hill sits adjacent to a linear boundary (Figure 2.20; Hawkes, C. F. C. 1939) that separates areas partitioned by field systems and open areas given over to pasture (Bellamy 1991: 75–6). Similarly Danebury lies adjacent to, and overlooks, a large area of open land to the west that contrasts with dense field systems to the north, east and south (Davis pers. comm.).

There are no Sussex hillforts close to a river, though there is an insub-stantial and undated enclosure at Castle Hill, Newhaven, where the Ouse meets the sea. The lack of interest in the river valleys of Sussex may be because the downlands are a relatively narrow strip of high ground. Most of the early hillforts are located either on the northern escarpment or on prom-inent hilltops on the edge of the coastal plain (Hamilton and Manley 1997,

---

[39] Casterley Camp, Vespasians Camp, Ogbury and Old Sarum; and south of Salisbury, Clearbury Rings and Castle Ditches, Whitsbury.

[40] The source of the Wylie lies immediately to the north of Whitesheet Hill, though this hillfort is looking south and probably unconnected with the Wylie and there are no other hillforts in the first stretch of the river as it heads north. However, when the valley opens out, and turns to run south-east, it becomes the focus of many hillforts. On the right side of the valley are Cley Hill, Battlesbury, Scratchbury, Knock Castle, and Codford Castle (though these are unusual hillforts) and Yarnbury. On the left side are Bilbury Ring and Groveley Castle.

[41] Sidbury, Quarley, and Figsbury Ring. The first two are set well back from the valley.

[42] Hambledon Hill, Hod Hill, Buzbury Ring, Spettisbury, Badbury Rings, Dudsbury, and eventually Hengistbury Head, at Christchurch Harbour. Badbury Rings is set well back from the river.

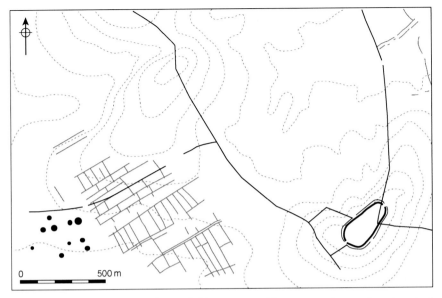

Figure 2.20 The linear boundaries, field systems and barrows to the north and west of the hillfort at Quarley Hill, Hampshire (after Cunliffe 2000, fig. 7.1).

2001). In both locations the hillforts are close to a clear natural boundary in the landscape.

The linear arrangement of hillforts on escarpments and along river valleys has encouraged people to suggest they were built to control routeways through the countryside, though this ignores the significant morphological and chronological differences within the linear groups. The most recent argument for the importance of a Ridgeway route was made by Bell and Lock (2000) in relation to the Berkshire Ridgeway, which connects Segsbury, Rams Hill, Uffington, and Liddington. They argue that the easiest way to cross the downlands in an east-west direction is along the Ridgeway and that this therefore existed as a route for moving animals early in prehistory. Furthermore the east-west orientation of the gateways to the hillforts of Segsbury and Uffington suggests the route initially passed through the hillforts. However, this interpretation ignores Fowler's argument that the Ridgeway is post-Roman and 'demonstrably later than the (prehistoric) landscape it overlies and cuts' (Fowler, P. J. 2000: 22).[43] Furthermore, if the Berkshire escarpment

---

[43] Admittedly, the authors are looking at different parts of the Ridgeway, but both areas appear to be traversed by linear boundaries.

was chosen as a location for hillfort construction because it acted as a route-way then one would expect the other escarpment locations also to mark routeways. However, this is difficult to argue as many of these escarpments are penetrated by coombes that would have hindered movement along the Ridgeway. The current Hampshire Ridgeway between Walbury and Ladle Hill avoids Beacon Hill because it is surrounded by steep coombes, and the hillforts on the Dorset and Sussex Ridgeway are frequently separated by substantial coombes. The argument that these escarpment forts mark a long-distance route therefore seems unconvincing.

The most recent argument for the importance of rivers as routeways was made by Sherratt (1996), who suggests that the rivers of Wessex provided a passage across southern England to Wales and the Midlands that avoided a difficult trip around Cornwall. This argument fails to convince as 'it deliberately conflates monuments of different periods' (Sherratt 1996: 220), it assumes a controlling relationship between rivers and hillforts, such as Danebury and Maiden Castle, which clearly does not exist, and it is inconsistent in failing to explain the absence of important hillforts on several apparently strategic rivers, notably the lower Avon and almost all of the Test. Environmental work in the river valleys of Wessex suggests that the rivers were not free-flowing, nor substantial water courses in the Iron Age (see page 22), and the historical evidence clearly demonstrates that even in the post-Roman period these valleys were not used as routes (Fowler, P. J. 2000).

The above arguments assume that there was considerable organized move-ment of people, animals, and commodities during the Iron Age. The existence of structured routes implies regular long-distance movements across the landscape, from producers to consumers, but the motivation for the creation and repeated use of these routes is seldom discussed. As I will argue in subsequent chapters, the evidence for exchange in the Iron Age is minimal, and it was most likely based on small-scale gift exchange between neighbour-ing communities. The principal feature of Early Iron Age societies is their autonomy. The bounded communities, indicated by the construction of hillforts, rejected contacts with other communities (see Chapter 3), and their members did not participate in regular long-distance movements. We therefore have to come up with another explanation for the location of hillforts along escarpments and valleys.

An important feature of these linear locations is that they lie on boundaries between two distinctive landscapes, and our understanding of these locations is dependent on how we interpret the environment of these adjacent land-scapes. The river valleys were relatively inhospitable, and the limited evidence we have from excavation suggests these areas were not densely occupied

(Evans, J. G. *et al.* 1993). The presence of widespread deposits of alluvium would have limited agricultural activity. Similarly, the escarpments were located between the intensively cultivated downlands and the damp and wooded clay vales. Detailed fieldwalking of the Vale of Wardour (Gingell and Harding 1983), the Vale of Pewsey (Tubb pers. comm.) and the Vale of the White Horse (Tingle 1991) have failed to identify any significant later prehistoric activity in these areas.[44] There is also very little evidence for Early or Middle Iron Age occupation in the coastal plain and the Weald in Sussex (Hamilton 2003).

There may therefore be a link between the decision to build a hillfort on an escarpment or the edge of a valley; both are boundaries between domesticated, partitioned landscapes (the downlands) and wilderness zones of relatively uncontrolled landscapes (river valleys and clay vales). However, despite the lack of evidence for the occupation of these landscapes it is likely they were regularly visited. The wild landscapes contained two important resources that were relatively rare on the downlands: water and timber. These resources were crucial for the reproduction of the downland communities. Water is not routinely available in the high downlands where the hillforts are located, and drinking water may have had to be brought up from the base of the escarpment or the river valley on a daily basis. Cattle would similarly require access to reliable water sources and would have to be taken regularly to water every day. Most of the Early Iron Age hillforts have timber-framed ramparts, which required the destruction of a substantial acreage of carefully managed woodland and the most likely sources of timber were the clay vales or the valleys.[45]

The importance of these boundary locations appears to have diminished in the Middle Iron Age and it is noticeable that many, though not all, of the developed hillforts have quite different locations. One that retained its location

[44] The juxtaposition of the permeable geology of the chalk and the impermeable geology of the underlying greensand and/or clay will result in the appearance of numerous chalk rich springs along the base of the escarpment. These calcareous springs enhanced the soils of the surrounding land and in Pewsey this created localized concentrations of settlement at the base of the escarpment (Tubb pers. comm.).

[45] These wooded landscapes may also have other functions which are both practical and symbolic. Many important Bronze Age hoards are known from these locations, and rivers and boggy areas are known to be favoured for certain types of depositional activity. There is a suggestion that hoards of metalworking tools and evidence for metalworking activity is concentrated in these areas, whereas the downland hoards are more standardized collections, dominated by axes. The burnt mounds are also ambiguous monuments. Some suggest they are cooking locations, possibly for hunted animals, but others would argue that they are saunas. If the latter explanation is accepted then these locations may be special liminal places where individuals go to purify themselves. Most of the evidence for the use of these areas relates to the Bronze Age but it does indicate the potential symbolic significance of a relatively unused part of the landscape.

is the developed hillfort of Yarnbury; though associated with the Wylie valley, it has no visual sightlines to the valley. It is on a very low hill, which, although commanding good views of the surrounding chalk downland, is not a significant feature in the landscape, and it could not be said to have spectacular views comparable to hillforts on the valley sides. Badbury Rings is in a very similar location. Neither Maiden Castle nor Danebury were located on important river valleys but were instead each sited within a large area of chalk downland.[46] This locational preference may be comparable to that observed by Hamilton and Manley (1997, 2001) in Sussex. They argue that in the Middle Iron Age only four hillforts were occupied (The Caburn, Cissbury, The Trundle and Torberry) and that these were located in the centre of the downs. Their visibility is more restricted and regional than the earlier hillforts, which had extensive views from the escarpment. However, they are situated on distinctive hills that are recognizable from some distance away. Central locations appear, therefore, to characterize the developed hillforts of the Middle Iron Age.

Hillfort and Enclosure Relationships

Having examined the uneven distribution of hillforts, small enclosures and banjo enclosures, it is important to consider how these different forms of settlement relate to each other. Various models for the relationship exist in the archaeological literature and I will discuss a couple of these before examining the basic chronological and spatial patterning of these different settlement forms in the area around the hillfort of Danebury. Cunliffe proposed a model where 'the hillfort was the residence of king and retinue, the larger "farms" should be seen as the residences of the noble families, the smaller enclosures and open settlements being the homes of the lower ranks of the client farmers' (Cunliffe 1983: 168–9). In this model all the different settlement elements discussed above were part of a contemporary settlement system, and status was directly reflected by the size of boundary and enclosure. Hill provided an alternative model, which again assumed that all the different settlement elements were contemporary but that society was based on autonomous farmsteads and that hillforts were 'locales for corporate gatherings and rituals, activities outside the normal bounds of culture, economics and social interaction' (Hill 1995a: 53). In contrast, Hingley (1984) provides a model of settlement whereby the presence of a boundary reflects the corporate

---

[46] Maiden Castle, unlike Danebury, is not on a prominent hill, though it does have excellent views. However, this probably reflects the distinctive topography of this part of Hampshire rather than a particular desire of the occupants.

identity of the social group. In his study of the upper Thames valley, isolated bounded settlements were located in the uplands, whereas dense open settlement was the norm in the lowlands. All these studies can be criticized for assuming a stable chronological pattern of settlement throughout the Iron Age and a relatively homogeneous pattern across the Wessex landscape. I have already established that there were significant spatial differences in Wessex and, before we reconsider the relationship between settlement types, we should consider the nature of chronological variability.

The systematic programme of excavations in and around the hillfort of Danebury provides an opportunity to examine the complex chronological relationships between hillforts and enclosures. In this area five hillforts (Bury Hill, Woolbury, Danebury, Balksbury, Quarley Hill) and ten simple enclosures (Houghton Down, New Buildings A and B, Nettlebank Copse, Little Somborne, Meon Hill, Lains Farm, Grateley South, Suddern Farm, and Old Down Farm) have been excavated and the chronological relationship of the different sites is relatively secure (Figures 2.21, 2.22). The examination of the animal bones and crop remains from the Danebury Environs excavations has also explored the possibility of seasonal occupation of these settlements which further complicates the nature of the relationship between different settlement types (Campbell and Hamilton in Cunliffe 2000).

The first enclosures were constructed in the Late Bronze Age/Early Iron Age transition period. Balksbury (Ellis, C. J. and Rawlings 2001) was a large and sparsely occupied enclosure that contained isolated four-post structures and three houses (Wainwright and Davies 1995). The small enclosures at Houghton Down (Cunliffe and Poole 2000e), New Buildings A and B (Cunliffe and Poole 2000c), Meon Hill (Liddell 1933, 1935), and Old Down Farm (Davies 1981) were also occupied at this time.[47] Cunliffe suggested a distinction between small farmsteads with single houses, such as Old Down Farm, and larger 'nucleated' settlements with several houses, such as Houghton Down (Cunliffe 2000: 170), but only Old Down Farm has been completely excavated and the number of houses present in any of these enclosures is unclear. The enclosures at Houghton Down and Old Down Farm contained substantial houses as well as a range of pits and four-post structures. An unenclosed settlement dating to this period appears to have been present at Boscombe Down West, site Q (Richardson 1951), just to the west of the study area.

The only one of these sites to produce any seasonal data was New Buildings. The absence of evidence for lambing suggests it was not occupied in the early spring, but there was evidence for occupation in the late spring/early summer

---

[47] Cunliffe has argued that an enclosure at Danebury was also built in this period (Cunliffe 1995: 16) but the evidence presented for this enclosure has not convinced me.

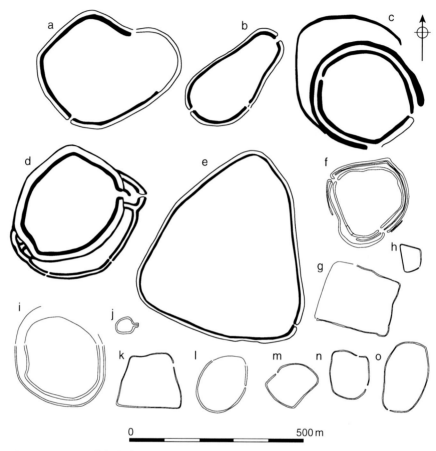

Figure 2.21 Simplified plans of the enclosures and hillforts in the Danebury Environs region: a) Woolbury, b) Quarley Hill, c) Bury Hill, d) Danebury, e) Balksbury, f) Suddern Farm, g) Flint Farm, h) New Buildings, i) Boscombe Down, j) Nettlebank, k) Rowbury, l) Meon Hill, m) Old Down Farm, n) Little Somborne, o) Houghton Down (after Cunliffe 2000 and Cunliffe and Poole 2008).

and autumn/winter (Hamilton in Cunliffe 2000). The plant remains include evidence for autumn activities, waste from threshing and winnowing, and hazel nuts, but the absence of bracken remains, used for winter bedding, suggests the site was not occupied in the winter (Campbell in Cunliffe 2000).

The hillforts of Quarley Hill, Bury Hill I, Danebury and, possibly, Woolbury were constructed at the beginning of the Early Iron Age. Quarley Hill and Danebury are smaller than Balksbury, but Bury Hill I is intermediary in size and this may indicate a slightly earlier construction date (Cunliffe 2000: 164).

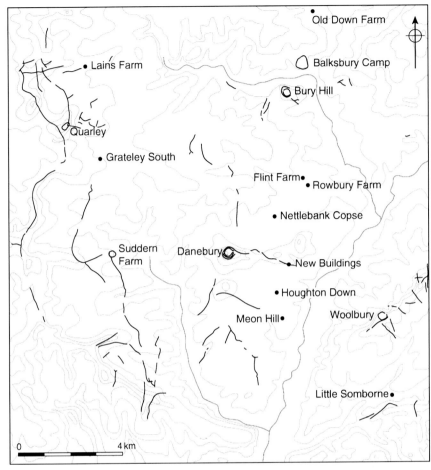

Figure 2.22 The location of the excavated enclosures in the Danebury Environs study area (after Cunliffe 2000 and Cunliffe and Poole 2008).

Danebury produced evidence for occupation comprising a dense spread of pits and four-posters, and rows of small houses arranged along roads that traverse the interior. In contrast, limited excavation and geophysical survey of Bury Hill and Woolbury suggest these hillforts may have had very little occupation. Most of the established small enclosures continued to be occupied in the Early Iron Age and additional enclosures were constructed at Little Somborne (Neal 1980), Lains Farm (Bellamy 1991) and Suddern Farm (Cunliffe and Poole 2000b). The size and shape of these enclosures are very variable.

The situation changed at the beginning of the Middle Iron Age when Cunliffe (2000: 166) suggests the hillforts at Bury Hill, Woolbury, and Quarley Hill were abandoned. Only Danebury continued to be occupied, and developed an increasingly substantial boundary and elaborate entrances. Most of the small enclosures were occupied but it is possible that the boundaries of many were infilled, both naturally and deliberately, and that the settlements were effectively unenclosed. A new, and very small, settlement also appeared at Nettlebank Copse (Cunliffe and Poole 2000d); it was probably enclosed.

Seasonal information is available from the enclosures at Suddern Farm, Nettlebank Copse, and Houghton Down (Campbell and Hamilton in Cunliffe 2000). The latter two sites were permanently occupied; slaughtering of animals occurred throughout the year and all stages of crop processing were present. Houghton Down had a spring peak in sheep mortality, probably related to lambing, but summer deaths were rare. The sheep mortality data from Suddern Farm indicate a substantial number of deaths in the winter and early spring, including perinatal animals, and so indicates lambing. There is very little evidence for summer or autumn deaths and, though threshing debris was present, there were no hazelnut shells. Large numbers of the older animals had periodontal disease and this is argued to indicate culling of the herds gathered together over winter. A similar pattern was noted for Danebury, though this was not assessed in the same way. The absence of evidence for crop threshing in Danebury implies that this activity was taking place at other settlements before the crops were brought to the hillfort (Jones in Cunliffe 1984a: 494–5; Jones in Cunliffe 1995: 45).

Danebury continued to develop throughout the Middle Iron Age but, by the beginning of the second century BC, all of the small enclosures close to Danebury were abandoned. The only firmly attested settlements at this time were at Old Down Farm and inside the enclosures at Woolbury and Balksbury, though these should be regarded as unenclosed settlements inhabiting ancient monuments (Cunliffe 2000: 182). These settlements were all some distance from Danebury and may be outside the territory controlled by the hillforts inhabitants.

At the end of the Middle Iron Age, sometime around the end of the second century BC, a new hillfort was constructed inside the old enclosure at Bury Hill. This has a distinctive form, comprising two massive dump ramparts with a deep, intervening ditch. However, its occupation was short-lived and, during the first century BC, the inhabitants moved to an area immediately around and outside the east entrance (Hawkes, C. F. C. 1940; Payne *et al.* 2006). The abandonment of Bury Hill coincided with the abandonment of Danebury, but also with the redefinition of the old enclosure at Suddern

Farm. This enclosure was redefined by two substantial ditches but it is unclear if these represent a contemporary feature or a sequence of construction. Suddern Farm is not situated on a prominent hilltop and is not normally classed as a hillfort. The settlements at Old Down Farm and Balksbury maintained their limited occupation in the Late Iron Age and Houghton Down, Meon Hill, and Nettlebank Copse were reoccupied. Many of these settlements are characterized by rectangular enclosures (e.g. Old Down Farm, Houghton Down) and these often include multiple, conjoined enclosures, which Cunliffe refers to as clustered enclosure settlements. However, the reoccupation of the settlement at Nettlebank Copse involved the creation of a small banjo enclosure (Cunliffe 2000: 166). Unfortunately, the nature of the settlement in this enclosure is unclear, and activity is largely represented by the deposition of rubbish in and around the ditch.

The Late Iron Age occupation of Nettlebank Copse appears to have been restricted to the autumn or winter and there is a very strong autumn peak for sheep mortality, which might indicate a specific cull. The plant remains also indicate specialized crop processing in the autumn, drying barley and using spelt waste, as well as activity from autumn through to early spring. Other unusual features of the site are the consumption of mature pigs and wild animals, and the presence of large numbers of spindle whorls. The Late Iron Age evidence from Houghton Down was quite different from the pattern of the Early Iron Age. Most of the animals were old and were killed in the autumn or winter, suggesting specialist wool and/or milk production and a more limited period of occupation. The Late Iron Age mortality pattern from Suddern Farm is more evenly distributed throughout the year, but winter mortality is again high. Winnowing and threshing evidence is present and indicates the processing of local crops and the importation of processed crops. It is argued that this site also shows a greater emphasis on wool production.

In summary, in the Early Iron Age people were living in permanently occupied enclosures, both small enclosures and hillforts. Most of these enclosures were economically self-sufficient but Danebury imported grain from other sites and New Buildings had a limited period of occupation that involved processing grain to be consumed elsewhere.[48] This undermines Hill's model, which assumes that hillforts were not permanent settlements but seasonally occupied with an enhanced grain storage facility and an important

---

[48] New Buildings might also be connected with the summer grazing of cattle. It does seem likely that it is closely related to Danebury particularly since a linear earthwork links the two sites and there is very little evidence for occupation activities inside the enclosures at New Buildings.

ritual function (Hill 1995a: 53).[49] Detailed analysis of the finds assemblages from a range of small enclosures and hillforts (Stopford 1987; Marchant 1989; Hill 1996) does not support Cunliffe's argument that there was a significant difference in the status of people living in the enclosures and the hillforts. In fact, the inhabitants of some of the small enclosures were constructing larger houses than those in the hillforts (see Chapter 4). However, the prominent hilltop location of hillforts, such as Danebury, and the size of the enclosing banks and ditches, indicate a significant difference between hillforts and smaller enclosures and suggest that the occupants of small enclosures had a more restricted perspective on the world.

In the Middle Iron Age the situation is dramatically changed and the increasing importance of developed hillforts, such as Danebury, is indicated by the abandonment of surrounding hillforts and small settlements, and the deliberate infilling of the settlement boundaries. These patterns can be demonstrated in other areas of the Wessex landscape. Analysis of the landscape around Maiden Castle suggested that developed hillforts were surrounded by an inner and an outer zone (Sharples 1991a, 1991c). In the inner zone, all the settlements, both hillforts and small enclosures, were abandoned and their inhabitants were absorbed within the boundaries of the hillfort. In the outer zone, hillforts and enclosures may have had continuity of occupation, but the surrounding boundary was either neglected or deliberately reduced.

A good example of the changing nature of a small settlement in the outer zone is visible at Winnall Down/Easton Lane in Hampshire (Fasham 1985; Fasham *et al.* 1989). The chronological sequence began with an open settlement in the Late Bronze Age and this was replaced by an enclosed settlement in the Early Iron Age which was built so that the enclosure entrance was built above the abandoned settlement. In the early Middle Iron Age an open settlement was created to the north-east of the enclosure but this was short lived and in the late Middle Iron Age a new open settlement was created on top of the abandoned enclosure. In the Late Iron Age a rectangular enclosure was created on the east side of the open settlement and this continued to be occupied in the Roman period. The abandonment of the enclosure boundary in the Middle Iron Age appears to have been a significant event and suggests the independence of the community was undermined. The inhabitants may have become closely

---

[49] The principal evidence for seasonal activity derives from an interpretation of the houses as insubstantial and temporary (following Stopford 1987), and comparable to the seasonally occupied lake village of Meare. However, this is an inappropriate comparison: the Danebury houses are similar to the houses at Glastonbury, which are not thought to be seasonally occupied, and are directly comparable to the houses present on most small settlements in the Iron Age (see Chapter 4 for a detailed discussion).

affiliated with a much larger corporate entity, such as the community occupying the hillfort at St Catherine's Hill or the large enclosure at Orams Harbour.

These patterns might not be applicable to every area of Wessex and it is possible that in some areas, relatively distant from developed hillforts, small enclosures might maintain their boundaries and even develop increasingly complex morphologies. This may explain the large numbers of enclosures in areas such as Cranborne Chase and the development of complex banjo enclosures, such as those on Gussage Hill. This is an area where hillforts appear to be relatively peripheral.

Neither Hill's nor Cunliffe's model clearly describes the relationship between small settlements and hillforts in the Middle Iron Age and it is therefore necessary to consider the model presented by Hingley (1984). He suggests that boundaries and settlement densities reflect the strength of corporate ties between communities. The development of the hillforts would therefore indicate an increasingly tightly bounded corporate group which was challenging the autonomy of the smaller enclosures. These autonomous settlements had three potential responses:

- to identify completely with the corporate group and live in the hillfort—archaeologically indicated by the absence of settlements around a hillfort;
- to become aligned to the corporate group but live apart from it—archaeologically indicated by the removal of the boundaries, which act as indicators of independence;
- to maintain their autonomy as part of a loosely structured corporate group—archaeologically indicated by a dense distribution of small enclosures.

It would be misleading to describe the relationship between the occupants of an unenclosed settlement and a hillfort as reflecting the status of the inhabitants. Both were members of the same corporate group and it is the status of the corporate group in relation to other such groups that was important. These communities had a conception of status that was focused on competition with the adjacent enclosure community. These ideas are explored further in Chapter 5.

There were significant changes throughout the region in the Late Iron Age. Settlement forms become much more diverse and range from hillforts, through substantial enclosures, to small unenclosed settlements. The animal bones and crop remains suggest an increasingly complex agricultural economy with mono-crops of wheat and barley, and the introduction of new crops such as peas and oats. This might coincide with a much more integrated economy, with some communities specializing in certain agricultural

activities and sites, such as Nettlebank Copse, which may have been seasonally
occupied. These complexities are also reflected in the increasing importance
of material culture and in particular the importance of exchange and the
development of coinage, which will be discussed in Chapter 3.

FROM SIMILARITY TO DIFFERENCE: PATTERNS OF SETTLEMENT OFF THE CHALK

The area surrounding the chalk downland is characterized by distinct localities, which have their own archaeological peculiarities that require separate
analysis. The three main regions are: the Dorset Heaths and the New Forest;
the Coastal Plain of Sussex and Hampshire; and the Thames Basin Heaths. I
will not attempt to discuss the landscapes to the west of the chalk downlands
(though some of their characteristics were mentioned in relation to the Vale
of Pewsey above) and my discussion of the Dorset coast will concentrate on
the Isle of Purbeck.

The Dorset Heaths and the New Forest

Fieldwork in the New Forest and the Dorset Heaths has been relatively
restricted. In Dorset there has been a considerable amount of work in and
around the urban conurbations of Bournemouth and Poole (Figure 2.23;
Calkin 1962) and the development of the oil industry in Poole Harbour has
resulted in excavations on the islands and along the southern shores of Poole
Harbour (Cox and Hearne 1991; Woodward, P. J. 1987a). Gravel quarrying
has also recently led to an extensive excavation at Bestwall Quarry on the
western edge of Poole Harbour (Ladle and Woodward, A. 2003). Work in
Hampshire has been much more limited but the New Forest has recently
been subject to a detailed survey (Smith, N. 1999b) and there have been
important excavations at Hengistbury Head in Christchurch Harbour
(Cunliffe 1987).

There is extensive evidence for Bronze Age burials in both the Dorset
heathlands and the New Forest, and these include many examples that can
be dated to the later part of the second millennium BC (Calkin 1962;
Petersen 1981; White 1982). Settlement evidence is more difficult to identify, but recent work at Bestwall Quarry has revealed a substantial Middle
Bronze Age settlement (Ladle and Woodward, A. 2003) surrounded by a
field system. Field systems were also revealed in the valley of the Corfe river

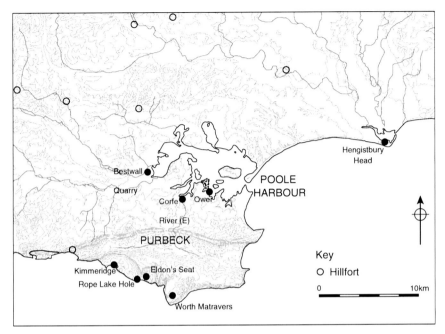

Figure 2.23 The topography of the Dorset Heaths, Poole Harbour and Purbeck, showing the location of sites mentioned in the text.

(Cox and Hearne 1991: 225–6) and in the Bournemouth area (Gardiner 1987: 335), though they are still missing from the New Forest (Smith, N. 1999b: 45–6).

Examination of the soil and pollen evidence from the Dorset Heaths around Poole Harbour indicates that the agricultural exploitation of the Middle Bronze Age quickly exhausted the relatively fragile soils of the tertiary sands and gravels (Cox and Hearne 1991: 226); and the heaths that characterize the area today developed during the Early to Middle Bronze Age. Evidence for substantial Late Bronze Age settlement is absent from the heath, but burnt mounds identified in the New Forest may date to this period and suggest transient occupation (Pasmore and Pallister 1967; Smith, N. 1999a). It has also been argued that the sustained presence of heathland vegetation in the first millennium BC could only have occurred if the vegetation was consciously maintained by grazing and controlled burning (Allen, M. J. and Scaife 1991: 217).

Iron Age activity is characterized by a scatter of hillforts concentrated along the rivers Stour and Avon (Smith, N. 1999b) and around the coast at estuaries and natural harbours. This probably reflects the enhanced productivity of the soils in these environments. The most important site is Hengistbury Head, a coastal promontory fort that was occupied in the Late Bronze Age/Early Iron Age transition. Occupation continued into the Early Iron Age and contemporary settlements occupy the gravel terraces of the Stour valley (Cunliffe 1987: ill. 231). There is very little evidence that these settlements continued to be occupied in the Middle Iron Age though occupation at Hengistbury Head reappears at the very end of the second century BC (Cunliffe 1987: 339). The evidence from Poole Harbour indicates the reoccupation of the coastal littoral in the second century BC (Cox and Hearne 1991: 228–9).

Activity intensified in the first century BC and this reflects an increased exploitation of the resources of the coastal littoral, particularly salt production, and the development of two important centres that had close contact with the Continent: Hengistbury Head (Cunliffe 1987) and Ower (Cox and Hearne 1991; Woodward, P. J. 1987a). Both sites were located on promontories next to sheltered harbours, but Hengistbury Head was developed in the old fort, whereas Ower was a new location. Hengistbury Head appears to be particularly important in the first half of the first century BC but Ower is more important in the period immediately prior to the Roman conquest. Poole Harbour has also provided evidence for a number of other Late Iron Age settlements that seem to be associated with salt production (e.g. Corfe river) and shale working (particularly at Ower) and somewhere in the harbour area there should be a substantial pottery production centre. Fabric analysis of pottery assemblages from Dorset and the surrounding areas makes it clear that in the Late Iron Age most of the ceramic needs of the region were being supplied by Poole Harbour products (Brown, L. 1997).

The Dorset Coast

The Dorset Coast has been subject to only a limited amount of survey and excavation (Radcliffe 1995; RCHME 1970) but as far as is known the Weymouth Lowlands have an archaeological record that is comparable to the downland areas of south Dorset. Hillforts, such as Chalbury and Abbotsbury Castle, appear by the Early Iron Age, and there are many relatively unexplored settlements and a characteristic group of burials of Late Iron Age, Durotrigian type (Fitzpatrick 1996). The Isle of Purbeck, in contrast, has a distinctive archaeological record that differs from most of the other areas of Wessex. The area is characterized by extremely rich Late Bronze Age/Early Iron Age settlements. These have been most recently examined at Eldon's Seat (Cunliffe and Phillipson 1969), Rope Lake Hole (Woodward, P. J. 1987b) and Compact Farm (Graham *et al.* 2002), but other sites are known (Calkin 1949). These sites produce very large ceramic assemblages and evidence for the extensive exploitation of Kimmeridge shale for the production of armlets. They are comparable in artefactual productivity to the midden settlements of the Vale of Pewsey but, unlike sites such as East Chisenbury and Potterne, they also have evidence for houses that include stone-walled structures (Woodward, P. J. 1987b). Occupation continued through the Iron Age at Rope Lake Hole and in the Late Iron Age the area seems to have been densely occupied, with many settlements, including Rope Lake Hole, closely involved in the production of shale bracelets.

The Coastal Plain of Sussex and Hampshire

The coastal plain of Sussex appears to be densely occupied in the Late Bronze Age. Recent excavations of Late Bronze Age settlements include several on Selsey Bill (Seager Thomas 1998, 2001), Rustington (Rudling 1990; Rudling and Gilkes 2000) and Yapton (Rudling 1987) and a burnt mound at Patching (Stevens, S. 1997). These settlements are characterized by scatters of boundary systems, scoops and wells, but houses are not particularly well represented. A detailed examination of the inter-tidal archaeology of the tidal inlet of Langstone Harbour (Allen, M. J. and Gardiner 2000), which lies between the harbours of Chichester and Portsmouth, indicates that the inlet was largely formed in the Iron Age, though salt marsh first appeared in the Late Bronze Age. Bronze Age activity was present but this was not intensive and comprised a number of Middle Bronze Age burials in the northern part of the harbour and scatters of potsherds of Late Bronze Age date. It is possible that salt extraction took place in Langstone Harbour in the Late Bronze Age but the evidence is not conclusive and most of the briquetage scatters, which indicate salt-working, belong to the Late Iron Age/Roman period.

There is almost no evidence for Early or Middle Iron Age activity in either Langstone Harbour or the Sussex coastal plain, and it seems that the area was largely unoccupied for most of the Iron Age. On the west Sussex plain several small settlements dating to the end of the Middle Iron Age have been excavated (North Bersted: Bedwin and Pitts 1978; Ounces Barn: Bedwin and Place 1995; Copse Farm: Bedwin and Holgate 1985). They are characterized by ditched rectangular enclosures and roundhouses. Industrial evidence is present at several sites and at Ounces Barn there are moulds for coin blanks. The chronology of these settlements is problematic but they probably

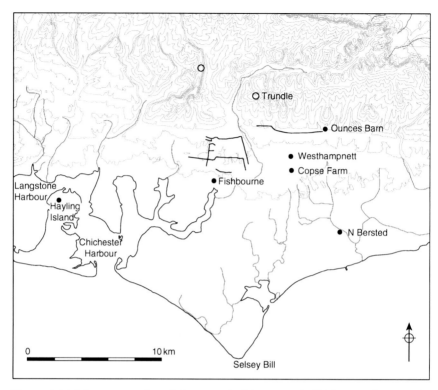

Figure 2.24 The topography of the coastal plain around Chichester, showing the location of sites mentioned in the text (after Fitzpatrick 1997: fig. 4).

appear no earlier than the second century BC, and it has been argued that several sites are abandoned at the end of the first century BC, prior to the Roman conquest (Davenport 2003: 105).

These settlements lie to the east of the Chichester Dyke system, which seems to enclose the estuary of the River Lavant, which in turn provides access to Chichester Harbour and the Channel (Figure 2.24). The area enclosed includes the Roman town of Chichester, and the early Roman palace at Fishbourne, and though neither location has produced substantial evidence for pre-Roman structures, the dyke system probably indicates that this was a Late Iron Age centre or *oppidum*.[50] The difficulty of separating pre-conquest and post-conquest structures, plus the urban spread that covers the area,

---

[50] The Roman term *oppida* is used to describe major Late Iron Age settlements in central and western Europe, most of which are defined by substantial boundaries. Some of these were documented by Caesar and other classical authors, and it is clear that they were important

makes it difficult to identify Late Iron Age settlement activity (Davenport 2003: 106). The most convincing evidence for the importance of the location is the discovery of an exceptionally large cremation cemetery at Westhampnett (Fitzpatrick 1997), which lies just to the west of the Chichester earthworks. The burials at Westhampnett were deposited in the first half of the first century BC and are earlier than any of the earthworks, though their chronology is not secure. The presence of an important pre-Roman temple on Hayling Island (King and Soffe 2001), to the west of Chichester Harbour, may also be significant.[51]

Thames Basin Heaths

The Middle Bronze Age archaeology of the Kennet valley is concentrated on the valley floor (Figure 2.25) where there is extensive evidence for burials (Field Farm: Butterworth and Lobb 1992), ditched field systems (Reading Business Park: Moore and Jennings 1992), and metalwork (Rowlands 1976). Settlements are not common but a good example is Wier Bank Stud Farm at Bray on the Thames (Barnes and Cleal in Barnes *et al.* 1995) and it is possible that some of the Late Bronze Age settlements have earlier precursors (Bradley *et al.* 1980). Settlement became much more common in the Late Bronze Age, principally on the valley floor (Lobb and Rose 1996: 81), but there is also evidence for an expansion onto the plateau gravels on the valley sides (Hartshill Copse: Collard *et al.* 2006).

The Late Bronze Age settlements exhibit several features that make them extremely important in any study of the later prehistory of central southern England. Reading Business Park (Figure 2.26; Moore and Jennings 1992; Brossler *et al.* 2004) was located on the first gravel terrace of the Kennet and is a very large Late Bronze Age settlement with at least two important foci.[52] Settlement in both areas was characterized by post-built roundhouses, many of which have been repeatedly rebuilt on the same spot, shallow pits, and deeper waterlogged water holes, four-post structures and a large elongated spread of

---

political and economic centres. The archaeological evidence for the continental *oppida* is relatively consistent (Collis 1984a) but in Britain this term has been applied in a more liberal fashion to almost any large Late Iron Age settlement (Haselgrove 1989). Most of the British *oppida* are not circumscribed by a single boundary and evidence for dense settlement is not normally present. They are characterized by complex arrangement of linear earthworks, burials of status, a historical association with rulers and the evidence for coin production.

[51] Other temples are known from the Sussex Downs, e.g. Lancing Down (Bedwin 1981).

[52] Pollen analysis indicates the terrace was cleared of woodland by the Late Bronze Age (Scaife in Brossler *et al.* 2004: 112) and after the settlement was abandoned it was sealed by alluvium.

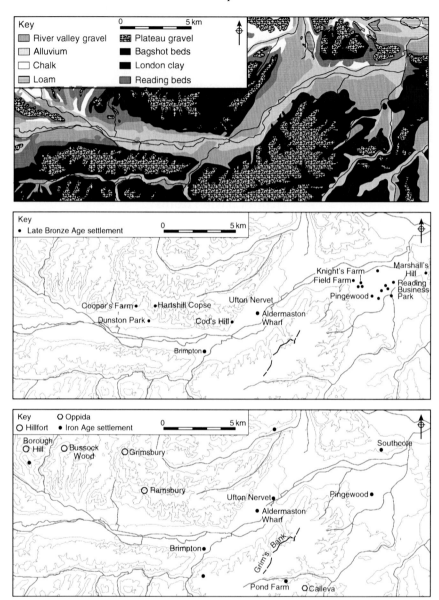

Figure 2.25 The geology of the Kennet valley and the location of Bronze Age and Iron Age settlements (after Lobb and Rose 1996: figs. 5, 15 and 16).

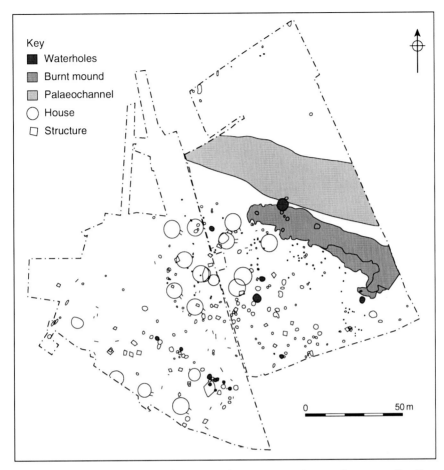

Figure 2.26 A detailed plan of an area of Late Bronze Age settlement at Reading Business Park in the Kennet valley (after Brossler *et al.* 2004: fig. 3.7).

burnt flint. The material culture present on the site is not particularly rich, but the large ceramic assemblage includes both plain and decorated Post Deverel Rimbury Wares which suggest the settlement extends into the Late Bronze Age/Early Iron Age transition. This settlement is comparable to large settlements on the river gravels in the Upper Thames Valley (Shorncote Quarry: Hearne and Adam 1999) but there is still little obvious explanation for its size.

Another important feature of the Late Bronze Age settlement record is the early evidence for iron working. The site at Hartshill Copse on the Plateau Gravels above Thatcham (Collard *et al.* 2006) has bloom smithing debris from contexts dating back to the *c.*1000 cal BC. This is within the Late Bronze Age, but as the authors demonstrate there is evidence for a limited number of iron objects in Late Bronze Age contexts from Britain and adjacent areas of the Continent. The site is close to the Late Bronze Age/Early Iron Age transition site at Coopers Farm, Dunston Park (Fitzpatrick in Barnes *et al.* 1995) and there is evidence for primary smelting of iron ores at Hartshill in the Early Iron Age. It seems likely that these sites are exploiting local iron ores; either siderite concretions in the London Clay (Young in Collard *et al.* 2006: 398) or ironstone concretions in the greensand, which outcrops only 10 km to the south-east (Collard *et al.* 2006: 403).[53]

Many of the Late Bronze Age settlements were abandoned by the beginning of the Early Iron Age,[54] and there is a dearth of settlement evidence for the first couple of centuries of the Iron Age on the river gravels (Lobb and Rose 1996: 84). There are a number of hillforts immediately to the north of the valley at Membury, Bussock Wood, Grimsbury, and Ramsbury, and the latter hillfort is very close to the iron-working sites at Hartshill and Dunston Park. The hillforts are presumed to date to the Early Iron Age but very little excavation has been undertaken.

By the Late Iron Age the valley terraces were again densely occupied and several rectangular enclosures have been shown to date to this period (e.g. Thames Valley Park; Barnes *et al.* 1997). However, the most significant development at this time is the creation of the *oppidum* of Silchester, Calleva Atrebatum, on the plateau gravels to the south of the Kennet valley, between 25 and 15 BC (Fulford in Fulford and Timby 2000: 546). This was built in an area of poor quality land that has no evidence for extensive later prehistoric activity and could well have had a significant forest cover when the site was occupied. Unlike most of the other British *oppida* (such as Chichester), Silchester appears to be a relatively focused settlement that may even have been surrounded by a continuous ditch (though evidence for the eastern circuit is still missing). Excavations at the centre of the Roman town have also revealed a street grid imposed on an earlier, less structured settlement at the beginning of the first century AD, at the latest. The material recovered from the site indicates there were close contacts with the developing tribal polities to the east and that the site lay on the boundary between these territories and those developing on the south coast.

---

[53] It was argued that the Late Bronze Age settlement at Hartshill had a specialist function due to the relatively small quantities of crop remains, and the presence of two unusual timber alignments may even indicate a ritual role, but the evidence is not particularly convincing.

[54] Hartshill is an exception (Collard *et al.* 2006).

CONCLUSION

This chapter has attempted to provide an introduction to the landscape—archaeological, geographical, geological and political—of an area of southern Britain that has been the subject of sustained archaeological exploration for well over a century. The exploitation of the land by the later prehistoric occupants was not only informed by the physical characteristics of the environment but also by its ancient history. Monuments created by the Neolithic and Early Bronze Age inhabitants covered the landscape and the daily activities of people and animals had a dramatic effect on the vegetation and the soils of the region. By the beginning of the first millennium BC the landscape had a human history and structure that differentiated locales and regions and provided a complex system of signification that we can only vaguely interpret. Clearly, monuments such as Avebury and Stonehenge stand apart from the domestic landscape, but how they were interpreted and how they influenced later prehistoric religion and society is difficult to understand. The region was dominated by extensive grassland, but woodlands must have existed to provide timber for houses, boundaries, and other artefacts, and these areas, probably the river valleys and areas off the chalk downlands, would have to be controlled and maintained. Some areas were intensively cultivated for cereals and these have been partitioned to control movement and access in a manner that was very different from other areas of the landscape.

At the beginning of the first millennium BC regional diversity and difference become increasingly apparent. On the chalk downlands most people lived in small unenclosed settlements embedded in fields systems that were by then probably several hundred years old. The landscape was in the process of being further partitioned into small territories by the creation of substantial linear boundaries, and a group of large, sparsely occupied enclosures was being created that presaged the developments of the Iron Age. This landscape is quite different from that of the adjacent non-chalk environments, which had their own distinctive characteristics. In the Vale of Pewsey and the Isle of Purbeck, substantial midden mounds were created that involved the destruction of enormous quantities of artefacts, including elaborately decorated ceramics. Massive numbers of animals were present and these were consumed in vast feasts. In the Kennet valley contemporary settlements were extensive, but in contrast to the midden mounds these are represented in the archaeological record by horizontal spreads of relatively ephemeral features, largely houses, waterholes, and pits. Some of these settlements were associated with the exploitation of local iron and produced examples of the earliest iron

objects in Britain, but otherwise the material culture was relatively impoverished compared with the midden sites.

On the chalk, the Early and Middle Iron Age was a period of enclosure and
though the form of the enclosures varies quite considerably they expressed a
desire to define communities of people and to tie them to particular places in
the landscape. The importance of enclosure differentiates the landscapes of
the Iron Age from the preceding periods. These enclosures are not uniformly
distributed in the landscape, despite the apparent uniformity of the chalk
downland environments. Hillforts were initially concentrated in visually
dominant positions at the edge of the downlands, overlooking the more
ecologically varied river valleys and clay vales. Smaller enclosures were built
in much less prominent positions that are usually visually focused on the
constrained landscapes of the chalk coombes. These locational characteristics
are common throughout the region but there are disparities in the overall
distribution of the different classes of enclosure. Neither hillforts nor small
enclosures are evenly distributed and several regions have notable concentrations, or absences, of either, or both, types.

Detailed exploration of the landscape around the hillfort of Danebury
suggests a period when a variety of enclosure types were present and when
the differences between enclosure types were not as pronounced as they seem
to be now. However, as one moves through the Iron Age the smaller enclosures gradually disappear, the number of hillforts is reduced, and the size of the
boundary and density of occupation in the remaining hillforts increases
considerably. These complex hillforts are not found everywhere, and in this
period, at the end of the second century BC, it seems likely that some areas, far
from the developed hillforts, developed alternative settlement strategies that
emphasized small enclosures or possibly even unenclosed settlements.

Evidence for Early to Middle Iron Age settlement is difficult to find in the
off-chalk areas. In the lower reaches of the Stour and the Kennet valley, the
presence of hillforts suggests that the settlement pattern was not very different
from that on the chalk, but very few of these enclosures have been extensively
excavated (Hengistbury Head is the exception). However, in other areas, such
as the Hampshire–Sussex coastal plain and Poole Harbour, the absence of
hillforts and any other evidence for Middle Iron Age settlement might
indicate a complex, possibly transhumant occupation by pastoralists.

At the end of the second century BC, the off-chalk areas begin to develop a
very rich archaeological record that contrasts dramatically with the record
from the chalk. All the off-chalk areas show some similarities in the
precocious development of elaborate settlements that appear to be intimately
related with production and exchange of material culture. The precise nature
of these unusual settlements varies between each region. In the north the most

important settlement is the heavily Romanized settlement of Silchester, which appears to lie on the border between the developing eastern polity, based to the north of the Thames, and the southern polity, based around the Solent and the East Sussex coastal plain. At the centre of the latter polity is Chichester, which was surrounded by an enigmatic complex of linear earthworks, finds, rich settlements, and the exceptional cemetery of Westhampnett. The interpretation of the Chichester complex is problematic, but it certainly indicates a political centre that was recognized as such by the invading Romans. In the west there is nothing comparable to these political centres, but the coastal settlements at Ower and Hengistbury Head were clearly important conduits for contact with the Continent in the Late Iron Age; and these sites, and others in Poole Harbour, became increasingly important centres of production, particularly for pottery.

The Late Iron Age changes on the periphery were much more dramatic than the changes that were occurring in the chalk. The hillfort-dominated landscapes of the second century BC become increasingly more complex with a range of enclosures indicating a functionally more differentiated settlement pattern. Material culture is much more important in linking individuals together; many hillforts in the east, such as Danebury, are abandoned and the pre-eminent centres in the west, such as Maiden Castle, appear to be undermined. It seems that the development of the important centres in the Late Iron Age was directly related to their unimportant position in the preceding periods of the Middle Iron Age. These issues will be considered in detail in Chapter 3.

3

Creating a Community

In the summer of 1979, when I was working on my undergraduate dissertation in the National Museum, I became involved in an interesting piece of field-work that has direct relevance to the material that we are going to examine in this chapter. A Mrs MacDonald came into the museum to enquire whether some objects she had in her possession were of any archaeological signifi-cance. She had been encouraged to make this visit by a recent television programme where the presenter discussed and exhibited objects that were similar to those in her possession. She explained to the curator that the objects had been found by a family member during ploughing and had been kept in the kitchen drawer for the last two decades, though they were often brought out for the children to play with. She then removed, from her shopping bag, a gold bracelet and a gold 'dress fastener' of distinctive Late Bronze Age type. This had the immediate effect of rendering the museum curator speechless—these were in the days before metal detecting had become a popular hobby, and new finds of this significance were seldom made. The most recent discovery of comparable objects was in the nineteenth century. Further discussion of the nature of the discovery revealed that the location of the find was still remembered; it was just behind the farmhouse. It was also thought that other objects were discovered at the time, but these were discarded, as they were not so interesting. As there was a possibility that objects were still present in the field it was decided that a team would be sent by the museum to explore the finds location. I was dispatched, with two other students then working in the museum, and a metal detector, purchased specially for the occasion, to see what we could find.

I have to say that metal detecting must be one of the most boring pastimes ever invented. In our youthful enthusiasm, we decided to be thorough and systematic. We set out a grid that covered the area where the gold had been discovered and began work. One of us marched up and down putting in flags every time the detector identified a metal find, whilst the other two followed along digging them up. It is amazing how much farm machinery lies in most ploughed fields. I am sure we could have built our own tractor by the time we were finished. By the end of the week, the tedium had become unbearable and we agreed that it was time to quit. We decided to work Friday morning to complete the examination of the gridded area and then head off to visit our friends, who were digging a proper site nearby. The next morning we found the largest Bronze Age gold hoard that had been found in Britain in the twentieth century. The moment of discovery was a shock: scrape, scrape, scrape, bright shining gold. It is that sudden: unlike most materials, pure gold does not tarnish or corrode, so when you dig it up it is as good as new and after a light brushing you could wear it and no one would know it had been in the dirt for three millennia. This is probably why people who find gold seldom think it is very old, or very valuable; it is too gold-like to be gold.

By the end of the day, we had found four bracelets, two 'dress fasteners', and one corrugated band, all made from gold. They were clustered together in a thin layer of ploughsoil directly above the bedrock. There was no sign of any pit or container and they had clearly been disturbed and damaged every time the field was ploughed. I had used the week to have a good look around the landscape and, though there are several roundhouses and a rather interesting Neolithic burial chamber in the locality, the hoard was not located anywhere near these monuments. It appears to have been deposited on an unmarked hillslope, though it did have a rather beautiful view. It is therefore difficult to understand the context of deposition, which makes the hoard comparable to thousands of other deposits of Late Bronze Age metalwork.[1]

The discovery I have just described occurred in northern Scotland but it could just as easily have been southern England, since the absence of any contextual information is a characteristic of most of the Wessex hoards. The most recent discovery in this region is a large hoard of 303 axes, or axe fragments, at Langton Matravers in the Purbeck region of Dorset (Wessex Archaeology 2008; Roberts pers. comm.). This was discovered by metal detectorists, but a team of professional archaeologists from Wessex Archaeology was brought in to examine the location. The careful excavation of two areas, roughly 20 m², resulted in the identification of the four pits that contained the hoard, and two post holes, but did not clarify why the material was deposited where it was.

The national occurrence of this Late Bronze Age phenomenon of metalwork deposition is emphasized by similarities in the form and materials deposited. Gold is not common in most of Britain, but it is present on the south coast, particularly in Sussex. Bracelets are also a relatively common Late Bronze Age ornament throughout Britain, though there are some differences in the precise form that differentiate those of north Britain and Ireland and those of south Britain and the adjacent areas of the Continent. Clearly, these were valuable objects that were worn by important people, and

[1] A full report on the hoard has been published (Clarke, D. V. and Kemp 1984).

the availability of these rare materials indicates a system of redistribution that was of considerable importance to the inhabitants living in areas such as Wessex that had no gold, copper, or tin naturally available.

GIFT AND COMMODITY

In this chapter, I consider the social relationships of the communities that occupied this landscape. Any analysis of the community must begin by discussing the means by which relationships are formalized between individuals. The traditional anthropological method for carrying out this analysis has been the examination of kinship, and there is a voluminous literature devoted to the theory and methodology of kinship studies. Unfortunately, the nature of the archaeological record makes it impossible to study kinship directly, and very few archaeologists have attempted to introduce kinship theory into prehistory (Rowlands 1980; Thomas, R. 1998). An alternative to this interpretive approach is the examination of the nature of exchange relationships and in particular the role of gift exchange. A detailed consideration of the nature of gift exchange provides an important theoretical basis for reconsidering the significance of artefacts in the first millennium BC. It provides new insights into the role of monument construction and particularly the appearance and development of hillforts.

Since the seminal work *The Gift* by Mauss, first published in 1925 (Mauss 1990), a substantial body of anthropological literature has built up that demonstrates the close relationship between the movement of people and the movement of material culture (Appadurai 1986; Bazelmans 1991; Frow 1997; Godelier 1999; Sahlins 1972; Weiner 1992). It is clear that material culture plays a crucial role in creating communities by establishing relationships between individuals and by mediating relationships between groups. The literature includes various alternative positions that could provide quite different perspectives on the archaeological record, but it is not possible to go into these differences in detail here. Instead, I will outline some of the main points and give a basic explanation of how gift exchange differs from commodity exchange.

The recent anthropological discussion of exchange (Godelier 1999; Weiner 1992) has suggested that we can divide 'goods' in circulation into three different classes of material:

- sacred items of ancestral significance that should not be exchanged;
- items that are exchanged as gifts and thus create social debts;
- items of equivalent value that are exchanged as commodities and create no social debt.

The cultural significance of the transaction increases as one moves from commodity to sacred object, and the significance the transaction plays in defining community relationships likewise increases. However, the role of the objects is not dictated by aesthetic criteria (*contra* Godelier 1999: 161–2), rarity value or use value (Gregory 1982). It is theoretically possible for any object to begin its life as a commodity, to be exchanged as a gift and, for a small number, to be transformed into sacred objects. It is also possible, though less common, for objects to lose their sacred status and become commodities (Godelier 1999: 165).

Christopher Gregory (1982) has argued that the primary distinction between gift and commodity exchange is that the former is about the relationship between people, whereas the latter is about the relationships between things. Maurice Godelier (1999: 11–12) goes even further and suggests the movement of objects is only a by-product of gift-giving, as the primary goal of the exchange is to establish friendship between the giver and the receiver of gifts. These relationships are the formative bonds that create group identities and mediate contact between groups. Gift exchange is closely connected to the creation of kin relations through marriage, and the provision of a wife often forms the source of a long-term relationship of gift-giving and receiving. Commodity exchange, in contrast, involves the exchange of things with no associated human attachments. These things have a comparable value and therefore the process of exchange involves the simultaneous cancelling of any debt. Commodity exchange has no long-term significance and does not create a relationship between the individuals involved in the exchange.

Anthropologists would generally agree that there is a spectrum of exchange relationships in most contemporary societies, but that gift exchange tends to be a dominant feature of clan-based societies, whereas commodity exchange is a defining characteristic of class-based societies. Economies based on commodity exchange are characterized by an emphasis on production to maximum capacity. The individuals involved maximize profit by the reduction of labour cost and are fundamentally concerned with the conversion of resources held in common, into goods owned by individuals (Frow 1997: 139).

Ownership is an important concept, as it is fundamental to how we understand the development of exchange. The freedom of any individual to dispose of property is crucial to their ability to participate in a commodity exchange, though individual rites of ownership over anything, including labour, are a subject of considerable debate (Frow 1997). In contemporary society, controversy rages over our ability to sell human sperm or eggs, or to control the reproduction of our image and the words we write. John Frow (1997) has argued that the ability to define and appropriate property previously held in common is one of the principal features of capitalism.

In societies dominated by gift-giving, individuals cannot acquire ownership of land, resources, or possessions. Ownership is partial, freedom to participate in exchange relationships is restricted by obligations to other members of kin, age, gender, and status-related groups. Marilyn Strathern (1988), in her work in Papua New Guinea, has argued that it is almost impossible to identify anything that is not governed by some form of communal or bipartisan ownership. Even the crops produced by the labour of one person are regarded as belonging to a family unit and can seldom be disposed of without acknowledging the rights of others. As a consequence of the inalienable nature of these collective claims of ownership, the gift cannot simply be cancelled by the return of the object at a later date. Gift exchange creates a relationship that ensures that future gifts will continue to pass between individuals or groups for some time to come. To quote Godelier, 'the giving of gifts and countergifts creates a state of mutual indebtedness and dependence which presents advantages for all parties' (Godelier 1999: 48). It is these lines of indebtedness that create 'the social relations which constitute the framework of a specific society' (Godelier 1999: 48).

Gregory (1982: 61–9) has also emphasized that a theory of gift exchange must incorporate a theory of production and consumption. Human labour is a gift, which creates obligations. This gift can be clearly seen in the coming together of individuals in acts of communal construction. Participation in these acts creates an obligation that is not simply disposed of by feeding the participants, but which requires future participation in reciprocal acts. Similarly, the cultivation of food and the production of artefacts require labour in resource acquisition and craftsmanship. Raw materials and crop fertility can be conceived of as gifts given by deities. They bind the recipient into reciprocal acts of gift-giving which can take the form of prosaic daily offerings or elaborate ceremonial festivals. These transactions are rituals that invoke relationships between people and gods, or between the living and the dead. The incorporation of these acts of creation and consumption into a theory of the gift is an attempt to make this an all-encompassing theory, which provides an explanation for all social action (Barraud *et al.* 1994).

It goes without saying that the identification of gift exchange in the archaeological record is problematic. I would argue that the most important means of distinguishing the significance of gift-giving in any society is through our understanding of the significance of individual ownership and the role of production. I have discussed the ownership of land in the previous chapter and argued that, despite the recent suggestions of J. D. Hill (1995a) and Roger Thomas (1997, 1998), there is no evidence that individual, or even household, ownership of land or resources, such as animals, timber, and minerals, exists in the first millennium BC. It is possible that all the material present in the archaeological record for the first millennium BC is the result of gift exchange. However, it seems likely that there are a large number of transactions that do not involve the creation of significant social debts, even within societies dominated by gift exchange.[2]

Sacred Items

Godelier has argued that sacred items 'affirm deep-seated identities and their continuity over time' (Godelier 1999: 33). These items would be held by a community leader and could be accompanied by a detailed biographical history that relates them to the prestigious owners they have had and the important events with which they have been involved. In many cases, this biographical history will be related to the origin myth of the group and these objects may be ancestral figures transformed into corporal reality.

The nature of the objects can be very variable. Annette Weiner (1992: 49–56) has shown the importance of the elaborately decorated cloaks and blankets of the Maori.[3] These would be brought and worn by high-status individuals during sacred festivals. However, sacred objects in the highland areas of Papua New Guinea are frequently insignificant items that would be undetectable if found on an archaeological site. Godelier (1999: 125) eloquently describes the reverence that these superficially mundane items have.

Even before I arrived, I had felt that something unusual was afoot. A heavy silence hung in the air. The village was suddenly deserted. Everyone had left, having caught wind of something serious in the offing. Then the men arrived . . . I was not expecting this. The two men came into the house and sat down, one at either end of the table. I put my head out to make sure no one could listen in, and saw two or three men from the Bakia clan, armed with bows and arrows, discreetly posted round the house, so that no one could approach. The man opened his netbag and took out a long object

---

[2] Gregory (1982: 50) argues that most low status exchange of subsistence goods will be regarded as commodities and that these exchanges will be restricted to within the group. Alternatively, it has been argued (Sahlins 1972) that exchanges of subsistence goods between kin are gifts and that the continual flow of these goods facilitates the more intermittent higher-level exchanges. These gifts act to reinforce relationships at a day-to-day level, which are created by a significant act of gift-giving.

[3] 'From swaddling an infant to wrapping a ruler, cloth delineates all levels of social relations, all supports for political alliances. Further, because of its variation in style and technical production, cloth has an almost unlimited potential as an emblematic marker of age, sex, status, rank and group affiliation. As a repository of human labour, cloth can convey complex meanings that symbolize the tying together of kin and political connections, humans to gods, the power of cosmology and history and in the Maori case, the complex spiritual world of the hau' (Weiner 1992: 48–9).

wrapped in a strip of red bark. Without a word, he laid it on the table, untied the strip and began undoing the packet. This took some time. Carefully and delicately, his fingers spread the bark. Finally, he opened it completely, and I saw, lying side by side, a black stone, some long pointed bones, and several flat discs.

I was unable to say or ask anything. The man had begun to cry, silently, keeping his gaze averted from what lay before him. He remained in that posture several minutes, sobbing, his forehead on his hands, which were resting on the edge of the table. Then he raised his head, wiped his reddened eyes, looked at his son and, with the same delicacy and the same precautions, reassembled the packet and wrapped it in the red *ypmoulie.*   (Godelier 1999: 125)

By their very nature, these objects will not be frequent archaeological discoveries. They are related to the fertility and successful regeneration of the community/group and should therefore be handed down, exchanged between generations to ensure the successful continuation of the group. To exchange one of these items with another group would compromise the independence of the group and could only arise if the cosmological power surrounding the objects became seriously undermined by significant changes in the social context. In later prehistory, the most obvious time for such changes would be around *c.*800–600 BC when bronze is rejected as the medium of personal display (Taylor 1993). Another period of considerable change is the transformation that occurs immediately prior to the Roman conquest.

The nature and prestige of these objects may be directly related to the scale of the groups involved. Sacred objects are likely to exist for various groups at different levels within the societies of the first millennium BC. Every household may have a number of objects and these would be quite different to those used by large communities. The frequency and rate of deposition of these objects is also likely to vary: objects sacred to a household may be discarded or deposited quite often as these households have a limited lifespan. In contrast, large kin groups have a history that outlives the household, and therefore their associated objects may be retained over many generations. These variations might be reflected in the archaeological recognition of objects deposited in house destruction levels. Indeed, it might explain the placement of objects in these deposits. If the destruction of a house marked the end of a household, then it would be appropriate also to destroy their sacred objects by burying them in the house.

Consumption

The creation of relationships between people and the gods highlights the significance of the conspicuous consumption of objects in acts of mass destruction. These are famously a feature of the tribes of the north-west coast of America, such as the Kwakiutl, but it is a matter of dispute how widespread this phenomenon is. Mauss defined any form of competitive exchange (or agnostic total prestation) as potlatch and so regarded it as a widespread phenomenon. Godelier argues that the term should be restricted to 'public destruction of wealth' (Godelier 1999: 155) and that destruction on the scale witnessed in the north-west coast was exceptional. This can be accepted as an anthropological observation but the archaeo-logical evidence suggests that conspicuous consumption in mass acts of destruction is a relatively frequent occurrence (Bradley 1990). The large copper alloy hoards at the beginning of the first millennium BC are possible examples, as are the elaborately decorated shields and helmets, dating to the last two hundred years BC, found in the rivers of eastern England (Fitzpatrick 1984).

Anthropological understanding of elaborate consumption rituals is dom-inated by discussion of potlatch, a term derived from the Kwakiutl tribe of the north-west coast of America (Boas 1966). In this region, a potlatch was a large festival organized by one individual where vast quantities of objects ranging from trade blankets to elaborate 'coppers' were gathered together and then either given away as gifts to the participants or destroyed. Potlatch events were often related to lifecycle rituals, such as weddings and funerals, but could also be necessary if a taboo had been broken or a competitive rival required humiliation. A distinctive feature of these festivals was the destruction of items, particularly the extremely important 'coppers' (Rohner and Rohner 1970: 103–5). This occurred when there was a particularly bitter competition for status and position between two equivalent individuals. Destruction is an important feature of this competition because it is a public demonstration of an individual's ability to perform a symbolic role. Any competitor who aspired to a particular status within the community would be required to destroy a substantial quantity of material and the quantity of material destroyed would have to be at least as much or more than that destroyed by a rival vying for the same position. However, by the act of destruction, the competitor has reduced the amount of material in circulation within the community, thus making it more difficult for a rival to accumulate this material.

To carry out a potlatch, the protagonist would accumulate gift debts over a lengthy period of time. Once they had accumulated sufficient debts to achieve a show of strength that could not be emulated, they would call in the debts and assemble the material required for the potlatch. However, it is likely that rivals would also have had debt relationships with the same people and so the timing was crucial. If they waited too long the material owed might be used to pay a rival's debt, but if they went too early they might not amass sufficient material to make it impossible for a rival to surpass this achievement. It was this complexity that makes the game competitive and worth playing.

EXCHANGE IN THE LATER BRONZE AGE

Ideas about gift exchange have been current in the archaeological literature for some time and many authors (Barrett 1985; Barrett and Needham 1988; Bradley 1990; Fontijn 2003; Rowlands 1980; Taylor 1993) have considered them in some detail in relation to the Later Bronze Age. There seems to be a general agreement that gift exchange was the dominant practice, accountable for much of the movement of metals. The absence of sources for copper, gold, and tin in the lowland areas of southern and eastern Britain necessitates some exchange mechanism.[4] It seems likely from analysis of the alloys (Northover 1982; Rohl and Needham 1998), typological characterization of the artefacts (Burgess 1991) and the presence of shipwreck cargoes (Muckelroy 1981), that central southern England was largely supplied with metal from the adjacent areas of the Continent.

A principal area of contention is how important commodity exchange was in these Later Bronze Age societies and how commodity and gift exchange can be differentiated archaeologically. Richard Bradley (1990) has argued that significant differences in the material present in dry land and wet land hoards (Needham and Burgess 1980) indicate a difference between utilitarian and votive deposition. The objects found in utilitarian hoards, on dry land, were interpreted as commodities exchanged through balanced transactions or barter (Bradley 1990: 145). However, in the recent reprint of *Passage to Arms*, Bradley (1998b: xviii–xix) suggests this was a 'weakness' and that the whole process of production, circulation, use, and deposition should be regarded as shrouded in ritual.

---

[4] Mined copper sources have been located and excavated in Wales (Dutton and Fasham 1994; Timberlake 2003) and Ireland (O'Brien 1994). Many of these date to the Early Bronze Age, but occupation continues into the Later Bronze Age at Great Orme (Dutton and Fasham 1994) and Copa Hill (Timberlake 2003). Trace element analysis of these objects has been undertaken (Northover 1982; Rohl and Needham 1998) and though this has shown distinctive regional and chronological groupings, it has not proved possible to relate these to source material. It has proved almost impossible to link mines with regionally distinctive artefacts. Similarly, it has proved impossible to discern which of the source areas for tin (Cornwall, Brittany, or Iberia) are the most important for alloying with British copper.

John Barrett and Stuart Needham (1988) would take a similar view and accept that both dry and wet hoards represent ritual deposition of material acquired through gift exchange. However, they still wish to identify a role for commodity exchange in the Bronze Age and suggest that the movement of material from the Continent to Britain represents commodity exchange. This is based on two lines of interpretation: an ethnographic generalization and an interpretation of the cargo of the Dover wreck. They accept Marshall Sahlins's (1972) position that commodity exchange occurs largely between groups on the edge of bounded territories where the participants involved have no kin relationship. This suggestion is clearly contradicted by Gregory (1982: 50), who argues that subsistence products were regarded as commodities and exchanged by barter within local groups. Early Greek literature also documents the importance of gift-giving in creating diplomatic alliances between distant and alien societies and the emerging Greek polities (Herman 1987: 78). The Dover cargo has been argued to indicate commodity exchange because the composition of the material is completely different from the material found in Britain and is difficult to parallel on the Continent (Muckelroy 1981). The material would appear to have been assembled from a wide range of geographic areas, and this would seem to be best explained in terms of the travels of an itinerant scrap merchant. This might well be the case, but the exceptional nature of this discovery makes it impossible to generalize, and Needham has re-evaluated his position (Needham and Dean 1987).

The most detailed explanation of the nature of exchange networks is the analysis of the Middle to Late Bronze Age material from southern England by Mike Rowlands (1976, 1980) and Ann Ellison (1980a, 1980b, 1981). Ellison provides a detailed model of Deverel Rimbury societies in southern England, which integrates the ceramics, metalwork, and settlement evidence. Rowlands carried out a detailed analysis of the metalwork and also developed Ellison's analysis with a discussion of the period from 1500 to 600 BC. This provides a theoretical overview of exchange relationships, placing the evidence from southern Britain into the wider geographical perspective of the Bronze Age of the Atlantic seaboard and its contacts with the Urnfield and Hallstatt areas of central Europe and the Mediterranean.

Ellison's and Rowlands's original analyses were primarily concerned with the Deverel Rimbury societies of the period 1500–1150 BC, and this forms the basis for the analysis of Late Bronze Age society. Both authors emphasize that a hierarchy of exchange relationships is visible in both the ceramic and metalworking evidence:

1. At a local level the distribution of Ellison's 'everyday wares' identifies units that cover an area of approximately 10–20 km.[5]

2. Regions are defined by the distribution of 'fine wares' and these tend to correlate with the distribution of axe and ornament sub-classes (Rowlands 1976: 163, 1980: 33).[6]

3. Rowlands (1976: 117–18) then divided southern England into 'metal-working centres' on the basis of the principal concentrations of metal-work and the relationship between tools, weapons, and ornaments within the distribution.[7] These centres coincide with some of the regions defined by the ceramic record.[8]

The distribution of weapons, particularly large objects such as rapiers, swords, and basal-looped spearheads cuts across these regions. Weapons seldom exhibit the regionally distinctive features that are present on axes or ornaments (Rowlands 1976: 178). They are found in large quantities in the Thames valley,[9] which seems to be the source region for many of the objects found, but are rare on the south coast and Dorset. The stylistic changes these weapons undergo follow similar patterns on the Continent and indicate close contact between Continental artisans and those working in the Thames valley (O'Connor 1980).

Rowlands argues that the regional distributions 'represent the extent of food giving and other exchange relationships existing between settlements which were linked in a hierarchy of alliance and exchange' (Rowlands 1980: 33). The elites are involved in competition for power through the acquisition of titles that relate them to the ancestors. Competition involves the manipulation of exchange relationships to achieve victory in conflicts, which could range from relatively peaceful feasts to violent warfare. Competition operates

[5] Approximately nine types of everyday wares were identified in Wessex. Variation was greatest in Dorset where the different types overlap to a considerable extent.

[6] Three regions were defined by fine wares in Wessex; type 1 vessels are found in central Wessex, type II vessels in south Dorset and type III the Avon and Stour valleys. The definition of these fine ware types is not as clear as the everyday wares (Ellison 1980a). However, it is interesting to note that south Dorset is distinctive, as the pottery from this region continues to be different throughout the first millennium BC.

[7] Five main centres were identified: East Anglia, the Thames valley, the south coast (south Hampshire/Sussex/Kent), south Wiltshire/Dorset and Somerset/Devon. South Wiltshire/Dorset is not a principal metalworking centre but appears to be a transitional zone under the fluctuating influence of the south coast and Somerset/Devon centres.

[8] The boundary between south Wiltshire/Dorset and Somerset/Devon coincides with the division between those areas that use Deverel Rimbury Wares and those that use Trevisker Wares. The division between south Wiltshire/Dorset and the south coast coincides with the distribution of distinctive Deverel Rimbury fine wares.

[9] Another centre appears to be the Cambridge region and there are some smaller centres, for example in south-east Devon (Rowlands 1976: 167).

at various levels. The distribution of high-status metalwork 'for example, forms one system of circulation which is directly politico-ritual in function and operates as a kind of pump to stimulate the production of food and other forms of surplus' (Rowlands 1980: 46). It must be stressed that this does not indicate centralized production or a redistributive economy. This perpetual competition means that these societies are very unstable. The constant pressure to increase the number of exchange relationships means that they have a tendency towards expansion and collapse (Rowlands 1980: 47).

Rowlands goes on to argue that upland areas such as Wessex have a dependent relationship with the metalworking centres in coastal or riverside situations. He suggests that this relationship involves the exchange of agricultural resources and in particular cattle for bronze. Access to bronze is controlled by the coastal regions because communities in these areas have exchange relationships with the Continent.[10] The 'economic base of the riverside/coastal communities lay in specialist craft production (particularly metalwork), in the processing of raw material for exchange and in the supply of manpower, skills and technology for riverside, coastal and marine transport' (Rowlands 1980: 35–6).

The control over elaborate weapons is an important indication of the status of the Thames valley area. These weapons indicate the establishment of long-distance exchange relationships between groups dispersed along the Atlantic facade of Europe and throughout the British Isles. The relative absence of these important objects from Wessex and the south coast suggests that communities in these regions were excluded from these prestige relationships. Access to the 'greater sources of wealth available (in the Thames valley) would imply greater displays of consumption, more inflationary cycles of gift exchange for the establishment of political dominance and ranking, and very much larger support groups for local political leaders' (Rowlands 1980: 35).

This model has been criticized by Barrett and Needham, who argue that 'metal circulated as tools, ornaments and dress decoration in a quite secondary role to social status established by other means' (Barrett and Needham 1988: 136). They justify this argument on the basis that there is no archaeological evidence for the accumulation of surplus at sites such as Blackpatch and Itford Hill. Nor is there much evidence for an important role for metalwork on these settlements. They see no evidence for larger political structures in this region and suggest the primary political concerns are gender and kin relations and that these are resolved through boundary construction.

---

[10] They may also have had exchange relationships with Wales, and from there to Ireland, but the British sources of copper do not seem important in the Late Bronze Age for southern England.

However, this critique is flawed by the limited scale of the analysis. Rowlands would argue that surplus production is exported from the region to be consumed in core areas such as the Thames valley or the south coast, and therefore there is no need for excessive storage capacity in the downlands. The absence of bronze artefacts from the locality of the settlements is not surprising, if this is a relatively impoverished periphery. Barrett and Needham's suggestion that boundaries are an important expression of political developments is based on the work at South Lodge in Cranborne Chase (Barrett *et al.* 1991). However, it is worth noting that the importance of the boundary at this site is enhanced by the deposition of several copper alloy artefacts in the ditch, which was deliberately infilled soon after it was dug. This supports Rowlands's view of the importance of metalwork in these societies.

Metal

Much of the discussion of the Late Bronze Age and Late Bronze Age–Iron Age transition period has been based on generalizations of the nature of bronze deposition in south-east England that have ignored regional differences. However, it has been pointed out by R. Thomas (1989) that there are significant differences between the nature of the material present in Wessex and that present in the Thames valley, and it can be demonstrated that within Wessex there are yet further variations. The most important differences are the relative quantities of material of the Ewart Park and Llyn Fawr traditions (the former belongs, with the Wilburton tradition, in the Late Bronze Age, whereas the latter defines the Late Bronze Age–Early Iron Age transition). In the lower Thames valley, the quantities of Llyn Fawr material are negligible compared to the vast quantities of Ewart Park material present.[11] Most of the Llyn Fawr material comprises isolated Gundlingen swords, and there are no definite Llyn Fawr hoards. In Wessex, in contrast, the distinction between the two periods is negligible. The region is noted for the number of Llyn Fawr hoards (O'Connor 2007) and these suggest that bronze exchange and deposition, and the social system that supported this, continued much longer in this area than it did elsewhere in Britain.

---

[11] Unfortunately, our understanding of bronze deposition in the first half of the first millennium BC is hampered by the absence of a detailed catalogue of the material found. It is possible to produce a list and plot the distribution of the bronze hoards found but, though the isolated finds from Dorset and north Wiltshire have been examined (Pearce 1983; Barber 2005), there is no catalogue of isolated finds that is comparable to the detailed catalogue of the Middle Bronze Age finds produced by Rowlands (1976).

Most of the Ewart Park material is found in the north, in Wiltshire and Berkshire, whereas the Llyn Fawr material is more evenly distributed across the region. It is also noticeable that there are very few hoards, of both periods, on the Tertiary sands and gravels of Dorset and Hampshire, where many Middle Bronze Age hoards were found (Taylor 1993). The Late Bronze Age hoards from the Sussex Plain are restricted to the east, where there is only a limited area of plain between sea and the chalk downlands (Bedwin 1983).

The size of the hoards also distinguishes Wessex from the Thames valley, where many substantial Ewart Park hoards are found (the Petters Hoard: Needham 1990). The two largest Late Bronze Age hoards from Wessex come from Blackmoor and Bentley in Hampshire. The Bentley hoard contains 139 pieces, mostly scrap, but including large numbers of sword, spearhead, and axe fragments (Lawson 1999: fig. 11.7). The Blackmoor hoard is estimated to contain over 90 objects (Colquhoun 1979) and is dominated by large numbers of spears and swords. These hoards belong to the Wilburton tradition, which dates to the earlier part of the Late Bronze Age (c.1130–1020 BC) and the Blackmoor hoard belongs to the end of this period and has sometimes been used to characterize its own phase in the Late Bronze Age succession. The largest hoards from the Ewart Park phase of the Late Bronze Age are from Yattendon in Berkshire, and Ashley Wood and Winchester in Hampshire. Yattendon (Figure 3.1) has about 59 pieces, roughly half of which are spearheads or spearhead fragments; both Ashley Wood (Figure 3.2) and Winchester have about 30 pieces, again mostly spearheads, though some sword fragments are present (Burgess *et al.* 1972). The largest Llyn Fawr hoard is the new hoard from Langton Matravers, Dorset (see page 91) but substantial hoards are also known from Fawley in Hampshire and Tower Hill on the Berkshire Downs. Langton Matravers consisted of 303 largely 'Portland Type' axes or axe fragments (Wessex Archaeology 2008), Fawley comprised 68 Armorican axes (O'Connor 2007: 75) whereas Tower Hill was a more mixed hoard comprising 46 axes (22 complete) and a large amount of ornamental material and scrap (Miles *et al.* 2003). Roughly, 18 out of 25 Ewart Park hoards have fewer than ten pieces whereas five out of 12 Llyn Fawr hoards have fewer than ten pieces.

Wessex also provides good evidence for the use of other metals. Gold objects have been recovered from a number of areas, notably Chickerell in Dorset (Woodward, P. J. 2002) and Tisbury in Wiltshire, and gold is a frequent discovery in Sussex, where finds include lock rings from Highdown Hill (Curwen 1954: 186: fig. 67) and Harting Beacon (Bedwin 1979: 24; Keef 1953). Iron is also found in Late Bronze Age contexts in Wessex. Two iron spearheads are loosely associated with a hoard of two bronze spearheads and a knife blade from Melksham, Wiltshire (Gingell 1979).

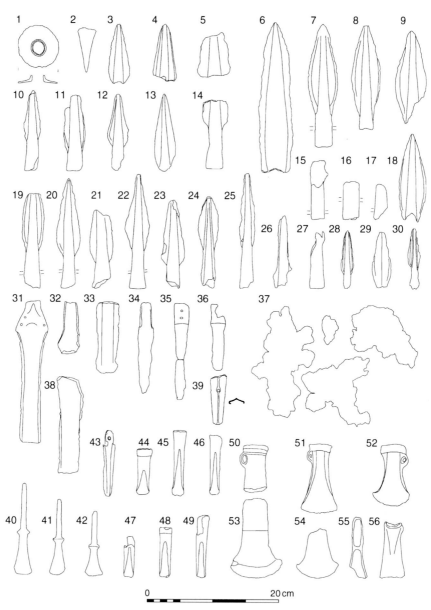

Figure 3.1 The Late Bronze Age hoard from Yattendon, Berkshire: 1 a disc; 2 a ferrule; 3–30 spearheads and spearhead fragments; 31–36, 38, 43 swords and knives; 37 four fragments of sheet metal; 39 chape; 40–42 chisels; 44–49 gouges; 50–56 axes (after Burgess *et al.* 1972: figs. 15–18).

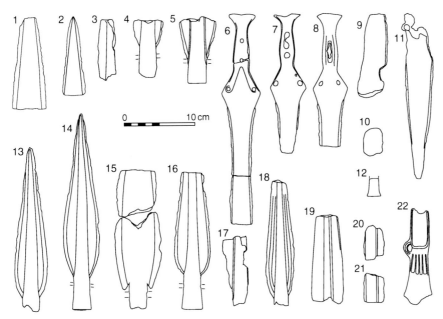

Figure 3.2 The Late Bronze Age hoard from Ashley Wood, Hampshire: 1–5, 13–21 spearheads and spearhead fragments; 6–11 sword fragments; 12 ferrule; 22 palstave (after Burgess *et al.* 1972: figs. 19 and 20).

The nature of the discovery, unfortunately, does not enable us to securely place the iron spearheads with the dateable hoard material, but its form is reminiscent of the iron spearhead from the Llyn Fawr hoard itself.

Of considerable importance has been the recent discovery of iron metal-working debris from the site at Hartshill Copse in the Kennet valley, Berkshire (Collard *et al.* 2006). An otherwise apparently simple settlement of two round-houses associated with pits, ancillary structures of various forms, and two unusual palisades, was found to contain large quantities of hammerscale and iron spheroids that indicate the presence of extensive iron working, though not iron production.[12] A detailed analysis of the distribution of this material suggests bloom smithing in one house and blacksmithing in the other, and an extensive suite of radiocarbon dates indicates this was taking place around 1000 BC. There is also an Early Iron Age settlement that has produced evidence for several areas of metalworking, including primary production.

[12] There is a lack of substantial pieces of slag in stratified contexts and it is possible that the micro-residues may have been deposited in the Late Bronze Age contexts by soil processes and belong to a much later phase of activity. The authors have addressed this concern but they were not able to completely exclude the possibility from my mind.

The site is close to the settlements at Dunstan Park and Coopers Farm (Fitzpatrick 1995), which have also produced iron working activity.

The evidence outlined above clearly demonstrates that whilst Wessex was on the periphery of the bronze distribution networks of the Ewart Park period, in the Llyn Fawr period it became the centre of depositional activity. Furthermore, the importance of bronze does not appear to be related to access to iron, since the Hartshill evidence would indicate iron was being exploited from the start of the first millennium. Instead, it represents the social importance of copper alloys in developing relationships with other communities in Britain and on the Continent.

EXCHANGE IN THE EARLY IRON AGE

Their [hillforts] massive storage capacities imply the stockpiling of goods for redistribution, while the occurrence in some quantities of bulk raw materials . . . produced outside their immediate territories, indicates that it was probably to the forts that these materials were transported before being redistributed to the settlements in the hinterland.   (Cunliffe 1991: 533)

Much of the debate about exchange relationships in the Iron Age has focused on the validity of Cunliffe's interpretation of hillforts (Cunliffe 1984a: 556–62, 1991, 1995). This model isolated the economy from social and religious activity and effectively argued that material culture circulated as commodities and that the production and distribution of these commodities were controlled by an elite, who were living in a hillfort. This model has been subject to sustained criticism (Bowden and McOmish 1987; Ehrenreich 1991; Hill 1995a, 1996; Morris, E. L. 1994, 1996; Sharples 1991a; Stopford 1987) and it has been emphatically demonstrated that the occupants of hillforts did not have a pre-eminent role in either the production or distribution of commodities. Indeed, the evidence for specialist production of any form is remarkably rare in the Early Iron Age. This can be demonstrated by examining the evidence for production and exchange, focusing initially on iron and pottery, as these are particularly informative.

Iron Production

The second half of the first millennium witnesses some dramatic changes in metal technologies. Iron becomes the primary metal and though bronze is occasionally used, it is reserved for decorative objects, mainly small personal ornaments. The nature of the iron objects produced is also in marked contrast to those produced in bronze in the first half of the millennium. Large weapons and tools almost disappear from the archaeological record and there is no suggestion that high-status objects similar to those produced in the Bronze Age are important. The nature of the depositional context also changes. A characteristic feature of the Bronze Age was the presence of large collections of objects (hoards) in isolated contexts separated from the evidence of domestic activity. These metalwork hoards disappear at the end of the sixth century BC and iron objects are deposited on settlements, though in very small quantities, with other broken and discarded fragments of material culture. This change in the significance of metal suggests that long-distance exchange of raw iron was not a feature of the Early Iron Age.

In contrast to copper and tin, iron ores are widely available throughout the British Isles. Wessex is surrounded by important sources of high-quality iron ores in the Weald, the Forest of Dean and, slightly further afield, Northamptonshire, all of which were extensively exploited in the Roman period.[13] The most important contrast with the Bronze Age is the presence of low-grade iron ores across the whole of southern England (Figure 3.3; Ehrenreich 1985: 19; Salter and Ehrenreich 1984: 147–8). The tertiary basins of Hampshire and the Thames valley contain hard pans, which are water concentrated iron deposits in the gravel and sand. Similar deposits appear in the greensand. The chalk produces iron sulphide ores in the form of marcasite nodules that can be reduced to oxides by roasting.

The technology of iron production is very different from that used in copper alloy production (Tylecote 1986: 128–31). The most important difference is that iron melts at $c.1540°C$, a temperature that could not be achieved until the introduction of the blast furnace. However, it can be created by reduction of its ores at much lower temperatures; notionally at $c.800°C$ but, in practice, temperatures of $c.1150°C$ are required because of the presence of

[13] To the east are the sources in the Weald. These are siderite ores occurring as nodules or thin beds in the Wadhurst clay formation. To the west are the Carboniferous limestone deposits of the Forest of Dean and the Mendips. These deposits are largely limonite but also contain large quantities of haematite and goethite. Further to the north is the Jurassic Ridge and the oolite and lias deposits contain important carbonate ores, which are concentrated in Northamptonshire. These ores are noted for their high phosphorous concentrations. Other important sources include haematite ores present in the granite outcrops of the south-west, and a particularly important source may be the Great Perran Lode of Newquay, Cornwall, where haematite, limonite, and carbonates are found. Carbonates produce a distinctive high cobalt, high nickel iron (Ehrenreich 1985: 16–19).

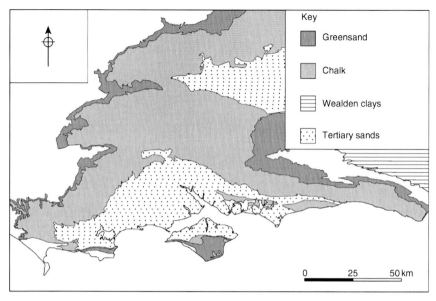

Key
- Greensand
- Chalk
- Wealden clays
- Tertiary sands

0   25   50 km

Figure 3.3 A simplified geology of southern Britain showing the iron ore bearing deposits (after Salter and Ehrenreich 1984: fig. 10.2).

impurities. At this temperature, the impurities liquefy and can be removed as slag. These high temperatures require a furnace, and large quantities of charcoal are essential to achieve the heat and as part of the reduction process. Unfortunately, no well-preserved furnaces have been found in Wessex. The iron produced is known as a bloom and in its initial state it is 'a porous, slag-rich lump with large cavities' (Ehrenreich 1985: 23). The production of iron capable of making tools was undertaken by the repeated heating and hammering of the bloom. This purified the bloom by removing the cavities and forcing out the residual slag. It was therefore possible, in the second half of the first millennium BC, to use raw materials that were readily available in the landscape to produce the basic tools that were required for day-to-day existence.

The archaeological evidence for iron working in the Early Iron Age is poor but it does suggest the routine exploitation of local sources prior to the third century BC.[14] A number of sites such as Longbridge Deverill in Wiltshire

[14] Hingley has suggested that in the Early Iron Age metalworking is specialized (Hingley 1997: 10) and possibly even centralized (Hingley 1997: 16) but this argument is based on the absence of evidence, which can never be particularly convincing.

(Tylecote 1986: 139) and La Sagesse, Romsey, in Hampshire (Green in Fitzpatrick and Morris 1994) have evidence for smelting in the seventh to fifth centuries BC. Recent, yet unpublished, excavations at Rooksdown Hospital, Basingstoke, have produced 149 kg of slag from both smelting and smithing and 70% of this is securely stratified in contexts that date to the late fifth to fourth century BC (Andrews and Laidlaw 1996). At Maiden Castle (Sharples 1991a), excavation of deposits dating to about 400 BC produced large plano-convex hearth bottoms, which probably indicate primary smelting (Salter in Sharples 1991a: 167). This material was not found associated with a furnace but was incorporated into settlement contexts.

Early smithing slags have been found in excavations at Hartshill Copse (Collard *et al.* 2006), and Coopers Farm, Dunstan Park in Berkshire (Fitzpatrick 1995), Potterne, Wiltshire (Lawson 2000), and Area 4 Andover, Hampshire (Rawlings pers. comm.). The Hartshill Copse material has been dated to around 1000 BC, well within the Late Bronze Age, but the Coopers Farm and Potterne material appears to be dated to the seventh century BC. Both the sites of Swallowcliff Down in Wiltshire (Clay 1925) and Winklebury Camp in Hampshire (Bayley in Smith, K. 1977: tbl. 6) have produced slag in contexts dating to the seventh to sixth centuries, but it is not clear if this is from smelting or smithing activity.[15]

Despite this evidence for iron metalworking, it is noticeable that several extensively excavated settlements have produced very little evidence for metalworking activity. There is nothing from Easton Lane/Winnall Down (Fasham 1985; Fasham *et al.* 1989) or Balksbury (Ellis, C. J. and Rawlings 2001; Wainwright and Davis 1995) and there is very little evidence for metalworking in the early phases of the hillfort at Danebury (Salter in Cunliffe 1995).

Ceramics

One of the most important features of the archaeological record in Wessex is the large quantity of ceramics found on most archaeological sites. However, the significance of this material has still to be fully realized. From the beginning of the first millennium BC the ceramic record is essentially split by a distinction between fine ware bowls and coarse ware jars, though fine jars, coarse bowls, and cups are also present (Figure 3.4; Barrett 1980). This distinction continues into the Iron Age, when the cups disappear and the

---

[15] There is a surprising reference to tap slag from All Cannings Cross (Cunnington 1923) which suggests reasonably sophisticated smelting in the period prior to the third century BC.

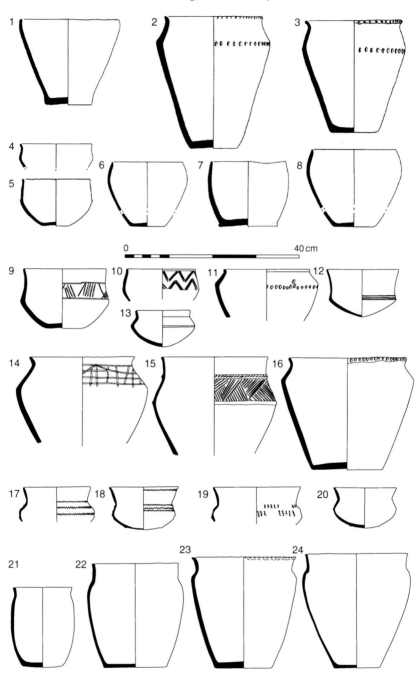

0   40 cm

qualitative difference between coarse ware jars and fine ware bowls becomes increasingly marked. The bowls are often elaborately decorated, very carefully manufactured and often finished to produce a highly polished red surface, which imitates rare forms of copper alloy vessels (Cunliffe 1991: 65). Slight variations in the form of these fine ware bowls distinguish separate regions in southern Britain, and in the Early Iron Age Cunliffe (1991: fig. 4.4) was prepared to discriminate between distinctive regional assemblages in south Dorset, Somerset, Wiltshire/Hampshire, and Sussex. He suggested (Cunliffe 1991: 461) that these represented specialist production zones. Elaine Morris (1994), in her survey of the pottery from Britain, argued that there was 'a limited presence of specialized fine ware production of bowls' in central Wessex but the industry was 'based predominantly on localized production for local consumption' (Morris, E. L. 1994: 377).

Locating the source of these production centres and estimating the importance of specialist production at any one site has proved problematic. The ability to identify sources is hampered by the geology of the region. Most of the Wessex uplands are chalk, and flint provides an acceptable temper that was used throughout the region. Flint cannot be sourced and therefore it is often impossible to ascertain whether the pottery is produced locally or from a specialist production centre some distance away. It is only when the ceramics are tempered with material from the geologies surrounding the chalk that it is possible to identify imported ceramics. At Potterne (Morris in Lawson 2000: 166), the early deposits (*c.* eleventh to tenth centuries BC) suggested non-local material was very rare, but as the deposits accumulated non-local material increased until in the final deposits (dating to the eighth and seventh centuries BC) it was almost 20% of the assemblage.

Of particular significance is the observation (Morris in Lawson 2000: 172) that there was little morphological difference between the vessels that derived from exchange relationships with communities some distance away and those that were made in the vicinity of the site. Similar patterns were observed in the Early Iron Age at Danebury (Morris, E. L. 1997) where a large proportion of the vessels examined were demonstrated to be made from non-local fabrics and again there was little morphological difference between these vessels and those made close to the hillfort. Elaine Morris (1997) has suggested that these

---

Figure 3.4 A selection of pottery, showing the changes that occurred in the first half of the first millennium BC: 1–8 Late Bronze Age pots from Reading Business Park, Berkshire (Moore and Jennings 1992); 9–16 pottery of the Late Bronze Age–Early Iron Age transitional period from Potterne, Wiltshire (Lawson 2000); 17–24 pottery of Early Iron Age date from the hillfort at Danebury, Hampshire, 17–19 are scratch cordoned bowls (Cunliffe 1983; Cunliffe and Poole 1991).

ceramics were exchanged to create relationships between the different communities involved, and they were not concerned with acquiring pots that had
superior qualities. It may be that the exchange of pots was closely connected
with visits by the members of other communities and that a visit was the
occasion for a feast that involved the destruction of a selection of vessels (Hill
1995b). This interpretation suggests we are dealing with gift rather than
commodity exchange.

CHANGE IN THE FIRST HALF OF THE FIRST MILLENNIUM BC

This review of the evidence for the nature of exchange relationships in the
first half of the first millennium BC emphasizes the methodological differences in Bronze Age and Iron Age studies. In the former, a detailed
theoretical understanding of the exchange process is placed at the centre
of the interpretation of Later Bronze Age society and emphasizes the role of
gift exchange. In contrast, Iron Age studies have taken a minimalist approach to understanding the process of exchange. A commodity-based
approach to exchange processes dominated in the 1970s and 1980s, and
though the model has been discredited, it has yet to be replaced by a
widespread appreciation of the significance of gift exchange. Analysis of
exchange is largely relegated to specialist studies and little attempt has been
made to move from the identification of imported material to a theoretical
understanding of exchange relationships. In part, this is due to the nature of
the archaeological record. The important role of copper alloys in the Bronze
Age makes it impossible to avoid discussion of exchange. In contrast,
the evidence from iron is much more ambiguous. Local and non-local
sources were important, but it is impossible to quantify the significance
of either. We have to address these historiographical problems if we are
to define the character of changes in exchange relationships in the first
millennium BC.

The evidence from the Bronze Age appears to demonstrate that complex,
stratified exchange networks were present and that these not only created
local communities but bound regions with other regions some distance away.
These long-distance networks of exchange are important as they were closely
related to the creation and definition of hierarchies in the Late Bronze Age.
The ability to manipulate the distribution of bronze was crucial to anyone
who had aspirations to status at this time. Rowlands (1980) argues that there
was considerable competition for positions within this society and that access

to these positions was restricted to certain individuals and groups who controlled the movement of bronze. It is quite likely that society in southern England was split into groups who had access to long-distance exchange networks, such as those in the Thames valley, whereas those on the downlands had more restricted exchange networks. The Thames valley groups were associated with weapons and it is perhaps appropriate to refer to them as a warrior aristocracy. However, even within the downland groups the deposition of hoards of lower-status metalwork, such as axes, indicates competition was just as important.

In a paper on the replacement of bronze by iron, Needham (2007: 49) outlines three possible models for the transition that can be paraphrased as:

1. *Steady transition*: prolonged development of iron working as bronze use diminishes.
2. *Iron undermining bronze*: sudden abandonment of bronze because of a sudden uptake in iron use.
3. *Bronze crisis*: massive reduction in the use of bronze but not connected to substantial uptake of iron could be caused by:
   a. A crisis in supply that leads to stocks declining.
   b. A crisis of confidence in the special qualities of bronze leads to reduced social significance and use.

The logical basis for the first two interpretations is open to question as it is assumed that there is a direct relationship between the decline and eventual abandonment of bronze and the use of iron. There is unlikely to be a connection between these two processes. The primary purpose of bronze production was to facilitate the maintenance of relationships between people; its use to make tools, weapons, and ornaments was mainly subsidiary to its role as a medium for exchange. Iron, because of its widespread availability, has no role or only a very limited role in exchange relationships in either the Late Bronze Age or Early Iron Age and it is very unlikely that these societies would have considered its function as equivalent to that of bronze. Contemporary archaeologists make this assumption because these materials are both classed as metals and because the three-age system, which structures prehistoric chronology, assumes a technological development that relates the different materials, stone, bronze, and iron. This leaves the third of Needham's models for consideration, since this makes no assumption about the relationship between bronze and iron.

Needham (2007) suggests that the evidence indicates there was, at the end of the Ewart Park phase (*c.*800 BC), either a massive dumping of bronze metalwork as hoards, or that the hoards that would previously have been retrieved and recycled were left in the ground because the social value of bronze had been undermined. He suggests this cannot be due to a crisis in supply, because of the quantities of metal available for deposition, and so it must represent the devaluation of this material. However, he does not really explain how this devaluation occurs.

It is certainly significant that in the Thames valley 'the deposition of bronze fell away to relatively negligible proportions, especially as far as the deposition of hoards, and socketed axes was concerned' (Thomas, R. 1989: 271). This area had the closest links with the Continent, the most complex range of artefacts types, the largest quantities of material, and the most complex depositional practices, and yet it is the first region to abandon bronze in Britain. This would suggest an external stimulus was important. If we are correct in assuming that the metalwork deposited in the Thames area derived from gift exchange with the Continent then any rejection of the symbolic significance of bronze by their exchange partners on the Continent was bound to undermine confidence in the value of copper alloys.

The pattern discussed above is not relevant to the position in Wessex, where 'the amount of bronze deposited actually seems to have increased in the Llyn Fawr phase' (Thomas, R. 1989: 272) despite the evidence for early iron working that is documented at Melksham and Hartshill (Collard *et al.* 2006). The increasing quantities of metalwork found in this area do not represent dumping of waste material by the entrepreneurs of the Thames valley. It would not make sense to build long-lived gift exchange networks using material that was devalued in the eyes of some of the participants. Furthermore, analysis has clearly demonstrated that the Llyn Fawr material has a very different composition from the Ewart Park material and therefore does not indicate that this metalwork has been recycled (Rohl and Needham 1998: 110).

Instead, it seems likely that the source for Llyn Fawr metalwork is the re-establishment of direct gift exchange networks between Wessex and the Continent. Large quantities of Armorican axes were being imported from Brittany in the Late Bronze Age–Early Iron Age transition (*c.*800–600 BC).[16] These relationships were strong in the Middle Bronze Age but seem to have been in abeyance in the Late Bronze Age (O'Connor 1980).

The establishment of gift exchange networks with the Continent might appear at this time precisely because the Thames area was no longer participating in long-distance exchange. If Rowlands is correct to assume that Wessex had a subsidiary role in the exchange relationships of the Ewart

[16] It may be that the sheltered anchorage of Weymouth was a point of contact between the two areas.

Park period and was dominated by the core area around the Thames, then the collapse of the exchange networks linking the Continent to the Thames area would also lead to the collapse of the exchange relationships between the Thames and Wessex. This would empower the inhabitants of Wessex and allow them to renew direct relationships with the Continent. The non-functional aspects of the exchange process are emphasized by the nature of the objects circulated: the most common axes of the Llyn Fawr period, the Breton and Sompting axes, were not designed to be used as tools (Megaw and Simpson 1979: 337).

The evidence suggests that communities in Wessex were using bronze to create relationships much later than were the communities of the Thames valley. However, it must be emphasized that the Llyn Fawr bronze industries do not dominate Wessex. The quantities of metalwork present are not sub-stantially greater than those of the preceding Ewart Park phase and are much smaller than those deposited in the Middle Bronze Age. It seems likely that metalwork use was limited to certain groups within society and that other groups were exploring alternative strategies for building relationships.

The ceramic evidence is more difficult to characterize than the metalwork, but there does seem to be an increase in the movement of ceramics in the transitional period and in the Early Iron Age. It is clear that the exchange of pots has a symbolic significance and does not indicate a trade in commodities. These exchanges indicate the development of contacts between local commu-nities, rather than the long-distance exchange indicated by the copper alloys. The deposition of pottery in settlement contexts probably indicates meetings in the domestic sphere and the function of pots for storage, cooking, and serving food suggests these exchanges were closely associated with the con-sumption of food, perhaps at feasts.

The end of the Llyn Fawr tradition marks the demise of long-distance exchanges; there is very little evidence in the Iron Age for any contact or movement between Wessex and the Continent.[17] The collapse of these exchange networks did not simply result in the inhabitants having problems acquiring copper alloys; it removed the glue that held society together. The most dramatic indication of the fundamental nature of these changes is the disappearance of hoards; there are no hoards of any type of metalwork in the period from 500 BC to 300 BC. This suggests that social competition was no longer focused around the acquisition and consumption of material wealth.

---

[17] There is evidence for the continuation of some contact between eastern England and the Continent, and Stead (1984) provides a sceptical summary of the evidence for cross-Channel trade throughout the Iron Age.

LABOUR AS POTLATCH

In the initial discussion of exchange at the beginning of this chapter, it was emphasized that exchange was not simply restricted to the movement of material. Exchange was a much wider phenomenon that encompassed, amongst other more esoteric constructs, the exchange of human labour. In this context, it is perhaps essential that we rethink the significance of the architecture of the first half of the first millennium BC. The period from 800 to 600 BC is characterized by the appearance of settlements surrounded by large boundaries (see Chapter 2 for examples) and some of these contain very large houses (discussed in detail in Chapter 4). Both of these phenomena must involve the exploitation of exchange relationships.

The definition of settlement boundaries would involve the labour of a considerable number of individuals. Even a relatively small enclosure such as Little Woodbury (Figure 3.5; Bersu 1940) would involve large numbers of people. The earliest boundary was a timber palisade and involved the use of large quantities of prime timber. These trees would have been grown in a carefully managed woodland and indicate the consumption of resources that were not widely available, and were probably owned by the community. The construction of this enclosure, and the large house at the centre of Little Woodbury, is likely to have involved a group of individuals brought together by the future occupants. The participants would provide resources, such as timber, and their muscle power, because they were bound by relationships with the occupants that were long standing and involved the regular exchange of food and basic material culture. Integral to the construction event would be feasting and other ritual activities.

Many of these Early Iron Age settlements have substantial boundaries. The recent work at the hillfort of Segsbury included a detailed estimate of the labour required to excavate the ditch and create the rampart (Figure 3.6; Lock *et al.* 2005: 143). The authors calculate that approximately 1,950 cubic metres of chalk was moved and that this would have taken 889 person days, 20 people for 44 days, assuming one person can move 0.8 cubic metres per hour. However, most early hillforts, including Segsbury and the nearby hillfort at Uffington (Figure 3.6; Miles *et al.* 2003), have timber revetments that involved the use of large quantities of good-quality structural timber. Assuming the interpretation of the phase 2 rampart at Segsbury is correct (see below), this was fronted by large timber posts spaced just over a metre apart (Lock *et al.* 2005: 102–4: fig. 3.48); an estimated 1,250 large split timbers were used. The revetment would require further horizontal timbers to retain the chalk rubble and, though these might have been small

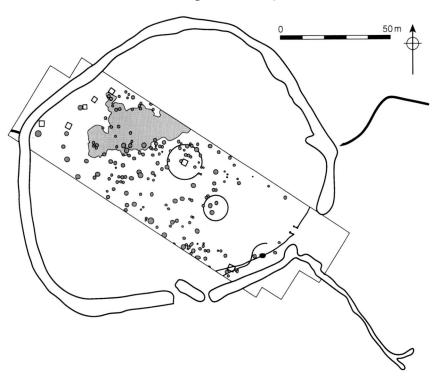

Figure 3.5 A plan of the settlement at Little Woodbury, Wiltshire showing the location of the houses, pits, and the large 'working hollow' (after Bersu 1940: pl. III).

branches, planking would have been more reliable. Acquiring, preparing, and moving the timbers used in this rampart would have been a time-consuming and labour-intensive job, which would have considerably increased the numbers of people required and/or the number of days worked to create the rampart.

A variant of these timber-revetted ramparts used stone cladding between the upright timbers, and at Maiden Castle the second phase of the eastern entrance involved the use of large quantities of limestone (Figure 3.7; Wheeler 1943: pl. xc, xci). The limestone could not have been quarried on site and the nearest source was on the other side of the South Dorset Ridgeway, several kilometres from the hillfort. An interesting feature of the construction of the later rampart at Segsbury was the creation of internal chalk rubble revetments that were made from a type of chalk not present on the hilltop (Lock *et al.* 2005: 143). This material was carried some distance to the site but is practically indistinguishable from the local chalk, quarried from the ditch of the hillfort.

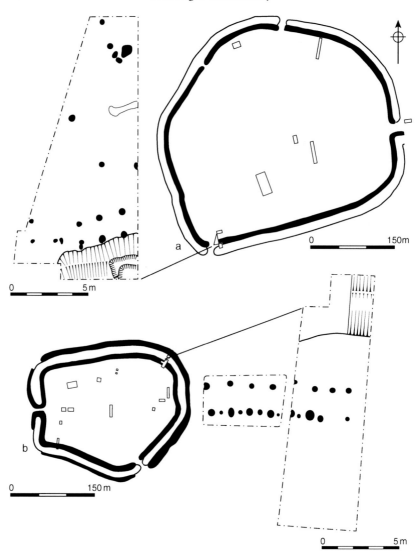

Figure 3.6 The hillforts of a) Segsbury, Oxfordshire and b) Uffington, Oxfordshire, showing the timber structures beneath the ramparts (after Miles *et al.* 2003: figs. 6.1 and 6.2; and Lock *et al.* 2005: figs. 1.2 and 3.48).

These resources were not necessarily required because they were crucial to the structural integrity of the ramparts; it seems more likely that they were a means of creating physical links between the landscape, its inhabitants, and the monument. Anyone walking into the hillfort of Maiden Castle through

Figure 3.7 The limestone revetment that provides an elaborate frontage to the east entrance at Maiden Castle (reproduced with permission of the Society of Antiquaries of London).

the eastern entrance would have been visibly reminded of the relationship between the people in the hillfort and the people on the other side of the Ridgeway. The presence of timber in a rampart might also be recognized as coming from a particular location, as the environmental evidence (Chapter 2) indicates that the Wessex landscape was largely devoid of trees at this time. The evidence from Segsbury of hidden exotic materials is surprising, and suggests these relationships may be quite complex and deliberately concealed.

The enclosure boundary, though it appears to originate in the Late Bronze Age–Early Iron Age transition, is a feature that achieves universal significance in the Early Iron Age. In contrast, the construction of large, resource-rich houses is a feature only visible in the Late Bronze Age–Early Iron Age transition (see Chapter 4). It may be that the construction of large houses was an attempt by some Late Bronze Age groups to use an existing and well-established tradition of house construction to emphasize their status. If this was the case, then the strategy failed; many of the large houses are in settlements that were abandoned or drastically restructured in the Early Iron Age (e.g. Pimperne and Dunstan Park) and there is little indication that they were occupied for more than a couple of generations.

Developments in the period from *c.*500 BC to 200 BC suggest that the mobilization of resources for boundary construction was the principal medium for elite competition. Enclosures are the dominant form of settlement type in Wessex in the Early to Middle Iron Age (see Chapter 2). However, the range in form of these enclosures is dramatic. Boundaries can be relatively simple palisades (e.g. Little Woodbury), indicative of little more than a couple of weeks, work; or enormous multiple ramparts and ditches (e.g. Maiden Castle), under constant construction for generations (Sharples 1991a). Hillforts that show signs of substantial enhancement of the boundary are known as 'developed hillforts', and this act of enhancement is often associated with the enlargement of the enclosed area and the creation of multiple boundaries. The density of occupation inside an enclosure is variable, and though it seems unconnected to the size of the area enclosed it does seem to correspond to the complexity of the boundary. In general, sites with substantial boundaries, such as Beacon Hill (Eagles 1991), Danebury (Cunliffe 1984a, 1995; Cunliffe and Poole 1991), and Hambledon Hill (RCHME 1996) were densely occupied (Figures 3.8, 3.9).

Chronological trends are also visible in the smaller enclosures. Palisaded sites, such as Little Woodbury, developed ditched and banked boundaries with elaborate entrances (Bersu 1940), whereas others, such as Winnall Down (Fasham 1985), were abandoned or had their boundaries infilled. Both large and small enclosures often have complex histories with periods of enhancement, growth, and abandonment that do not occur in any straightforward sequence.

The significance of these enclosures can best be explained by the analogy of the potlatch discussed at the beginning of this chapter, and is directly comparable to the role of metal in the Late Bronze Age. If we regard the construction process as related to the gift of labour and resources, then the construction of increasingly larger and more complicated enclosure boundaries is effectively the conspicuous consumption of restricted resources. Communities were in competition to attract larger and larger numbers of people to help in the process of construction. These acts of construction were possibly seasonal events or festivals, and the successful organization of the event would define the relationship between the communities involved. The construction of the boundary represented the consumption of the labour resource in an act that was largely symbolic. The ramparts existed as a visible indication of the relationship created between the people who spent most of

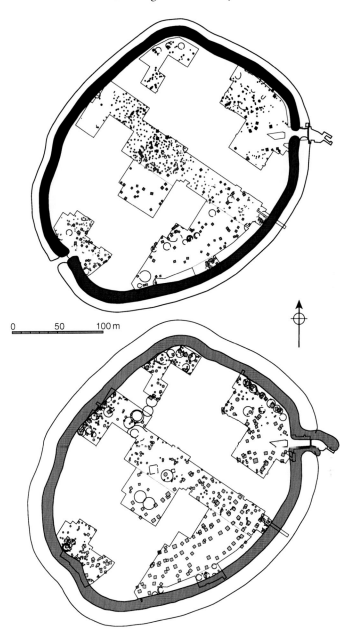

Figure 3.8 The early and late phases of activity at the hillfort of Danebury, Hampshire. Note that in both plans there is a large area to the west of the central transect, that was not fully excavated. No pits are shown in this area because it is impossible to phase the unexcavated pits. (after Cunliffe 1995: figs. 8 and 9).

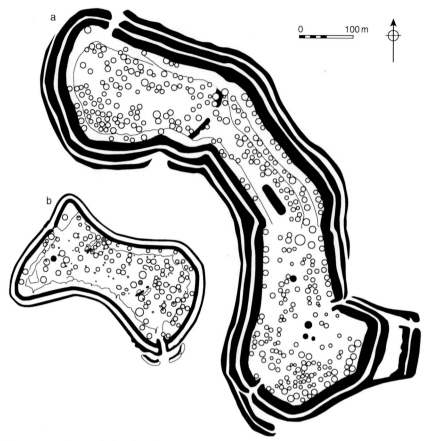

Figure 3.9 Plans of the distribution of houses inside the unexcavated hillforts of a) Hambledon Hill, Dorset and b) Beacon Hill, Hampshire (after RCHME 1996: fig. 17; and Eagles 1991: fig. 1).

their time in the hillfort and the other people who may have participated in the construction of the hillfort, but who spent most of their time in the surrounding countryside.

The large numbers of people attending these construction events would have required large quantities of food: animals and grain. The importance of food is demonstrated by the provision of substantial storage facilities. These are one of the dominant features of the Wessex hillforts and appear to have provided resources for communities much larger than those occupying the enclosure (cf. Hill 1995a). It is also interesting that 'four-post granaries' were often arranged around the edge of hillforts. Their location enhanced the visibility of the stored foodstuffs; in some cases, these structures would have been the only feature visible inside the ramparts to someone on the outside.

Food was clearly of great symbolic importance to these communities and important animal bone deposits are often found in abandoned grain storage pits at these settlements (Hill 1995b and see Chapter 5). Food was acquired not only through intensified production, but also by the creation of exchange relationships with neighbouring communities. The careful manipulation of these exchange relationships would be required to accrue sufficient surplus to stage a construction event. It is this process of manipulation, which results in the rise to prominence, and I would argue dominance, of one hillfort over another. To compete, a community would have to reside in an advantageous location, as this allowed the inhabitants to create sufficient surplus to enter the competition. However, this only provides a baseline and does not explain why certain hillforts, such as Maiden Castle, appear to have developed much more substantial boundaries and enclosed much larger communities. This can only be explained by the competitive abilities of the individuals that belonged to that community. These abilities would rise and fall as generations passed and may explain why the development of some hillforts appears to be quite erratic.

The success of a hillfort construction event depended on not only the available labour and resources but also the ability to keep everyone content by supplying them with food and alcohol. The best time to undertake these construction events would have been in the summer, when crops were growing and the weather was relatively benign. In the summer, people would be consuming cereals harvested in the previous autumn, and these cereals would have had to be stored over the winter. It is possible that they were placed in granaries constructed on the circuit of the proposed hillfort prior to the construction event, perhaps as early as the previous autumn.[18] A visible display of food would certainly have been

---

[18] The complexity of the relationship between timber post structures and the dumped bank of chalk from the ditch is highlighted by the results of the recent excavations at Segsbury (Lock *et al.* 2005). Cutting the old ground surface immediately behind the ditch are two lines of paired post holes. Normally this arrangement would be interpreted as indicating a box rampart, and this would be a fairly typical example of Early Iron Age date. However, in this case such an interpretation appears untenable as one post was left in place and is visible as a void in the rampart, whereas three of the four posts of the inner line were clearly cut off just above the old ground surface. The outer line of posts, next to the ditch, had no stratigraphic relationship with the rampart as this had been destroyed by erosion. There was no sign of a revetment between any of the posts. It was argued by Lock *et al.* (2005) that the evidence indicates a phased sequence that begins in phase 1 with a timber palisade (the inner post line) which is followed relatively quickly by phase 2, a chalk rubble bank with a timber revetment (the outer post line). However, it seems problematic to refer to a barrier of posts over a metre apart as a palisade, as

an incentive for people to gather at the hill and to become involved in the construction process. As the construction of the rampart proceeded, the four-post structures then either became incorporated into the rampart structure, forming the basis for a box rampart, or were dismantled and removed. The incorporation of the structures into the rampart is an interesting piece of symbolism creating a clear link between fecundity and the settlement boundary.

This explanation may also help to explain the difference between Early Iron Age hillforts that frequently have timber-framed ramparts, and the formless dump ramparts that characterize Middle Iron Age hillforts. The construction of a hillfort in a new setting required the creation of food storage facilities because large numbers of people were being encouraged to come to a location that had no previous history of settlement or activity. The Middle Iron Age constructions may well represent the refurbishment of the boundary around an established settlement with storage facilities, and the work requirement could have involved fewer people over a longer period.

DEVELOPMENTS IN THE LAST THREE CENTURIES
OF THE IRON AGE

The period when large hillforts dominated the landscape of Wessex appears to have lasted from about 450 BC up to the beginning of the first century BC. However, during that time there seem to have been some considerable changes in the role of material culture. Artefacts are much more frequent discoveries in general; metalwork, both iron and copper alloys, become relatively common-place; pottery becomes increasingly fine and elaborately decorated; and a number of other material categories, such as stone, become important. There are also significant changes in the technical abilities displayed in the production of these objects, and the quality of the finished products is increasingly complex. The growing importance of the artefactual record coincides

---

the term is normally reserved for close-set posts that cannot be passed through. Furthermore, this interpretation does not explain the close relationship between the inner and outer alignment of posts. An alternative explanation is that the two post lines are contemporary and indicate timber structures that precede the digging of the ditch. The arrangement of the posts is strongly reminiscent of the lines of four-post granaries that are frequently found inside these hillforts.

with a gradual decline in the emphasis placed on building and rebuilding hillfort ramparts at the traditional sites. However, many of these hillforts continued as major centres of settlement and some substantial new enclosures were constructed at Suddern Farm (Cunliffe and Poole 2000b) and Bury Hill (Cunliffe and Poole 2000a). Many of these changes suggest that craft specialization and the exchange of commodities, such as trade iron and copper alloy objects, were becoming more important and that they are an essential precursor to the developed trading economies of the Roman conquest. In the following sections, I will review the development of these material categories over the last three hundred years BC, beginning with the categories that have been argued to represent local exchange, before examining the development of important Late Iron Age centres.

Ceramics

The physical characteristics of the ceramic assemblages began to change during the fourth century BC. The contrast between jars and bowls became less distinctive, the quality of the pottery declines significantly and decoration became less and less common. These features make it difficult to identify regional characteristics, and it seems likely that they indicate the declining importance of classifying status and gender distinctions in the household environment by daily food consumption. However, by the beginning of the third century BC, this transitional period came to an end and a distinctive series of new ceramic forms became established. The quality of the vessels improved, and decoration became increasingly important. Yet the assemblages remained standardized (Woodward, A. 1997: 29) and as Brown (in Cunliffe 1995: 54) has pointed out, the forms at Danebury exhibit 'a remarkably limited range of vessel types for most periods. During the main phases of occupation only two, or perhaps three, significant forms appear to have been current'. Cunliffe (1991) identifies regional traditions in the south-west (Glastonbury Wares), Dorset (Maiden Castle/Marnhull Style) and in a large region extending from the Welsh borders to the Sussex coast (the Saucepan Pot continuum) (Figure 3.10). The decoration of 'saucepan pots' is further classified into several style zones that subdivide this region into smaller sub-regions.

Elaine Morris (1994: 384) has argued that the development of these regional styles coincides with the development of specialist production centres and that some areas, such as Dorset, had completely abandoned domestic production. The significance of specialist production in Dorset

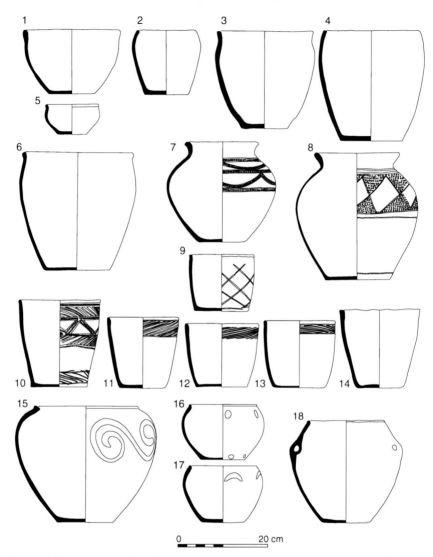

Figure 3.10 A selection of Middle Iron Age ceramics: 1–5 belong to the early Middle Iron Age; 6–19 to the later Middle Iron Age. 1–14 come from Danebury (after Cunliffe 1983; Cunliffe and Poole 1991); 15–18 from Maiden Castle (after Wheeler 1943).

reflects the location of the production centres on the geologically distinctive sands around Poole Harbour. These are clearly identifiable, and detailed analysis of the fabrics from assemblages at Maiden Castle and Gussage All Saints (Brown 1997) indicates the growing importance of Poole Harbour production in the last three centuries and in the first century AD. Ceramics from Poole Harbour dominated the assemblages of the adjacent areas of Somerset (Williams and Woodward in Barrett *et al.* 2000: 259–61) and Hampshire (Brown in Cunliffe 2000: 124). In other areas of Wessex, the identification of local or regional production is more difficult due to the geological homogeneity of the chalklands. In the north, the use of clays from the greensand that surrounds the chalk is indicated by the presence of distinctive glauconite inclusions (Morris in Bellamy 1991) and this suggests the movement of ceramics over long distances. However, in most of Wessex a simple flint temper is used that is impossible to source. Some authors have argued that this indicates local production (Morris in Cunliffe 1995: 244) but the homogeneity and quality of the vessels suggests more central-ized production, and there may have been a specialist production centre near Winchester (Vince 2003).

It is important, therefore, to consider the nature of the assemblages studied. Classification of the pots into a series of types is not enough. The significance of these types must be the object of discussion and analysis. Are the different types of vessels produced because they reflect the various functions of these containers or do they have a more symbolic function, differentiating groups by status or location? What do the regional style zones defined by Cunliffe indicate, and would individuals living in the first millennium BC have recog-nized them? Work on these problems is only beginning, and it is still very difficult to make quantified comparisons between assemblages at different sites (Brown in Cunliffe 1991; Woodward, A. 1997).

There are a number of contemporary vessel forms known in the Middle Iron Age (Woodward, A. 1997), indeed there is a marked increase in the range of forms present from this earlier phase, but the alternative forms are only a small proportion of the assemblage compared with the saucepan pots that dominate most assemblages (Woodward, A. 1997). The restricted function of the ceramics is also demonstrated by the restricted size of the saucepan pot form. Ann Woodward's (1997) analysis of the rim diameters from four sites indicates that the size range of these vessels is very restricted. These vessels could be used for a range of functions such as cooking, serving, and food storage, and this is partially supported by the range of residues present in these vessels (Brown in Cunliffe 1995: 55). However, they are not ideally suited as vessels for drinking or eating, nor are they capable of storing large quantities of grain or other foodstuffs. These functions seem better served by the range of vessels present in the earlier and later periods. The name 'saucepan pot' in some sense indicates the nature of the vessel. They are probably best suited for the cooking of a stew or a gruel.

The relatively high quality of the finish and the presence of decoration on these saucepan pots suggest they also had a symbolic function, which might be best identified and displayed through their use as serving vessels in communal meals. The number of people involved need not have been great, perhaps a large household or a couple of households, but it would have been sufficient to provide a framework within which social positions were negotiated, and the quality of the vessels passed from one to the other would have been a significant feature in these negotiations.

The nature of pottery industries changed in the first century BC with the development of distinctive high-shouldered jars with moulded or faceted bases. These were clearly emerging in the first half of the first century BC, as they are present alongside traditional saucepan pots in the cemetery at Westhampnett (Figure 3.11; Mepham 1997). Cunliffe (1991: 151) believes this 'Southern Atrebatic' style is an indigenous development but Mepham (1997: 131) suggests the influence of Continental material is important and points to the similarities with some of the Armorican imports at Hengistbury Head. None of the vessels at Westhampnett was definitely wheel-turned and the evidence suggests local production for the bulk of the assemblage. The diversity of the Late Iron Age assemblages increased towards the end of the millennium when the influences of the imported Gallo-Roman wares (discussed below) resulted in the appearance of platters, dishes, beakers, and lids. However, the substantial assemblage from the first phase of the *oppidum* at Silchester (Timby in Fulford and Timby 2000) is still overwhelmingly dominated by jars. This assemblage is made from a distinctive grog-tempered fabric which, though locally produced, is characteristic of the Late Iron Age settlements in Hertfordshire, Essex, and Kent. In the first century AD, a local flint fabric became increasingly dominant and indicates the appearance of Silchester Ware. This suggests specialist production in the vicinity of the site for the local region and local industries also seem to have developed to supply the region around Chichester (Hamilton in Bedwin and Holgate 1985: 222). Neither the Silchester nor the Chichester industries developed a distribution network comparable to that of the Poole Harbour industries, and it may be that the elite access to Gallo-Roman imports in these areas restricted the development of the local industries.

Stone

At the same time as the exchange networks for pottery were becoming important, there is evidence for the increasing importance of specialized stone sources for objects such as decorative rings, whetstones, and querns.

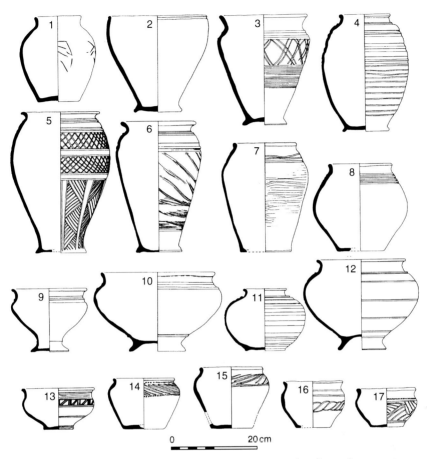

Figure 3.11 A selection of early first century BC ceramics from the cemetery at Westhampnett, Sussex: vessels 1–12 are new types characteristic of the Late Iron Age, whereas vessels 13–17 are more traditional forms of saucepan pots (after Fitzpatrick 1997; reproduced with the permission of Wessex Archaeology).

The rings are one of the few purely decorative items of material culture that were used throughout the first millennium BC, and an assemblage of 67 fragments was scattered throughout the deposits at Potterne (Figure 3.12; Wyles in Lawson 2000: 209). Rings were largely worn on the arm, and I shall refer to them as armlets.[19] The material of choice for these armlets was

[19] They are normally referred to as armlets or bracelets, but they could have been worn around the arm, wrist, leg, or ankle. Three examples have been found on burials: a Middle Iron Age male, less than 15 years old, at Winnall Down (Fasham 1985: 84) had a ring on his left

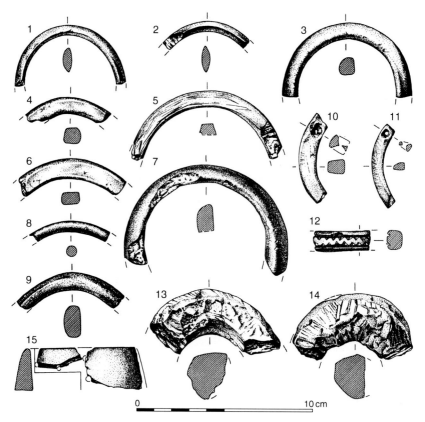

Figure 3.12 A selection of objects made from Kimmeridge shale found at Potterne in Wiltshire: 1–12 are bracelets (10 and 11 have been reworked into pendants); 13 and 14 are rough-outs that have broken in the process of making a bracelet; 15 is a very rare vessel fragment (after Lawson 2000: figs. 80 and 81; reproduced with the permission of Wessex Archaeology).

an oil-rich shale, worked using simple flint tools, that can be polished up to a lustrous black colour. Shale is present at a variety of sources but in southern England the preferred material is Kimmeridge shale that outcrops on the Dorset coast in Purbeck.[20] In the Iron Age, the industry seems to be solely

forearm; a Late Iron Age mature male buried at Tollard Royal, Dorset (Wainwright 1968: 118) had a ring on his left wrist; and an adult female buried in the War Cemetery at Maiden Castle (Wheeler 1943: 355, P33) had a ring on her right arm, just above the elbow.

[20] Two sites have been excavated immediately above the source, Eldon's Seat (Cunliffe and Phillipson 1969) and Rope Lake Hole (Woodward, P. J. 1987b). Both have produced large

concerned with the production of armlets that are hand carved. In the later Iron Age lathe technology was introduced (Cox and Mills in Cox and Hearne 1991: 170), and the range of products expanded to include discs or plates. Large quantities of waste are found on many of the settlements in Purbeck, indicating that production of these armlets was not tightly controlled. Further afield, the presence of roughly cut rings of shale from sites such as Danebury (Laws in Cunliffe and Poole 1991: 368), South Cadbury (Bellamy in Barrett *et al.* 2000: 262), and Meare (Coles, J. 1987) suggests unfinished armlets were being circulated after the initial preparation stage, though probably alongside finished examples. Armlets are widely distributed throughout southern England, but they are not particularly numerous after the abandonment of the Late Bronze Age/Early Iron Age middens.[21]

Our understanding of the lithology of the simple whetstone has been transformed by Roe's analysis of the relatively large assemblages from Danebury, Maiden Castle, and South Cadbury. This indicates the use of a distinctive fine-grained sandstone (Staddon Grit) that comes from the south coast of Devon near Plymouth Sound, close to the important site of Mount Batten (Cunliffe 1988b). This source produced nearly half of the whetstones from Danebury (Roe in Cunliffe and Poole 1991: 387), all of the recently excavated whetstones from Maiden Castle (Roe in Sharples 1991a: 232) and the majority (79%) of the whetstones used at South Cadbury (Roe in Barrett *et al.* 2000: 265).[22] All these whetstones are naturally formed pebbles that have been collected from the beach rather than quarried from an outcrop. It therefore seems unlikely that they represent specialist production but, rather, represent knowledge of, and access to, a particular section of the coastline that was known to produce stones ideally suitable for the task of sharpening iron blades. It may be significant that objects associated with the maintenance of metal tools came from a region that is a potential source of metals (iron, copper, and tin) and it may well be that these rather simple, functionally useful, objects were introduced by people who were primarily concerned with the movement of other more socially significant material.[23]

---

assemblages of shale that reflect different stages of the manufacturing process (Cox and Woodward in Woodward, P. J. 1987b). Occupation at these sites begins in the Late Bronze Age–Early Iron Age transition and continues through the Iron Age and into the Roman period.

[21] Danebury produced only seven bracelet fragments and ten other shale pieces (Laws in Cunliffe and Poole 1991: 368) and there were only 28 bracelet fragments[21] from South Cadbury (Bellamy in Barrett *et al.* 2000: 190–2).

[22] The hones present in the assemblages from the Somerset Lake Villages (Roe in Coles and Minnitt 1995) were made from a different type of sandstone (Hangman Grit) probably sourced to the north of the levels.

[23] Roe has argued that these stones follow the seaborne trade in metals along the south coast between Hengistbury Head (Cunliffe 1987) and Mount Batten (Cunliffe 1988b). However, this

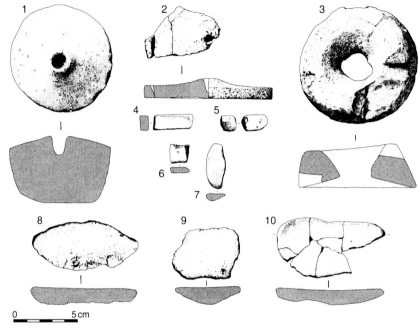

Figure 3.13 A selection of stone tools from the Iron Age enclosure at Gussage All Saints, Dorset: 1–3 are rotary querns; 8–10 are saddle querns; 4–7 are whetstones (after Wainwright 1979: figs. 68–71; © Crown copyright).

The largest stone tools used in these Middle Iron Age settlements are querns, an essential item for transforming grain into flour (Figure 3.13). In the first half of the first millennium saddle querns were being used, but some time after the middle of the millennium, these were replaced by rotary querns.[24] Recent studies of quern lithology have demonstrated that these objects were being produced at specific sources and then distributed over a wide region (Peacock 1987; Roe in Barrett *et al.* 2000). Several quarries have been located in southern England: Beacon Hill, an Old Red Sandstone source in the Mendips; May Hill, a Silurian sandstone from north of the Forest of

is difficult to accept, as these two sites have not produced substantial assemblages of whetstones and the largest number of Staddon Grit whetstones appear to belong to the Early and Middle Iron Age and therefore do not correspond to the period when these sites are important.

[24] Rotary querns have been recorded in Early Iron Age contexts at Danebury (Laws, Brown, and Roe in Cunliffe and Poole 1991: 396) but these may not be securely dated. Rotary querns only become numerically more significant than saddle querns in phase cp 7, the Late Middle Iron Age.

Dean; and two Upper Greensand sources, Pen Pits on the Somerset–Wiltshire border and Lodsworth in West Sussex. Several other sources with limited exposures are known (see Roe in Barrett *et al.* 2000: 264).

Despite the identification of these quarries, there have been few systematic attempts to quantify products from these sources.[25] The most detailed study of a source is that at Lodsworth (Peacock 1987). Both saddle and rotary querns were made from Lodsworth stone and the latter continued to be produced well into the Roman period. The sourced saddle querns have a fairly local distribution; most are found within 40 km of the source, and their variability suggests that the raw 'material was procured by direct access to the quarry site' and 'would be fashioned to the desired shape at home' (Peacock 1987: 76). The rotary querns in contrast are relatively homogeneous and appear to have been finished at the quarry. They are much more widely dispersed across the landscape of southern England, with Iron Age examples known as far west as Gussage All Saints, as far north as Odell in north Bedfordshire, and as far east as Bishopstone in East Sussex. Peacock argued that by the Late Iron Age production and exchange was in the hands of specialists. The assemblage from Danebury was overwhelmingly dominated by greensand (117/152) and it was estimated that about 30% of this was from Lodsworth.[26]

The distribution of specific stone types clearly confirms that exchange in basic raw materials was taking place throughout the first millennium BC, though the quantities of Kimmeridge armlets at Potterne and All Cannings Cross suggest exchange was much more important at the end of the Late Bronze Age. The exchange is most likely to be part of simple gift exchange networks that were discussed in the first part of this chapter. However, the evidence suggests that the production of querns became increasingly tightly controlled by groups of specialists at the end of the Iron Age. These artisans may also have controlled the exchange networks that distributed the querns.

Iron Production

In the Middle Iron Age, iron becomes increasingly important. We can begin our consideration of this by examining how much of it was in circulation. The most detailed assessment of the amount of material discarded per year on

---

[25] Tom Moore (2006: 184–90) has recently provided a detailed discussion of the western sources and some of the sites in Wessex.

[26] Danebury also produced a substantial group of 26 quern stones from a hard limestone characteristic of Potterne on the west side of the Vale of Pewsey (Laws, Brown, and Roe in Cunliffe and Poole 1991).

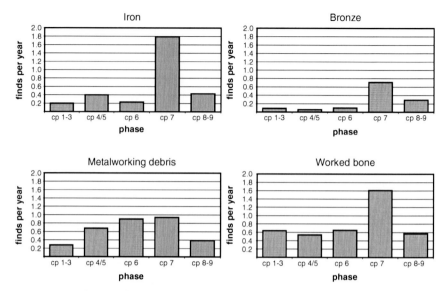

Figure 3.14 The distribution of a selection of material categories through the occupation of the hillfort at Danebury. The vertical axis is the estimated number of finds deposited each year. The horizontal axis shows the principal phases of the occupation of the hillfort, beginning with the Early Iron Age on the left side and ending with the Late Iron Age on the right side (based on data provided by Osgood in Cunliffe 1995).

any site was carried out at Danebury (Osgood in Cunliffe 1995: 204–6). This is one of the few sites where a large enough sample was excavated to estimate the amount present across the settlement, and where the chronology is sufficiently secure to estimate the number of items present in each phase from the fifth century BC through to the first century BC. The pattern identified suggests a steady rate of deposition over the first two to three hundred years, with a dramatic rise sometime in the third century BC (Figure 3.14). The latter part of the Middle Iron Age (cp 7) contains over 16 times more iron items than the Early Iron Age (cp 3). There is a sharp drop in the final phase of the occupation of the site, but this may reflect a decline in the occupation of the hillfort rather than a decline in the availability of iron.

A similar pattern is visible at Maiden Castle, where there was a dramatic rise in the number of iron objects (Laws in Sharples 1991a: 162) between the earlier and later part of the Middle Iron Age (phases 6F and 6G) which probably dates to the end of the second century BC.[27] These patterns are

---

[27] This pattern has not been adjusted to provide an estimate of the number of finds per year.

generally not visible at the small settlements, as these tend to produce proportionately fewer artefacts. However, both Winnall Down (Winham in Fasham 1985: tbl. 4) and Gussage All Saints (Wainwright 1979a: 104–9) show similar marked increases in the number of iron objects present in the latter Middle Iron Age phases, which would seem to confirm the more detailed trends visible at Danebury and Maiden Castle.[28]

The nature of the objects recovered is also very important as it provides an impression of the role of exchange in the last three hundred years BC. Peter Crew (1995) has recently examined the presence of trade iron at Danebury and demonstrated that it makes up nearly 40% of the total weight of iron found at the site. This material appeared on the site in the latter part of the Middle Iron Age (cp 7) and included currency bars and hooked billets that are widely distributed across southern England in the final three centuries BC. Crew suspects other forms of smithed blooms and billets were circulating at this time, but these are less distinctive and more difficult to identify. Currency bars are one of the best studied artefacts of the Iron Age (Allen, D. F. 1967; Crew 1994; Fox 1946; Hingley 1990b) and they can be split into three basic types, ploughshare, spit, and sword-shaped.[29] The general form of the currency bar, long and thin with one end pinched, served at least three functions: it indicated the quality of the iron used, it could be easily cut up to make tools (Crew 1994: 346–7), and it made a symbolic reference to warfare and agriculture (Hingley 1990b: 94).

Over 90% of the currency bars come from hoards, and it is rare for the large currency bar hoards to include any other objects (Crew 1994: 345). The presence of these hoards, and other large iron hoards in the last two centuries BC, is important, as these are not visible in the Early Iron Age. It suggests there was a significant relationship between the deposition of hoards and the trade in metal ores. However, the placing of the Iron Age hoards was somewhat different from that of the Bronze Age hoards. In Wessex, currency bars were deposited on settlements (Hingley 1990b) and almost all of the currency bar hoards, as well as other iron hoards, were placed on settlement boundaries, either in ditches or in pits cut into the back of a bank (Hingley and Haselgrove 2006).[30] It may also be significant that these hoards appear to have been placed in boundaries that were no longer under

---

[28] All these sites indicate a slight drop in the number of iron objects present in the final stages of the Iron Age, though again this may reflect the length of the period examined.

[29] Crew (1994) has provided a more detailed classification that divides currency bars into 20 different types.

[30] Three iron hoards were found at Danebury (Cunliffe and Poole 1991: 354) and all were associated with houses placed immediately behind the rampart. Two of the hoards lie on the south side of the hillfort and one lies immediately to the north of the south-west entrance.

construction. As noted above, the principal period of the construction of hillfort boundaries was over by the end of the third century, whereas most iron hoards were deposited in the second or first centuries BC. It could be argued that hoard deposition was used to emphasize the continuing importance of the boundary; deposition may have been a symbolic act of refurbishment.

Locating the source of this trade iron is problematic. Some iron sources have very distinctive chemical signatures that are believed to be sufficiently distinctive to survive smelting and to be recognized by analysis. A study by Robert Ehrenreich (1985: 95) identified four iron types on the basis of trace element analysis: a high cobalt and nickel iron, a high sulphur iron, a high phosphorous iron and an iron with none of these impurities.

The only known source of high cobalt nickel iron is near Newquay in Cornwall and Ehrenreich (1985: 98–9) suggests that this source was supplying a limited amount of iron in the Early Iron Age but the number of analysed objects with this type of impurity is very low. Iron objects with a high sulphur content are even rarer, and their significance is unclear. Phosphorous-rich iron comes from two principal sources—the Jurassic Ridge and the south Wales Coal Measures—and this type became more significant during the Iron Age (Ehrenreich 1985: 95).[31] Currency bars frequently have this chemical signature (Crew 1994: 346) and the examples found in Northamptonshire are almost certainly made from local sources. However, Crew (1995: 278) has argued that the examples with high phosphate content found in Wessex are of a type not present in Northamptonshire and must be made from an alternative source. The final group have no distinctive trace element signature and could be made using ores from the Weald, the Forest of Dean, the Lower Greensand, or the Continent (Ehrenreich 1985: 97). However, this kind of currency bar tends to cluster to the west near the Forest of Dean, and Crew (1994: 346) has suggested this is a likely source area.

Evidence for iron working is remarkably rare on settlements occupied during the last three centuries BC. There is some evidence for metalworking in the later phases of Danebury but it is restricted to smithing: the best evidence comes from a single pit dating to the latter part of the Middle Iron Age (phase cp 7). Chris Salter (in Cunliffe and Poole 1991: 414) argues that the material from this pit represents nine separate phases of blacksmithing activity spanning periods ranging from two hours to a day. These were probably the consecutive acts of a specialist blacksmith present on the settlement for only a

---

[31] The hillfort of Hunsbury in Northamptonshire is located on a very good source of phosphorous-rich iron and is associated with a range of iron objects. This is often used to argue that the Northamptonshire sources are more important than the Welsh sources, but the evidence is not conclusive.

limited period. Evidence for intensive metalworking is very limited from most of the other settlements of Middle Iron Age date and it is particularly noticeable that the extensive excavations at Winnall Down and Easton Lane (Fasham 1985; Fasham *et al.* 1989) failed to identify a smithing area.

The evidence is slightly better for the half-century preceding the Roman conquest, when some important metalworking areas have been identified. At Maiden Castle, an activity area was found in the earthworks in front of the eastern gateway to the hillfort (Sharples 1991a). This consisted of three separate layers of metalworking debris, which probably resulted from the intermittent use of an old house platform by an itinerant smith in the first half of the first century AD. Salter (in Sharples 1991a: 170) estimates over 200 kg of finished artefacts were produced. This is the most productive Late Iron Age smithing site known from southern England.

Another very important site is Gussage All Saints, but the evidence from this site is poorly dated and analysed (Wainwright 1979a). Over 750 kg of smelting slag is reported to have been found in a quarry hollow on the south side of the entrance to the site. This is very close to the location of a pit full of bronze working (discussed below), and suggests that the area around the abandoned enclosure entrance might have been an important focus for metalworking in the final period of the site's use. Unfortunately, our knowledge of this activity is restricted to a comment that an iron-smelting furnace was present and that it could be dated to the late first century AD (Spratling in Wainwright 1979a: 125). Some specialists (Clough 1985) have suggested that the dating is in error and that this is pre-Roman activity. If this is the case, it represents one of the most important primary production sites in Wessex.

The archaeological evidence for iron working is therefore poor, but it does suggest a change from the Early Iron Age patterns. Prior to the third century BC, sites such as Maiden Castle have evidence for smelting, though this is only on a fairly small scale and represents the exploitation of poor local sources. Iron working appears to be located within the domestic sphere rather than separated out as a specialist industry. During this period, the number of iron objects recovered by archaeologists is small and it seems the objects produced were carefully curated and recycled. After about 300 BC the pattern changes; there is very little evidence for primary iron working and it appears that local production has been replaced by the importation of raw material from sources outside Wessex. The most important sources appear to be in the Jurassic and Carboniferous limestone deposits to the west. This material came to Wessex in a variety of forms, the most conspicuous of which are the currency bars. The evidence, from Old Down Farm, Danebury, and Maiden Castle, suggests that this stock iron was being imported into both small enclosures and hillforts and cut up to create tools as and when these were required. The presence of concentrated blacksmithing areas at Danebury and Maiden Castle suggests specialist blacksmiths came to these settlements to work for a restricted period.

The increasing importance of iron and, in particular, the use of iron that was produced or sourced outside of the hillfort-dominated areas of Wessex, may have given the metal, and the individuals associated with the manufacture of objects from this metal, a special significance. The comparative rarity of evidence for iron working is noteworthy, particularly when compared with its relative prominence in the Early Iron Age. It suggests that local production was no longer acceptable. Similarly, the few complex smithies that have been identified are located on the periphery of the settlements (at Maiden Castle this was close to a cemetery) and appear to represent short-lived phases of intense production and perhaps the existence of itinerant blacksmiths. Richard Hingley (1997) has argued that iron working was shrouded in taboo and represented a class of arcane knowledge that was restricted to certain groups within society.[32] Production was surrounded by ritual and would have provided a potent sexual metaphor for fertility and reproduction. However, Hingley's interpretation should be applied with circumspection, as it is ahistorical and utilizes evidence from widely different Iron Age societies in Britain.[33] There appears to be no evidence for restrictions on the production of iron in the Early Iron Age but these do seem to appear in the Middle Iron Age. It is likely that the restricted nature of iron working in Wessex was a specific function of a desire to produce more complex and sophisticated artefacts in the Middle Iron Age (Figure 3.15), which required the importation of high-quality iron from areas some distance away. To acquire this material required the development of exchange networks that did not exist in the first half of the Iron Age, and which were counter to the community-based power structures that were symbolized by the hillfort ramparts. This resulted in the appearance of a group of specialist metalworkers/artisans, who facilitated the movement of materials from other regions into Wessex, and who undertook the transformation of these materials into complex objects. The peripheral social status of these artisans may be indicated by the location of settlements that have produced evidence for metalworking and other complex transformative industries.

[32] Hingley's (1997) interpretation is heavily dependent on the ethnography of Herbert (1993).

[33] The social control of iron production is likely to have varied greatly in different areas of Britain. The regionally distinctive nature of the British Iron Age makes this very likely, but it is also clear that some areas were important production zones, whereas other areas consumed iron.

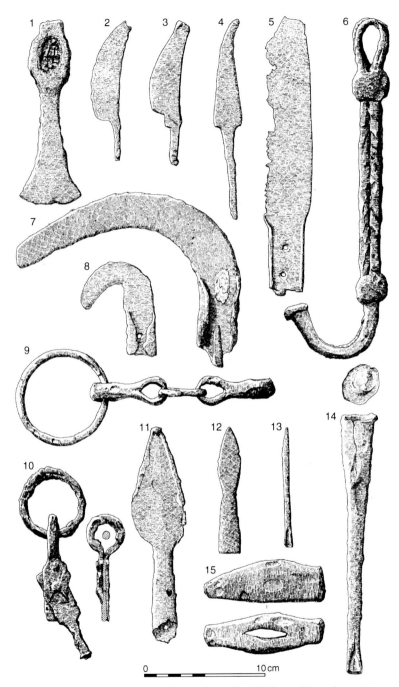

Figure 3.15 A selection of iron objects from the hillfort of Danebury: 1 axe; 2–4 knives; 5 saw; 6 cauldron hook; 7 and 8 sickles; 9 and 10 bridle bits; 11 and 12 spearheads; 13 and 14 gouges; 15 socketed hammer (after Cunliffe 1984; Cunliffe and Poole 1991; reproduced with the permission of Professor B. W. Cunliffe).

Copper Alloys

The use of copper alloys during the early part of the Iron Age was severely limited and is restricted largely to the production of fibula brooches and other small decorative objects (Figure 3.16). Fibula were used to fasten garments and represent one of the few pieces of personal adornment available to the inhabitants of Wessex during the Iron Age. They may have been used to differentiate individuals but the process of differentiation could not have been complex, since although the brooches change through time, they are largely homogeneous in each period, until the Late Iron Age. The British examples are also very small objects with little evidence for non-functional decoration and contrast with Continental types that can be extravagantly decorated.[34] In the first century BC, there was a significant change in the quantity and diversity of the brooches present in Britain. A range of new types (of Continental influence) became available, which included forms that can be classed as decorative; and brooches became much more common (Haselgrove 1997; Jundi and Hill 1998).

The first century BC rise in brooches is well documented by a recent analysis of the brooches recorded by the Portable Antiquities Scheme (Worrell 2007: 376). The data collected by this scheme also provide some valuable evidence for the range of copper alloy objects present in Wessex. The bulk of the objects recorded are brooches but there are significant quantities of horse gear, other items of personal adornment, and toggles/fasteners.[35] The quantity of horse gear recorded is low compared with other areas of the country, such as East Anglia, Lincolnshire, and the Midlands. It is interesting, therefore, that horse gear is well represented in the excavations of Wessex settlements. Isolated pieces of horse gear have been recovered from many settlements; there was a hoard of horse gear from Bury Hill (Cunliffe and Poole 2000a) and waste from their production was found at Gussage All Saints and Silchester.

The production debris from Gussage All Saints is of considerable importance as it provides some of the best evidence for copper alloy working in Britain. The evidence derives from a pit located just inside the entrance to the original enclosure, close to where the iron working activity occurred (Wainwright 1979a). It is unclear if the original enclosure ditch was functioning at this point, but it is obvious that the bronze working activity was peripheral to the main areas of activity in the enclosure. The base of a typical grain storage pit was crammed with metalworking waste from the production of copper alloy

[34] In Bohemia, the sculptural qualities of these brooches make them important artworks.
[35] The bulk of these objects come from Hampshire, but this might simply reflect the early start of the Portable Antiquities Scheme in this county.

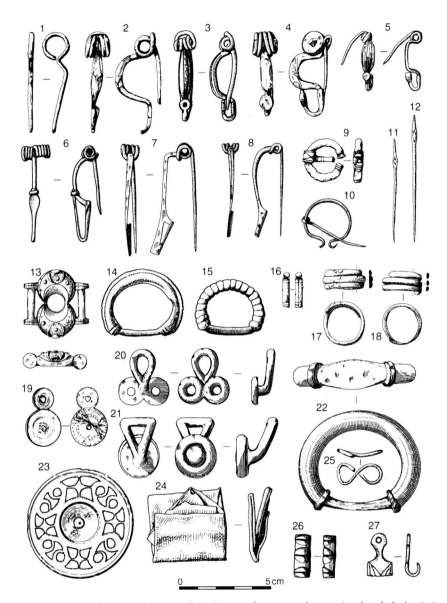

Figure 3.16 A selection of copper alloy objects of Iron Age date. 1 ring-headed pin; 2–8 fibula brooches; 9 and 10 penannular brooches; 11 and 12 needles; 13 strap junction; 14, 15 and 22 terrets; 16 cylinder with coral; 17 and 18 spiral rings; 19, 26 and 27 decorative attachments; 20 and 21 button and loop fasteners; 23 openwork disc; 24 folded sheet; 25 twisted wire. 1, 2, 9 and 25 are from Gussage All Saints (after Wainwright 1979: figs. 84, 85; © Crown copyright); 3, 4, 6, 7, 8, 10, 13, 14, 15, 19, 20, 21, 22, 23, 24, 26 and 27 are from Danebury (after Cunliffe 1984: fig. 7.6; Cunliffe and Poole 1991: fig. 7.5; reproduced with the permission of Professor B.W. Cunliffe); 11, 12, 16, 17 and 18 are from Maiden Castle (after Sharples 1991a: fig. 129; © English Heritage) 5 is from Balksbury (after Wainwright and Davies 1995: fig. 31; © English Heritage).

Figure 3.17 A selection of copper alloy objects and metalworking debris; 2–5 and 7–10 are from Gussage All Saints, 11–17 from Silchester. 1 copper alloy terret from Hod Hill; 2–5 fragments of terret moulds; 6 copper alloy linchpin from Owslebury; 7–10 fragments of moulds for linchpins; 11 and 12 crucibles; 13–17 pellet moulds for the production of coins. (1–10 after Wainwright 1979a: figs. 101–5; © Crown copyright; 11–17 after Fulford and Timby 2000: 187 and 189; with the permission of Professor M.G. Fulford and the Society for the Promotion of Roman Studies.)

chariot fittings. In total there were 7,174 mould fragments from this pit, and a further 26 fragments from elsewhere on the site.[36] Mansel Spratling (in Wainwright 1979a) estimates that these represented the debris from the production of roughly 50 sets of chariot fittings (Figure 3.17). Also in the pit were nearly 600 crucible fragments, several pieces of bronze and iron scrap (including a composite steel and bronze bridle bit), large quantities of tuyere fragments, an elongated billet of tin bronze and four finely made bone implements that are assumed to be modelling tools for shaping the wax prototypes.

In the original report (Wainwright 1979a), Spratling suggested that the production of chariot fittings might have been a long-term specialization of the inhabitants of the enclosure, as there were small quantities of waste from a number of features other than the principal pit deposits. Jennifer Foster (1980), on the other hand, argues that these worn and abraded fragments are largely derived from a single restricted period of activity and suggests 'that these are the products of a temporary workshop set up by the itinerant metallurgists to accomplish one particular job' (Foster 1980: 37). I would agree with the latter assessment and would emphasize that the job was the casting of metal artefacts not the production of chariots. These 50 sets of chariot fittings may have been a supply that was meant to last for many years and to be exchanged between groups of people rather than attached to chariots. The large number of chariot fittings at Bury Hill (Cunliffe and Poole 2000a) represents a deliberate deposit placed in a pit as objects, rather than chariot fittings. This metalwork, therefore, possibly had a social role that was separate from its use as chariot fittings.

Most settlements produce very little evidence for copper alloy metalwork. At Maiden Castle, a collection of small fragments of sheet and strip was found in the south-west corner of the hillfort, associated with limited evidence for iron

---

[36] These included the fragmentary remains of 1,100 moulds for side links of bridle bits, 722 moulds for central links of bridle bits, 638 moulds for side or central links, 903 moulds for gates, 66 moulds for stop knobs, 34 moulds for linchpins, 20 moulds for strap unions, 41 moulds for flat pieces, three for button and loop fasteners, 46 unidentified moulds, and 2,500 other fragments (Foster 1980).

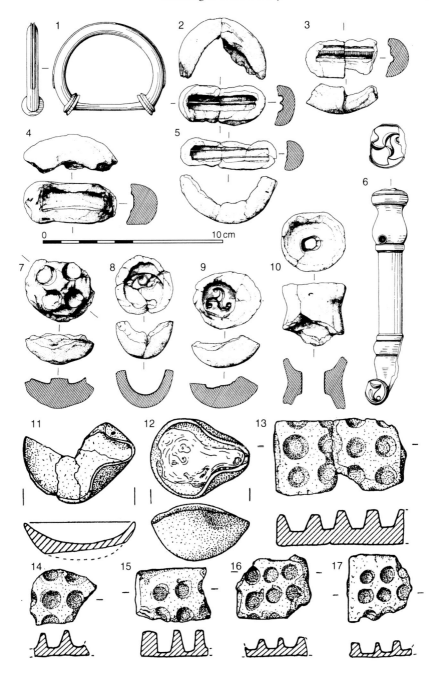

smithing, which suggests the systematic dismantling of sheet metal vessels (Northover in Sharples 1991a).[37] No moulds, ingots, crucibles, or large pieces of slag were associated with these bronze fragments, but it seems likely that they indicate the break-up of substantial sheet metal vessels into pieces suitable for recycling. This pattern is replicated at Danebury (Northover in Cunliffe and Poole 1991) where the material recovered was dominated by fragments of sheet and binding strips, particularly in the later Middle Iron Age (cp 7). At Danebury, there was a small collection of crucibles and fragments of bellows guards (Cunliffe 1995: 67), but again nothing that would indicate that the production of copper alloy (or precious metal) objects was a regular activity.

Evidence for complex metalworking was identified at Hengistbury Head (Cunliffe 1987). This site has evidence for primary metalworking that includes the smelting of chalcopyrite, possibly to produce both copper and iron, and the amalgamation of cassiterite ores to produce bronze. Analysis of the crucibles (19 were found) suggests the refining of copper, alloying of silver and the melting of bronze and silver. It is clear that bronze casting was occurring, and it seems likely that both silver and base metal coinage was being produced (Northover in Cunliffe 1987: 95–6). There was a considerable amount of metalworking taking place on this site;[38] it was undertaken by skilled artisans who had access to important sources of raw material from a wide range of sources, including the surrounding locality, south-west England and the Continent.

In the east, evidence for copper-based metallurgy is minimal and there is noticeably little evidence from Hampshire sites, such as Balksbury, Winkle-bury, and Winnall Down/Easton Lane. A collection of mould fragments for the production of horse gear was recovered from a Late Iron Age pit, beneath the Forum Basilica of Silchester (Fulford and Timby 2000: 31). The pit is an isolated feature at the southern edge of the excavated area and though it appears to be a rubbish pit, it was also used as the receptacle for an extended inhumation of a young adult male. The pit contained mould fragments for the production of various types of terrets, rings, multiple or spiral rings (some of which were bracelet size), penannular brooches, linchpins, strap unions, flat moulds, button moulds and coin moulds, as well as related waste from gates and crucibles (Figure 3.17; Northover and Palk in Fulford and Timby 2000). The metalworking debris was accompanied by a large quantity of

---

[37] The debris comes from two pits and a soil layer, which may be associated with the occupation of a house that is similar to other houses in the excavated areas.

[38] This probably included iron production and though this was not well represented in the recent excavations, it was identified in the early excavations of Bushe-Fox (1915).

pottery that included central Gaulish and Gallo-Belgic imports. Metallurgical debris was present in other parts of the site in the Late Iron Age and included crucibles and pellet moulds, but nothing connected to the production of horse gear. The pellet moulds indicate the presence of coin production, and metal analysis of the crucibles identified ternary alloys that were compatible with Atrebatic coin issues.

In Sussex, some of the settlements on the coastal plain have produced evidence for metalworking. Ounces Barn, Boxgrove (Bedwin and Place 1995: 64), produced fragments of pellet mould for the production of coin blanks, fragments of several crucibles, and some slag. This came from an enclosure ditch located at the end of one of the principal linear boundaries defining the Late Iron Age centre at Chichester.

Peter Northover (in Sharples 1991a: 161–2) has suggested that there is a significant difference between the copper alloy metalworking debris found on hillforts and on non-hillfort settlements. Both these settlement types could be distinguished from sites such as Hengistbury Head and Silchester, which showed evidence for primary production. Hillforts produce large quantities of waste from the recycling of sheet metalworking, whereas non-hillfort settlements produce evidence for the casting of vehicle and harness fittings. The distinction was primarily based on the contrast between the evidence from Maiden Castle and Danebury and that from Gussage All Saints, Beckford, Gloucestershire, and Weelsby Avenue, Lincolnshire. The observation has to be treated with caution as it is based on only a limited number of sites that have produced substantial evidence for copper alloy metalworking, and because these sites include settlements from areas of Britain with quite different settlement patterns. Furthermore, the recent publication of the excavations at South Cadbury in Somerset, a developed hillfort comparable to Maiden Castle and Danebury, has revealed an assemblage that includes evidence for both casting waste (143 pieces) and fragments of sheet and strip (80 pieces; Barrett *et al.* 2000: 291–301). The assemblage includes moulds for terrets, a possible horn cap and a bridle bit side link, which suggests activity very similar to that present at Gussage All Saints (Figure 3.17). It has been suggested that this unusual assemblage might indicate a reorganization of metalworking at the end of the Late Iron Age but the material seems to be scattered throughout the use of the hillfort in the Middle Cadbury phase, which spans the last three centuries BC and the first century AD.

The Cadbury assemblage clearly undermines the distinction between hillfort and non-hillfort copper metallurgy, but rather than completely discarding the distinction, I think the relationship between the process of metal use and metal production needs to be reconsidered. In the first case, it is clear that the evidence from Danebury and Maiden Castle is not directly comparable to that from Gussage All Saints. The scrap present at both these sites represents the destruction of sheet bronze vessels. These are being broken up into little pieces that can be melted down in the small crucibles available. A few crucibles are present at both sites and whilst it seems possible that this scrap was being melted down on site there is no evidence from either site that sheet metal vessels, or any other specialized product, were being produced. The evidence therefore indicates not an interest in the production of sheet metalworking, but an indication of the presence of sheet vessels that were damaged beyond repair and broken up for recycling. The presence of sheet vessels, such as cauldrons or buckets (Hawkes, C. F. C. 1951), may be an indication of the importance of communal feasting at hillforts, as these feasting events would have provided the obvious opportunity to use, and abuse, metal vessels. Large-scale feasting events would have been uncommon on smaller settlements and therefore it is not surprising that there is less evidence for sheet metal vessels in these contexts.

The primary transformation of the alloys appears to have been undertaken, as it was for iron, at sites such as Hengistbury Head, located on the periphery of the densely occupied downlands. The production of coins, which involved the careful preparation and mixing of several metals, also took place in these peripheral locations. The production of copper alloy artefacts is less controlled and though the concentrated and localized nature of the evidence suggests this work is, like iron working, undertaken by specialist artisans, these objects could have been created on downland settlements, at both hillforts and non-hillforts, and their production may well have formed a spectacular piece of visual entertainment.

Coinage, Gold, and Silver

The study of coinage is of crucial importance in how we understand relationships, status, and identity at the end of the Iron Age.[39] Colin Haselgrove (1996) divided the use of coinage into nine phases and three main periods (Table 3.1) and these will be explained briefly, before I discuss the possible role that coinage plays.

---

[39] The clearest explanation for the overall development of coinage in Britain is provided by Haselgrove (1993, 1996), the most innovative recent interpretation is by Creighton (2000), and the most recent regionally specific analysis is by Bean (2000). The most detailed catalogue of the individual coin types is by van Arsdell (1989) though his interpretation has been criticized by many authors (Burnett 1989; Kent 1990; Haselgrove 1990) and will not be examined in detail here.

Table 3.1 Haselgrove's (1996) division of the coinage of Britain

Period	Phase	Duration	Character
I	1	Mid–late 2nd cent BC	Earliest systematically imported coinages; Gallo-Belgic B and early Gallo-Belgic A
	2	Late 2nd cent BC	Later Gallo-Belgic A gold; earliest British potins
	3	Early 1st cent BC	Flat linear potin series; latest Gallo-Belgic A and earlier C gold, but little imported
II	4	*c.* 100–60 BC	Later Gallo-Belgic C and Dc and their earliest British derivatives (British A, B, O, etc.)
	5	*c.* 60–50 BC	Gallic war coinages Gallo-Belgic E and F and their immediate British derivatives (British Qa, La)
	6	*c.* 50–20 BC	Earliest struck bronze; silver relatively limited; latest British potins; legends very rare
III	7	*c.* 20 BC–AD 10	Includes TASCIOVANVS legends, ADDEDO-MARUS, DUBNOVELLAVNOS and TINCOMMIVS
	8	*c.* AD 10–AD 40	Includes CVNOBELINVS, subdivided in early and late issues, EPILLVS and VERICA
	9	*c.* AD 30–AD 45	Includes some EPATICCVS and CARA, some overlap with later Phase 8 issues

The earliest use of coinage extends from the beginning of the second century BC, or possibly earlier, through to the beginning of the first century BC, and represents the period when coins were largely being imported into Britain from the Continent. The imports comprise two distinctive coin types: gold coinage ultimately derived from coins of Philip of Macedon and potins that imitate the bronze coinage of Massalia.[40] The earliest substantial gold coinage to circulate in Britain, Gallo-Belgic A and B, was concentrated in the Thames Basin, Kent, and Essex (Bean 2000: figs. 1.3 and 1.7) and very few coins are found on the south coast. It has been argued by several scholars (e.g. Haselgrove 1987) that Gallo-Belgic B was manufactured on both sides of the Channel and it is possible that some of the Gallo-Belgic A coins were also produced in Britain. In the beginning of the first century BC a new coin Gallo-Belgic C appeared. This was not as plentiful in Britain but it has a more widespread distribution that includes a scatter along the south coast, and it was the first coinage to be regularly deposited in hoards.

The most important feature of period II, beginning roughly 100 BC (Haselgrove pers. comm.), is the production of British copies of these gold coins.

---

[40] Potin coinage is now believed to be amongst the earliest coinage in Britain; it was imported as early as the beginning of the second century BC, perhaps earlier, and a recent reanalysis suggests it was being manufactured in the early second century BC in Kent (Haselgrove 2006: 25). However, these coins are concentrated in Kent, with only a thin scatter throughout the rest of south-east England. They are not directly relevant to the study area.

British A is the most important early issue; it can be split into A1 and A2. The latter type is found south of the Thames with a concentration on the Hampshire coast (Bean 2000: fig. 2.2). British B is concentrated in Hampshire and east Dorset. The coin issues are relatively large and standardized, which suggests a limited number of issues and some control over their production. Continental gold coinage continues to be imported (Gallo-Belgic C and D) during period II, and is found on the south coast, particularly in East Sussex and West Hampshire. The early British issues are swamped by the quantities of imported material in the middle of period II, which may reflect the use of coinage to acquire British support for the opposition to Caesar during the Gallic Wars. Large numbers of Gallo-Belgic E, and to a lesser extent F types, were imported into Britain in the middle of the first century and these coins have an extensive distribution, extending into the Cotswolds and the Severn valley, up to the Peak District and the Humber estuary (Bean 2000: fig. 1.10).

Contemporary with the appearance of these coins was the appearance of a large and complex series of British derivatives. South of the Thames, the gold staters that appear in this period include British Q, which is based on a Gallo-Belgic F, and British Lz3 and M, which derive from a north Thames type. These coins are concentrated in Wiltshire, Berkshire, and west Surrey but they are also present on the south coast (Bean 2000: figs. 3.1–3.4). Contemporary with the staters are a very diverse series of quarter staters (British Qc) that are distributed widely but which include varieties that are concentrated on the coastal plain around Chichester (Bean 2000: fig. 3.7). Another important feature of this period is the introduction of a silver series of coins, which is numerically more important than gold coinage in the southern region. Simon Bean (2000: 60) identifies 61 different types of silver coin in this region, and this is likely to be a conservative estimate. Most of these types are represented by only a handful of coins and they all have a south coast distribution. A distinctive issue of bronze coins has also been identified around Chichester (Burnett 1992), but this appears to be short lived, and bronze coinage does not develop in this area in numbers comparable to those north of the Thames. Bean has suggested that the weight and quality of many of these smaller issues, both gold and silver, 'suggest the absence of a central authority' (Bean 2000: 112). However, there does seem to have been increasing control towards the end of this period, 50–20 BC, when the amount of coinage circulating was reduced and when the first inscribed coins of Commius appeared.

At the same time as these developments occurred in central southern England, a separate group of coins appeared in Dorset, which is known as the south-western or Durotrigian series. These derive from British B and mark the beginning of a regionally distinctive series that extends from the middle of the first century BC through to the Roman conquest.

Period III is characterized by the widespread adoption of inscriptions and Roman designs (Haselgrove 1996: 71). The principal inscriptions in southern England are to Tincomarus, Eppilus, and Verica, all of whom claim to be the sons of Commius, though this may be more generally interpreted as belonging to the family of Commius (J. H. C. Williams 2001). The earliest of these coins appear to be those issued under the name of Tincomarus, which are concentrated in the south coast, around Chichester in particular. His coinage can be split into an earlier series, which uses traditional (Gallo-Belgic) designs comparable to those of Commius, and a later series that uses Roman designs. The coins of Eppilus, in contrast, are concentrated around Calleva (Silchester) (with a separate series concentrated in Kent) and he actually aspires to the title Eppilus King of Calleva. His coins are all modelled on Roman designs and it is suggested he took over, or established, the *oppidum* of Calleva slightly later than Tincomarus. However, these two individuals were probably contemporary rulers for some years, and there is a short-lived Kentish coinage that suggests an alliance between Tincomarus, Eppilus, and Verica, and marks the earliest appearance of the latter. Verica seems to have succeeded both Tincomarus and Eppilus, and he produced two separate series of coins, one minted in Calleva and the other minted in the south, near Chichester (Bean 2000: 173–96). Verica, as king, was forced to flee to Rome either as a result of an attack on his kingdom, by Epaticcus and Caratacus from north of the Thames, or because of internal unrest (Creighton 2000: 122–3).

Throughout period III the Durotrigian/south-western coinage of Dorset continued to develop from the original design of British B. However, this design was gradually transformed and became increasingly abstract until, by the Roman conquest, the head was represented by a line and the horse by a series of isolated pellets. No inscriptions were ever placed on Durotrigian coinage and they never adopted Roman designs.

The introduction of coinage indicates an interest in two very important metals, gold and silver. Gold had been used to make elaborate ornaments in the later Bronze Age, but silver had rarely previously been used in any quantity in the British Isles. Both gold and silver were used to produce ornaments in the Late Iron Age, but these ornaments are very rare. The most important group of ornaments are torcs, and though these are concentrated in Norfolk, and in particular at Snettisham, the Wessex region has produced gold examples from Clench Common, near Marlborough, and the remains of three broken examples, twisted together, from Hengistbury Head (Jope 2000: 84–5). Evidence for the production of coinage at Hengistbury Head may indicate that these gold objects were collected as scrap for recycling (Northover in Cunliffe 1987).

A very important recent discovery was the set of jewellery known as the
Winchester Hoard (Hill *et al.* 2004). This comprised two unique necklaces,
four fibula (two pairs, one with attached gold chain), and two bracelets, all in
gold (Figure 3.18). These objects were scattered across a field but must
originally have been from a single deposit and probably represent a matching

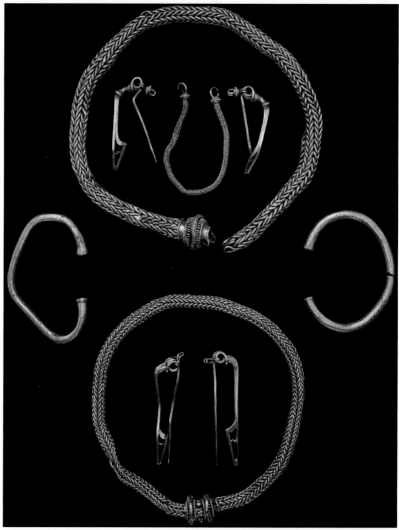

Figure 3.18 A collection of high status gold ornaments from near Winchester,
Hampshire (© Trustees of the British Museum). There are two pairs of fibula, one
pair connected by a chain, two torcs and two bracelets.

set of jewellery for two people. The necklaces have a unique loop in loop construction style that makes them very flexible when worn, and they are closed with a clasp that is decorated in Hellenistic or Roman style. The brooches in contrast are of a north-west European style that is found in Britain, though never in gold, and can be dated to between 80/70 BC and 40/30 BC. They are made from gold of over 90% purity, much purer than the gold used for British coinage, and almost certainly originating in the Mediterranean. If it had not been for the discovery of the brooches, the necklaces would have been assumed to have been deposited after the Roman conquest, but it seems clear they belonged to an extremely wealthy individual, who came to the south coast of Britain in the middle of the first century BC.

The gold used in most British coinage is a ternary alloy made from a mixture of gold, silver, and copper. The original proportion of gold in the Gallo-Belgic A and B coins was relatively high (just under 80%) but the introduction of the new British issues and the development of local coinage resulted in the gradual reduction of the gold content. Detailed analysis of these coin types (Cowell 1992; Northover 1992) reveals a carefully controlled reduction in the gold content. This was achieved by adding silver and copper (in 2:1 ratio), and the appearance of the gold retains a silvery gold colour similar to that of the earliest coins. However, in the latter part of phase II there is a significant change in the colour of these coins, due to the addition of much higher quantities of copper. Interestingly, the areas of Britain, such as Dorset, that continue to follow the earlier traditional designs try to maintain the silvery gold colour, even though the amount of gold present in the coins is frequently less than 20%.[41]

The visual impact of the coins is also demonstrated by their designs. In a recent analysis of the coins of south-east Britain, John Creighton (2000) has argued that the designs used are of considerable symbolic significance and can tell us about the changing nature of British society in the period leading up to the Roman conquest. His comments can be split into two separate areas of debate, concerning the Gallo-Belgic imagery used in periods I and II, and the classical imagery of period III. Both debates emphasize the importance of the royal use of gold and argue that 'torcs [*are*] the insignia of Kingship, or at least the paramount lineage, whilst coinage represented portable and transferable symbols of that authority' (Creighton 2000: 31). If gold was closely associated with kingship then it might suggest that a different view of kingship existed south and north of the Thames, as silver coinage is much more important on the south coast.

[41] The Snettisham torcs also tend to favour a silvery gold colour, but they have a much broader range of alloys that range from pure to debased gold.

The symbolic representations on British gold coinage ultimately derive from the coins of Philip II (the father of Alexander the Great), which were decorated on the obverse with the head of Apollo and on the reverse with a chariot being pulled by two horses. These coins were copied and recopied by the peoples of central and Western Europe[42] until, by the time they reached Gallia-Belgica, the chariot had been replaced by a horse surrounded by abstract symbols. In Britain the period I designs of the Gallo-Belgic A and B coins are quite stylized but still clearly recognizable. At the beginning of period II the issues available in southern Britain, that is, Gallo-Belgic C and D, British A2, B, and D, frequently delineated both the horse and the head as abstracted symbols (Figure 3.19; 1–3). The horse in southern Britain was often associated with a wheel and what appears to be a sun symbol (Figure 3.19; 7, 8, 11, and 9, 10 respectively). More unusual symbols include a lyre and bird (the latter symbol is visible on Fig. 3.19; 11), and these indicate close contact with Gaul during the period of the Gallic Wars. The head is less consistently represented; the wreath and the hair curls become increasingly emphasized and stylized and the eyes become abstract crescents. These motifs are arranged in a very distinctive cruciform pattern on several of the southern coin types (e.g. Bean Ma1-3). However, there are other coins with very naturalistic heads (Figure 3.19; 6, 7, 10) and a group of these have been interpreted as having helmets (e.g. Bean QsT1–4).[43]

Creighton (2000; Williams and Creighton 2006) has argued that the abstractions of these symbols are very deliberate and that they represent trance images that result from the drug-induced visions of shaman druids. He suggests a threefold division of entoptic imagery that can be related to the process of any trance (Lewis-Williams and Dowson 1988):

1. universal images such as dots, grids, parallel lines, zig-zags, nested curves, and filigrees that move, rotate, and form complex patterns;
2. culturally specific images such as sacred animals that coalesce with the abstract patterns of the previous phase;
3. transition through a tunnel of light, which is associated with flying or swimming, into vivid hallucinations where the participant is often transformed into an animal.

All these visions can be associated with images on the early coins, and examples from the appropriate entoptic stages are illustrated (Williams and

---

[42] These coins were also copied by Alexander and his successors and it is probably the late issues that are copied in Europe (Haselgrove pers. comm.).

[43] There are also groups that have the head replaced by boars (e.g. Bean QsT3-1) or pairs of horses (e.g. Bean QsT2-3).

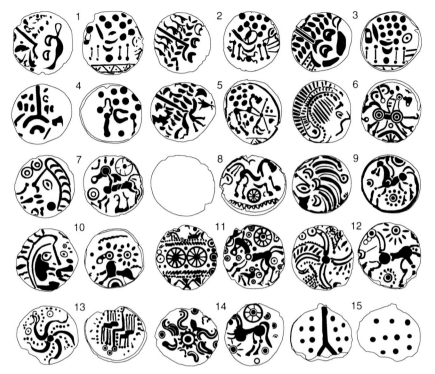

Figure 3.19 A selection of British coins decorated with designs ultimately inspired by coins of Philip of Macedon. 1 gold stater, British A, VA202. 2 gold stater, British B, VA1205. 3 silver stater, Durotrigian/British A, VA1235. 4 silver stater, Durotrigian, VA1235. 5 gold stater, British C, VA1220. 6 silver unit, British Lz7, VA264. 7 silver unit, British Lz8, VA355. 8 gold stater, British Qb, VA216. 9 silver unit, British QsD. 10 silver unit, British QsD. 11 gold quarter stater, British Qc, VA236. 12 gold quarter stater, British Qc, VA256. 13 silver quarter stater, Durotrigian (starfish type), VA1270. 14 Gold quarter stater, British Qc. 15 bronze cast unit, Durotrigian, VA1344. Note these are not to scale.

Creighton 2006: fig. 3). The stage 1 images used are related to rotational images that derive from the transformation of the head (Figure 3.19; 12). The stage 2 images are related to disassembled horses (Figure 3.19; 3, 4), particularly clear on coins in the south-western series (Dorset). The stage 3 images are divided into spiral images that suggest the tunnel (Figure 3.19; 12); winged horses, or spirit heads that imply weightlessness or out-of-body experiences; and animism, such as a horse with a human head.

These interpretations are undoubtedly interesting and are supported by an analysis of the British archaeological record that suggests drug use and specialist ritual practitioners, comparable to north European shamans, might well have existed in the Late Iron Age (Williams and Creighton 2006). However, there are problems with Creighton's selective use of the coinage. It is odd that the images used to illustrate the different trance stages are often quite regionally specific. The abstract symbols, for instance, are a feature of the south-western series, whereas the horses with human heads are a feature of Armorican coinage. It seems strange that one group should choose to illustrate one aspect of the visions and not all the stages. It is also not explained why, when shamanistic rituals and drug-induced trances are assumed to be long-lived cultural practices, the entoptic images of stages 2 and 3 were not previously represented in other media. The symbols found on coins are quite different from the decoration present on pottery and on other categories of decorative metalwork. Furthermore, the coinage with the most abstract and apparently drug-induced imagery (Gallo-Belgic C and D, British A2, B and D) does not form the prototype for later period II issues in central southern Britain. Later issues are modelled on the less stylized Gallo-Belgic F type and instead of becoming more abstract both the horse and the head become increasingly naturalistic (e.g. British Ma and Lz3; Bean 2000: 99).

It is possible that the short-lived importance of entoptic imagery can be related to the appearance of formalized druidic religion in the middle of the first century BC. This is certainly the period when archaeologically recognizable religious structures are identified (e.g. Hayling Island) and it might suggest that an increase in the production of coinage was directly related to a restructuring and formalization of religious practice in the first half of the first century BC. However, if this is the case then it is short lived, as entoptic imagery is rare in the second half of the first century BC (arguably only present in Dorset) and instead the symbolic representations are of an increasingly powerful secular elite of individual rulers closely aligned with Rome.

The introduction of classical imagery (Figure 3.20) occurs with the coins of Tincomarus and is associated with a change in the colour of the alloys used from a yellow gold to a red gold. Creighton (2000) argues that the images used do not indicate a random selection of the images available on Roman coins circulating in the north-west provinces of the Roman empire, but instead represent the specific adoption of symbols that were closely associated with the assumption to power of Octavian/Augustus; a mounted horseman with spear, star, sphinx, and so forth. The detailed understanding of contemporary Roman symbolism demonstrated by these coins must indicate a close contact between these individuals and Rome. Creighton believes this was because these individuals, the sons of the leading British families at the time of Caesar's invasion of Britain, lived as hostages in Rome, or other centres of classical learning, for an extended period after the invasion. The taking of hostages was normal practice at the end of a campaign, as it guaranteed

Figure 3.20 A selection of coins decorated with designs inspired by Roman coinage. 1 Eppilus, silver unit, eagle, noting his position as REX at Calleva (Silchester). 2 Eppilus, gold quarter stater, lion/horse, noting the connection with Calleva (Silchester). 3 Eppilus, silver unit, Capricorn, noting his relationship with Commius. 4 Tincomarus, silver unit, winged victory making sacrifice at altar. 5 Tincomarus, gold stater, traditional design. 6 Tincomarus, gold stater, rider on horse, noting his relationship with Commius. 7 Verica, gold quarter stater, horse. 8 Verica, silver unit, boar, noting his relationship with Commius. 9 Verica, gold quarter stater, horse, note use of the term REX and relationship with Commius. 10 Verica, silver minim. 11 Verica, silver minim, star and bird. 12 Verica, gold stater, vine leaf and armed rider on horse. Note these are not to scale.

the support of the conquered tribes. It was not perceived as a punitive strategy, since the hostages were treated as guests and educated in Roman ways.[44] The similarity of the images used in Britain and the images used on coinage in other client kingdoms also indicates a close link between the rulers of these kingdoms; there may even have been intermarriage between the dynasties of kingdoms at opposite ends of the empire (Creighton 2000: 118). Creighton may be over-interpreting the evidence but it is clear that the tribes of south and east England were closely aligned with the Roman empire from the end of the first century BC.

---

[44] There is historical evidence for the presence of a number of conquered dependants in Rome but not for the presence of British tribal leaders.

The most important feature of early coinage that we have yet to consider is what it was used for. Most of the authors discussed above have been content to ignore this issue, but there is an explicit assumption in many of the texts that coinage is a standard used to encourage trade in commodities. However, it must be emphasized that coinage is not equivalent to money and does not necessarily indicate the development of commodity exchange in the Late Iron Age. These issues have been most thoroughly explored by Haselgrove (1987), who was very critical of previous suggestions (Collis 1971) that a market exchange system was developing. He provides four uses for money: a means of payment (for services rendered); storage of wealth (accumulation of valuables); a standard of value (unit of account for different commodities) and a medium of exchange (to acquire other objects). All these roles can be separated, but Haselgrove assumes money must fulfil all four roles.

Coinage, in contrast, is much more limited: it is a 'piece of metal of a determined standard issued by a competent authority...a particular issue must have approximately the same weight and fineness in order to be useable and...bear the mark of a specific authority' (Haselgrove 1987: 20). It can be used in several different ways:

1. as a primitive valuable to acquire status and to give status to other people;
2. as primitive money, a medium for transactions;
3. as early cash, where production is controlled and use is restricted to political obligations.

It seems very unlikely that the early gold coinage of phase 1 could have been used as either primitive money or as early cash, as gold coins must have been very valuable items. It is difficult to imagine anything more valuable than gold coins, or gold artefacts, in circulation during the Late Iron Age. A more likely interpretation is that coinage was used as a primitive valuable, operating as the highest level of a tiered gift exchange system. Haselgrove's (1987) analysis of the gold coinage of south-east England went some way to supporting the interpretation of gold as a primitive valuable since it was evenly spread throughout the region and could be contrasted with bronze coinage, which was concentrated around early *oppida*. Most gold coins are found as small hoards, between two and ten coins. These are rarely found on settlements but instead are located in the surrounding landscape, placed close to rivers and other watery places.[45]

---

[45] Haselgrove notes that gold coins were particularly rare discoveries at the important *oppida* of Braughing, Canterbury, and St Albans (Haselgrove 1987).

These results generalize the picture from southern England, and it has to be remembered that the southern region (Hampshire, Berkshire, and Sussex) and the south-west (Dorset) have quite distinctive patterns. The southern region has more silver than gold coinage, particularly in period II, and very little evidence for bronze coins. The symbolic importance of these coins is clearly illustrated by their deposition at the temple of Hayling Island, which lies just to the west of the Chichester complex (King and Soffe 2001). Excavation of a Roman temple revealed a Late Iron Age shrine with two construction phases (Figure 3.21). The first phase is a rectangular building, which lies immediately

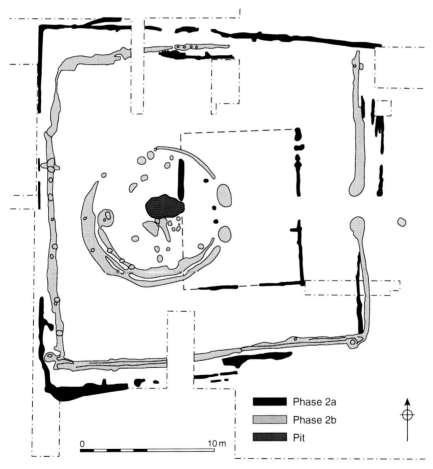

Phase 2a
Phase 2b
Pit

0   10 m

Figure 3.21 The Late Iron Age temple at Hayling Island, showing features belonging to the two structural phases (after King and Soffee 2001: fig. 7.1; reproduced with permission of Hayling Island Excavation Project).

in front of a large hollow, and was surrounded by a trapezoidal enclosure. This was replaced by a circular building, which is centred on the large hollow and surrounded by a roughly square enclosure. Both structures have eastern orientations. The large hollow appears to be an important focus within the enclosure and it might represent a place where deposits/offerings were originally laid, or it could have been the location of a large upright post or stone, though its primary use has been erased by later activity.

Haselgrove (2005) would argue that the first enclosure belongs to the first half of the first century BC, the second phase may date to around 30 BC, and the final Roman phase is immediately post-conquest. His dating is based on a detailed analysis of the impressive group of about 165 coins that were recovered from the excavations. Most of these coins were found in the south-east corner of the enclosure and they are associated with other votive offerings, which include numerous brooches, two currency bars, shield binding, iron spearheads, vehicle fittings (with Continental parallels), a Neolithic and a Mesolithic axe, broken Middle Bronze Age spearheads, and an assemblage of animal bones dominated by pig and sheep (King and Soffe 2001).[46] These discoveries emphasize the religious significance of coinage in the Late Iron Age. These objects are being deposited as a gift to the gods and it seems likely that most of the period I and II coinage found in southern England may have been deposited as offerings in contexts that, though less elaborately delineated than the formal temple of Hayling Island, were still of considerable religious significance.

The overall pattern of early coin deposition is therefore quite similar to that of later Bronze Age metalwork and it seems likely that it functioned in quite a similar fashion within Late Iron Age societies. However, coinage does have some quite specific characteristics that indicate it carries additional functions that distinguish it from bronze use at the beginning of the first millennium BC. The designs that decorate the coins are clearly much more symbolically important to the communities using coinage than the designs on bronze axes. In period III the areas to the north of the Thames, and in Kent, develop low-value bronze coinage, which may be 'early cash'. However, the principal use of the coinage in the south continues to be as a primitive valuable. The classical

---

[46] The assemblage of coins includes a large number of early Gaulish types that probably arrived before the Gallic Wars. They indicate contact with a very large area of Gaul; mostly Belgic Gaul and the Normandy/Loire area, but there was also material from east Gaul and Armorica. The assemblage is similar in character to the other early material from the Chichester area and quite different from the Armorican-dominated assemblages from Hengistbury Head (De Jersey in Cunliffe and De Jersey 1997) and the assemblage from Silchester, which arrived via the Thames. The other temples known in southern England tend to have much more restricted assemblages of local coins. These differences may represent the different political allegiances of the groups using the temple at Hayling Island.

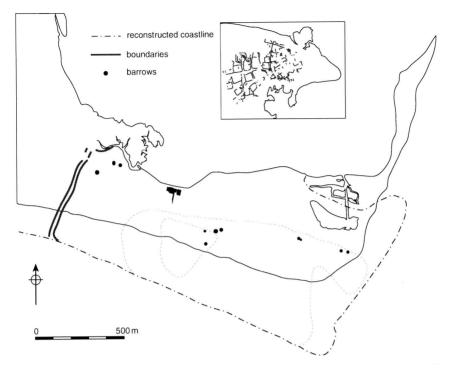

Figure 3.22 A map of the promontory fort at Hengistbury Head on the south side of Christchurch Harbour and, in the inset, the settlement at Ower on the south coast of Poole Harbour (after Cunliffe 1987: illus. 3, 6 and 12; Cox and Hearne 1991: fig. 31).

images and inscriptions identifying rulers, and their political centres, are clearly of considerable symbolic significance in creating the political allegiances that provided the basis for these emerging dynasties.

LATE IRON AGE CENTRES

Four sites seem to represent significant new developments, and have evidence for a range of innovative features that characterize the Late Iron Age in Wessex: Hengistbury Head and Ower in Dorset, Chichester in West Sussex, and Silchester in Berkshire.[47]

[47] There may also be Late Iron Age foci at Arundel in Sussex (McOmish pers. comm.) and Savernake Forest in Wiltshire (Bowden pers. comm.), but further work is required.

Hengistbury Head is a promontory on the south side of Christchurch Harbour (Figure 3.22; Cunliffe 1987). The promontory is defined by a substantial boundary but it is unclear when this was constructed. The interior was extensively trenched and a large assemblage of finds was recovered from activity areas on the north shore of the promontory (Bushe-Fox 1915). One of these settlement foci was explored by Cunliffe (1987: 66) who exposed a densely occupied area with eleven phases of activity, four of which were placed in later prehistory. The earliest phase of human activity was split between a concentration of Early Iron Age buildings, covering the east half of the trench, and an isolated scatter of Middle Iron Age buildings, in the west half of the trench. These structures were partially covered in sand by a short-lived flood event, caused by higher sea levels. This was followed by two phases of Late Iron Age activity: Late Iron Age 1 and 2, and the latter includes the construction of the first enclosure ditches. Enclosure ditches continue to be an important feature in the Roman phases of activity, which are also characterized by the deposition of extensive gravel spreads. A small trench excavated to the north, in the marsh on the edge of the harbour, revealed a sequence of Late Iron Age deposits interleaved with natural water-lain deposits.

Ower is currently located at the end of a promontory projecting into Poole Harbour. The promontory appears to be a late development, created by rising sea levels. Originally, the location was on the edge of a much larger promontory that included Green Island and Furzey Island (Cox and Hearne 1991: fig. 91). Poole Harbour was reoccupied some time in the second century BC, but during this period occupation appears to have been concentrated on the coast of what is now Furzey Island. Only when this was cut off from the mainland, around 50 BC, did the new promontory of Ower become important. The site was characterized by a complex of irregular, rectangular enclosures (Figure 3.22; Woodward, P.J. 1987a: fig. 31),[48] and whilst excavation has confirmed the Late Iron Age date of these enclosures, no substantial associated structures have been located.

The *oppidum* at Silchester (Calleva) provides the most convincing evidence for a planned densely settled Late Iron Age centre in Britain. It was enclosed by at least two substantial earthworks that defined an inner and outer enclosure (Fulford 1984), though the east side of this enclosure still eludes identification (Figure 3.23). Excavation at the centre of the settlement, underneath the Roman Forum-Basilica, identified three phases of settlement, with the last one spanning the Roman conquest. The first phase, which dates to some time

---

[48] Unlike Hengistbury Head, there is no evidence for a substantial boundary separating the peninsula from the hinterland.

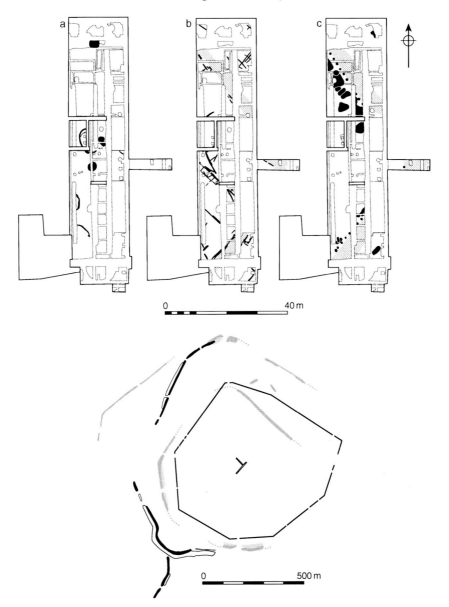

Figure 3.23 A plan of the Late Iron Age earthworks and Roman wall of Silchester. At the top is a plan of the excavated area in the centre of the Roman town showing the Late Iron Age activity below the Forum-Basilica: a) phase 1; b) phase 2; c) phase 2/3 (after Fulford and Timby 2000: figs. 4–7 and 232).

after 50 BC, comprised a number of gully-defined round or oval houses that were associated with several wells. These appear to be replaced around 15–5 BC by a planned system of ditch-defined roads flanked by rectangular buildings (Fulford and Timby 2000). Phase 3 involved the metalling of the road and the replacement of the infilled ditches first by a palisade and then by lines of pits. There is no structural evidence for settlement but the pits were infilled with occupation debris. It is argued that the settlement covered most of the area enclosed, but these observations need to be tested by further excavations.

In contrast to Silchester, Chichester is perhaps the most ill defined of all the British *oppida*. The principal feature is a series of substantial linear boundaries on the coastal plain between Chichester Harbour and the River Arun (Figure 2.24). The principal boundary (the Devil's Ditch) runs along the base of the chalk scarp of the downlands, and there is a series of boundaries running parallel, and perpendicular, to this boundary which are concentrated in, and to the north of, the Roman town of Chichester.[49] The boundaries define a focal point somewhere around the Roman town, or close to the Roman palace at Fishbourne (which lies immediately to the west of the town)[50] and Iron Age coin finds suggest a focus beneath the Roman town (Haselgrove 1987: 149). However, no nucleated Late Iron Age settlement has been found in this area and extensive excavations have revealed only three insubstantial structures close to a large ditch to the east of the town (Down 1989: fig. 12.2), and a substantial ditch to the west of the town, adjacent to Fishbourne Palace (Manley and Rudkin 2005). The latter ditch contained a collection of pre-conquest Gallo-Roman fine wares and amphora, and smaller collections of this material have also been found during excavations in the town and at Fishbourne Palace (Manley and Rudkin 2005: 58). Some scholars (Creighton 2001: 9–10; Manley 2003: 138–9) have suggested

[49] These boundaries are closely related to the alluvial flood plains of the river valleys that cut across the coastal plain, which around Chichester include the River Lavant, Fishbourne Creek, and Basham stream.

[50] The boundaries also impede access to Selsey Bill, and some people have suggested there was an *oppidum* on Selsey Bill that was eroded away by the sea but this has now been fairly emphatically dismissed (Bedwin 1983). The importance of the broader region is emphasized by the discovery of the temple at Hayling Island (King and Soffe 2001) and the cemetery at Westhampnett (Fitzpatrick 1997). There are also several settlements to the east of the town; including Copse Farm, Oving (Bedwin and Holgate 1985) and Ounces Barn, Boxgrove (Bedwin and Place 1995) that provide valuable evidence for Late Iron Age activity. The cemetery at Westhampnett contains 161 burials and is one of the largest cremation cemeteries known from south-east England, comparable to the cemetery at King Harry Lane, St Albans (Stead and Rigby 1989). Both cemeteries are associated with dyke systems defining major Late Iron Age centres. The cemetery at Westhampnett and the temple at Hayling Island date to the first half of the first century BC (Fitzpatrick 1997: 204, Haselgrove 2005) and pre-date the dyke system and the Late Iron Age features from both the town and the palace. Nevertheless, it is difficult to accept Fitzpatrick's (1997) suggestion that Westhampnett represents the dead from a couple of small settlements such as Copse Farm. In contrast, these structures seem to indicate large groups of people who were experimenting with new ways of socialization.

a pre-conquest date for the earliest buildings at Fishbourne Palace[51] and it is possible they represent early first century AD activity.

These sites all have certain similarities that suggest their origin and function may be related. The most obvious is their position in the landscape. Hengistbury Head and Ower are located on natural harbours at the mouth of the Rivers Avon and Stour, and Frome and Piddle, respectively, and their immediate hinterland is the tertiary deposits of the Dorset Heaths and the New Forest. Chichester is located at the landward end of the natural inlet of Chichester Harbour; the sea would be accessible along the Fishbourne channel.[52] Silchester, in contrast, is situated a long way from the coast on the plateau gravels that form a large area of inhospitable uplands on the southern edge of the tertiary deposits of the Kennet valley. The locations occupied were inhabited in the Middle to Late Bronze Age but were largely deserted during the Early and Middle Iron Age. Ower and Silchester are in locations that have very little evidence for earlier activity of any date.[53] The West Sussex coastal plain appears to have been reoccupied only in the second century BC, after a period of abandonment of about 300–500 years (Davenport 2003: 104–5). Only at Hengistbury Head was the Late Iron Age settlement associated with an earlier occupation.[54]

The environment at all of these sites is ill suited to arable agriculture as they are all, except possibly Chichester/Fishbourne, surrounded by nutrient-poor soils that support heath or woodland. However, it would have been possible to find small areas of suitable land within the catchments of all the sites. Hengistbury produced mixed assemblages of grain, chaff, or weeds, though chaff was poorly represented (Nye and Jones in Cunliffe 1987). Peas, flax, and beans seem to have been introduced as crops during the Late Iron Age, and

[51] Phase 1a at Fishbourne comprises two timber buildings, T1 and T2, that were interpreted as storage structures that belonged to a post-conquest military depot on the site. Manley (2003: 139) suggests that the principal dating evidence for these structures relates to their dismantling and that material from this part of the site includes Arretine pottery that must date earlier than AD 25. However, he does not argue that the buildings represent a high status native settlement, though this is the logical outcome of his argument. Creighton (2001) has also argued that the distinctive structure of these buildings has similarities with other Late Iron Age buildings. Both Manley and Creighton imply that the Fishbourne evidence might indicate a pre-conquest Roman military presence in southern England.

[52] The sea was probably also accessible down the River Lavant to Pagham Harbour on the east side of Selsey Bill.

[53] Silchester was constructed in a woodland clearing (Wooders and Keith Lucas in Fulford and Timby 2000: 532–3).

[54] It has been suggested that settlement on the promontory was continuous as a small area of Middle Iron Age activity was located in the recent excavations. However, it is not clear how early or long lived this Middle Iron Age occupation was, or whether it might be largely contemporary with the Late Iron Age 1 activity. There is a strong possibility that a period of abandonment occurred in the Middle Iron Age and Cunliffe (1987: 339) suggests this could last from c.400 to 100 BC.

figs were being imported (Cunliffe 1987: 339). Silchester also produced very little cereal-processing debris (chaff) despite extensive wet-sieving (Fulford in Fulford and Timby 2000: 555) and it is suggested that this might indicate the site was dependent on other agricultural settlements.[55]

The animal bone assemblages from these settlements are distinctive but not consistent. Silchester produced the largest assemblage of animal bones (Grant in Fulford and Timby 2000) but there are small and interesting collections from the ditch at Fishbourne, Chichester (Sykes in Manley and Rudkin 2005), and at Hengistbury Head (Grant in Cunliffe 1987) and Ower in Purbeck (Coy in Woodward, P. J. 1987a). The early assemblages from Hengistbury Head and Silchester are linked by the dominance of cattle bones; the fragments make up 81% of the principal domestic species at Hengistbury and 54% of the main species in the first phase at Silchester (they decline to only 37% in phase 3). It would be very unusual for cattle to play such an important part in the economy of a chalk downland site in the Middle Iron Age, as sheep dominate these assemblages. Furthermore, the age of death of the cattle at Silchester is unusual. All of the animals appear to be over two years old, which suggests the settlement was not associated with the breeding and rearing of animals, but instead was provided with mature animals for consumption.

Pigs were also important at Silchester; in the first phase they were numerically comparable to the sheep but they increased in importance to become 33% of the assemblage in phase 3. Pigs were significant in most of the Late Iron Age settlements of south-eastern England and the numerical importance of the Silchester assemblage is comparable to other sites. However, pig is even more important in the assemblages from Fishbourne and Ower; at the former they make up 73% and at the latter 51% of the assemblages, though both are small, 251 and 471 bones respectively. Nevertheless, these assemblages do seem to emphasize a trend towards Continental eating habits at these settlements that differentiates them from adjacent settlements, such as Copse Farm, Oving (Browne in Bedwin and Holgate 1985), where sheep were still numerically dominant.

The evidence suggests the inhabitants of these sites may have been receiving primary foodstuffs from adjacent communities. Initially these foodstuffs were cattle, which may reflect the prestige of these animals in the local downland settlements. However, as time progressed these communities began to receive much more pig and this may represent the development of animals that more directly reflected the nature of prestige food consumption in the peripheral communities. Pig was the most common foodstuff in the areas of the

---

[55] The evidence from Ower and Chichester is not sufficient to assess the nature of arable agriculture at these sites.

Continent closely connected to these sites and may be more suited to the dining activities adopted in these centres.

These settlements are also connected by evidence for exchange and production at a level categorically different from that found on most chalk downland sites. The best evidence comes from Hengistbury Head, which has been much more extensively excavated than the other sites. The Late Iron Age industries include 'bronze working, glass working, the turning of Kimmeridge shale to make armlets, and the use if not extraction of salt' (Cunliffe 1987: 339); iron working is also likely to be present. These industries were dependent on the importation of raw materials, as only iron and salt could be sourced on the site. Ores from the south-west (including Callington on the Devon/Cornwall border), and the Mendips, have been identified, and these connections would also explain the presence of Glastonbury Ware on the site.

Large quantities of imported Armorican pottery were found at Hengistbury Head (Figure 3.24). Estimates suggest the imported ceramics could be as high as '6,300 fine Black Cordoned vessels, 5,000 Rilled Micaceous vessels and 1,500 Graphite-coated vessels...[and]...an estimated 1,000+ amphora' (Cunliffe in Cunliffe and De Jersey 1997: 47) all of which, together with over 26 Armorican coins and a piece of purple glass, are likely to be derived from Brittany. Continental contact appears to be most important in the period from 120 to 60 BC (Cunliffe in Cunliffe and De Jersey 1997: 51),[56] but the site continued to be occupied in the century preceding the Roman invasion and, though there is evidence for the importation of some Roman and Gaulish material during this period, the evidence of the amphora, in particular, indicates a decline in contacts with the Continent.[57]

In contrast to Hengistbury Head, there is only limited evidence for industrial specialization at Ower, Chichester, and Silchester.[58] This may reflect the relatively small areas of excavation at these three settlements and it is clear that pottery production centres must be located in their locality as all three sites appear to have been supplied by local industries. The Poole Harbour industries were becoming increasingly

[56] Most of the imports from the recent excavations were restricted to three main deposits: from an isolated trench through the marsh deposits on the northern fringes of the promontory; from a large quarry in the centre of the main excavations; and in a soil accumulation layer on the slopes down from this area (Cunliffe in Cunliffe and De Jersey 1997: 49). None of these deposits could be described as within the settlement and this suggests that the imported material was carefully curated and deposited in peripheral locations.

[57] The quantities of Dressel 1B and Dressel 1 Pascual 1 are significantly smaller than the quantities of Dressel 1A.

[58] Both the Fishbourne ditch and the Copse Farm settlement have produced evidence for iron smithing but this is no more than one would expect on a domestic settlement.

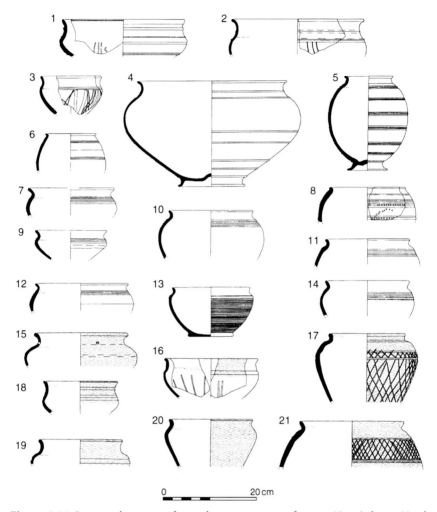

Figure 3.24 Imported pottery from the promontory fort at Hengistbury Head, Hampshire. 1–6 black cordoned ware; 7–14 micaceous ware; 15–21 graphite-coated ware (after Cunliffe 1987; reproduced with the permission of Professor B.W. Cunliffe).

important during the occupation of Ower. The large quantities of coins around Chichester and Silchester are also important (Bean 2000), and coin production is demonstrated by the discovery of pellet moulds at Ounces Barn, Boxgrove, near Chichester (Bedwin and Place 1995: 64) and from various locations at Silchester (Northover in Fulford and Timby

2000).[59] Both sites have associated crucibles and metalworking debris, and at Silchester the analysis of this material indicates the melting of ternary alloys, with a composition comparable to the local coinage. Silchester also had evidence for the production of horse harnesses comparable to those at Gussage All Saints.

The exceptional nature of Ower, Chichester, and Silchester is distinguished by the assemblage of imported Continental pottery present at these sites.[60] In contrast to the assemblage from Hengistbury Head, the assemblages from these sites are dominated by Roman forms, some from the Italian peninsula, but mostly from newly created production centres in Gaul (Figure 3.25). The imported fine wares include early Arretine wares, Terra Rubra and Terra Nigra, Gallo-Belgic Whitewares, Lyons ware, and vessels from Saintes and the Roanne. Most of the imported vessels are tablewares: cups and flagons, beakers and plates, and these imports represent an increasing concern with the social arena of food consumption. Amphora were also present, and these contained olive oil, Catalonian and Italian wines, and fish paste from southern Spain. The presence of both Dressel 1 Pascual I and Dressel 2–4 differentiates Silchester, and Chichester, from Poole Harbour, where only the former was present. It suggests Silchester may have been attached to an eastern supply route that was not reaching Poole Harbour. The relative quantities of imported pottery present vary considerably on all four sites. At Ower imports never contribute more than 4% of the assemblage, whereas at Hengistbury they form between 25% and 51% of the assemblages (Fitzpatrick in Cox and Hearne 1991: 230), at Fishbourne they form 39%,[61] but at Silchester they are only between 5 and 6% (Timby in Fulford and Timby 2000: 294, 297).

Several Middle to Late Iron Age sites have been excavated around these settlements and it has been consistently demonstrated that though a few pieces of imported ceramics, mostly amphora, may be present, these are insignificant compared with the large numbers present on the main settlements. Continental material is also very rare on the major downland settlements. The significance of these sites is not to act as a conduit for the dispersal of imported commodities; instead, they act as buffers that absorb raw materials from the Continent, and other areas of the British Isles, and transform them into materials that are desired by the

---

[59] Ounces Barn is an enclosure attached to the eastern end of the outer dyke of the Chichester earthworks.

[60] The Ower pottery is reported by Timby in Woodward, P. J. 1987a; Chichester is reported by Lyne in Manley and Rudkin 2005; and Silchester is analysed by Timby in Fulford and Timby 2000.

[61] By weight the imports were 25% and by EVE's 46% (Lyne in Manley and Rudkin 2005: 75).

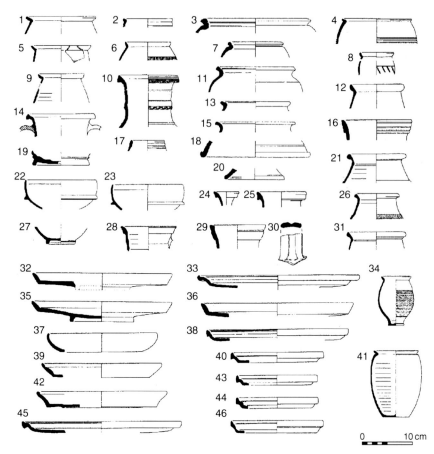

Figure 3.25 Imported Roman pottery from the Late Iron Age deposits at Silchester (after Fulford and Timby 2000; reproduced with the permission of Professor M. G. Fulford and the Society for the Promotion of Roman Studies).

introverted hillfort communities of the interior. The artisans living at these sites may well have been directly involved in the dispersal of this material into the interior and they may have been actively involved in barter exchange for foodstuff, such as cattle and grain.

CHANGE AT THE END OF THE FIRST MILLENNIUM

In this chapter, I have explored the way in which people have used the exchange of objects and labour to establish relationships and create communities.

The first half of the chapter explored the theoretical background and examined changes in material culture and settlement architecture that occurred as Wessex moved from the Late Bronze Age through to the Middle Iron Age. My interpretation of the transformation of that society has been laid out in pages 112–15. In the second half of this chapter, I have concentrated on the evidence for the last three centuries of the millennium. I have described the changing character of several important artefact categories and the development of new political centres in the period immediately prior to the Roman conquest. In this conclusion I will attempt to relate these descriptive accounts of artefacts to the exchange theories outlined at the beginning of the chapter and explain how control over the production and distribution of objects transformed the settlement landscapes of the Late Iron Age.

The main driving force for the changes at the end of the first millennium BC has often been assumed to be the expanding influence of Rome, particularly after Caesar's conquest of Gaul. The nature of the Roman impact on Britain has normally been interpreted using core periphery models, or world systems theory (Cunliffe 1988a; Haselgrove 1982), which argued that change in southern Britain was driven by the demand for raw materials in the growing commercialized economies of the Mediterranean. Commodities produced in very large numbers by Romans, or by Romanized industries in Gaul (Woolf 2000), could be exchanged with the tribes on the periphery of the empire for raw materials, such as 'grain, cattle, gold, silver and iron...also hides, and slaves and dogs' (Cunliffe 1991: 435, quoting Strabo *Geog.* 4.5.2). The contacts established between Roman traders and the indigenous peoples of Britain would be directed, and restricted, to individuals of status and influence, people who would be reliable contacts, and who could guarantee the supply of important raw materials. The restricted and long-lived nature of these contacts would naturally result in the status of the 'chosen few' being enhanced, as they would have had privileged access to the desirable commodities produced by Rome. Their access to these commodities and their ability to distribute these commodities within Britain would lead to status enhancement and consolidation of hierarchical structures. It also created, on a smaller scale, a core periphery structure within Britain. As complex hierarchical polities developed in southern Britain (which had easy access to Rome and the Continental sources of wealth and commodities), these relied on other peripheral regions of Britain to supply them with raw materials, slaves, and so on. These trading relationships would in turn enable the development of privileged elites in these regions.

These core periphery models assume a universal desire for Roman commodities by the people of the regions that surrounded the empire, and that the agency of the imperial power will always override the agency of the indigenous people. This has proved to be a very misleading assumption for both contemporary and past societies (Webster and Cooper 1996). The very erratic and idiosyncratic distribution of material culture outside the empire clearly indicates that local groups were able to make choices about what they wanted and it is noticeable how few imported tablewares are found in the chalklands of Wessex. Furthermore, the assumption that the Roman economy is a pure form of commodified exchange is problematic: there is clear evidence that gift-giving was an important aspect of Roman policy and was targeted at certain individuals and groups who would be amenable to the interests of the Roman state.

Creighton (2000) has recently put forward a reformed version of the core periphery model, which argues that instead of Rome spreading its influence through generalized economic development; it had a much more targeted policy that spread Roman influence through individual indoctrination. He argues that, after Caesar's conquest of the island, aristocratic individuals were taken to Rome as a guarantee of the acquiescence of the native polities. In Rome, they were treated as honoured guests pampered and fully assimilated into Roman manners and mores. On returning to Britain, presumably to accede to their inheritance, they would be fully Romanized individuals with a desire for Roman materials and an understanding of the nature of Roman statecraft. It has also been suggested that they might have had the ability to use Roman military personnel, if this was required, to suppress any native unrest (Creighton 2001; Manley and Rudkin 2005).

Neither of these approaches provides much of a role for the indigenous inhabitants of the British Isles, nor do they fully account for the manner in which change occurred in the two hundred years prior to the Roman conquest. I would like to suggest an alternative: that Late Iron Age societies developed from indigenous societies. They are the result of the success of these societies and their requirement to transform themselves because of this success.

One of the principal motors for the development of the Late Iron Age is the success of the hillfort polities of the Wessex chalklands. It is clear that some developed hillfort societies became the centres for very large areas of the landscape. The hillfort at Danebury is thought to have exerted control over a territory 25 km by 30 km (Cunliffe 1995: 178: fig. 4.28), and the influence of Maiden Castle would seem to cover most of south Dorset, as there are no comparable hillforts until one encounters Hambledon Hill and Hod Hill, about 29 km to the north. These territories are too large to be inhabited by the populations living in the hillforts; generally, agricultural workers will not walk for more than 1 hour (5 km) to their fields (Renfrew and Bahn 1991: 224). This suggests the presence of dependent settlements scattered across the landscape in areas some distance from the hillfort.

It was argued (pages 120–3) that in the Middle Iron Age the dispersed communities' relationship to the developed hillfort was defined by regular participation in monument construction. This not only involved seasonal movement of individuals into the hillfort to participate in construction events, but also the willing, or unwilling, contribution of part of their annual cereal crop to the communal grain stores that are such a significant feature of the interior of developed hillforts. However, by the second century BC, the evidence for the continual renewal and renovation of hillfort ramparts appears to be declining (Sharples 1991a: 261). It seems that monumentality had only a limited capacity for integrating large territories and that the coordination of these much larger communities required the re-creation of exchange relationships. This has been defined here as the movement of material culture that binds individuals and families into larger communities by social indebtedness.

The increasing importance of exchange in the latter part of the Middle Iron Age is demonstrated by the development of regional pottery production, such as the Poole Harbour industries, the development of specialist quern production centres, and the increasing importance of complex metalworking. Good-quality iron was moved long distances for the production of both simple tools and elaborate decorative objects, and copper alloys were imported to make horse harnesses and large sheet metal vessels. Pottery and stone tools, in contrast, were embedded within local gift exchange networks, at least until the first century AD, but this does not seem to be the case for metals. The evidence from Gussage All Saints, Danebury, and Maiden Castle suggests specialist artisans retained control over the most important stages of metalworking. Metalworking appears to be only an occasional activity and production is often restricted to the periphery of the settlement.

The presence of specialist artisans may well be seen as problematic in these hillfort communities, as they had been essentially self-sufficient, and peculiarly introverted, for the first three hundred years of the Iron Age. These artisans provided essential materials for the expansion and cohesion of these societies, but they also provided contacts with the outside world, which introduced the possibility of contamination and pollution (see Chapter 5 for a fuller discussion of pollution). In this situation, it seems likely that production and exchange were carried out by groups or individuals, categorized as different and otherwise excluded from society. These groups may have been based at settlements located on the periphery of the chalk. Peripheries were advantageous locations for a number of reasons: they naturally facilitated exchange with other communities outside the region; they were isolated from the potentially antagonistic hillfort groups and were surrounded by landscapes that were not densely settled, or of great agricultural significance.

This would explain the importance of complex metalworking activities at the settlements of Hengistbury Head and Silchester.[62] The absence of metalworking or other craft activities at Chichester and Ower may be important, but these sites are still very imperfectly understood.[63]

The relationship with these artisans/traders enabled the development of hillfort communities and provided a mechanism for the integration of territories that were much larger than the original territories, organized through monument construction. However, these developments also undermined the communities based in these hillforts. By isolating a group of specialist artisans, primary production was removed from the process of gift-giving between hillfort communities, and a barter economy developed. The act of producing and distributing material became separated from the role material culture played in creating social links between the hillfort communities. This does not remove the distinction between commodities and gifts, it simply places certain relationships into one or other of these categories. In this situation, the relationship between the producers and distributors of the raw materials and specialized objects is undertaken for immediate return probably through barter, because no social relationship was desired from these exchanges. However, the movement of the objects created within the hillfort societies was still undertaken on a gift exchange basis and probably occurred in heavily socialized ritual events.

These changes increased the significance of exchange and enhanced the importance of certain individuals who were presumably closely involved in exchange activities. The ability to manipulate exchange relationships would have given certain people the cultural capital to enhance their social significance within the hillfort societies. It is possible to identify a gradual decline

---

[62] It might also explain some of the characteristics of the Somerset Lake Villages of Glastonbury and Meare.

[63] The ethnic identity of these groups is likely to be mixed. There presumably would be groups that had always lived in these peripheral locations, and who had adopted their subsistence activities to cope with the specialized environments that existed in these places. There would also be people who though brought up in a hillfort society chose to leave for one reason or another. Both of these groups are likely to be using material culture that is directly comparable to those of the hillfort societies. The third category of person, who could be present in these peripheral locations, were individuals from neighbouring societies who were involved in the production and distribution of specialized goods. These people may well bring in objects that appear quite alien and this might explain the situation at Hengistbury Head where large quantities of pottery were present that appear to have been imported from Armorica. It has always been difficult to explain the significance of these imports, as they are almost never found on the contemporary inland settlements. The most likely interpretation is that the vessels had no economic significance, but reflect the presence of Armorican traders who may have been living seasonally, or permanently, in what was almost certainly a multi-ethnic centre for artisans and traders.

in the significance of monumental architecture, which coincides with the re-emergence of individual settlements, as the bounded societies of the chalklands became more and more permeable.

The use of coinage may be a good example of the relationship between gift and commodity. Coinage was produced in centres set up on the periphery by the artisans and traders. In the initial stages, this was exclusively associated with an extremely valuable and symbolically significant metal: gold. In hillfort societies, coinage must have circulated between elites in highly significant gift exchanges and it may well have been desired as a raw material to produce prestige objects such as torcs. Individuals could wear torcs, but torcs could also have been a badge of office, or community leadership, rather than a personal possession (Hill pers. comm.). However, in the later stages of the Iron Age, coins surpassed torcs in their social significance and it was the torcs that were melted down to produce gold coinage on sites such as Hengistbury Head. This transformation coincided with the reconfiguration of the power relationships in central and eastern Wessex. It seems that the increasing wealth of the peripheral communities in the period of the Gallic Wars undermined the power relationships of the hillfort communities of Hampshire and Sussex. The chalk downland societies of the eastern part of Wessex became a periphery that provided agricultural produce to the elite centres at Chichester and Silchester.

Coinage in these societies became a medium for conveying a message to a dispersed community that did not regularly gather together. Communities were connected by the movement of small groups of people to the centres of ceremonial power where they encountered important 'leaders'. These centres, that is, Chichester and Silchester, did not need to be totally encircled by a boundary because these places did not symbolize the community. At no point did the communities of these Late Iron Age polities coalesce as a group, nor did they conceptualize themselves as a single indivisible community distinct from other indivisible communities. They were instead bound together by networks of personal allegiance that were symbolized by coinage. The centres represented the focal points of these networks and were places that people passed through, and were connected with, by objects.

4

The House as a Cosmology

One of the most popular sub-disciplines of archaeology is experimental archaeology, the re-creation of items, structures, and practices of past societies in the present day. This area of study has a long pedigree in Continental Europe, but was a relatively late development in Britain. One of the pioneers of this approach was Peter Reynolds, who created the Butser Ancient Farm Research Project to explore life in the Iron Age (Reynolds 1979). When it was set up, in the 1970s, experimental archaeology was undertaken with full scientific rigour. Important goals included the quantification of resources required to create a house, the management of ancient breeds of domestic animals, the productivity of fields of ancient cereals, and the function of pits. All these tasks were carried out with a critical attention to detailed data recording and scientific rigour. More recently, experimental archaeology has become geared towards the general public, and though Butser Farm has retained a scientific core to its activities it also caters for a wider public, providing both knowledge and entertainment about past societies.

I had a brief experience of this work in 1977 when I took part in a week-long field school at Butser Farm, organized by Glasgow University. This was a key period in the development of the Iron Age farm. The original farm had been created on a spur near the top of Butser, specifically away from easy public access and in a very exposed location. Public interest in the experiment had become difficult to manage and a new site had just been located in the Queen Elizabeth Country Park, a much more accessible location near the main road from Portsmouth to London. The new location was designed to be a public amenity that would attract visitors to the Country Park and represented a move from 'Laboratory to Living Museum' (Reynolds 1979: 93).

The main job we were to undertake was to help with the construction of a large roundhouse that would form the centre of the new farm. Two previous timber houses had been built up on the hill, but both had been fairly modest affairs; one was based on a house plan from Wheeler's excavation at Maiden Castle, the other was slightly larger and based on the excavation of a house in the Balksbury enclosure, Hampshire (Reynolds 1979). Both were successful to a certain extent, but the Balksbury house had major structural problems that derived from a misinterpretation of what was a badly plough-truncated site. These problems were informative rather than disastrous and had encouraged Reynolds to attempt the reconstruction of one of the largest houses so far excavated in southern Britain; the Pimperne house (Harding *et al.* 1993). The excavated evidence was of the highest quality and the resultant reconstruction was extremely important and will form an important focus for discussion in this chapter.

When we arrived at Butser the basic structure had been erected and provided a somewhat gaunt skeleton of the house that was to be created. It was an immensely impressive structure even at this stage, and we were told how difficult it had been to manoeuvre the roof supports, over 10 m long, into position above the centre of the house, one of the few jobs that required real skill and immense strength. Our tasks were less complicated—we were to start work on the roof and finish the outside wall. The walls were wattle and daub; this involves weaving the hazel poles through the uprights of the wall and covering the resulting basket-like structure with a coat of clay, dung, and straw mixed with water. This is one of those simple activities that now feature in almost any Celtic-themed visitor attraction (many now exist). It is extremely messy, which appeals to the child in all of us, and is essentially a communal activity which everyone, mum, dad, and the kids, can participate in. It is energetic without being exhausting and requires no skill whatsoever. It provided an excellent mechanism for bonding a group of students and encouraged us to head out that night to slake our thirst at the local pub (although that was not difficult for most of us).

The other job I remember undertaking was putting on the roof purlins. These were hazel rods, slightly thicker than those used for the walls, tied horizontally to the rafters of the roof, that would be used to tie down the thatch. I don't particularly like heights, and would not normally stand on the edge of a tall building, so when I started on this job I wondered how long it would take before my fear of heights undermined my bravado. Strangely it never did. I worked up the roof, slowly getting higher and higher until I was standing 5 or 6 metres above the ground—and yet I felt totally secure. My security may have been based on the knowledge that I had attached the ties on which I was standing and felt confident in my workmanship, but I think it was more likely to be the stability of the structure that impressed and reassured me. It was obvious that the architecture of the circular house was immensely stable, everything was tight and immovable. We had been lectured on the distribution of forces and how this made a stable structure, but there is nothing like standing on a hazel rod 6 metres above ground level to make you realize just how robust a simple timber structure can be.

The reconstruction of the Pimperne house became widely known and highly influential in Iron Age studies. The process of building it revealed in some detail the large quantities of resources required to build such a house, and the scale of the reconstruction forced everyone to reconsider how sophisticated our Iron Age ancestors were. It was immediately apparent, for instance, that an upper floor, or loft, was possible, if not likely, in these structures, which would almost double the floor area provided by the building. The results of the reconstruction were disseminated not simply by the detailed publication (Harding *et al.* 1993) but by the inspiration this had on artists who attempted to recreate Iron Age life (see Figure 5.2).

I do not feel any pride in my contribution to this iconic building as it was minimal, and all credit for this construction must go to Peter Reynolds. However, participating in the construction certainly influenced my understanding of the social significance of houses. I was slightly surprised to read in the published report on the construction of the house that its creation was best done by a restricted group of perhaps two or three people and was not likely to be a communal event; this is not my recollection. I came away from this field school impressed with just how productive this event had been for creating friendships within our group and understanding the character and skills of the different participants. I firmly believe that the construction of a big house would have been an event involving many people and an excuse for much enjoyment. The construction of the Amish barn in the film *Witness* conjures up the situation perfectly; the flirtation between the hero (Harrison Ford) and the heroine (Kelly McGillis) is central to the event.

THE HOUSE IN LATER PREHISTORIC STUDIES

One of the characteristic features of the archaeological record of Britain in the first millennium BC is the presence of houses. These have been found in almost every area of the island and, though numbers vary through time and from region to region, the essential characteristics remain very similar. The most significant feature of British houses is that they are almost universally circular in shape. This is a distinctive feature of British later prehistory that differentiates Britain from the adjacent areas of mainland Europe, where houses are generally rectangular in shape.[1] Roundhouses were not present in

---

[1] There are areas on the Continent where roundhouses have been excavated, and roundhouses are certainly a significant feature of the domestic architecture of the Iberian peninsula (Gonzáles-Ruibal 2006). It has also been argued that the house architecture of Britain is more

the later historic periods, though they continued to be built during the Roman occupation, and Neolithic and Early Bronze Age houses, though difficult to identify, seem to be predominantly rectangular rather than circular. This phenomenon invites detailed consideration in any analysis of British prehistory and forms the central focus for this chapter.

Houses are an extremely important aspect of the archaeological record, and they would have dominated the perceptual geography and psychology of individuals in prehistory; they were a constant feature of the prehistoric world, encountered if not occupied, on a daily basis from birth to death. The structure (shape and layout) of a house was designed to provide shelter from inclement weather and was a place to carry out essential activities that range from sleeping and eating to simple craft activities. However, the structure also had a great symbolic significance; it provided a physical analogy for society, and by choreographed routine activities, houses helped to establish social relationships and embed these into the memory of the occupants. Moving around a house children learned their relationship to the adults and other children who were present within the structure. They also became aware of the distinction between members of the household and outsiders who visited the house. These social relationships are analogies for the relationships that position the domestic group in the wider society outside the house; they are rarely discussed openly but are derived from the repeated and recurrent use of certain space by certain people on a daily basis (Bourdieu 1977).

Contemporary interest in the social importance of the prehistoric house began with the re-evaluation of the site of Glastonbury Lake Village by David L. Clarke (1979). Clarke's paper had superficially limited methodological aims and was reported as a work in progress, but in reality it set out a vision of Iron Age society, which in detail and scale has seldom been attempted. He claimed to be undertaking a re-examination of 'the kinds of evidence that might be recovered from the spatial relationships involving the site, its artefacts, structures and features, as a system within a hierarchy of other sites, distributed in an interconnected network over a landscape distorted by distance' (Clarke, D. L. 1979: 365). He was pushing a particular model of Iron Age society to its limits in order to highlight assumptions that could then be tested by further work. Unfortunately, the data used to create the

---

similar to areas of Brittany and Normandy than previously thought. There have been a number of circular houses discovered in recent years in these two regions (Menez *et al.* 1990) and these are particularly common on later Bronze Age settlements, such as Malleville-sur-le-Bec (Mare and Le Goff 2006). However, this appears to be a feature only of these two regions, and the domestic architecture of central France and the northern European plain, up to and including the Pas-de-Calais, is dominated by rectangular buildings (Audouze and Büchsenschütz 1991; Gerritsen 2003; Roymans 1990).

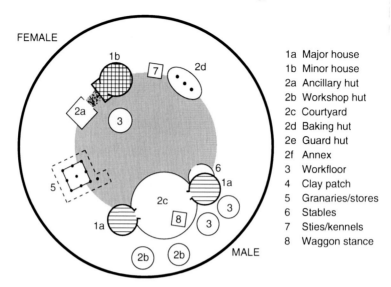

Figure 4.1 Clarke's model of the settlement structure in the Glastonbury Lake Village; note that examples of 2e, 2f and 4 are not shown on the diagram (after Clarke 1979: fig. 1).

model was not fully published and it is difficult, using the published paper, to justify the analysis presented. However, the paper still highlights issues that are directly relevant to our understanding of later prehistoric houses.

One of the primary goals of the paper was to highlight the wide variety of structures present at Glastonbury. Eleven basic structural types were identified, and an analysis of location and associated finds suggested 14 functional categories of space (Figure 4.1). Clarke argued that these structures were organized into compounds and that each compound was split in two on the basis of gendered activities. The male side was defined by a pair of major houses (1a), facing each other across a courtyard (2c), and was associated with workshop huts (2b), workfloors (3), and stables (6). The female side was defined by the minor house (1b), and ancillary hut (2a), and was associated with a baking hut (2d), workfloors (3), a granary (5), and sties or kennels (7), though not all the ancillary buildings were present in every compound. Each compound could have held an extended family or lineage of between 15–20 individuals. More controversially, Clarke argued that there was evidence to support the claim, reported by Caesar, that these kin groups had shared wives.[2]

---

[2] Clarke suggested that the site grew from an initial group of four compounds to seven compounds in the final phase of the site. On the basis of the presence of a variety of high-status objects he suggested that one compound, in the centre of the site, was pre-eminent. This compound may have had a relationship to the other compounds similar to the relationship between the major

This work was highly influential and has appeared in numerous general textbooks on British prehistory. Unfortunately, it has been shown to present a misleading picture of the settlement evidence. John Coles and Stephen Minnitt have provided a detailed critical analysis of the excavations at Glastonbury that they hoped would 'eliminate Clarke's model for good' (Coles, J. and Minnitt 1995: 180). They demonstrate that the structural types identified above are not clearly, or even vaguely, delimited by either the structural evidence or the artefact distributions suggested by Clarke. To illustrate the problems I will summarize their analysis of the major house type (Coles, J. and Minnitt 1995: 183–4). These structures are supposed to have timber floors, stone slab doorways, and porches, but re-analysis suggests that, though eight of the 13 identified major houses had wooden floors, only two of the 13 had porches and none had slab doorways. These houses are supposed to have a variety and abundance of finds and, whilst some do (M62 and M5), several examples (e.g. M14, M29, and M13) have very few finds; they are supposed to occur in pairs but examination of the phasing of the mounds suggests that none of the potential pairs of houses was ever contemporary; instead, they occur sequentially and indicate a shift in the location of the single major house. Of the 42 identifiable structural units that Clarke suggests were major houses, only 16 can be interpreted as roofed structures. These major houses have the clearest descriptive signature of any of the structures identified by Clarke, and Coles and Minnitt's analysis of the ancillary buildings was even more dismissive. They were also extremely critical of the presence of well-defined compounds and find no evidence for an obvious gender split between dominant craft-oriented male activities and subsidiary female cooking and storage structures.[3]

house and the subsidiary house. There may also have been some specialization of household activity as certain compounds had greater evidence for agricultural and/or craft production.

[3] Coles and Minnitt dismiss Clarke's phasing as perverse and demonstrate that it completely ignores Bulleid's description of the stratigraphic relationships between mounds. Their new phasing highlights a steady growth in the settlement, though they consider two possible influxes of people from outside, followed by a drastic reduction in the first century BC that culminates in abandonment around the middle of the century. The early phase consists of four 'units' (which we must presume to be households as they are defined by houses). The middle phase consists of ten units (but 11 houses), with 30 accompanying spreads (surfaced areas for outdoor activity) and some shelters. The late phase, when the site has reached its overall limits, comprised 13 houses, six shelters and 57 clay spreads. Coles and Minnitt suggest 14 self-sustaining units but there were also large surfaced areas outside of these units. The final phase consists of only five houses, but there were many associated clay surfaces and Coles and Minnitt suggest these might indicate an increasingly seasonal occupation. Unfortunately, this phasing is no more convincing than Clarke's. It seems to be based on stratigraphic relationships that are not fully explained and appears to rest on the simplistic assumption that the clay floors are systematically replaced at evenly spaced intervals. It also ignores the chronology provided by the material culture from the site.

Ann Ellison (1981) developed a model for house use in the Middle Bronze Age that was directly derived from the approach taken by Clarke. She set out to use the distributions of finds found on Middle Bronze Age settlements 'to deduce the distribution of different activity areas within the settlement' (Ellison 1975: 352). She acknowledged that there were very few sites that had been excavated with sufficient care or recorded in sufficient detail to provide an accurate understanding of past activity but felt that it was still possible to undertake the analysis. She isolated four structural types (Ellison 1981: 419):

- major residential structures. These were large circular houses with an entrance porch and internal pits. They were associated with pottery concentrations, particularly fine ware, a stone assemblage, dominated by tools for production and maintenance, tools for textile production, and any status items, such as bronze objects;
- ancillary structures. These were smaller and more oval structures that seldom had a porch, but did have pits. They were associated with querns and scrapers, for food preparation, and sometimes concentrations of animal bones. The ceramic assemblages are smaller and are dominated by coarse wares;
- animal shelters. These had worn floors and the structural evidence was poor. They produced very few finds;
- weaving huts. These were small structures with weaving equipment, but no evidence for food preparation, storage, or consumption.

The influence of Clarke is clear and was emphasized by her suggestion that the major house was for male and female tasks, whereas the smaller ancillary huts were for female activities. The small kin groups present in these Bronze Age modular units were specifically contrasted with the larger extended families associated with Clarke's modular units at Glastonbury (Ellison 1975: 378).

These ideas were almost immediately tested by the large-scale excavations of a Middle Bronze Age settlement at Blackpatch in Sussex (Drewett 1982). The excavation of Hut Platform 4 revealed a slightly larger than expected Middle Bronze Age settlement which comprised five huts.[4] A systematic attempt was made to characterize the assemblage from each building and to define function by the presence of particular artefacts types (Figure 4.2). The following functions were ascribed (Drewett 1982: 340):

- Hut 1—food preparation hut;
- Hut 2—animal stalling, flint knapping;

---

[4] The structures at Blackpatch are consistently referred to as huts despite Drewett demonstrating that these were substantial buildings, easily justifying the label 'house'.

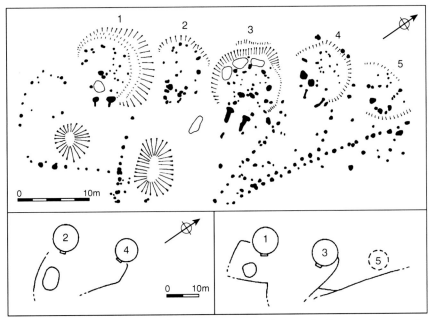

Figure 4.2 A simplified plan of the settlement at Blackpatch, Sussex, showing the revised phasing of Russell (after Drewett 1982: fig. 4; and Russell 1996a: fig. 2).

- Hut 3—craft and storage;
- Hut 4—craft, storage and food preparation;
- Hut 5—animal stalling, flint knapping.

It was also tentatively suggested that Hut 3 was a 'head person's (man or woman) hut', though the ambiguity is slightly undermined by pairing it with Hut 1, which was interpreted as a 'wife's hut'. The relative isolation of the different occupants of each house was enhanced by the presence of fence lines that separated different houses. These clearly distinguished Hut 4 as a partially autonomous unit and led to the suggestion that it may be for 'grandparents' or alternatively 'unmarried siblings'. The analysis concludes that the settlement was a 'joint family compound' (Drewett 1982: 342) significantly larger than most of the settlements identified by Ellison.

This interpretation of the site was radically altered by the suggestion that the settlement had two quite distinct phases. Russell (1996a) argued that the arrangement of the fence lines and the apparent overlap of houses 1 and 2, as well as the generally congested nature of the house platforms, made it likely that there was a sequence of building with only two or three houses present in any period. He suggested that houses 2 and 4 were the earliest and that these were replaced by houses 1 and 3. House 5 could not be closely associated with either phase. This re-analysis makes the site much more like the other Middle Bronze Age settlements that have paired major and ancillary buildings,[5] and therefore brings the settlement into line with the model presented by Ellison (1981).

Surprisingly, the influence of the Glastonbury paper, in the 1970s and 1980s, was largely restricted to the discussion of houses belonging to the second millennium BC, and not the first millennium houses that Clarke had been interested in. During these decades, a large corpus of first millennium house plans was accumulated by excavation, but analysis of these was largely limited to debate about the correct interpretation of the archaeological record. A particular interest was the relationship between the archaeological plan of post holes and the size and form of the structure above ground (Guilbert 1981, 1982). However, in the early 1990s there was a change in the nature of the debate. A number of papers (Fitzpatrick 1994; Giles and Parker Pearson 1999; Hingley 1990a; Oswald 1997; Parker Pearson 1996, 1999, and Parker Pearson and Richards 1994) were published that reasserted the social significance of the house and argued that it provides a central metaphor for the interpretation of Iron Age society (Hingley 1990a; Parker Pearson 1999).

Richard Hingley (1990a) was one of the first authors to approach the subject, and his paper is also important in providing a social model of the house that is significantly different from the model that has come to dominate the literature (Figure 4.3). Hingley argued that large single houses, containing households, dominated the archaeological record for the first millennium BC. These houses gathered together the individuals and tasks previously dispersed in several small houses (following Barrett 1989) and were divided into a central and a peripheral space. This division was often marked architecturally by the ring of posts that formed the main structural support to the roof, but even in small houses where this feature is absent, these areas were conceptually differentiated by their distance from the central hearth. The differentiation of these spaces was fundamental in the structuring of daily activities. The central space was dominated by the presence of a hearth and thus was used for cooking and other activities, such as eating and craft production, which would require light and heat. The peripheral space, in contrast, was dark and restricted and would have been used for sleeping and storage. Furthermore, the characteristics of these spaces meant they were conceived as respectively public and private zones: the former open to outsiders, the latter restricted to members of the household.

[5] The only other settlement location fully excavated as part of the Blackpatch project, Hut platform 1, had a pair of structures, one of which was notably larger than the other (Drewett 1982: 343).

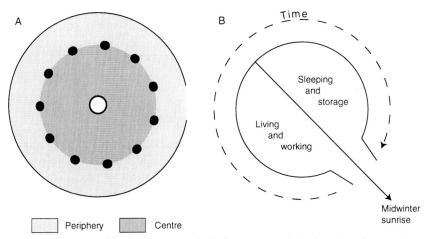

Figure 4.3 Two models for the cosmological structure of the Iron Age house. A was produced by Hingley (1990a) and is based on the centrality of the hearth. B was produced by Parker Pearson (1996) and is based on the importance of the entrance and the position and movement of the sun.

Hingley (1990a) expands on this fairly straightforward analysis by using a structuralist model that relates the observable dichotomies in the house with other deeper dichotomies such as culture and nature, cooked and raw, life and death, male and female. He argues that these divisions were fundamental to the inhabitants' perception of their position in life. Furthermore, the division between centre and periphery was used to structure space on the larger scale of the settlement, and may have acted 'as a metaphor for the spatial organization of the territory of a single community' (Hingley 1990a: 133). Danebury and Winnall Down provide good examples of settlements that appear to have a core–periphery structure: central spaces either occupied by shrines at Danebury, or left empty at Winnall Down, and a peripheral area adjacent to the enclosure boundary where houses were built.

An alternative model is argued primarily by Mike Parker Pearson (1996, 1999) and Andrew Fitzpatrick (1994). In this model the authors stress that the architecturally significant feature of the house is not the central hearth but the entrance (Figure 4.3). They contrast the size and significance of the post holes that mark the entrance to a house with the relatively ephemeral nature of the central hearths.[6] The cosmological importance of the entrance is further

---

[6] Parker Pearson and Richards (1994) have observed that the entrance is occasionally marked by the deposition of animal remains and an example at Haddenham is referred to. The author also excavated a house at Maiden Castle (Sharples 1991a) where the entrance was marked by a slot in which sheep mandibles had been laid.

indicated by its consistent orientation. In a detailed study of the orientation of the entrances to 280 circular houses, Alastair Oswald (1997) demonstrated that there was a significant cluster of houses oriented east, to sunrise at the equinox, and south-east, to sunrise on the midwinter solstice, with minor clusters focusing on midsummer sunrise and sunset, and sunset at the equinox.

The orientation of the entrance creates two structuring devices: an axis through the centre of the interior which splits the house in two and a direction for movement, sunwise, that dictates the manner and sequence in which people encounter the interior of the house. The evidence for the former is supported by the presence of axial symmetry in the arrangement of the posts that define the house (Guilbert 1982) and the differential distribution of material culture in the interior of some houses, notably Longbridge Deverill, Wiltshire (Hawkes, S. C. 1994) and Dunston Park, Berkshire (Fitzpatrick 1994). The evidence from Dunston Park consists of the distribution of material in the post holes of the house structure, as unfortunately no floor layers survived the recent cultivation of the site. In contrast, the material from Longbridge Deverill was found as a pottery concentration within the soil overlying the floor, and this is believed to be material preserved by the destruction of the house in a fire (Hawkes, S. C. 1994).

The concept of movement implicit in this relationship with the sun has been used to argue that the division of the interior reflects the division of the day, and the year, into cycles of activity. Thus the orientation of most entrances on sunrise suggests that during the day the south side of the house was used for daytime activities, such as cooking and craftwork, and as day progressed to night, people moved to the north side of the house, an area for sleeping. Seasonally, the axis from the entrance may mark a split around the time of midwinter. The south side can be seen to be associated with craft activities, food processing, and possibly butchery, whereas the north side may be associated with crop storage, the overwintering of animals and possibly a concern with the sexual reproduction of both humans and animals.

This structure and cycle of activities has also been claimed to be visible in the spatial organization of settlements, and congruent patterns have been observed at Winnall Down and Danebury. However, most of the authors (Hill 1995b; Parker Pearson 1996, 1999; Fitzpatrick 1994) applying this metaphor have restrained themselves from relating these structural dichotomies to more general principles such as life/death, male/female, and so forth.

The most recent examination of the second millennium house has been by Jo Brück (1999). She assembled a considerable database of information on Early and Middle Bronze Age settlements and structures in southern England

and reviewed the evidence for the division between major and ancillary buildings, identified by Ellison and Drewett, and the relevance of the cosmological views of Hingley and Parker Pearson. Her analysis of the Middle Bronze Age record indicates that the evidence for a clear division of the finds, assemblages present in major and ancillary buildings is problematic. Only three of 48 structures had an assemblage that could be characterized as appropriate to a major structure, whereas 14 of 48 had an assemblage appropriate to an ancillary structure. Most of the buildings examined had mixed assemblages. Brück's analysis undermines the idea that clear-cut divisions between male and female space exist in the Middle Bronze Age, though she avoids specific mention of gender divisions.

Brück identifies certain characteristic features that indicate how these structures were used. The entrance, which is marked by a porch or substantial door posts, is preferentially oriented towards the south and south-east and there is a concentration of activity in the front of the house near the entrance. The houses have an internal post ring, which creates a peripheral space that can be used for storage, and the posts are often laid out with axial symmetry based on the entrance orientation, but this does not appear to affect depositional activity during the use of the house.[7]

These observations are not consistent enough to suggest a rigid cosmology, such as that defined by Hingley or Parker Pearson. However, despite this lack of evidence, Brück has no doubt that the house would have structured social interaction. She argues that the murky and ephemeral patterns visible are all we are likely to identify because of the vagaries of human agency. The house simply provides a range of possibilities that could be drawn upon by the inhabitants if they had the opportunity, resources, and desire. The divisions of space that were implicit in the structure of the house could also be drawn upon at different periods in the use of the house and ultimately leave a confused and muddled picture of activity in the archaeological record.

Brück (1999) also identified another distinctive feature of the Middle Bronze Age house which has hitherto been missed. She observed that these houses, in contrast to houses of the Late Bronze Age, seldom showed evidence for repair, and that this indicated a restricted lifespan for the occupation of the house. This temporality is not likely to be constrained by environmental or economic factors and must therefore indicate a social constraint. She suggests a strong metaphorical link between the social life of the occupants and the structural life of the house. The house may have been constructed to coincide with the establishment of an individual's social

---

[7] The exception is Hut 3 on platform 4 at Blackpatch, which is discussed above.

maturity/independence, which might be by marriage, and its use may have come to an end when the individual was no longer socially independent, either through death or infirmity.

All these works provide a rich source of ideas and information that are crucial to our understanding of the organization and structure of households in later prehistory. In recent years the cosmological interpretations of Parker Pearson, Hingley, and Fitzpatrick have been criticized by Pope (2007) and Webley (2007), and whilst I would not agree with the generally negative views expressed in these critiques, these cosmological interpretations cannot be applied without close attention to the archaeological record. Many of the works have focused on isolated examples taken from a large body of data and they have often not been clear about the temporal and regional specificity of the source data. Whilst the review presented in the following pages cannot claim to provide a total examination of all the evidence for houses in Wessex, it will, nevertheless, attempt to examine the relevance of the ideas expressed above, through time and in a comprehensive manner.

FAMILY, HOUSEHOLD, OR RESIDENTIAL UNIT

One of the questions that arises from these studies but which has been ignored by many archaeologists is the composition and social significance of the inhabitants of the structure referred to as a house. Are we dealing with a family, a collection of kin-related individuals, or should we be more cautious and refer to them as a household? Is even this term too specific? Would the most accurate term simply be co-resident group? These terminological distinctions might appear to be semantic nit-picking by many archaeologists but they do highlight some important points that are much debated in anthropology and require consideration (Carsten and Hugh-Jones 1995).

The problem with the assumption that a house contains a genetically linked family is that it can be demonstrated that houses frequently contain occupants who have no genetic link. They could include individuals who are closely connected with the genetic group and individuals who have no connection but are simply lodgers. In many societies adoption or fosterage can be a useful means of co-opting additional family members, and this is a well-known feature of later Celtic societies (Parkes 2006). In some societies these people can become members of the 'family' and would have the same privileges and inheritance rights as any genetic member of the family, but in other societies expansion of the domestic unit would not be so generous and the incoming individuals could be regarded as servants or slaves with a very limited set of rights.

The use of the term household ignores the potential kin-based nature of the group and concentrates on the functionality of the unit physically defined by the architecture.[8] A recurrent problem with the use of this term is that anthropologists frequently assume that a household is a functionally significant group both outside and inside the architectural structure. However, there is no reason to assume that a household will own common property that they farm collectively; there are many examples of married sons living within the house, but owning property that they farm separately. There may even be differences between the land farmed by the husband and wife in relatively small households. Even within the house, multifunctional groups can exist. In polygamous societies a husband can have several wives and these can cook and eat food with their offspring in spatially segregated areas (Goody 1966: 75). These complexities have led many anthropologists to suggest that the term household is unhelpful leaving us with the term co-resident groups, which implies little. However, in this text I would prefer to follow Verdon (1998: 37) in using the term household in its restricted sense of a co-resident group without any assumption that this group has any extended functional significance.

THE UNUSUAL NATURE OF THE BRITISH HOUSE

The existence of houses as a dominant feature of the social landscape and the physical geography of prehistoric southern Britain cannot be taken for granted. It is often assumed that the domestication of Europe, at the beginning of the Neolithic, placed houses at the centre of society (Hodder 1991). However, whilst this does seem to be the case across much of Europe, it is a distinctive feature of the British archaeological record that houses are not common prior to the Middle Bronze Age. The relative absence, or scarcity, of houses from the Neolithic and the Early Bronze Age suggests that the early agricultural communities of Britain were essentially mobile communities moving around an underpopulated and unbounded landscape with their herds of cattle and sheep (Edmonds 1999). Cultivation was a subsidiary activity and cereals would probably have been planted in small plots and

---

[8] Anthropologists can be rather generous with their definition of an architectural unit as a house. This is often expanded to include several closely related roofed structures in a compound, something that would be defined as an enclosure in the archaeological record.

left relatively untended for most of the growing season (Fairbairn 2000). A sense of place and connection to the landscape was provided by the construction of impressive monuments that vary in form and use but are closely associated with the manipulation of death rituals and the seasonal gathering together of large groups of people (Bradley 1998a).

This picture has been challenged in recent years by the discovery of several Neolithic buildings. In lowland Scotland, substantial timber halls have been found with large quantities of carbonized cereal grains that indicate the households occupying them were carrying out intensive arable agriculture (Barclay *et al.* 2002). The increasing frequency of rescue excavation in Ireland has resulted in the discovery of large numbers of small rectangular houses (Armit *et al.* 2003). In England there have been several important discoveries of rectangular buildings comparable to the Irish examples, which suggests houses may be present in greater numbers than some people thought (Darvill and Thomas 1996).

Most of these houses date to the beginning of the Neolithic, in the period immediately after the introduction of agriculture. Evidence for houses in the Late Neolithic and Early Bronze Age is still elusive, although the general feeling is that people were still relatively mobile in this period. The most important recent discoveries are from the excavations of the massive ritual centre of Durrington Walls (Parker Pearson *et al.* 2006), which appears to be the focus for the gathering together of large numbers of people. In an area adjacent to, and underneath, the large enclosure bank, where the conditions for preservation were exceptional, seven buildings have been discovered, which provide good evidence for the nature of Late Neolithic houses. These houses are defined by a roughly square floor of chalk plaster and have a central hearth. The outer walls supported the roof and were made of wattle and daub and, in two places, of chalk cob.[9]

These buildings could be dismissed as exceptional and misleading, since they are associated with the ritual activity taking place inside the henge, but the structures closely resemble the buildings found at two contemporary settlements, Woodcuts in Dorset (Green, M. 2000) and Trelystan in Powys (Britnell 1982). It may also be significant that these houses resemble the Late Neolithic houses at Skara Brae and several other settlements in Orkney (Richards, C. 2005). The evidence seems consistent and suggests that, in the Late Neolithic, people occupied relatively small square structures that are very different from the circular roundhouses so characteristic of the later Bronze Age and Iron Age.

---

[9] In the chalk downlands of southern England cob is a mixture of crushed chalk, water, and straw that was used to make substantial buildings until the twentieth century (Keefe 2005).

There have been numerous attempts to undermine the significance of circular houses and many archaeologists have attempted to identify a rectangular building tradition in Britain (Harding, D. W. 1973; Moore 2003). It is important to recognize that square buildings, defined by four, six, or occasionally eight large post holes are relatively common. These appear in the Bronze Age and are increasingly common in the Iron Age. They numerically dominate the interior of many hillforts (e.g. Danebury; Figure 3.8) and are often found in linear arrangements alongside routeways that traverse the interior. The interpretation of these structures is problematic as they are not generally associated with floors and cannot be linked with distinctive artefact assemblages. Some archaeologists (e.g. Stanford 1974) have interpreted them as structures that people lived in and have used their presence to suggest densely occupied terraced housing in some of the hillforts of the Welsh Marches. Others have isolated linear arrangements and suggested they represent the central supports for large timber halls (Dixon 1976; Moore 2003). Neither interpretation is convincing. The more widely accepted interpretation is that they represent above-ground storage facilities, although there is a range of alternative possibilities, including excarnation platforms and defensive watchtowers (Ellison and Drewett 1971).

The lack of any strong similarities between the later prehistoric roundhouses and the Late Neolithic structures suggests that we have to look to a different source for the architectural inspiration behind the domestic architecture of the later Bronze Age. This inspiration was clearly not coming from Continental Europe, as I have already noted that the dominant house form on the Continent is the rectangular house, and these are large elaborate structures in the Early Bronze Age (Fokkens 2003). The limited evidence for circular houses in this area is likely to derive from British architecture. The solution is to look not to the domestic buildings but to the ritual architecture of early prehistory. Large religious monuments appear to have a crucial role in the Early Neolithic, the Late Neolithic, and the Early Bronze Age, and in the last two periods these monuments are distinctively circular in form.

The most numerous circular monuments in this period are Early Bronze Age round barrows (Last 2008). These are closely associated with burial rituals and, in Wessex, most barrows cover a central inhumation in a grave pit. These barrows may originally start off quite small but they often have extended histories which encompass subsequent burials inserted into the mound, which in turn can be enlarged to become a much more monumental feature. Round barrows are also often associated with timber constructions, which include circles of posts that have sometimes been interpreted as buildings (Ashbee 1960: 62–5). Barrows are very common in the chalk downlands of Wessex, and large cemeteries are known throughout the region.

Henges and timber and stone circles are important, though less frequent, monument types that were first built in the Late Neolithic but continued to be built in the Early Bronze Age (Barnett 1989; Harding, J. 2003). Henges are enclosures, defined by a ditch and an external bank, that are normally accessed by either one or two entrances. These enclosures can be circular and this is a feature of the two earliest examples, Flagstones in Dorset (Smith, R. J. C. *et al.* 1997) and Stonehenge in Wiltshire (Cleal *et al.* 1995), but many examples are oval, or irregular, in form. In southern England these enclosures are closely associated with timber circles and, in the examples at Woodhenge, and inside the larger enclosure at Mount Pleasant, a ditch is placed immediately outside the timber circle and effectively controls access to these structures (Gibson 1998). Timber and stone circles are also found without any enclosing ditch.

The interpretation of the timber circles is open to debate. Many archaeologists (e.g. Piggott, S. 1940; Lees 1999) have argued that they represent elaborate timber houses and might be the homes of the priests officiating at the great stone circles, but this seems unlikely. Many of the most famous examples have multiple rings of tightly spaced posts and the size of the posts used is enormous, too large and unwieldy to be an efficient way of building a house. Furthermore, some timber circles are replaced by stone circles and if these are a simple transformation of material type then they clearly demonstrate that the initial monument was not a roofed building. Timber circles are now generally considered to be free-standing circles of posts that served some purpose in the ritual activities undertaken on a seasonal basis at the enclosures. The precise nature of these ritual activities is unknown but many archaeologists believe that these included a close observation of the sky that attempted to predict the movements of the sun and perhaps also the moon and the stars. It also seems likely that these observations were at least partially recorded by the construction of the timber and stone circles. These monuments became theatres in which the predictable effects of astronomical events could be used to impress the less knowledgeable members of the community.

The construction of these large monumental structures stops in the Early Bronze Age, though there are indications that smaller monuments, particularly post and stone alignments, continued into later periods. One of the few well-dated later Bronze Age monuments is at Ogden Down in Dorset (Green, M. 1992) where a round barrow is surrounded by two rings of posts and an avenue leads off to join this monument to another barrow. This monument is relatively small compared with the timber circles of Mount Pleasant and Woodhenge, and does little to undermine the basic belief that large gatherings of people at major enclosures were uncommon in the later

Bronze Age. The use of round barrows continued for another four centuries, and some archaeologists have suggested they became structurally similar to the houses that increasingly dominate the landscape (Bradley 1998a: 155). They are certainly built in close association with each other.

Barrett (1994a: 136) has suggested that the end of this period of monument construction, and the emergence of a domesticated landscape of houses and fields, represents a transformation of two separate concepts of time. In early prehistory, human history was 'a process of becoming', a series of journeys that led to the timeless location of the ancestors. This could be seen as a metaphysical journey through time, but also metaphorically represented the annual cycle of movement around a landscape, that ended up at a monumental representation of the ancestors (Parker Pearson and Ramilisonina 1998). In later prehistory people had 'a sense of being' (Barrett 1994a: 147); they were located at the 'centre of a domain' and were conscious of the cyclical effects of the seasons upon the land that they resided in. Attitudes to time play a crucial role in the transformations of the first half of the second millennium BC. It seems that the role the timber circles had in measuring time, in the Late Neolithic and Early Bronze Age, was used as a template to create a domestic house that would chart and control time in the Middle Bronze Age.[10] The circular structure of both buildings mirrors perceptions of the sky and enables orientations and celestial events to be documented by significant alignments and allows daily, monthly, and yearly cycles to be easily observed.

THE CHARACTER OF LATER PREHISTORIC HOUSES

As a result of the extensive excavations of the last fifty years, the pattern of house construction in the first millennium BC is fairly well understood. However, examination of houses and the development of the cosmological

---

[10] An analogous change appears to have occurred in Ireland during the first millennium BC. Throughout most of the Iron Age, domestic architecture is very difficult to identify. Indeed, the absence of a tradition of domestic architecture at this time has made the identification of the Irish Iron Age a problem (Cooney and Grogan 1994). This problem is resolved only in the first millennium AD when domestic settlements, in circular raths, appear in their thousands. Circular structures have been identified in Ireland in the Iron Age at Navan (Waterman 1997) and Dun Aillinne (Johnston and Wailes 2007), though these structures appear to have a religious role; they do not define domestic space but create arenas for religious events (Warner 2000). These Irish structures are very similar to the structures found in henge monuments in Britain dating to the Late Neolithic/Early Bronze Age and it is a peculiar coincidence that, in both instances, religious structures appear prior to domestic structures.

models mentioned above rarely involve any synthetic presentation of the overall patterning visible in the archaeological record. Instead, the normal practice is to isolate certain particularly well-preserved or thoroughly examined structures and use these as representatives of the idealized house. There are reasons for this type of approach and I will adopt it later on in this chapter, but it is important to create an overall impression of the archaeological record for houses, as this highlights historically significant patterns. In the following section I will briefly describe the evidence available for later prehistoric houses in central southern England, pointing out changes in size and entrance orientation, before providing a more detailed examination of the evidence from individual houses. It is, unfortunately, not possible to provide a general survey of the evidence for the Late Iron Age, as very few house plans are known that can be dated conclusively to the century before the Roman conquest.

Size

Assessing the overall dimensions of these houses is not as simple as it might first appear. The archaeological evidence for house structure is problematic; it is often possible to identify the location of a house securely but to have little idea of its size. Houses can be delineated by three significant features: the principal structural posts, which are normally inside the house, a wall line, and occasionally, a surrounding gully, which is assumed to control rain water running off the roof. The internal structural support is indicated by a circle of post holes, and it has been fairly convincingly argued that this has a direct relationship with the size of the structure (Guilbert 1981). However, it is important to emphasize that small structures do not require an internal post ring and that structural posts need not be placed in post holes. The outer wall can be revealed by a variety of features, such as a stone wall, a line of stakes, a ring of posts, a gully, or a chalk cut scarp, and most of these features are open to reinterpretation as internal or external features. A gully is a particularly ambiguous feature: in some cases these can be used to hold the external wall of the house but in other cases this might be an open ditch that surrounds the house. A detailed analysis of the fills should reveal which is the case, but the evidence is often ambiguous. A house could be represented by a post ring, a wall line, and an external ditch but it is very unusual for all three features to be present. Most houses are represented by one or other of these features. To get an overall picture of the change in house size throughout later prehistory, the measurements for both post rings and wall lines have been collated in Figure 4.4. Only by

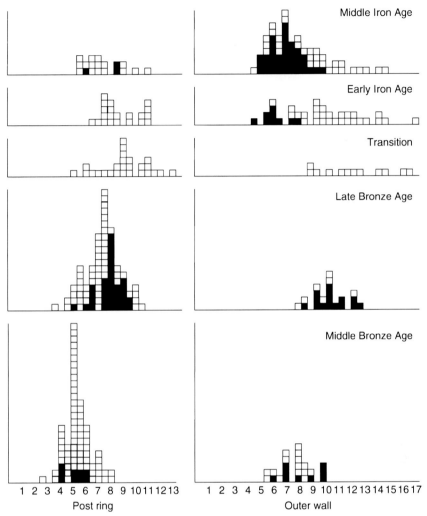

Figure 4.4 A histogram showing the changes in the diameter of the post ring and outer wall for later prehistoric houses in Wessex. Each box represents a single house. The infilled boxes indicate the most important site numerically in each phase. In the Middle Bronze Age this is Itford Hill, in the Late Bronze Age it is Reading Business Park, and in the Early and Middle Iron Age it is Danebury.

examining both features do we get a consistent indication of chronological change from the middle of the first millennium BC through to the end of the first century BC.[11]

---

[11] In most cases I have used the dimensions quoted in the text rather than measure them from published plans. People's preference for round numbers may explain the detailed pattern

The dataset from the Middle Bronze Age is one of the best available, and consists of 85 houses (Figure 4.4). These come from 24 sites that are spread throughout the region and most of the sites have relatively small numbers of houses; Itford Hill (Burstow and Holleyman 1957) and Easton Lane (Fasham, Farwell and Whinney 1989) are the two largest groups with 13 and 11 houses respectively. Houses of this date are normally represented by an internal post ring, but they are often terraced into a hillside, which gives some indication of the location of the external wall, and in some excavations evidence for a stake wall has been located.[12] In general the houses are small and include some very small structures. The diameter of the post ring varies from 2.5 m to 8.5 m with a prominent mode between 5.0 m and 5.5 m. The number of houses with an accurate measurement for the outer wall is low but indicates these houses would normally be between 5.5 m and 10.5 m in diameter.

The number of house plans available from Late Bronze Age settlements is substantial, comprising 106 houses (Figure 4.4). However, the dataset is not as good as that for Middle Bronze Age houses, since although the houses are found on 13 settlements, the overwhelming bulk of the measurable house floors come from two sites: Reading Business Park, Berkshire (35 houses: Moore and Jennings 1992), and Shorncote Quarry on the border of Gloucestershire and Wiltshire (22 houses: Hearne and Adam 1999). Both sites lie on the northern boundary of the study area and are quite different from those dated to the Middle Bronze Age as they lie on the terraces of major rivers and not on the chalk downland. Nevertheless, the number of downland sites, of Late Bronze Age date, has increased in recent years (e.g. Dunch Hill: Andrews 2006; Twyford Down: Walker and Farwell 2000) and these suggest that the houses present at Reading Business Park and Shorncote Quarry are representative. Our understanding of these structures is also hampered by the nature of the remains. All the structures identified are clusters of isolated post holes. On some sites complete rings can be

---

of clustering on specific dimensions. External gullies are relatively rare in Wessex, so the dimensions of these have not been collected.

[12] The precise position of the outer wall has been the subject of considerable debate over the years. A characteristic feature of these houses is their location on hill slopes and this requires the creation of a terraced platform. Originally it was argued that the house was a free-standing structure built on the terrace and that the post ring, as well as being the principal structural feature, was also the outer wall (Burstow and Holleyman 1957). This idea was rejected in the 1970s when a number of authors (Avery and Close-Brooks 1969; Musson 1970) pointed out that these houses had an outer wall and that this was clearly indicated by the position of the door posts. The reconstruction of the Blackpatch houses (Drewett 1982) argued that the wall sat along the top edge of the scarp, making the houses considerably larger. The excavations at Mile Oak (Rudling 2002) revealed stake walls at the base of the scarp inside the terrace of house I, but on the top of the scarp for house II. It seems there was no fixed rule in later prehistory.

clearly identified, such as 'structure 26' at Coburg Road (Smith, R. J. C. *et al.* 1992), but in other cases, repeated rebuilding on the same spot results in a confused mass of post holes and sometimes only partial rings are present. In these cases houses can be interpreted only with considerable caution. Despite these caveats, the data is consistent and indicates that houses have increased in size. The post ring diameters lie between 4.5 m and 11.0 m and there is a clear mode between 7.5 m and 8.0 m. The number of wall lines identified is again small, but all the houses have walls with diameters between 8.0 m and 13.5 m, and the mode is between 10.5 m and 11.0 m.

A small group of 32 houses can be identified that belong to the Late Bronze Age/Early Iron Age transitional period (identified by the presence of furrowed bowls). These houses come from ten sites and the largest group of houses were the six recognized in the hillfort of Winklebury (Smith, K. 1977), though this includes one structure rebuilt three times (Guilbert 1981). These houses are widely dispersed across the Wessex landscape and include both classic chalk downland sites (e.g. Houghton Down: Cunliffe and Poole 2000e) and river terrace sites (e.g. Dunston Park: Fitzpatrick, Barnes, and Cleal 1995). These houses are often spectacularly large (Figure 4.4). The internal post rings have diameters that range from 5.4 m to 13.3 m, with a mode between 9.0 m and 9.5 m. The outer wall is often clearly visible and most of the houses have external diameters that range from around 9 m at Overton Down (Fowler 2000) to 16.5 m at Winklebury. It seems unlikely that everyone in the Late Bronze Age/Early Iron Age transition period lived in large houses, and it is possible that the fine wares used to characterize this period are not present in smaller contemporary houses, which have been dated instead to the Late Bronze Age.

A total of 51 houses have produced data that can be used to describe the Early Iron Age house (Figure 4.4). These houses come from ten settlements and there are substantial groups from Danebury (Cunliffe and Poole 1991), Hengistbury Head (Cunliffe 1987), and Winnall Down (Fasham 1985), all in Hampshire. There is a distinct change in architectural form and an increasing number of houses with a clearly identifiable outer wall but no recognizable inner post ring (e.g. the Danebury houses: Cunliffe and Poole 1991: figs. 4.6–4.8). The diameters of the post rings range from 6.5 m to 11.1 m and seem to indicate a binary distribution. There are a group of small houses with a mode between 7.5 m and 8.0 m that are comparable to the Late Bronze Age houses, and a group of large houses, such as Little Woodbury (Bersu 1940), Pimperne (Harding, D. W. *et al.* 1993), and Flint Farm (Cunliffe and Poole 2008), that are comparable to the large houses of the Late Bronze Age/Early Iron Age transition. The distribution of the outer wall diameters is much less clustered than previous distributions, ranging from 4.5 m to 15 m. Small houses are characteristic of the hillfort at Danebury but there is a group of well-defined large houses which also have a massive internal post ring.[13]

The architectural trends that began in the Early Iron Age become even more emphatic in the Middle Iron Age. Most of the houses are represented by walls and only a few internal post rings are identifiable. A total of 91 houses from 12 settlements has produced useful information (Figure 4.4). The dataset is dominated by houses from Danebury (Cunliffe 1984a; Cunliffe and Poole 1991) and these are predominantly small houses which have an outer wall diameter that lies between 4.5 m and 10.5 m, comparable to the size range of Middle Bronze Age houses. This size range also encompasses houses from Hod Hill (Richmond 1968), Maiden Castle (Sharples 1991a), and Pilsden Pen (Gelling 1977), all substantial hillforts dating to the end of the Middle Iron Age. However, there are a number of houses that appear to be substantially larger than this group and these come from the Middle Iron Age phase at Winnall Down/Easton Lane (Fasham 1985; Fasham, Farwell, and Whinney 1989).[14] This dichotomy might indicate that people living outside hillforts were living in larger houses than those inside hillforts, but it is noticeable that the houses in the Middle Iron Age enclosure at Mingies Ditch in Oxfordshire (Allen, T. G. and Robinson 1993) were comparable in size to those from the hillforts. The houses at Glastonbury (Coles, J. and Minnitt 1995) were also directly comparable to the Danebury houses, in both size and structure.[15]

Despite the problems of the dataset, a clear pattern has emerged. Houses are generally small in both the Middle Bronze Age and the Middle Iron Age. At the beginning of the first millennium BC there is a tendency for size to increase and there is a particularly noticeable group of large roundhouses

---

[13] Groundwell Farm, Wiltshire (Gingell 1982), has three houses that are comparable to the other large houses of this and the preceding period. However, the final house has a suggested diameter of 17.5 m which would make this the largest house known from southern England. The interpretation of this structure as a roofed building is not convincing. It seems likely that a house of this size would require a substantial internal post ring to support the roof, and though these are present in the three smaller houses, only three isolated post holes were found in this structure. It is therefore difficult to accept this was a roofed structure.

[14] It might be possible to reinterpret these large houses. The outer wall is unusually defined by a wall gully and though post holes were identified in the gullies perhaps these indicate external fences that surround the house.

[15] The excavations at Glastonbury produced a large number of house plans and in the recent re-analysis of the site, Coles and Minnitt (1995: 181) claim to have recognized fewer than 40 houses, circular buildings with roofs, on 22 mounds. Unfortunately they never list these houses and it is only possible to create a list by examining the published phase plans (figs. 4.9–4.12), which depict 32 or 33 houses; the remaining half dozen probably represent the rebuilding of houses during a phase.

The primary evidence used to identify a house is a clay floor, a hearth, and a ring of stakes. The clay floors and hearths are frequently replaced, which can indicate a complete rebuild of

constructed in the Late Bronze Age/Early Iron Age transition that continue to be built in the Early Iron Age. The presence of relatively small houses in the Middle Iron Age is important as it suggests that the significance of the house as an arena for social interaction between different households was declining. The house may have become an intimate arena for social display between household members. John Barrett (1989) and Roger Thomas (1997) have suggested that the transition from small to large houses at the end of the Bronze Age marked a change from exogamous to endogamous marriage arrangements. This was represented by combining the separate male and female space of the Middle Bronze Age in the large houses of the Late Bronze Age. If this is an acceptable interpretation of the evidence then the importance of small houses in the Iron Age indicates a return to space divided into functionally and socially separate spheres of activity.

The chronological patterns outlined here are not followed in other areas of Britain. The development of large houses appears to occur later in the Iron Age in eastern England (Hill pers. comm.), and in southern Scotland and Atlantic Scotland large houses appeared at the beginning of the Iron Age and developed increasingly monumental attributes as the Iron Age progressed (Sharples 2007).

Orientation

The recent reinterpretation of the social significance of Iron Age houses has been closely related to the realization that roundhouse entrances were carefully and consciously oriented towards midwinter sunrise and the equinox,

---

the structure. However, this is not always the case and it is also clear that some clay floors were re-laid inside standing buildings. The presence or absence of a full ring of stakes is frequently used by Coles and Minnitt to distinguish between houses and shelters (without roofs). However, this distinction does seem to be rather arbitrary as several of the houses defined as houses by Coles and Minnitt have irregular wall lines, whereas some of the rejected structures, with only partial wall lines, have very well-defined walls and floors. The presence of incomplete arcs of stakes may be due to the removal and reuse of some posts and it is unclear if Bulleid would have recognized stake holes as opposed to stakes and given the malleability of the underlying organic substrate these might have been very difficult to identify.

Another problem with using the Glastonbury data is that most of the dimensions quoted by Coles and Minnitt, and Bulleid, relate to the clay floors, which do not necessarily reflect the size of the houses. Several houses have walls that lie inside the edge of the clay floors (e.g. M14) and in some cases it is clear that the walls lie outside of the clay floor (e.g. M61 and arguably M69). It is also clear that the houses need not be circular and some houses, notably mound 9, floors 1/2/3, were distinctly oval. Nevertheless, despite all these caveats, it is still possible to assemble dimensions from 37 houses and they provide a pattern that is very similar to that obtained from Danebury.

south-east and east respectively (Oswald 1997). Whilst these orientations had been noted by other archaeologists (Guilbert 1975), they had previously been interpreted as an attempt to compensate for strong western winds in the winter and to maximize sunlight in the interior (see also Pope 2007). Oswald (1997) undertook a detailed analysis of this issue that convincingly demonstrated these simplistic functionalist explanations would not have resulted in the very distinctive patterns observed in the archaeological record.[16] Wind direction is affected by local topography and would create a much more generalized spread of orientations. Furthermore, there are major regional differences in the direction of bad weather between the east and west coast of Britain that should be visible in the archaeological record, if this was important in the construction of the house.

No regional study of the orientation of roundhouse entrances in Wessex has been published, so the opportunity has been taken to produce a chart demonstrating that Wessex houses conform to the patterns present throughout the rest of Britain (Figure 4.5). The Middle Bronze Age pattern is dominated by a large number of houses oriented towards the south-east, with a significant spread towards south-south-east and south, and only a few outliers around these directions. Late Bronze Age houses have a similar focus but there no longer appears to be an interest in the south, with east becoming more important, and there are considerably more outliers, including a group of three west and west-south-west facing houses at Winnall Down (Fasham 1985). The number of houses in the transitional phase is quite small and most are facing south-east or south-south-east; three large houses, two from Haughton Down and one from Winklebury, are oriented to the west (west-north-west and west-south-west). In the Early Iron Age the south-east orientation retained its significance but there was now a substantial group of houses oriented to the east and a general spread of houses oriented in a northerly direction (from west-north-west to east-north-east). The Middle Iron Age dataset has a pattern not dissimilar to that of the Early Iron Age. The preferred orientation is to the south-east but a general spread to the south and to the east is visible. Three houses point to the north-west and there are isolated houses pointing in almost every direction.

It has been suggested by Hill (1996) that the unusual nature of hillforts places them outside the norms of society and Parker Pearson and Richards (1994: 54) suggested that the houses at Danebury are preferentially oriented towards the interior, the ritual centre of the settlement. However, a detailed analysis of the evidence from the Middle Iron Age period at Danebury

---

[16] A recent attempt to undermine these observations is not convincing (Pope 2007).

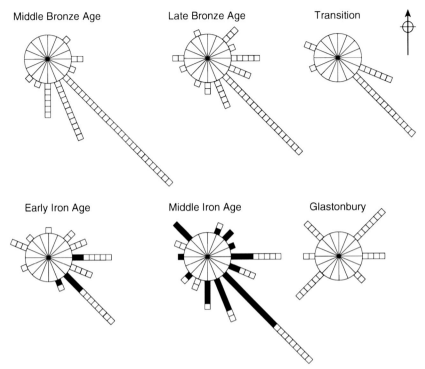

Figure 4.5 A diagram showing the orientation of Wessex roundhouse entrances through time. Each box represents a single house. The infilled boxes indicate the houses at Danebury.

(Davis 2002) shows that this is not the case.[17] About 38% of the Middle Iron Age houses at Danebury have entrances oriented towards the south-east, and the next favoured orientation is to the east (17%); there is only one house facing west, so there is no great divergence from the Iron Age norm. However, there is a significant number of houses with orientations to the north-west and north-east and these do suggest some special circumstances. Some of these houses are tucked in behind the southern rampart (e.g. CS22) and it might be expected that practical necessity would force them to open to the north but several houses in this situation (CS70, CS40) are positioned slightly behind the rampart in a position that allows an eastern orientation. A more important influence on the orientation seems to be the relationship with work areas and storage zones. This is

[17] The confusion might be caused partially by Cunliffe referring to an arbitrary grid north which is 215° west of north in the text. In volume 1 (Cunliffe 1984a), all the northings point north-west, but in the later volumes both grid north and north are indicated on the plans.

particularly clear in the north-west corner of the hillfort where houses CS38 and CS39 are oriented towards pits, four-post structures and activity areas. Another site with a large number of houses is Glastonbury, but our understanding of the orientation of these is confused. In the original report, only seven doorways were observed (Bulleid and Grey 1911: 59), and these covered almost the full range of possible orientations.[18] In the recent re-analysis of the settlement (Coles, J. and Minnitt 1995) 28, or 29, entrance orientations were identified by the presence of large horizontal timbers or by stone paving placed outside the wall line.[19] These entrance orientations are plotted in Figure 4.5 and they show an interesting pattern.[20] The orientations highlight an unusual north-east to south-west axis with a few houses pointing roughly towards the east and west. The number of south-west orientations is significant and was visible even in Bulleid's conservative examination of the evidence. The occupants of the settlement appear to be expressing their difference from the normal dry land settlements and they are doing this by emphasizing, and perhaps carrying out, rituals at quite different periods of the year, midsummer sunrise and midwinter sunset.[21]

The overall analysis of entrance orientations clearly confirms the general trends observed by Oswald (1997). The Middle Bronze Age pattern shows a more southerly orientation than the later Iron Age pattern but all periods focus on the south-east. East becomes important in the Early Iron Age, but is

---

[18] These houses were oriented north-east (x 2), east, south-east, west-south-west, west, and north-west.

[19] They claim to recognize 29 entrances but the orientations of only 28 are plotted (cf. Coles, J. and Minnitt 1995: 105 with fig. 4.6). They do not provide a list of the orientations by house and it is only possible to reconstruct them by examining the phase plans (Coles, J. and Minnitt 1995: figs. 4.9 – 4.12) where 27 entrance orientations are marked. Unfortunately, when these orientations are plotted the pattern produced is not similar to that illustrated in Coles, J. and Minnitt 1995, fig. 4.6, and also it conflicts with the textual descriptions of the mounds. For example no houses are oriented to the north-east in fig. 4.6, but on the phase plan, houses on mounds 3 (final), 13 (late), 23 (middle), and 61 (middle) are clearly shown facing north-east and two of these structures have substantial doorways recorded by Bulleid as oriented north-east.

[20] There is room for much ambiguity over these distributions. For example when a clay floor is identified does it indicate a reconstruction of the house and if the house is reconstructed does the entrance remain in the same place? I have counted a house on a mound only once for each phase identified by Coles and Minnitt no matter how many floors are attributed to that phase. I have also tended to assume that the entrance remains in the same place unless it can be demonstrated to have changed. For the record, the houses counted are north-east M13, M23, M27/4, M27/3/2, M61, M65; east M45, M57/4/2, M57/1, M69; south-east M18/4, M18/3/2; south no examples; south-west M14/3, M14/2, M35/4/3, M35/1, M42, M74/5, M74/4/3 (note the M74 houses are actually oriented WSW); west M9/8/9, M9/3/2/1; north-west M4, M29/10, M29/1.

[21] The emphasis on midwinter sunset is interesting at a wetland site such as Glastonbury. Some people have argued that the settlement would be seasonally occupied in the summer due to winter flooding. If this orientation is accepted as representing activity at this time of year then it supports Coles and Minnitt's (1995) argument that the site was occupied throughout the year.

perhaps less significant than in other areas of Britain (Oswald 1997: fig. 10.2). In all the periods but the Middle Bronze Age there are a few houses that point towards the west. However, these are exceptional and indicate a conscious decision to mark a house, and the activities undertaken within that house, as special. Only one site stands out as having a radically different pattern and that is the wetland settlement at Glastonbury in Somerset.

THE HOUSE AS A LIFECYCLE

During the Middle Bronze Age the traditions of domestic architecture exist in tandem with burial traditions, but in the transition to the Late Bronze Age, the evidence from burial traditions declines and eventually disappears (see Chapter 5). It is possible that there was a relationship between burial monuments and houses, and I would like to suggest that, in later prehistory, house architecture was a metaphor for the lifecycle. Support for this notion can be claimed from a number of different sources. Parker Pearson (1996) and Fitzpatrick (1994) have already suggested that house orientation and organization are being used as metaphors to structure and categorize two major temporal cycles—the day and the year. It therefore seems quite likely that the metaphor would be extended to encompass a third major temporal cycle, the occupant's life. Furthermore, the orientations visible in the houses can be linked to burial. In the Deverel-Rimbury tradition, 'satellite' cremations are normally situated in an area around the southern edge of the barrow and this coincides with the orientation of the houses during this period (Bradley 1998a: 152–8). Some houses have burials directly associated with the destruction of the house, such as Compact Farm in Dorset (Graham *et al.* 2002). It has also been noted by Brück (1999) that there is a striking pattern visible throughout the period of house use; houses seldom seem to be repaired but often seem to be completely replaced.[22] This suggests that house longevity may not be dependent on the inherent structural qualities of the material used but instead to the lifecycle of the occupant of the house.

Creation/Construction/Birth

The creation of a roundhouse begins with one of the most intangible processes: the decision to build. Allied to this decision is acquiring the right

---

[22] These patterns have also been noted by Gerritsen (1999, 2003) in his analysis of the Iron Age houses of the Damar-Meuse-Scheldt region of the Netherlands.

to build in the specific part of the landscape that you choose. Neither of these processes is particularly well understood by archaeologists, but the decision would probably represent one of the most significant events in the life of any member of the community. The ability to break away from an existing household/family and establish your own household is a clear demonstration of independence. The location of the house might also be an indication of status; in a landscape densely occupied and partitioned (see Chapter 2), the ability to choose a special or favourable location could well be a clear indication of a household's relative position in the community. It seems likely that the decision to construct a house is closely related to the coming of age of an individual within an existing household (Goody 1966). This might coincide with marriage, but there is no need to assume that this is always the case. In some societies, married couples frequently have to live in a parent's house until they acquire the resources necessary to start a new household (Bloch 1995b). Indeed, in societies with permanent houses built to span generations, it is common for married children to stay in the house to continue the relationship between lineage and structure (Bloch 1995b).

The decision to construct a house may well have been tied to a ritual event or process which we cannot fully understand. It has been argued (Guilbert 1975) that the timing of the construction of a house may have been carefully controlled, and this may be linked to the tight clustering of the entrance orientations. As discussed above, these point towards the south-east and midwinter sunrise, or to the east and sunrise on the morning of the equinox. Whilst this seems theoretically plausible, the suggestion that large numbers of houses were constructed in December is unlikely: mid-winter is not a good month to undertake any major building event, even in southern England.

As the opening of this chapter discussed, the more practical requirements for the construction of an Iron Age roundhouse have been well documented in recent years, as a large number of roundhouses have been reconstructed as educational resources in a variety of public centres. One of the most important reconstructions was of the house discovered at Pimperne in Dorset, which was recreated at the Butser Experimental Farm by Peter Reynolds (see page 174; Figure 4.6). This reconstruction was thoroughly documented and the information published in the final report on the excavations (Harding, D. W. *et al.* 1993). The house can be dated to the Late Bronze Age/Early Iron Age transition and is a characteristically large house, though not the largest known.

The Pimperne house had an outer wall line, 12.8 m in diameter, and an inner circle of posts 9.75 m in diameter. The outer wall used approximately

Figure 4.6 The reconstruction of the Pimperne house during construction at Butser Ancient Farm (photographs taken by Professor W. Hanson).

80 timbers,[23] and it was estimated that these should be 1.52 m tall to provide a reasonable roof height adjacent to the wall. The inner ring was comprised of 22 posts, 0.22 m in diameter, and these were joined by lintels, of a similar thickness, to form a timber ring beam on which the rafters of the roof could rest. Oak was used for all the principal uprights. The internal ring required trees approximately 45–55 years old to provide trees of comparable thickness to those identified by the post holes of the excavated house; 36 trees were used for the ring, the lintels and the porch around the door. The trees for the outer wall were 10–20 years old and the reconstruction used approximately 65 trees for this feature. The outer wall was bound together by coppiced hazel rods and an estimated 350 rods were taken from 50 stools. This was subsequently daubed with a mixture of clay, earth, and straw or other fibrous material, although the amounts used were not quantified.

[23] The precise figure is not mentioned in the report and some of the post holes were removed by later disturbance or are not clearly defined in the area around the rear entrance.

The reconstructed roof was pitched at 45°, the angle required to allow rainwater runoff. This required 55 trees of ash and elm, up to 10.36 m long, and they were tied together with an unquantified number of hazel purloins. The roof was thatched with reed straw and approximately 7 tons of thatch was required to create a layer 10 cm thick. As Reynolds (in Harding, D. W. *et al.* 1993: 103) points out, the thatch layer should have been 30 cm thick and skimping on the thatch resulted in the roof having to be repaired regularly throughout its life. Therefore, an appropriate roof would have required approximately 21 tons of thatch. This was the most time-consuming job and took approximately 36 days' work. It is not clear how much longer this job would have taken if the thatch was applied to its proper thickness. Likewise, the thatch used was commercial thatch and came cleaned and ready for use, and Reynolds noted that the preparation of straw thatch would have been a particularly time-consuming process in later prehistory.

Reynolds emphasized that the house 'can only have been built by a few people working for a long time' (Reynolds in Harding, D. W. *et al.* 1993: 106) as opposed to a lot of people working for a short time. He believed that the only activity which would involve many people was the creation of the daub and its application to the walls as this is best done in a very messy party atmosphere. However, I feel this is a matter of personal temperament rather than scientific observation (see page 176). A well-organized and experienced team who were used to working together could reduce the time taken to build a house quite dramatically. It is quite normal to see teams working on the re-thatching of a modern house roof, and many phases of the construction could easily absorb a large number of people. Indeed, it is difficult to understand how the resources required could have been assembled without the participation of a large team, and these people would require another support team to provide them with food. Some of the required resources are only seasonally available, mainly the straw, and skilled labour might have been available only for a restricted period. The longer the construction period, the more susceptible the partially completed house would be to storm damage. As Reynolds has pointed out, houses are very stable when they are completed but during construction they are susceptible to damaging winds and rain.

The resources necessary for the smaller houses of the Middle Iron Age would be very different from those used in large houses. The basic structural elements for Middle Iron Age houses are thin saplings from coppiced trees (Figure 4.7). The clearest description of the resources required for the construction of a small house is provided by Coles and Minnitt (1995: 106–7), using data from the experimental rebuilding of a Glastonbury house at the Peat Moors Centre in Somerset. They estimate that the wattle wall of a house 8 m in diameter would require about 80 vertical stakes, about 2 m tall, and about 690 m of

Figure 4.7 An imaginative reconstruction of a Danebury house (from Cunliffe 1996: fig. 4.9; reproduced with the permission of Professor B.W. Cunliffe).

horizontal rods. The Glastonbury stakes could be ash or alder but were normally made from oak. Their diameter was *c.*100 mm which would suggest a 10–15-year-old coppice. The rods were willow or hazel and the average diameter of 25 mm suggests they were 4–5 years old and about 3 m long. An estimated 4–5 tons of daub was required to complete the weatherproofing of the walls. At Glastonbury an estimated 8 cubic metres of clay was also needed to create a dry floor, but this was not normally a requirement in the well-drained environments of the downland settlements. The roof probably required about six major rafters, 7 m long, interspersed with about 29–34 shorter timbers held in place by a ring beam and interwoven with roughly 870 m of rods, and was covered by about 1,700 bundles of reeds. Coles and Minnitt estimate that this house could have endured for about 35–50 years.

It is clear that despite the considerable reduction in the size of these houses their creation still represented a considerable expenditure of resources and labour. Coles and Minnitt (1995) estimate seven people working for 14 weeks, though this seems too long. In the Somerset Levels it would have been relatively easy to source wood, clay and reeds, but for the communities living in downland settlements, such as Danebury, it was not likely to have been so straightforward. The bulk of archaeological thinking has gone into the recreation of the construction event, and it is impossible to estimate the effort required to assemble the raw materials. However, it is important to consider the problems involved in first sourcing these raw materials and then transporting them to the construction site. Environmental evidence has fairly conclusively demonstrated that the chalk downlands had been almost completely deforested in the Neolithic and Early Bronze Age (see Chapter 2) and any surviving woodland is likely to be restricted to deposits of clay with flints, or the river valleys. These restricted areas of woodland would have been under tremendous pressure since they would have provided fuel for warmth, cooking, and important craft activities such as metalworking; objects such as tool handles, ploughs, and vehicles; building materials for houses, granaries, palisades, bridges, and tracks.

The size of trees used in the Pimperne house would require a long-term investment in the creation of closed woodland that would have been carefully managed to restrict unauthorized use by people and grazing animals. To remove the number of trees required would have made a significant impact on this patch of woodland. The very large quantities of coppiced hazel or willow used also clearly indicate careful long-term management of the wood-land resource. Ownership would have been an important issue and one wonders whether the woodland was controlled by a special group, who managed it for the wider agricultural communities, or whether it was con-trolled by the larger community, who allocated time, within the annual cycle of activities, to woodland management. The first seems more likely but unusual communities are not easy to recognize in the archaeological record.[24] The isolated nature of the woodlands is also likely to have given trees and wood a special spiritual dimension that should be considered in this fairly prosaic consideration of house materialities.

There is a significant difference in the large quantities of mature timber used in Late Bronze Age/Early Iron Age houses, such as Pimperne and Long-bridge Deverill Cow Down, and the relatively infrequent use of mature timber

---

[24] Groundwell Farm (Gingell 1982) has exceptionally large houses for a Middle Iron Age enclosure and the evidence for a large proportion of pigs in the animal bone assemblage is also unusual for a Middle Iron Age settlement.

in Middle Iron Age sites such as Maiden Castle and Danebury. These changes parallel differences in the resources consumed in the construction of enclosure boundaries between the two periods (see Chapter 3). Early hillforts are characterized by the construction of a box rampart, which has a vertical timber wall face, built on a substantial timber framework using large posts. In contrast, the later dump ramparts of the Middle Iron Age seldom use any timber in their construction. If a revetment is required in this period it is normally constructed using stone.

The woodland resources required for the construction of both enclosures and houses in the Late Bronze Age/Early Iron Age transition would have been considerable and suggest the inhabitants of Wessex may have had a rather cavalier attitude to the natural environment in this period. This might indicate a breakdown of traditional power structures which left these resources unprotected and therefore open to appropriation by the strongest and most organized members of the community. It is noticeable that when the inhabitants return to occupying small houses in the Middle Iron Age, these have a slightly different design which no longer involves the use of a structural ring of substantial timbers, and instead they are constructed with fast-growing hazel or willow rods from a coppiced stool.

Is it possible that the environmental destruction of the Late Bronze Age/ Early Iron Age transition was irreversible and that substantial timbers were difficult to get hold of? This clearly is not the case at a site like Glastonbury where timber is available in large quantities and is used to create solid floors. Even in hillforts, such as Maiden Castle, some of the small houses were using timber for internal post rings. However, in the centre of the chalk downlands, access to mature oak was potentially much more difficult. Carefully managed mature woodland could have been completely consumed by the construction of the Early Iron Age hillforts and it would have been very difficult to regenerate this woodland once it had gone. Carefully managed and long-established woodland would have produced limited quantities of trees every year, and this would justify the effort put into its maintenance. The re-creation of destroyed woodland required just as much, if not more, maintenance, but would produce very little for the first 20 to 30 years.

Use/Life

Understanding the significance of houses requires an analysis of their use, and in particular, the organization of their internal space. This is not possible for most of the houses described above as these are normally ploughed almost to destruction. Very few internal floor deposits survive and generally all that is identifiable is a ring of postholes. It is therefore necessary to concentrate detailed analysis on the best preserved houses; houses where deposits were preserved in the interior and where the distribution of artefacts and the remains of occupation deposits have been analysed and provide some evidence for the nature of household activity.

The act of preservation is not random and prejudices the archaeological record to certain periods and types of site. For example, most small Iron Age enclosures are positioned on slightly sloping ground, and intensive ploughing of these sites means they produce very few well-preserved house plans. Hillforts, in contrast, are difficult, though not impossible, to destroy by ploughing and the accumulation of sediments in the densely occupied areas immediately behind the rampart results in the excellent preservation of house floor deposits. This means we have a good understanding of the structures inside hillforts but we can not say for certain that these are identical to the structures inside smaller settlements.

The Middle Bronze Age house

There is a tendency for houses dated to the middle of the second millennium BC to be constructed in a hollow, dug into the slope of a hill, and this preference results in the partial preservation of the house interiors. However, occupation deposits are seldom identified and it appears that the floors were normally kept clean. Our understanding of the structure of the occupation is dependent on the presence of sub-surface features, which include pits and post holes, and occasional objects and patches of debris lying directly on the floor. The clearest evidence for the activities carried out inside these houses comes from two well-preserved and representative houses that were excavated at Blackpatch in Sussex (Drewett 1982) and Rowden in Dorset (Woodward, P. J. 1991).

The settlement at Blackpatch is located on a rare area of unploughed downland in East Sussex. It comprises several terraces cut into a south-east facing hillslope. The terraces explored by excavation all seem to have evidence for houses. These houses are surrounded by field systems indicated by lynchets and on the edge of the field system are a number of burial cairns. The most detailed excavation was on site IV, which consists of a group of five houses probably built in two successive phases (see page 181; Figure 4.2; Russell 1996a), each with two houses and leaving one unphased structure. Houses 1 and 3 belong to the second phase and both have relatively rich internal deposits.

Drewett (1982: 342) suggested that house 3 was a headman, or head-woman's, house (Figure 4.8). There was no formal hearth but it is argued, on the basis of the distribution of burnt flint, that a hearth was located at the front of the house in the centre of the entrance. Arranged behind this was an area illuminated by light coming through the doorway that was suitable for craft (leather, wood, bone) working, though there is very little evidence for these activities. The rear of the house was split, by an axis running through the entrance of the house, into an area on the left-hand side provided with three shallow pits used for crop storage, and an area on the right-hand side with a concentration of loom weights that was used for weaving.[25] These activities lay between the main ring of structural posts and the external wall around the periphery of the house. Measurement of potsherd thickness suggests that there was a wide range of vessels present in this house (Ellison in Drewett 1982: fig. 33). A razor, a knife, and two awls or tracers were found on the floor and are thought to indicate the high status of the occupants of the house.

Drewett (1982: 342) suggested that house 1 was a wife's hut. Food preparation and cooking were indicated by the presence of pottery, flint flakes, and fragments of a quern. These activities appear to be occurring on the right-hand side of the house. The hearth is again difficult to locate as only limited quantities of fire-cracked flint were present and there was only one pit, immediately behind the entrance, that might indicate a storage function. Analysis of variations in potsherd thickness in this house suggests the assemblage was dominated by everyday wares used for cooking. Two spiral finger rings were found on the floor of the house and these were argued to indicate the relative status of the occupants.

Another very well-preserved Middle Bronze Age house was excavated at Rowden on the South Dorset Ridgeway (Woodward, P. J. 1991). The excavations examined a single south-facing house but it is likely that this is part of a pair of houses, with its partner about 20 m to the west, on the other side of a trackway. The house was oval, approximately 9 m long and 7 m wide, and the floor was sunk into a pit rather than a terrace (Figure 4.8). The chalk sides of the pit were lined by a flint wall but the main structural element was a ring of posts, approximately 4.2 m by 5.1 m. There was no evidence for a porch

---

[25] Cynthia Poole has argued (pers. comm.) that the cylindrical loom weights of the later Bronze Age are in fact hearth furniture. The argument is based on the association of these objects with hearth debris and the absence of any wear to indicate suspension of the weights. These two observations might indicate the weights were a form of oven brick used as a portable source of warmth. They could be heated at the fire then picked up by pushing a stick through the perforation and transported to where the heat was required. Their location at Blackpatch could indicate they were used to warm a sleeping place.

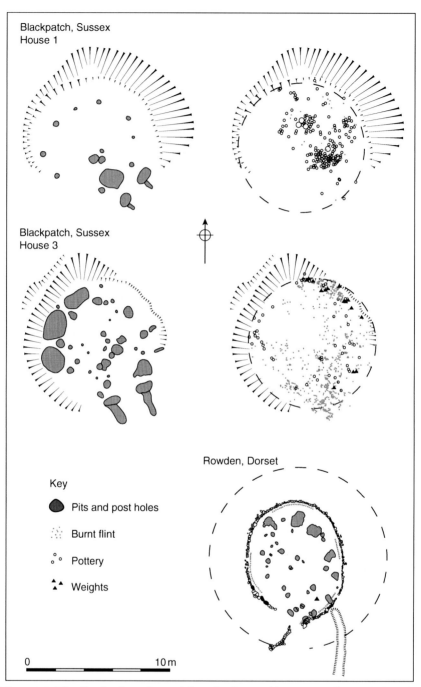

Figure 4.8 The distribution of material on the floors of houses 1 and 3 at Blackpatch, Sussex (Drewett 1982: figs. 6 and 10), and the structure of the house at Rowden, Dorset (Woodward 1991: fig. 23).

but a low flint wall restricted access from the west side of the entrance and on the east side gullies led into it.

When one entered the house, a timber screen encouraged movement to the right. This may have been designed to control access to the fire, which is interpreted as being placed adjacent to the wall immediately to the left of the entrance (several sarsens that show signs of burning were identified in the wall at this point). The principal 'interactive' zone was in the centre-front of the house and appears to be separated from the rear of the house by a timber partition. Four shallow pits were located to the rear of this house, between the timber circle and the house wall, and these are reminiscent of the pits in house 3 at Blackpatch. One of these pits contained a large quantity of carbonized barley, which had been carefully cleaned prior to combustion. Two areas of private space may be defined on either side of the house and that on the west side was associated with a copper alloy razor and arrowhead. The pottery from the house was dominated by fine wares and an almost complete vessel was placed in a post hole at the entrance during construction.

The difficulties involved in interpreting activities inside any building are highlighted by these houses. Even though they are the best preserved Middle Bronze Age houses in Wessex, the evidence still has to be stretched to make even a simple interpretation. For example, the absence of clearly identifiable hearths is glossed over and a few burnt stones are taken to indicate the position of a very simple fireplace unmarked by any architectural embellishment. This is surely surprising; a fire must have been one of the most important features of a house, as it provided much needed heat and light which would be essential for any comfortable occupation of the building. It would also be essential for cooking food and could be used to preserve foodstuffs by drying and smoking. The relative (in)visibility of this key feature must be significant. It is possible that it was deliberately removed and its location erased following the abandonment of the structures. There are many traditional societies where the fire symbolizes life, and was kept permanently lit, and when the house was abandoned the fire may have been taken out and moved to another location.

The abandonment of the house also raises questions about the significance of the artefacts present in the house. When these are valuable items, such as the copper alloy finger rings from Blackpatch, or the arrowhead from Rowden, should it be assumed that they were accidentally lost during the use of the house? It seems more likely that they represent objects placed within the house as part of specific lifecycle ritual processes related to its closure (Barrett and Needham 1988: 136; Brück 1999: 154). It is, however, still possible that some abandonment deposits reflect activities that had gone on in the house or the status of the inhabitants.

Despite these caveats there are some obvious patterns visible in these houses that are supported by a wider study of the Middle Bronze Age settlements of southern England (Brück 1999). The double-ring structure is a feature of house architecture in this period and the posts are often carefully laid out to create axial symmetry between the internal post opposite the entrance and the entrance itself. The double ring creates a space, which is automatically divided into a core area and a periphery. However, the evidence for the significance of this spatial division is ambiguous; when pits are present they are placed in the peripheral area and this suggests it performed a storage role. However, the concentric arrangement of space is undermined by the location of the hearth. In contrast to later houses, this is not placed routinely in the centre of the house; instead, it is found in the area immediately inside the entrance and is often part of an activity area marked by large con-centrations of finds. The importance of the axis created by the entrance to the house is also ambiguous. The doorway is a significant architectural feature; it was marked by larger post holes, provides the axial symmetry for the internal structure and is strongly oriented to the south-east or, to a lesser extent, south. However, Brück (1999) identified only four out of 23 houses where the axis of symmetry affected the distribution of finds or features; house 3 at Blackpatch was one of these structures.

Late Bronze Age/Early Iron Age Houses

I have already commented on the lack of any well-preserved Late Bronze Age houses. None of the houses identified at Reading Business Park has floors or any evidence for how they were used. It is only really with the appearance of the very large houses at the Late Bronze Age/Early Iron Age transition that we identify structures associated with house floors and artefact distributions. The two best-preserved houses of the period are the houses at Pimperne, Dorset (Harding, D. W. *et al.* 1993), and Longbridge Deverill Cow Down, Wiltshire (Hawkes, S. C. 1994).

The evidence from Pimperne, Dorset, indicates a single house inside a sub-rectangular or oval enclosure (Harding, D. W. *et al.* 1993). The enclosure was much larger than required simply to enclose this house, but the rela-tively limited excavation suggests the rest of the enclosure was largely devoid of any other structures. The house and enclosure are dated to *c.*500 BC by the pottery. The house was rebuilt once and the two phases are not concentric but have centres roughly 0.3 m apart. The outer walls of the two houses only align with each other at the entrance, which faces to the south-east. Both houses are structurally similar and have the same dimensions; Harding suggests there was little interval of time between the demise of one house and the construction of the other.

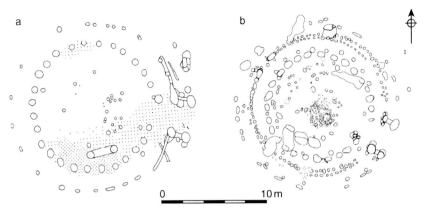

Figure 4.9 The Late Bronze Age/Early Iron Age houses at a) Longbridge Deverill Cow Down, Wiltshire and b) Pimperne, Dorset (after Hawkes, S. C. 1994: fig. 4; Harding *et al.* 1993: fig. 16; reproduced with the permission of the Hawkes Archive, Institute of Archaeology, University of Oxford; Professor D. W. Harding).

The principal structural feature is an inner ring of posts, defining a circle 9.75 m in diameter, and an outer ring of smaller posts, defining a circle 12.8 m in diameter (Figure 4.9). Outside this circle of posts was another 'intermittent circle of shallow scoops and elongated slots' (Harding, D. W. *et al.* 1993: 27). The entrance was a particularly substantial feature comprising a rectangular box projecting up to 1.5 m from the outer line of posts (Figure 4.6). It was impossible to identify the two separate phases in the post holes of the entrance structure, partly because they retained the same position, but also because it seems likely these posts were replaced more than once. The gap for the entrance was 3.04 m, creating a very substantial opening.

Unfortunately, no floor layers survive in the interior. There was a baked clay hearth which, though roughly in the centre of the house, was nearer the entrance. This was surrounded by numerous small features and, to the west, by a layer of flint cobbles, which Harding suggests may be a collapsed wall (Harding, D. W. *et al.* 1993: 29). Harding draws attention to a pair of large post holes to the south of the hearth adjacent to the inner post ring. He suggested these might indicate the position of a loom. Webley (2007: 139) suggests that pottery was concentrated in the post holes of the entrance and the post holes of the 'loom'. Other small finds, including a copper alloy ring and pin, appear to be concentrated in the post holes on the south side of the house.

At Longbridge Deverill, Cow Down, Wiltshire, four houses were identified in a large sub-rectangular enclosure (Hawkes, S. C. 1994). Hawkes suggested that these houses were built in a chronological sequence starting in the eighth century BC and ending in the second half of the sixth century BC. House 3 was a particularly impressive and well-preserved structure, with an entrance towards the south-east, which the excavator argued had been destroyed by fire. The principal structural feature is an inner ring of post holes, defining a circle 11.60 m in diameter (Figure 4.9). These holes contained posts 0.30 m in diameter and were spaced approximately 1 m apart. An outer ring of posts was identified, defining a circle 15.5 m in diameter. These were slighter, oval-shaped post holes set at more irregular intervals. A third ring of even more ephemeral and irregular posts is suggested but with less conviction. The rectangular entrance structure projected from the second ring of posts, which were defined by gullies on either side of the door. It provided an opening 3.40 m wide. The post holes of the entrance had been replaced at least once and provide the only evidence for modification of the structure.

Like the Pimperne house, the inner ring of posts was the principal structural support for the roof, and it is argued that the outer, irregular and ephemeral ring represents the end of the rafters. However, Sonia Hawkes (1994) argued that, in contrast to Pimperne, the outer wall of the house was on the line of the inner post circle, not the second circle. She based her argument on three factors: the closely-spaced nature of the inner ring of posts, the presence of large quantities of daub in the post holes of this ring, and the abrupt edge to the floor deposits along this line. She suggested the second ring was little more than a screen that separated the storage or byre area under the eaves of the roof from the worst of the weather.

No hearth was observed but it is presumed to have been in the centre of the house and to have been destroyed by Roman ploughing. Post holes suggest the presence of screens or a drying rack between the hearth and the entrance and another ring of post holes might indicate the construction of a gallery or platform inside the back half of the house. The distribution of pottery on the house floor was significant. A large and extensive spread covered the area from the entrance around the southern third of the floor, avoiding the central area. The only other spread was very restricted and lay against the north wall. At the centre of the main distributions of pot were two massive post holes, similar to those found at Pimperne, where they were interpreted as a loom. Hawkes sensibly argued that looms do not require substantial post holes and instead suggested that these features represent 'a fixed piece of furniture, an earth-fast table or dresser... on which the leading family's table service and festal meal would be displayed on grand occasions' (Hawkes, S. C. 1994: 68). This would explain the subsequent concentration of ceramics in this area in all the Longbridge Deverill houses and the Pimperne house. Loom weights were found in the south-west sector of the floor area, and directly opposite the main doorway were two spindle whorls and a bone gouge. One of the spindle whorls lay outside the wall line and it was suggested these finds might indicate a secondary doorway, as at Pimperne.

The appearance of these large houses in the Late Bronze Age/Early Iron Age transition marks a decisive break with the Middle Bronze Age traditions. The occupation evidence at Longbridge Deverill clearly provides the strongest evidence in support of the cosmological models suggested by Parker Pearson (1996, 1999) and Fitzpatrick (1994). There appears to be a clear split between the right- and left-hand sides of the house, with the left-hand side used for day-to-day activities that survive as a layer of occupation debris, whereas the absence of debris on the right-hand side suggests it was used for sleeping and storage. However, it could be argued that the interpretation of these patterns is simplistic (Webley 2007). Most of the pottery recovered from Pimperne, Dunstan Park, and Longbridge Deverill houses 1 and 2 came from post holes, and there is now good evidence from sites such as Houghton Down (Cunliffe and Poole 2000e) and North Popley (Wright pers. comm.) that the pottery had been packed deliberately into the post holes after the house had been dismantled and after the ceramics had been severely burnt (see below). However, the evidence from Longbridge Deverill house 3 is of a spread of pottery and other finds in the southern half of the house, which does suggest a more significant emphasis on this area. The structural arrangements also provide some evidence in support of Hingley's model. The presence of an inner ring of posts clearly splits the interior of the house into a centre and periphery, and at the Longbridge Deverill house the excavator argued that the periphery lay outside the house wall. The evidence from Pimperne suggests the central hearth has become a permanent and much more substantial feature of these structures.

The Middle Iron Age House

Due to the appearance of hillforts, and the opportunities they provide for the preservation of ephemeral layers and features in the area behind the rampart, the number of well-preserved house floors increases considerably in the period from 400 BC to 100 BC. However, I will restrict my detailed discussion to houses from the hillforts of Maiden Castle (Sharples 1991a) and Danebury (Cunliffe 1984a; Cunliffe and Poole 1991). The preservation of houses in other settlement forms is much more problematic and many sites with good evidence for occupation throughout the Middle Iron Age have no surviving house structures. An exceptionally well-preserved site is the enclosure at Mingies Ditch in Oxfordshire, which, though outside the study area, is worth discussing.

The best-preserved house discovered during the recent excavations at Maiden Castle (Sharples 1991a) lay in the south-west corner of the hillfort, in the quarry hollow immediately behind the inner rampart. It was the only one of a number of houses recovered in this hollow that was completely excavated and undisturbed by later activity. It was attributed to phase 6 F and an archaeomagnetic date of 200–150 BC was obtained from the central hearth. The diameter of the outer wall of the house was estimated to be 6 m and this was surrounded by a bank and gully, 9.3 m in diameter (Figure 4.10). The structural elements of the house were difficult to identify and it is not clear whether it had an inner circle of structural posts. In the original excavation report (Sharples 1991a) it was suggested that an inner post ring was present, which was indicated by clusters of stone that acted as post pads. However, these post pads never formed a complete ring and the four that were observed are not concentric to the house wall.[26] There may never have been an inner timber ring and the post pads may have served quite different functions, such as a hard standing for pots. Extending in front of the south-facing entrance was a rectangular limestone pavement.

In the centre of the house was a hearth, consisting of a flat surface of baked clay on a foundation of flint nodules, that was replaced twice, first by another similar hearth and then by an oven with limestone and clay walls. These replacements lay to the south-west of the central hearth and the opening to the oven pointed back towards the centre of the house. Surrounding the hearth to the west and south (left-hand side), was a sequence of charcoal layers that suggest domestic activity was concentrated in this area. Along the east (right-hand) side of the house interior was a shallow elongated hollow, which could be interpreted as a sleeping position. The only part of the interior to have a surface was an area of rammed chalk just behind the entrance threshold. The east (right-hand) side of this surface was edged by limestone rubble, which may indicate the location of a partition wall and would certainly have deterred people entering the house and turning in this direction.

A phosphate and magnetic susceptibility survey of the interior (Sharples 1991a: fig. 86) contrasted the area of the charcoal spread on the left (south-west) and the area of the hollows to the right (north-east). The charcoal spread was characterized by high phosphate and sporadically high magnetic susceptibility, whereas the area around the hollows had low phosphate and high magnetic susceptibility.

---

[26] The excavations at Glastonbury and Danebury indicate that the small houses that characterize Middle Iron Age hillforts do not need substantial inner post rings. However, the excavations at Maiden Castle demonstrate that some small houses (e.g. 6851 and 6852; Sharples 1991a: 75–8) did have internal post rings.

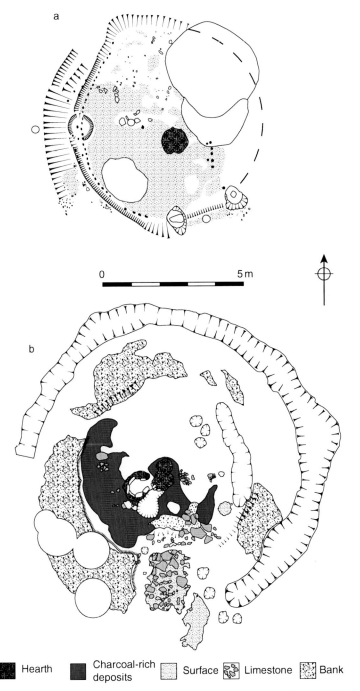

a

b

0   5 m

■ Hearth   ■ Charcoal-rich deposits   □ Surface   ▨ Limestone   ▨ Bank

Figure 4.10 Two Middle Iron Age houses from a) Danebury, Hampshire and b) Maiden Castle, Dorset (after Cunliffe and Poole 1991, fig. 4.46 and Sharples 1991, fig. 84).

A total of 73 houses was identified during the extensive excavation of the hillfort at Danebury, Hampshire (Cunliffe and Poole 1991: 39), most of which can be dated to the Middle Iron Age. The long sequence of activity and the repeated digging of pits mean that many of the house plans are incomplete and provide only a limited understanding of the internal occupation of the houses. Furthermore, only three houses had intact occupation layers that have been excavated and published (Brown in Cunliffe 1995: 185–92).

CS56 was situated in a row of houses located behind the rampart on the right-hand side of the eastern entrance (Cunliffe and Poole 1991: 86–9). The house was defined by a stake wall approximately 6.5 m in diameter, with the stakes placed about 0.2 m apart (Figure 4.10). As with most of the other Danebury houses there were no internal post holes to suggest any other structural elements were present. There were two lines of stakes on the west side and the excavator suggests these indicate a phase of rebuilding rather than a double wall. Two post holes joined by a slot indicate the frame and sill of a door approximately 1.7 m wide. The door faced slightly east of south and provided access onto 'road 6', which follows the northern rampart.

The interior had a chalk floor of rounded chalk lumps in a layer of puddled chalk. This was particularly well made, and smooth, to the front and south-west side of the house. A circular hearth was constructed of flint pebbles placed in a shallow hollow covered with puddled chalk and with a burnt surface, and this lay on the central axis of the house, slightly nearer the entrance than the back wall. A line of stakes was present just inside the door, apparently blocking access to the right-hand side of the house. This wall was destroyed by the digging of a pit that may be contemporary with the later occupation of the house. This pit and much of the floor was subsequently destroyed by the digging of another pit, some time after the house was abandoned.

A grey brown silt was interpreted as an occupation deposit contemporary with the use of the house. This generally had very low numbers of heavily abraded sherds scattered fairly evenly across the interior, but a concentration of sherds close to the south wall, near the entrance, may represent the smashing of a complete pot. At the back of the house there is a concentration of copper alloy sheet fragments, a whetstone and two iron fragments, which may indicate an area of small-scale metalworking (Brown in Cunliffe 1995: 185).

Forty-nine of the excavated houses at Danebury can be placed in the Middle Iron Age (post 350–300 BC) and all but one[27] of these structures had the walls defined by upright timber stakes which would have been woven together by horizontal hurdles to create a wattle wall (Figure 4.7). In some houses, the stakes are placed in a ring groove, whereas in others, individual

---

[27] The exception is CS1, which has walls made of vertical planks placed in a ring groove.

holes are created for the stakes. Cunliffe suggests that 'selected vertical poles, projecting above the woven wall, were bent inwards and joined at the apex to form a framework for the wattlework to continue upwards' (Cunliffe and Poole 1991: 43–5, fig. 4.9). He suggests reed was used to thatch both the roof and the walls of the house as there is very little evidence for clay daub. The entrance structures are standardized, consisting of two post holes joined by a slot. In the best-preserved examples, the presence of two posts in each post hole seems clear and this has been interpreted as a sliding door. In the 34 well-preserved houses, eight have hearths and ovens, 18 have hearths alone, and ten have neither feature. Wattle screens partitioning the interior are not common but can be observed in a couple of houses.

Several authors (Stopford 1987; Hill 1995a: 49) have suggested that the relatively flimsy structures at Danebury and Maiden Castle would be incapable of prolonged permanent occupation and that they indicate the seasonal occupation of hillforts. This interpretation fails to mention that the evidence from contemporary settlements is equally ephemeral. The settlement at Glastonbury provides detailed evidence for large numbers of structures that are very similar to those found on the hillforts; they have stake walls with no internal post ring and central hearths. The principal difference is that they have thick clay floor layers which are occasionally placed over elaborate timber foundations, but this probably reflects the wet environment in which they were constructed.

Mingies Ditch was a small enclosure located on the flood plain of the River Windrush in Oxfordshire (Allen, T. G. and Robinson 1993: 54–9). Five structures were located in the interior. Three of these appear to be houses and two are less substantial structures. The best-preserved structure was house 5 on the south side of the enclosure. This was defined by a stake wall, 8.4 m in diameter, which was in turn surrounded by a discontinuous gully. The entrance faced east and was defined by a pair of large post holes, one of which had been recut at least once. A gravel path led up to the entrance, which had limestone cobbling at the threshold. There are a number of post holes in the interior, but these do not create a ring concentric with the house wall, and it is suggested by the excavator that they may represent temporary roof supports. A large post hole was found in the centre of the house but the post had been removed and backfilled and covered with a clay hearth. This post hole was clearly not in use during the occupation of the house and may be connected with its construction.[28] The hearth was surrounded by a dark floor layer but this is not discussed in detail in the

---

[28] Central post holes were a feature of several of the Glastonbury houses and Coles and Minnitt (1995) have argued that these are not structural, but might have performed a marking-out function for the construction of the mound.

report. Another well-preserved house (3) at Mingies Ditch was defined by an internal ring of posts, 6.5 m in diameter, and a wall 8.5 m in diameter. It was surrounded by a gully and had an entrance facing east and a hearth located towards the front left as you entered the house. A shallow scoop was located at the centre of the house.

The houses of the Middle Iron Age are characteristically small, and there is evidence for clear functional variation between houses, most obviously demonstrated by the presence or absence of hearths in the Danebury database. Some of the better-preserved examples (such as Maiden Castle) clearly show evidence for an organization of internal activities that emphasizes the difference between the right- and left-hand sides of the house. This provides support for the presence of the underlying cosmological structure identified by Parker Pearson. Unlike the evidence from the large Late Bronze Age/Early Iron Age houses, the Middle Iron Age evidence is unambiguously derived from the occupation of the house. In contrast, the absence of a clearly identified inner ring of structural posts at most sites suggests the structural difference between core and periphery was much less significant in this period. Nevertheless, the hearths, in contrast to Middle Bronze Age hearths, were located near the centre of the house and were a carefully constructed feature. Well-built ovens also become an identifiable feature in this period.

The Late Iron Age house

The existence of a distinctively different Late Iron Age house seems likely but is as yet unproven. It has been difficult to identify houses on a number of Wessex sites that have good evidence for Late Iron Age occupation (e.g. Winnall Down) and it is assumed that rectangular houses were becoming more common. However, in some of the Dorset hillforts, such as Maiden Castle, Late Iron Age roundhouses are identifiable. This might indicate the conservative nature of Dorset, compared with Berkshire, Hampshire, and Sussex, but this remains to be proven.

The site at Compact Farm, Worth Matravers, Dorset, is a good example of a Late Iron Age house that continues the traditions of the Middle Iron Age (Graham *et al.* 2002). A small settlement dating from the first century BC to the second century AD was found during the excavation of a late Roman barn, and this contained two houses, the earliest of which was particularly well preserved. This house had a stone wall, 1.10 m wide, that enclosed an area 6.20 m in diameter (Figure 4.11). The entrance faced east-south-east and outside the house was an area 2.2 m², paved with limestone slabs which extended through the entrance passage up to the line of the inner wall face. At this point there was

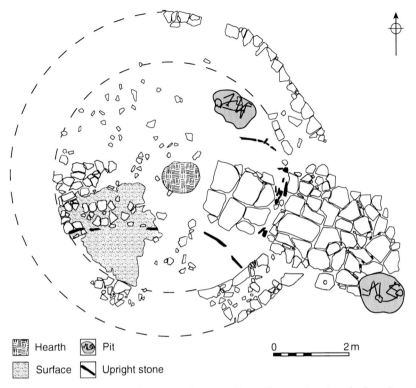

Figure 4.11 A Late Iron Age house at Compact Farm, Dorset showing the location of two later burials (after Graham *et al.* 2002: figs. 1.6 and 1.9).

a slot filled with small upright slabs, with a small post hole at the south end, which indicates the position of the door.

The principal feature in the interior of the house was a small baked clay hearth and between this and the doorway was another area of limestone paving. On either side of this paving, though well set back, were upright slabs which channelled people into the centre of the house. There was one other upright partition which ran from the south-west edge of the house towards the inner edge of the south entrance partition. Together they create a well defined space in the south half of the house. The west side of this area was covered with limestone fragments and the area to the north of this partition, the back of the house, also had a rough limestone paving.

A floor layer was present and it contained fragmented pot, animal bone, shale, and rounded pebbles. Pottery, shale, and bone were fairly evenly distributed across the interior (Graham, Hinton, and Peacock 2002) though concentrations were noted just inside the doorway and along the south edge of the house wall. Sieving of the floor layer also indicated blacksmithing debris was present and this was concentrated on the east side of the partitioned area in the south (left-hand) side of the house. The excavator relates this to the evidence for a hearth on the northern side of this partition and argues that the partition would have been too low to form a boundary between these two areas, though this seems a rather tenuous argument. Analysis of the carbonized plant remains from the floor also showed a difference between the clean grain from the north side of the house and waste material in the south side of the house.

The house was systematically dismantled and covered with rubble, but between these two acts, a grave was dug in the interior close to the destroyed north wall. A middle-aged male was placed in this grave in a crouched position on his right-hand side with his head to the west. This must have occurred very soon after the house was abandoned and it is difficult not to assume that the individual was connected in some way with the occupation of the structure, and that his burial position against the north wall is significant. Another grave was found just outside the entrance to the house, but this seems to be a Roman burial.

The house is unfortunately rather isolated and cannot be assumed a representative of Late Iron Age house use. Nevertheless, it does indicate the continued importance of circularity, central hearths, entrance orientation to the east-south-east and an occupation that differentiates between right and left sides of the interior. There is clearly considerable continuity with the Middle Iron Age forms discussed above, in this one area of Dorset.

Destruction/Death

The abandonment or 'death' of a house is a very important point, which again is seldom discussed by archaeologists (but see Gerritsen 2003: 95–102; Tringham 2005). This is partly to do with the poor quality of the evidence for houses on most settlements, but it is clear that there were distinctive practices associated with house abandonment that require highlighting.

In the 1970s and 1980s, there was a lengthy debate about how long a roundhouse would survive as a viable structure. How fast would decay eat away the principal timber and thatch elements in an Atlantic climate where rain is a problem? The pessimistic view taken by authors such as Drewett (1982: 343) is that decay was relatively fast, and that houses might last only 15–25 years; but a more accurate picture emerged in the 1990s when the experimental work that had begun in the 1970s matured.

The work on the Pimperne reconstruction is particularly important in emphazising the potential longevity of these structures (Harding, D. W. *et al.* 1993). When this structure was dismantled, 14 years after it had been built, it proved to have very little structural decay that would threaten the stability of the house.[29] The most problematic areas of rot appeared to have been caused by leakage during one of the periods of roof repair that resulted from the inadequately thin layer of thatch laid down when the house was built. The only area of persistent rot that is likely to be historically significant was around the entrance, and it was decided that the damaged posts had to be replaced. This proved to be a relatively simple and safe process that produced an archaeological signature that could be recognized in the original excavations.

This work suggests roundhouses were inherently stable structures that could last for a considerable period of time.[30] This hypothetical longevity is, however, a problem when we look at the archaeological record. There is little evidence for substantial repairs on later prehistoric houses and, when these are noted, they tend to be found in the area around the entrance that Reynolds highlighted as subject to early decay. Brück suggests that the most likely interpretation of this pattern in the Middle Bronze Age was that 'settlements might be established upon marriage, occupied throughout the life of the head of the household and his or her spouse and abandoned upon their deaths' (Brück 1999: 149); a lifespan was estimated to be 20–40 years. This would be very much at the lower end of the estimated life of a timber house. A short lifespan for houses appears to be supported by sites, such as Reading Business Park, where several houses were built one on top of the other without much evidence for a lengthy period of occupation. A short lifespan seems to be a cultural tradition that spans most of later prehistory and most of Britain.[31]

One of the distinctive features of the Middle Bronze Age settlement record is the absence of house sites that show repeated rebuilding. In Brück's (1999) analysis of the sites in southern England only five of 76 houses were found that

---

[29] It should be emphasized that the Pimperne reconstruction was not permanently occupied, which is likely to have exacerbated problems, particularly those of damp and rot. A permanently occupied house would have a fire constantly on the go, keeping the house warm, and the smoke generated by the fire would have helped preserve the thatch. The occupants would also have been much more diligent when it came to repairing the roof and it is unlikely they would have tolerated the floods that swept down the valley.

[30] Brück (1999: 149) quotes a claim by Reynolds that they would last over 100 years and a claim by Frances Pryor that they could last indefinitely.

[31] An exception to the rule is the Atlantic Province of Scotland where the inhabitants developed a tradition of monumental roundhouse construction at the beginning of the Iron Age that created houses that lasted generations (Sharples 2006).

had been completely rebuilt on the same spot,[32] and the overwhelming majority of the houses examined showed no sign of significant alteration to the earth-fast timbers (Brück 1999: 147). The pattern suggests there were taboos that prevented the reoccupation of a house site, and these restrictions created a distinctive settlement pattern for the Middle Bronze Age landscapes of southern England.

At Itford Hill in Sussex (Burstow and Holleyman 1957), what appeared to be a village, to the original excavator, was reinterpreted as a settlement of one family group that shifted location every generation (Figure 4.12; Ellison 1978). Similarly, the settlement at Blackpatch represented at least two phases with two major houses in each phase (Russell 1996a). In this case the later houses had been positioned to fill in the gaps between the earlier houses. In other situations, such as at Easton Lane, Hampshire (Fasham *et al.* 1989), a more dispersed pattern is visible and the houses were scattered across a landscape divided by fields.

This Middle Bronze Age pattern of relocation and short lifespans appears to be widespread across southern Britain and might explain the large numbers of houses that belong to this period.[33] This tradition has been explained by Brück (1999) as a fairly natural response to the dynamic nature of the households that occupied these structures. Following the work of Goody (1966), she envisages the household moving through a cycle of growth, maturity, and decline:

- the initial impulse to create a house coincides with the decision to commence reproduction;
- the household matures and reaches its maximum level of production when children are old enough to be used as a labour force; additional buildings may be required;
- upon adulthood the children disperse to create their own households and buildings are abandoned;
- inevitably the original inhabitants die or become too infirm to continue on their own and the settlement is abandoned or destroyed.

In this model the residential basis of the household was not continued and children are not encouraged to stay with the ageing parents, to inherit the farm and the land that surrounds it. This suggests that inheritance and property

---

[32] A good example of a Middle Bronze Age house rebuilt on the same spot is roundhouse IV at Patcham Fawcett, Brighton, East Sussex. The main structural post holes occur as pairs and the entrance has been slightly displaced (Greatorex in Rudling 2002: 273–4).

[33] A similar pattern is characteristic of the north European plain in later prehistory. Extensive spreads of houses appear to indicate the houses had short lifecycles and that later generations deliberately avoided building on top of earlier houses. This settlement pattern continued well into the Iron Age in northern Europe and only comes to an end during the Roman Iron Age (Gerritsen 1999, 2003).

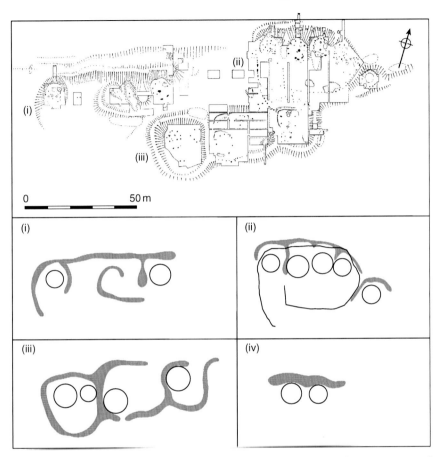

Figure 4.12 A plan of the settlement at Itford Hill, Sussex (after Burstow and Holleyman 1957: fig. facing page 168; reproduced with the permission of the Prehistoric Society) and the sequence of construction proposed by Ellison (1978). The final phase (iv) consists of two houses to the south of the main settlement area and these are not visible on the original plan.

ownership are not an important issue in this period. Andrew Fleming (1988) has argued, on the basis of his analysis of the field systems and houses on Dartmoor, that individual households do not own their own land and that instead this was owned by a community comprising several households, with the land farmed communally. A communal system of landownership is certainly one that would explain the lack of interest in household continuity visible in the Middle Bronze Age.

It has been a feature of recent writing on the household to stress the conflicts that are inherent within domestic units of males, females and children

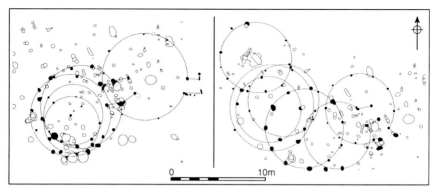

0   10m

Figure 4.13 Two Late Bronze Age house sequences at Reading Business Park (after Brossler and Allen 2004: figs. 13 and 16; reproduced with the permission of Oxford Archaeology). Houses are repeatedly rebuilt on the same spot, creating a confusion of post holes which can only be tentatively interpreted with careful analysis.

(Birdwell-Pheasant and Lawrence-Zúñiga 1999). Conflict is particularly common in households that contain several generations and include incoming wives or husbands who are competing with the indigenous patriarch or matri-arch. Such situations normally encourage fission, which would not be a problem in a landscape relatively under-occupied and in communal ownership.

This system appears to have changed in the later Bronze Age, as one of the characteristics of this period is the repeated rebuilding of houses on the same location. This is a feature of quite small single farmsteads on the chalk such as Coburg Road, Dorset (Smith, R. J. C. *et al.* 1992), where a cluster of post holes suggests that a row of three houses was rebuilt on the same spot twice (Figure 2.15). It is also a feature of the much larger settlements that are found on the Thames gravels. The extensive excavations at Reading Business Park (Moore and Jennings 1992; Brossler *et al.* 2004) revealed a number of areas that were densely occupied in the Late Bronze Age. Some of these areas had isolated houses but others were much more complex. In area 5 clusters of post holes suggest the presence of many houses built on the same spot (Figure 4.13).

This pattern of rebuilding on the same spot is also a distinctive feature of most of the large houses built in the Late Bronze Age/Early Iron Age transition period. The houses at Flint Farm, Little Woodbury, Dunstan Park and Pim-perne (Figures 4.14, 4.9) were rebuilt twice with only a marginal difference in the location of the building.[34] A slightly more complex situation is visible at

---

[34] The houses at Old Down Farm (Davies 1981) and Dunstan Park (Fitzpatrick *et al.* 1995) have not previously been interpreted as representing two phases but both houses have double post rings that are not concentric and the porch structures have intercutting post holes that

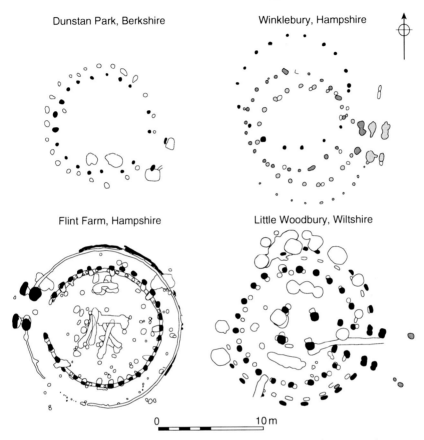

Figure 4.14 The plans of four large Late Bronze Age/Early Iron Age houses at Dunstan Park, Berkshire; Winklebury, Hampshire; Flint Farm, Hampshire; Little Woodbury, Wiltshire. Dunstan Park, Flint Farm and Little Woodbury have two phases of construction; Winklebury has four phases of construction (after Fitzpatrick 1984: fig. 35; Smith 1977: fig. 5; Cunliffe and Poole 2008: fig. 6.17; Bersu 1940: fig. 20).

Winklebury (Smith, K. 1977) where a less well-preserved house appears to have been rebuilt at least three times (Figure 4.14; Guilbert 1981: 301–2). Only at Longbridge Deverill, Cow Down (Hawkes, S. C. 1994), did the inhabitants choose not to rebuild on the same spot.

It may be significant that some of the Late Bronze Age/Early Iron Age houses are located in substantial enclosures surrounded by ditches. These

indicate two phases. These houses were heavily ploughed and it is quite possible that the outer wall posts have been destroyed by cultivation as they were at Winklebury. If the post rings represent two internal structures then these houses become comparable in size to the houses at Pimperne and Little Woodbury.

are quite different from the relatively loosely defined enclosures that surround the Middle Bronze Age settlements at Itford Hill and Blackpatch. The repeated rebuilding of the large house at Winklebury was not because there was a lack of space inside this hillfort and this is also true for the rebuilt houses at Old Down Farm and Dunstan Park. The builders of these houses chose to reoccupy the location of an earlier house. In all these replacements the area of the entrance is the least displaced. This seems to be used to orient the later house in relation to the earlier house and emphasizes the importance of the threshold. This is likely to indicate an increasing concern with place and might also suggest the growing importance of landownership.

The relationship of these consecutive large houses helps to clarify the social significance of these structures. The close juxtaposition of the structural elements suggests the time between the abandonment of one house and the construction of the other is quite short. If one accepts the evidence from the Butser experiment that these houses would have endured for a long time, then the demolition and reconstruction of these houses must have served a social purpose. The Butser experiment also suggests that the timbers of the original house would, with a few minor losses, have been capable of being used in the new house. Unfortunately, the evidence does not normally provide enough information to demonstrate what happens to the posts of the abandoned buildings.[35]

An important feature of the post holes of the Late Bronze Age/Early Iron Age houses at North Popley, Basingstoke (Wright pers. comm.), Houghton Down (Cunliffe and Poole 2000e: 25–9), Longbridge Deverill (Hawkes, S. C. 1994), and Brighton Hill South (Fasham, Keevil and Coe 1995) is the presence of large quantities of heavily vitrified pottery, which has clearly been deposited after the posts had been removed (Webley 2007). At Houghton Down the greatest quantity of debris came from CS2, which was the only structure to have another built directly on top of it. The sherds were concentrated in the post holes around the entrance, which remained in the same location despite the rebuilding.

The deposition of this pottery suggests a deliberate attempt to mark the end of the use of the house and the household that occupied it, and one may presume this also marks the death of the inhabitants, or at least the death of the pre-eminent inhabitant. Destruction suggests that there may have been no direct succession between the occupants and their descendants; in other

---

[35] It should be possible to tell from the post hole fills whether a post has been extracted or rotted in situ and whether the resultant hole was allowed to fill in gradually or was deliberately infilled. Unfortunately, despite the routine excavation of sections across the post holes and the identification of different fills, these are almost never discussed and interpreted in the reports.

words, there was no heir who could assume ownership. This would support
the argument that the social norm in the Bronze Age was for children to
establish their own household when they assumed adulthood. It would
suggest that any children present in the house when the household head
died would be unsuitable to inherit the house. The immediate reconstruction
of the house implies that the location, and association with the previous
household, was important. The new owners inherited or acquired a position
of influence by the act of re-construction and perhaps the physical appropriation of the timbers of the old house. The new owners may have been the
descendants of the original occupants, who were moving back to their old
home (and presumably abandoning a less auspicious house in the process),
but this need not be the case. It could be that a more distant relative aspired to
lead the community and that they made their aspirations known by the act of
occupation and rebuilding.

The symbolic significance of these large Late Bronze Age/Early Iron Age
houses appears to be emphasized by this distinctive process of house construction on the same location. It is noticeable that despite the appearance of
enclosures, and the increasing concern with residing in the same location,
many of the smaller Late Bronze Age and Early Iron Age houses continue
deliberately to avoid earlier houses. The settlement sequence at Winnall
Down/Easton Lane illustrates this quite clearly (Figure 4.15; Fasham 1985;
Fasham *et al.* 1989). The sequence began with a dispersed pattern of up to 11
Middle Bronze Age houses that were scattered across an area divided into
fields by shallow ditches. The most concentrated area of settlement comprised
three houses, a rectangular structure, and a fenced enclosure in the south-east
corner of the excavated area. This was replaced in the Late Bronze Age by a
group of three circular houses and an ancillary structure that lay approximately 150 m to the north-east. This new location was at the end of a
low ridge separating two dry valleys, which was a very characteristic Iron Age
settlement location. The Early Iron Age enclosure was subsequently built
behind these west-facing houses; the enclosure ditch cut through two of the
houses and the west-facing entrance of the enclosure opened onto the southern edge of the Late Bronze Age settlement. This must have been a deliberate
and highly symbolic orientation as most Iron Age enclosures, like the houses,
face to the east or south-east (Hill 1996: fig. 8.9). In the early Middle Iron
Age the settlement moved again. There were two principal clusters of houses;
one *c.*120 to 140 m to the north-west, and one almost directly west of
the enclosure, about 70 m in front of the entrance; neither area had
been previously occupied. In the late Middle Iron Age the settlement
returned to the site of the Early Iron Age enclosure, where the occupants
recognized and utilized the ancient enclosure boundary (Hill 1995b: 89).

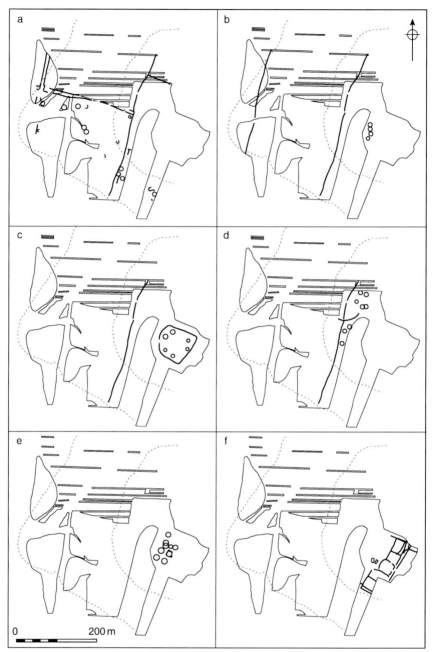

Figure 4.15 The sequence of settlement activity on the spur of land known as Winnall Down/Easton Lane: a) Middle Bronze Age, b) Late Bronze Age, c) Early Iron Age, d) early Middle Iron Age, e) late Middle Iron Age, f) Late Iron Age to Roman (after Fasham *et al.* 1989: figs. 30, 64, 66, 67, 72, and 75).

This was the first time the inhabitants of this area had moved onto a location that had been previously occupied.

The main focus for the Late Iron Age/Roman settlement lay to the south of the Middle Iron Age settlement, though the rectangular enclosures partially overlay the Early Iron Age enclosure and the late Middle Iron Age settlement. All these movements were located at the west end of a low east-west oriented ridge that looks across the valley of the River Itchen. The movements seem to represent an attempt to occupy a prominent place in the landscape without actually building houses on the same spot as the previous generation.

The increasing desire to occupy enclosures and hillforts in particular, in the Iron Age, appears to undermine the desire for residential mobility observed in the later Bronze Age. The construction of the ramparts of a hillfort indicates a long-term commitment to place (see Chapter 3) and implies that houses will be rebuilt on the same spot for many years. Hillfort construction might therefore be expected to encourage the adoption of structures that spanned more than one generation. In contrast, the small Middle Iron Age houses are less substantial structures than those constructed in the Middle Bronze Age and there is no evidence that they have a life prolonged beyond one generation. It is also difficult to identify structures that have been repeatedly rebuilt on the same spot that are comparable to the large buildings of the transition period. If we look at the plan of the interior of the hillfort at Winklebury, Hampshire (Smith, K. 1977), it is noticeable that only one of the small houses of the Middle Iron Age occupation overlapped with an Early Iron Age house and none of these houses overlaps with another. There seems to have been more than enough space in the interior of this hillfort to maintain spatial and temporal separation. Similarly, at Pilsden Pen, in Dorset, the excavation of a large area in the interior of a Middle to Late Iron Age hillfort exposed about 18 houses (Gelling 1977). Only one of these houses (hut 13) had evidence for repeated rebuilding and there is only one other location (hut 8) where two possible houses might have overlapped.

These two hillforts are arguably relatively short-lived places and it is clear that on developed hillforts, such as Maiden Castle and Danebury, the pressure on space was much greater and this inevitably resulted in the repeated construction of houses on the same spot. A good example of this is the quarry hollows around the periphery of the hillfort at Danebury where the evidence indicates a long sequence of activity (Cunliffe and Poole 1991). One of the largest areas examined in detail (area A/D) is located immediately to the north of the south-east entrance (Figure 4.16). The early activity in this area was destroyed by a quarry dug to provide chalk for the construction of rampart 3, at the beginning of period 5, about 270 BC (Cunliffe and Poole 1991: 228–31; Cunliffe 1995: 18). The creation of the quarry provided ideal

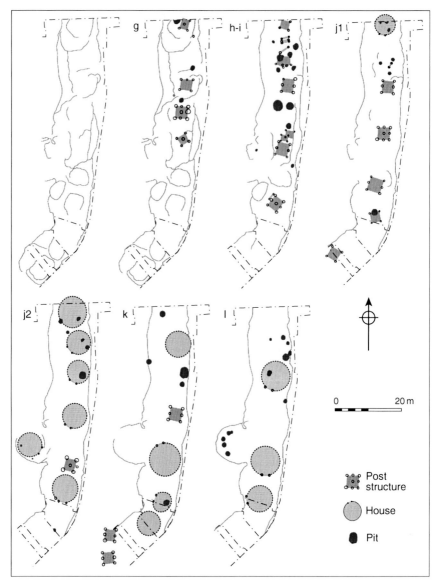

Figure 4.16 The sequence of activity in the quarry hollow to the north of the east entrance at Danebury (after Cunliffe and Poole 1991: figs. 106–12). In the early phases (g and h–i) the structural evidence consists of rectangular post-built structures that are normally interpreted as granaries. These structures are sealed by a relatively uniform and extensive layer that was interpreted as silt accumulating in this area during a period of abandonment.

conditions for the identification of an archaeological sequence since soil, eroding from the interior of the hillfort and the ramparts, naturally accumulated in the hollow and sealed the evidence for human activity.

The quarry was a continuous trench excavated immediately behind the inner rampart but within it there are deeper discrete quarry pits that may indicate work units, and these pits structure the later occupation of the area. The phases described in the caption to Figure 4.16 are all contained within period 6 which begins about 270 BC and should end around 50 BC. There are 12 events, including two silting phases of unknown duration, and these events span a period of approximately 220 years. This suggests that each event was roughly 18 years long. Clearly some of these events, such as the silting phases and the initial quarrying phase, may be shorter than the occupation of a house, but the time scale suggests each event was equivalent to, or less than, the adult life of an individual.

There is only one phase (j2) when a row of residential roundhouses exists in the quarry hollow. The following phase (k), which appears to be similar, comprised several working floors with hearths that are not interpreted as houses. Furthermore, none of the houses present in phase k has a hearth. This might indicate they were not residential structures but ancillary buildings for storage, or workshops. Alternatively it might indicate that the source of heat

---

The next phase of activity (j1) contained a roundhouse. This was a relatively small structure, 6.2m in diameter, but it had a central hearth, which was rebuilt, and an oven. Immediately adjacent to this house was a working floor (not marked) and further south were three pits and five granaries.

The following phase (j2) was a dramatic change: six roundhouses were built and only one granary; one house was built above the earlier house, one above the working floor, three replaced granaries, and the final house was built on the edge of the quarry in an area not previously used. All but one of these houses had a central hearth and high densities of bone and pot (Brown in Cunliffe 1995: 139–144). At the end of this phase there was another period of abandonment that sealed these structures under a thick layer of silt.

The following phase (k) involved the construction of three houses, extensive laid chalk surfaces (not shown), five pits and three granaries. None of the houses had hearths and only one was a direct replacement of an earlier house. Two of the structures had doorways oriented to the west and one of these had a noticeably low density of pottery, bone, and small finds. These structures were again sealed by a layer of silt.

The final phase of activity (l) had three houses and two pit clusters. The northern house was built over a working floor and was rebuilt during this phase. The central house is a rebuilding of an earlier house and it is very interesting to note that the entrances faced in opposite directions and there were two completely separate ovens placed in each half of the house. All of the surfaces and houses in this phase had high densities of pot and bone and small finds were frequent discoveries.

and light was less permanent than in previous periods and did not leave an archaeological residue.

Very few houses are rebuilt on the same spot without an intervening period of abandonment. The clearest examples, CS54 and CS7/8, are at the very end of the sequence. It would seem, therefore, that a prohibition on rebuilding on the same spot as a dead relative might still exist. Analysis of the finds (Brown in Cunliffe 1995) also emphasizes that most of the small finds associated with houses derive from the silt layer above these houses rather than from occupation deposits. This might indicate that the objects are deliberately placed after the abandonment of the houses in some sort of commemorative act.

The construction process is remarkably coherent. Despite a complex sequence of granaries, houses, activity areas, and silting, these maintained the spacing of the original quarry pits created over 200 years earlier.[36] If one assumes that the original quarries represent organized work groups that were constructing the phase 3 rampart, and that these gangs were organized around kinship links, then it seems quite possible that these kin groups established property rights over the area immediately adjacent to the rampart. These property rights appear to have been maintained throughout the remaining life of the hillfort and were possibly associated with the maintenance of the adjacent area of the rampart, though this seems to have been an increasingly minimal responsibility in later years.

It is also interesting that the quarry area was initially used for the construction of granaries and only later became the location for domestic settlement. Perhaps this simply represents the increasing density of people occupying the hillfort. However, it may be that the refurbishment of the hillfort required the construction of some conspicuously substantial grain stores that could be seen above the new ramparts.

A similar situation is visible in the area excavated behind the inner rampart of the expanded hillfort at Maiden Castle (Sharples 1991a: trench D). The initial structures in the area behind the rampart were four-post granaries; only much later were these replaced by houses. In one terrace, three houses were built one on top of the other. Each was a complete building which had its own structural timbers and floor layers. The floors were separated by *c.*20 cm of soil that appears to be fairly homogeneous silt, and which was initially interpreted as a natural accumulation. Soil micromorphological analysis subsequently indicated this was a midden layer, a deliberately placed organic

---

[36] These silting phases may indicate the abandonment of the hillfort, but it is difficult to explain the continuity of construction in the rampart area if there had been a long period of abandonment. I would envisage people occupying other areas of the hilltop during these silting episodes.

deposit, that attempted to cover over the house, prior to its rebuilding. The other houses, in what appears to be a row of houses behind the rampart, were also rebuilt, but the evidence for a period of separation before the rebuilding is less clear.

The analysis of the sequences at Winnall Down and Danebury suggests that, despite the evidence for increasing residential stability in the Iron Age, there was still a reluctance to reoccupy places that had been previously occupied by houses. This was clearly not as big a taboo as it was in the Middle Bronze Age and the decision to occupy permanent enclosures forced people into devising enabling rituals that allowed them access to previously occupied ground. Nevertheless, it highlights the unusual character of the Late Bronze Age/Early Iron Age period when the locations of large houses were almost always reoccupied.

CONCLUSION

This detailed analysis of the house has, I hope, demonstrated the complex social significance of domestic space in both the Bronze Age and the Iron Age. I have argued that the origin of the distinctively different circular houses of later prehistoric Britain is closely related to the abandonment of the large timber circles of the Late Neolithic and Early Bronze Age. The Middle Bronze Age houses adopted a circular structure that relates to the sky and the movement of the sun and which could be used to chart the temporal progression of days and years. The transformation at the end of the Early Bronze Age represents the secularization of time. Prior to this, the measurement of time was undertaken within ritual structures (free-standing post circles) that were possibly controlled by ritual elites and restricted to locations that were contained by enclosures (henges), which may well have acted to exclude the bulk of the population. After this, the ability to measure time was placed at the centre of routine daily practice in the house.

The alignment of the entrance and the position of the hearth in these circular buildings provided two key structures that ordered temporal movements and provided metaphors that clarified the individual's role within their family and in relation to other groups. Temporal cycles were marked by the movement of the sun from east to west and were reflected in the use of the southern and the south-western parts of the house as an activity area. The hearth, in contrast, provided a central feature that may well have acted as a metaphor for the central role of the household. It may be overly simplistic to suggest that the architectural visibility of the hearth and the entrance reflect the importance of the social metaphor in different societies, but it is clear that the adherence to these structures varied in different areas of Wessex, and in different periods of later prehistory.

In the Middle Bronze Age the absence of a well-defined hearth is significant and might imply that the central role of the household was less significant than in the Middle Iron Age when houses of a roughly similar size had very distinctive, well-made hearths. However, we must take into consideration the relationship of the house within the community. In the Middle Bronze Age the house was isolated in the landscape and there seems no need to question the social centrality of the household. In contrast, the Middle Iron Age houses of Danebury and Maiden Castle are located in densely occupied settlements; they are surrounded by rows and rows of identical structures. In this situation, the independence of the household may well have been severely constrained by the community (see Chapter 5) and the hearth may have been a symbol of that threatened status.

Similarly, the significance of movement and its relationship to daily and seasonal routines of work may be stressed at different points in the life of the house. It is clear that, in the Late Bronze Age/Early Iron Age transition, this feature of house architecture was strongly emphasized at the end of the life of a house when broken vitrified pottery was rammed into post holes on one side of the house and not the other. However, in the Middle and Late Iron Age the routine occupation of houses, such as those at Maiden Castle and Worth Matravers, created occupation deposits that commemorated these activities. This may simply reflect the unusually good preservation of these houses but it might be that there was a conscious decision to allow deposits to accumulate that were normally carefully removed from the house in order to mark these cycles.

The centrality of the household is also reflected in the constructional history of the house. Throughout later prehistory it seems that houses were built to last for a short period of time equivalent to the lifecycle of the adults who built and occupied them. This did not vary even though the structures themselves could be relatively flimsy or immensely substantial. The flimsy structures of the Middle Iron Age were relatively easy to remove and erase, whereas the massive structures of the Late Bronze Age/Early Iron Age transition required a specific act of destruction that might involve a spectacular fire or a sustained piece of systematic dismantling. The resources absorbed by the Late Bronze Age/Early Iron Age houses would have been substantial and, together with the evidence for the construction of hillfort ramparts and palisades, suggest that the period witnessed an unsustainable assault on the natural environment, which may well have accompanied the breakdown of traditional power structures in these communities.

Middle Bronze Age houses are slightly more substantial than Middle Iron Age houses, though the space enclosed is similar. This might reflect the relative availability of timber in the increasingly denuded environment of the chalk downland, but it is also possible that it reflects a relationship with the landscape. Middle Bronze Age houses are scattered across large territories broken up by field boundaries (see Chapter 2), and their substance may therefore reflect a desire to claim a relationship with the land that was held collectively. In contrast, Middle Iron Age houses are placed in well-defined locations that have long histories of occupation. The households do not require substantial architecture to establish their position, particularly as the settlements are separated from the agricultural landscape by enclosing boundaries and their location on hills. The house occupants probably spent long periods away from the house simply to undertake their routine agricultural tasks.

I would like to end this chapter by noting the absence of any substantive discussion of Late Iron Age houses. Some examples have been identified that seem to continue Middle Iron Age traditions but it is likely that the rarity of structural evidence in many Late Iron Age sites indicates the development of a new architecture that is more susceptible to destruction and is therefore invisible in the archaeological record. If we accept that the house had a central metaphorical significance throughout the later Bronze Age and Iron Age then the archaeological absence of Late Iron Age houses must represent a significant transformation of social relationships in the last century before the Roman conquest. The centrality of the household appears to have been undermined in this period—this will be one of the themes we explore in the next chapter, where I shall examine the importance of the individual.

5

Defining the Individual

During the 1985 excavation at Maiden Castle (Sharples 1991a), a large grain storage pit cut into the back of the rampart of the Early Iron Age hillfort was excavated. About half way down the fill of that pit the left femur of a mature adult was exposed. This bone was lying in a relatively sterile soil layer and it was not marked by any special finds or careful constructions; in many respects it could easily be dismissed as a discovery with little significance. Fifty years ago such bones would have been regarded as accidental losses, simply rubbish conveniently disposed of in a handy receptacle. It could be an indication that excarnation was the general means of disposal and that this occurred close to or actually inside settlements, but it might also indicate the accidental disturbance of human remains in graves located at the hillfort.

In recent years we have come to understand that these deposits are much more significant. A number of archaeologists (Whimster 1981; C. Wilson 1981; Cunliffe 1992) came to realize that the presence of human remains on Iron Age settlements was a distinct cultural tradition characteristic of central southern England. The work of J. D. Hill (1995b) has enhanced our understanding of this phenomenon by emphasizing that the deposition of human remains is part of a complex suite of actions which involves the arrangement of different categories of material in carefully placed deposits. The process of deposition was clearly intimately involved in the definition of social relationships in the Iron Age of central southern England.

It is difficult to imagine that if we, as archaeologists, could immediately recognize a human bone, our ancient pit diggers could not. The placement of this bone was a deliberate act, and the location of this deposit was carefully chosen. Hill (1995b) has shown that these pit deposits were carefully structured. Human remains are normally found in layers that are largely sterile, but a pit chosen for the deposition of human bone will normally have fills containing other carefully selected deposits. These mark the pit as a bank of socially constructed material.

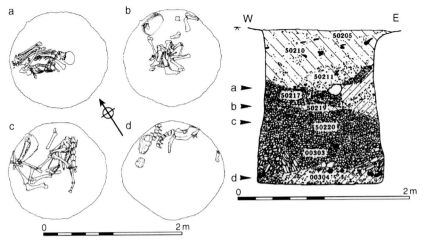

Figure 5.1 Special deposits placed in an Iron Age storage pit dating to the first century BC at Flagstones, Dorset. The four plans show the different deposits placed in the filling of the pit: a) an adult, probably female; b) a deposit of cattle limbs, a horse jaw, a dog skull and half of a large jar; c) the partial remains of an articulated horse and segments of cattle and cranial fragments of a child less than six months old; d) three cattle skulls and attached neck vertebral (after Smith *et al.* 1997: fig. 34; reproduced with the permission of Wessex Archaeology).

This is certainly the case at Maiden Castle; at the base of the pit containing the human femur was a complete weaving comb, and just above the human bone was a copper alloy brooch (Hull and Hawkes 1987: type 6), which was in use from the late second century BC to the first century BC. It is associated with another, rather less attractive, iron brooch of roughly the same date. Near the top of the pit there was yet another iron brooch of La Tène D2A type, in use from 75 BC to the end of the millennium. The presence of these rare artefacts is significant and is what Hill would expect, given the presence of human remains.

Another good example of the relationship between human remains and material culture is a pit from the first century BC settlement at Flagstones in Dorchester, Dorset (Smith, R. J. C. *et al.* 1997: 44).[1] This has four separate deposits (Figure 5.1): at the base of the pit were three cattle skulls; above this was a deposit of horse and cattle limbs which included the cranial fragments

---

[1] The Iron Age settlement was located inside a Neolithic enclosure, but it is unlikely that this was significant as the ditches of the enclosure were deliberately and completely infilled in the Neolithic.

of an infant less than six months old; above this was a deposit of cattle limbs, a horse jaw, and a dog skull, with half a Late Iron Age jar. Above this was the skeleton of an adult, probably female, in a crouched position on her right-hand side, and with her legs and arms pulled so tightly into her chest that it seems likely that she was bound in this position.

Many of the features of the Flagstones pit are characteristic of pit deposits throughout Wessex; the special animal deposits consist of cattle and horse rather than sheep, the most common animal in later prehistoric settlement contexts; a juvenile human bone was associated with the animal bones; but the complete adult female was isolated. However, as Hill (1995b: 74) has demonstrated, the stratigraphic relationships visible in these deposits change from site to site. At Winklebury, Hampshire, human remains are found in pits with both small finds and wild animals. In the Early Iron Age at Winnall Down, Hampshire, human remains in the Early Iron Age are associated with high pot densities, but in the Middle to Late Iron Age, they are associated with high densities of animal bones. The association of human and animal bones is also visible at Old Down Farm, Hampshire, in the Early Iron Age, and in the late phases of the occupation of the hillfort at Danebury, Hampshire. The location of the deposits within the pit also varies from site to site. At Danebury, complete human bodies are preferentially placed close to or on the base of a pit, whereas fragmentary remains of humans are generally found higher up the fill.

THE INDIVIDUAL

The presence of human remains, bodies, and body parts, is an important and much discussed feature of Iron Age studies. It raises all sorts of questions concerning the spatial and temporal organization of the relationship between people and animals (the culture/nature dichotomy), between people and artefacts, and between the whole and the part. All these relationships need to be considered since they have the potential to tell us a great deal about society in the first millennium BC. It is clear that attitudes to the individual were complex in this period, and in this sense they are reflected in the increasingly complex manner in which archaeologists have begun to theorize the nature of individuality in contemporary societies and in the past. These ideas have recently crystallized around the theory that the individual as a free agent, who can act independently of society, is a fiction arising from the 'radical individualism and liberal political theory of the eighteenth and nineteenth centuries' (Brück 2006: 308). Furthermore, the notion that individuals are wholly bounded by their bodies as an inviolate entity unchanged by different inter-personal relationships, the social and physical contexts in which they find themselves, or their passage through life, is again a cultural construct at variance with anthropological analysis of lived human society (Morris, B. 1994).

In Iron Age studies this idealization of the individual has focused on the warrior chief and to a lesser extent the queen. These individuals are often depicted in popular works on the Iron Age (James 1993: 65) and there is a widely held assumption that they are the prime motivators behind the presence of craft specialization and the creation of monumental structures in later prehistory. There is an almost religious aspect to the assumption that the existence of a complex monument, such as a hillfort, must have required the presence of an individual, who could plan the layout and organize the massive labour force required for its construction. In his discussion of the developed hillfort at Maiden Castle Wheeler refers to 'the work of a master-mind, wielding unquestioned authority and controlling vast resources of labour. The whole plan is now knit together into a single unit with a single personality' (Wheeler 1943: 45). These attitudes are somewhat comparable to the belief that the world is so complex, there has to be a god who has designed it. However, belief in 'intelligent design' or a hillfort master builder is undermined by the desire of most architects to make things simple and suggests at best a capricious, if not patently stupid, designer was responsible for many hillforts where the complex and long drawn-out nature of the construction process undermines the idea of a coherent plan (see Bowden and McOmish 1987 for a discussion of hillfort design).

This belief in the inevitable agency of the great 'man' was an abiding feature of both Iron Age and Bronze Age studies throughout the twentieth century. However, in recent years, there has been a problem in the identification of homes for these chiefs and leaders. It has long been assumed that these individuals occupied hillforts, but this was challenged by several authors (Hill 1993; Marchant 1989; Stopford 1987) who pointed out that the artefactual evidence for elite goods was poorly represented in hillforts, as was the evidence for prestige buildings (see Chapter 3). This has resulted in some archaeologists (Alcock 1962; Jope 1995) arguing that the chiefs occupied the smaller enclosures where there is evidence for large houses, such as Little Woodbury in Wiltshire, and also for the production of elaborate metalwork, as at Gussage All Saints in Dorset, conveniently ignoring the fact that these are chronologically quite separate phenomena. However, it seems more logical to accept that all-powerful chiefs do not exist in the Wessex Iron Age, and it has even been argued that societies in the Iron Age were relatively egalitarian (Hill 1995a).

The hierarchical view of Iron Age societies has relied upon a suite of evidence derived from a variety of disparate sources. Three principal areas of influence can be highlighted and are outlined below:

- In the Late Iron Age, when a literate society (Rome) was in contact with Britain, noble leaders were clearly identified in south-east England. For example: Caesar names Cassivellaunus and Mandubracius in his account of the Gallic Wars; abbreviations of rulers' names and occasionally the title rex were applied to the coinage of the period (Williams, J. H. C. 2001); and large burial mounds, such as that at Folly Lane, St Albans, are found adjacent to the pre-eminent settlements of the region, e.g. Verlamion, and are presumed to contain the remains of deceased kings (Niblett 1999).

- The archaeological record for central Europe is dominated by burials, marked by massive barrows, and accompanied by large numbers of grave goods (see Chapter 6). Some of the richest burials belong to the Early Iron Age (Hallstatt D and La Tène A), but in the Middle Iron Age there is still an extensive tradition of flat graves where grave goods, including weapons and jewellery, were used to differentiate gender, status, and age.[2]

- In Britain there is one regional tradition, in the Middle Iron Age, that clearly fulfils all the criteria for identifying elite individuals; this is the very distinctive group of burials in the Yorkshire Wolds (Stead 1979). Within this group, particular individuals were clearly distinguished from the bulk of the population by large barrows placed in small cemeteries that were separated from the large cemeteries, which contained the bulk of the population (Stead 1991a). These individuals were laid out in large grave pits amongst the dismantled remnants of the two-wheeled vehicles, 'chariots', that one presumes were used to carry the corpse to the place of burial. Associated with these burials were the elaborate metal fittings that belonged to the chariot, and other offerings that were deliberately placed with the burial. These included swords, mirrors, beads, strange sealed boxes, suits of chainmail, and joints of meat, all of which emphasized the ability of the deceased and their descendants to accumulate wealth.

The Yorkshire burials in particular personify what is felt to be the classic warrior chief, and these burials are the source for the materials carried or worn by the

---

[2] Interestingly, the introduction of cremation as the normative burial rite in the Late Iron Age coincides with a decline in wealthy grave goods that suggests a more egalitarian period immediately prior to the Roman conquest.

Figure 5.2 Peter Connolly's artistic interpretation of a 'British noble couple' (Photo: akg-images, London).

individuals depicted in Figure 5.2 (Stead 1991a). The couple stand in front of a massive Iron Age roundhouse, similar to the Pimperne house recreated at Butser Ancient Farm (see Chapter 4). Some of the more radical postmodern archaeologists may argue that we should deconstruct this image of the Yorkshire chief but I see no reason to doubt the significance of elite culture in the Yorkshire Wolds. However, all these phenomena, the Yorkshire charioteers, the Continental warriors, the Late Iron Age coinage, and historical references, are tightly defined both chronologically and spatially, and represent societies very different from those identified in Wessex.[3]

---

[3] It is worth noting that the few hillforts that have been identified in Yorkshire date to the beginning of the Iron Age, well before the elite burials appear. The Yorkshire elite does not appear to require elaborately bounded settlements or particularly substantial houses to define a status which is so well represented by the elaborate metalwork one finds in these graves.

Bronze Age studies have not been so focused on the identification of chiefs, but the discovery of large quantities of prestige metalwork, and weapons in particular, has suggested the presence of a warrior elite that dominated society. The nature of the elite is often embellished by comparison with early Greek texts such as the *Iliad* and the *Odyssey* (Rowlands 1980) that purport to describe societies roughly contemporary with, and with similar material attributes to, those in Continental Europe.

Paul Treherne (1995) examined the elaborate burial record in continental Europe and provided a detailed interpretation of these societies. He suggested the emergence of a clearly identifiable burial rite at the beginning of the Early Bronze Age that emphasized the location of identifiable ancestors, in contrast to the anonymity of the community of ancestors visible in the Neolithic, where human remains were jumbled together in large necropolises (Treherne 1995: 113). As the Bronze Age developed there was an increasing concern with the body, which is charted by the presence of toilet implements, such as razors, and weapons. Weapons are a means of extending the body, and play an important role in choreographing the movement of the body. Death challenges the memory of these deceased individuals, and only the remembrance of the dead in an appropriately monumental fashion enables them to transcend the stigma of death. The deposition of toilet implements and weaponry was possibly used to remember specific events in the life of the deceased, and emphasized the creation of a self, an individual personhood, which would have specific genealogical links with the mourners.

Contemporary with these Bronze Age warrior burials in central and northern Europe were a comparably elaborate group of female burials that have been studied by Marie Louise Sørensen (1997). Female burials became increasingly elaborate in the Middle Bronze Age, where it is clear that complex messages were being conveyed about regional and local identities, age groups and status, as well as gender. An interesting difference between male and female decoration was the presence of permanent ornaments attached to female bodies. These consist of arm and leg rings that, once grown into, could not be removed. These clearly restricted and constrained the freedom of the body and, in the Late Bronze Age, these constraints are further emphasized by the presence of leg ornaments that are chained together. These ornaments graphically indicate that status within these societies frequently constrains rather than enables freedom.

Unfortunately for British archaeologists, none of these elaborate Bronze Age burials has been identified in Britain, and though this period is marked by close contact with the Continent and the movement of large quantities of metalwork across the Channel, the material culture of Britain is markedly less complex than that found on the Continent. The archaeological record for Wessex in both the Late Bronze Age and Iron Age is in some ways even more impoverished that for the rest of Britain. There are very few rich graves comparable to the Iron Age graves of Yorkshire,[4] and nothing to compare with those found on the Continent. Even the existence of cemeteries is a matter of some debate prior to the Late Iron Age. There is a reasonable collection of metalwork from the Wessex Late Bronze Age (see Chapter 3), but the objects are not as elaborate or as plentiful as those in other regions, such as the Thames valley or the Fens. However, even these objects disappear at the beginning of the Iron Age where it is almost impossible to find any elaborate or complex object prior to the two centuries preceding the Roman conquest. Coinage appears in these two centuries, but named coinage is restricted to the last five decades and is not a universal adoption throughout the region (see Chapter 3).

It is surely the role of archaeology to devise a model of social relationships which does not conflate societies that have invested a considerable amount of energy in differentiating themselves, especially when these differences are clearly visible in the archaeological record. One of the ways we should start to differentiate between these societies is by appreciating what the burial record is communicating about the nature of individuality in later prehistory. The common occurrence of isolated bones or body parts in the archaeological record, or the incorporation of complete bodies with a series of other materials in grain storage pits, can be interpreted as the presence of individuals who

---

[4] Hunter (2006: 97–9) has suggested that prestige metalwork comparable to that in the Yorkshire burials is present throughout Britain. This view is probably widely shared by other archaeologists. It results from the slightly self-critical nature of archaeologists, who quite often believe that really we know very little about past societies and that much of the evidence is reflected in materials that we cannot recover either because they are organic and have completely decayed or because they have been systematically destroyed and carefully and deliberately hidden in places that archaeologists can never systematically examine (such as the sea). This negative view is undermined by the fact that archaeological work in well-explored areas such as Wessex seldom makes exciting new discoveries that transform our understanding of the Iron Age. The idea that the burial record in Yorkshire simply makes visible what is happening throughout Britain is a misunderstanding of the significance of the archaeological record and the role of material culture. This is not a representation of the past but is the active constitution of social relationships in the past. An elaborately decorated sword did not simply represent the status of that individual who wore it; it was through its ownership that the individual achieved that status. Likewise, the burial of an individual with a series of objects of high value was not simply an indication of the status of that individual but was a ceremony carried out by a group of living individuals who were establishing their own position by discarding a considerable amount of wealth. The archaeological record is not accidental but constitutes the past, and to expect the answer to be concealed from us is a misunderstanding of its reality.

are not indivisible but partible. The body can be broken down as components that represent not the whole body, but a quite different whole that cross-cuts the individual person.

The idea of partible or fractured individuals is one that has become fashionable in archaeological studies since the 1990s. It is particularly common in recent interpretations of the Neolithic (Fowler, C. 2003; Jones, A. 2005; Thomas, J. 2001; Whittle 2003), and body fragments and disarticulated bodies are a recurrent feature of the British Neolithic in settlement contexts and more formal arenas, such as enclosures. These archaeological studies have been influenced by a number of anthropological studies (notably Strathern 1988, Weiner 1992, and Busby 1997 in Melanesia; and Busby 1997 and Marriot 1976 in India). Andy Jones (2005) has expanded these discussions to include an analysis of Mesoamerican and Andean perspectives on the individual. All these anthropological studies emphasize the complex nature of an individual's sense of identity. Marilyn Strathern (1988) has been particularly emphatic in her description of a society where the individual is created through relationships that exist between people, and it is the complexity of these relationships that enable an identity to be created.

Discussions of partible personhood are rare in studies of later prehistory, but a recent paper by Brück (2006) has discussed the concept in relation to the later Bronze Age societies of southern England. Brück argues that the archaeological record is characterized by special deposits whose deposition was closely related to the lifecycle of individuals. Houses, pots, and possibly querns, had a metaphorical relationship with the human body; they 'provided ways of thinking about social relationships and of coping with such processes as biological and social ageing' (Brück 2006: 302). An important feature is the deliberate and thorough fragmentation, or burning, of objects and the association of the broken and burnt material with fertility. Brück suggests these activities indicate 'that life and death were linked in an unending series of transformative cycles through the process of fragmentation and burning' (Brück 2006: 307).

Much of the discussion of partible personhood has focused on the relationship between people and objects and has highlighted the relationships that can be created by the production and exchange of objects. These issues have been examined in detail in Chapter 3. Andy Jones (2005) has also emphasized the importance of architecture in creating and defining relationships, a theme we examined in Chapter 4. The interpretation of burial practices provides a key insight into social relationships and, in combination with the material discussed in previous chapters, provides the basis for a reinterpretation of the later prehistory in Wessex.

THE BURIAL RECORD

Death is undoubtedly a significant event in any society as it disrupts and transforms not just the life of the individual concerned but all those who knew him or her. It is not just that the direct relationships between the deceased and other people (kin, friends, colleagues) are broken but that indirect relationships between these people can be radically transformed by the event. Individuals will take on different roles to compensate for the absence of the deceased and some will be promoted by these changes whilst others will be disadvantaged. The practical necessities of burial combine with the social necessities of this disruption to create a process that is surrounded by symbolism and ritual. Burial not only results in the disposal of the corpse but demands a reconfiguration of social relationships and a reconstitution of society. The process tends to be structured into a number of separate events that require the movement of the remains of the deceased and indicate stages in the journey from the world of the living to the world of the dead, from flesh to dry bones. Anthropology has suggested that these rituals are structured in a threefold pattern (van Gennep 1909).

The journey begins with the movement of the corpse from the place of death to a place of repose, where the body is effectively in storage whilst resources are gathered together for the transformation. The location and significance of this place vary and, in part, depend on the time spent waiting for the process of transformation to begin. This time could be very short and in some societies it is very important that human remains are removed from the world of the living as soon as possible. However, this is not the only response: some societies try to maintain the presence of the deceased for as long as possible, which can lead to treatments that attempt to inhibit physical decay and allow the deceased to continue as a social being a long time after biological death. The location of the place of repose also varies considerably: people may have to be quickly removed from the domestic landscape or they may be able to stay there. Until quite recently it was common in British society for a body to be laid out in a room in the house prior to burial. This allowed people to come around and view the corpse and to pay their respects to the deceased and their living relatives. In contemporary British society this practice is much less common and would probably be regarded as rather peculiar behaviour. Instead, the body is taken away to the mortuary and very few people choose to view the corpse.[5]

---

[5] In contrast, in America a considerable amount of effort and expenditure goes into presenting the corpse to enable a sustained period of viewing to take place (Mitford 1963).

The next stage of the process is the transformation from flesh to bone. This process could occur in a concealed location such as a grave, out of sight and out of mind, but other societies prefer a much more public transformation. Two methods are particularly important, since they involve a very public display of the process and are designed to quickly reduce the body to dry bones: excarnation and cremation.

Excarnation is the public exposure of the corpse to the elements (Carr and Knüsel 1997). The variable effects of wind, rain, and sun will encourage decay, but this practice is also designed to encourage animals to consume the flesh. In Britain there are a few large mammals that are attracted to carrion, such as foxes, but the principal benefactors of this process would have been birds, particularly corvids, who would have been attracted by the smell of decaying flesh. A corpse will normally decay in predicted stages: first the limbs fall off the torso, then the ribs come off the spine, then limbs disintegrate and finally the vertebral column breaks apart. Animals might disrupt this process but the absence of large carnivores would reduce the impact of this disruption. The most convincing evidence for excarnation is the presence of articulated segments of the body, such as a spinal column, pelvic girdles, and articulated hands and feet. To survive as articulated segments, limbs and spinal columns have to be buried when there is still sufficient muscle tissue remaining to hold the bones together.

The practice of excarnation can vary considerably. It need not necessarily be associated with any structural evidence and there are contemporary well-documented practices in China where the body is exposed on rocky outcrops (Martin 1996; Wylie 1965). However, there are also well-documented cases in America (Bushnell 1927; Driver 1961), where platforms were constructed to lay out the corpse. The raising of the body above ground may have had a variety of symbolic meanings but it might also be to encourage consumption by birds rather than mammals. The process of decay can also be very carefully controlled with bodies laid out in covered platforms with guards set to impede unauthorized access by animals (e.g. Sloan 2007: 114–15: pls. 65–6).

Cremation is another common practice that controls and encourages the transformation of flesh to bone. In this case the body was normally transferred to a special location, the pyre site, where the act of cremation would take place. The lighting of the pyre was perhaps the most dramatic part of the process. It would be an event observed by many people. Even those not actually present but going about their daily routine might be able to observe the fire and would certainly have been able to see the smoke. The burning of the body would take time, normally a full day (Downes 1999; McKinley 1997a), and even once the fire had died away it would normally be necessary to wait for the ashes to cool before it became possible to collect the remains of the deceased.[6]

The end product of the practice of cremation and excarnation is a collection of bones that may be left at the pyre/exposure site, buried in specially allocated space, such as a cemetery, or returned to the domestic sphere. In British prehistory, cremated remains generally appear to be deposited at cemetery sites, which can either be at the place of cremation, or separated from it. The amount of the cremated bone present in formal burial is very variable, and it has been suggested (McKinley 1997a) that the amount of time spent collecting the bones is represented by the quantity of bone present, and this may in turn be a reflection of the status of the deceased. The collection process could be done carefully, by hand picking the bones from the ashes, or it could be hurried with the remains of the body raked into a pile and shovelled into a container along with the pyre debris of soil, charcoal, ash, and any offerings that were placed on the pyre. These remains could be placed in a variety of containers for the journey from the pyre site to the area chosen for burial.

The treatment of excarnated remains is more difficult to summarize, and interpretation is open to much more dispute. In Britain the practice is identified in the Neolithic (Hedges 1983: 269) and the Iron Age (Ellison and Drewett 1971; Carr and Knüsel 1997), though in both cases the interpretation may be disputed. In the Neolithic, the bones are brought to chambered tombs (ossuaries) where large quantities can be found,[7] but isolated bones are also present in many other contexts ranging from small settlements to large complex enclosures. In the Iron Age the assumption is that a limited number of selected bones are brought back to the settlements, but that the bulk of the bones are left behind at the exposure site to be consumed or destroyed by the elements. This possibly explains the great shortage of human burials from the region. There is little evidence that transportation of these bones was associated with any particular container, but I would presume that when articulated elements are returned they would be wrapped.

Burial is another opportunity for complex ritual. Choices had to be made about the time and place of burial, the preparation of the remains, the nature of any accompanying offerings, and how the remains were to be contained.

---

[6] The fire could be quickly cooled by water if this was required (Downes 1999: 23). The upland location of most Middle Bronze Age burials would make this an unlikely procedure, as water sources are not present. However, it is possible the pyre sites were much closer to water sources, which would enable the burnt remains to be cooled quickly and also allow for the remains to be washed.

[7] At Quanterness it was argued that over 300 individuals were present, and though this number is possibly inflated, there were a great many bones present (Chesterman in Renfrew 1979).

Of primary concern was the integrity of the remains: were they to be separated from the domestic sphere or were they to be incorporated into it? How were the remains to be contained—by a special container, such as a coffin, or by something that was more commonplace, such as a pot? Offerings could be placed with the dead, either in the container or beside it. Once placed in the grave the remains were covered, though there is evidence for periods of exposure before covering. The grave may then have been marked by a barrow, a post, or simply by the creation of intangible memories. The burial is assumed to be the final act of this three-stage process of transformation, after which the remains are left undisturbed. However, in some cases, the act of burial may be only one part of the process, and the remains may be exhumed and moved on at a later stage.

These events could be drawn out over a long period of time, with numerous pauses for reflection and the gathering together of people and resources; or they could be compressed into a fairly short period of time, marked by appropriate ritual events. Similarly, the location of the events could be quite restricted, occurring close to where the deceased lived, but they could also be spread across the landscape and perhaps reflect the area traversed by the deceased during his daily routine. All these events could be observed by large numbers of people and they could choose to use the occasion for a range of complex interactions. The various potentials do not necessarily reflect the cultural characteristics of a specific society, but might indicate the ritual circumstances of the deceased and his surviving relatives, or the wider cosmological cycle of events at the time of death.

The burial record is clearly crucial to understanding the nature of person-hood in the first millennium in Wessex, and though formal cemeteries and rich grave goods are exceptional, there is still a substantial collection of human remains. This corpus of material has been subject to extensive discussion since the 1980s, and though there appears to be a consensus on the overall nature of the assemblage, and how it was created, it will be shown that this consensus is misplaced. A detailed review of the deposition of human remains in Wessex, from the end of the second millennium BC through to the first century AD, is required to understand how pit burials and isolated bones project a sense of later prehistoric identity.

The analysis will be structured around four basic categories of disposal that are potentially important in this region:

1. burial in settlement contexts;
2. placement in rivers (or other watery places);
3. the use of formal inhumation cemeteries;
4. cremation.

Burials in Settlement Contexts

The presence of human remains in Iron Age settlement contexts has long been recognized as a feature of the southern British Iron Age (Pitt Rivers 1888: 60), but it was only in the 1980s, after detailed examination by Whimster (1981), Wilson, C. (1981) and Wait (1985), that these remains were recognized as a coherent phenomenon worth analytical examination. Wilson, C. (1981) studied settlement burials in southern Britain and identified six categories of deposit:

1. worked or utilized bone; rare in the Iron Age;
2. fragments; 30 sites identified;
3. disarticulated bone; 10 sites identified;
4. articulated joints; rare, but clearly present;
5. partial burials; rare, but clearly present;
6. complete burials; under 300 burials noted.

She drew attention to the problem of reliably categorizing many of the deposits, and emphasized that careful excavation was needed to differentiate these categories.[8] Much of her analysis concerned the nature of the complete skeletons and she identified recurrent traits in the arrangement of these bodies which indicated that this mode of burial was governed by particular rules. The bodies were generally moderately crouched, though flexed and tightly crouched bodies were also present. Amongst the latter were skeletons that were clearly bound, and other individuals could be observed whose hands had been tied together. Most of the burials were arranged with their heads to the north and north-east and were placed on their left-hand side. Obvious gender differences were not observed. Only a few Early Iron Age burials were known, and the increase in burials through time seemed to coincide with a move from peripheral locations to those within the settlement boundary. The low numbers from the Early Iron Age make it difficult to observe change through time, though complete bodies do seem to become more important in later periods. Most of the internal burials were placed in grain storage pits, but peripheral burials were often placed within graves, ditch fills or ramparts.

---

[8] Neonatal remains are a good example of the problems of categorization. It is common for the partial remains of neonatal burials to be found only during examination of the animal bones. The majority of these remains probably represent complete articulated burials unrecognized during excavation and where some of the relatively small bones of the skeleton were accidentally discarded. However, it is quite possible that partial burials or disarticulated remains of newborn babies were buried in a fashion comparable to the partial adult burials. Only very careful excavation would enable this observation to be made.

Wilson (1981) questioned the routinely held belief that excarnation was the source for the partial and disarticulated remains, as there was very little evidence for weathering or gnawing on these bones, and she noted that at least one skeleton, from Winklebury, had been exposed in a grain storage pit. She suggested that bodies might be wrapped and kept as artefacts or mummies. Over the passage of time the wrappings would periodically require replacement, which would lead to the gradual disarticulation of the remains and the loss of individual body parts. The different categories might therefore represent the length of time the body circulated and the increasing presence of complete bodies would indicate a reduction of this period of circulation in the Middle to Late Iron Age.

Wait (1985) had a different classification, which comprised:

1. single complete inhumation;
2. single partial inhumation;
3. multiple partial inhumation;
4. articulated limbs;
5. skulls;
6. individual bones.

His analysis was again focused on southern Britain but was limited to a selected sample of 28 extensively excavated hillforts and non-hillfort settlements, and he was particularly interested in the differences between these two categories and in chronological change. He suggested that partial burials and multiple inhumations are a feature of hillforts, and that skulls, though present on settlements, are more common on hillforts. He identified a clear chronological progression from the Early Iron Age, when isolated bones dominate, particularly in the settlements; through the Middle Iron Age, when individual burials become more common—particularly in settlements; to the Late Iron Age, when the burials in settlements are almost exclusively complete, but when hillforts also develop a range of complex burial rites that include multiple burials.

These changes could be linked to differences in the age and sex of the burials. In both settlements and hillforts, the Early Iron Age assemblage is dominated by adults, often present as isolated bones, but through time the settlements increasingly contained more and more children, invariably as complete burials. It was also observed that female burials are more frequent discoveries in the Late Iron Age. The hillforts had a significant bias towards males in the Middle Iron Age, but otherwise there was a fairly even division of sex in both settlements and hillforts prior to the Late Iron Age. Wait agrees with Wilson's observation that the burials start off in peripheral locations but become increasingly integrated into the interior of the settlement in the Late Iron

Age. He argues that the remains represent a non-normative burial rite, and that the complete burials could represent human sacrifice or outcasts from normal society, whereas skull fragments may indicate ritual activity or votive offerings.

Neither of these studies specifically considered the evidence from Late Bronze Age settlements, though they did incorporate some of the material from middens, such as All Cannings Cross, that would now be considered to begin in the Late Bronze Age. The first comprehensive analysis of Late Bronze Age burial practices was by Brück (1995). This study identified unburnt disarticulated bone in settlement contexts as the most common burial category. The appearance of these remains marked a distinctive break with earlier practices, as human remains were not an important feature of Middle Bronze Age settlements, appearing instead as cremations, or inhumations, in formal cemeteries (see above). A distribution map (Brück 1995: fig. 6) shows the deposition of human remains on Late Bronze Age settlements to be particularly common in southern Britain, whereas many of the other categories identified in this study, such as cremations, hoard, and cave burials, are only found to the north and east.[9] The domestic contexts that produce the bones normally also contain domestic rubbish. Skulls are the most common discovery, followed by long bones, and the remaining parts of the body make up only 11% of the record (Brück 1995: fig. 3). It was possible to make only a limited assessment of age and sex categories, but these showed that most of the remains were from adults and that males and females were roughly equivalent.

Structured Deposition

These studies of human remains are complemented by studies of animal bones, which have similarly wrestled with the presence of articulated, and partially articulated, skeletal material on settlement sites. During the 1980s, the debate was polarized between those who thought these remains were ritual deposits (Grant 1991; Wait 1985), and those who interpreted them as waste from butchery, or meat that had gone bad (Armour-Chelu in Sharples 1991a; Maltby 1985; Wilson, B. 1992). Barry Cunliffe (1992) suggested the deposition of human and animal remains in pits was a special pit burial rite and could not be separated from the deliberate placing of other finds (see also Bradley 1990). These debates culminated in a detailed analysis of depositional practice in the Iron Age of Wessex by Hill (1995b).

[9] This might well be simply a reflection of the poor preservation conditions on settlements outside the calcareous environments of southern and eastern England.

In contrast to the bulk of the work referred to in this chapter, Hill set out to systematically consider the archaeological record for deposition in Iron Age Wessex. His work considered all the categories of material recovered and provided a detailed analysis of their contextual significance in relation to pits and ditches.[10] The analysis was based on the premise that there was no strict distinction between sacred and profane acts of deposition, that deposition is a reflection of a general cultural classification of all materials and that everything is categorized and placed, more or less carefully, in its appropriate place. One of his principal conclusions was that the quantities of material recovered are so small as to represent only a tiny proportion of the activities taking place on a day-to-day basis in the past. This highlights the significance of all the large groups of well-preserved animal bones and pottery fragments. These must indicate very rare special events, feasts perhaps, which he calculated could be as rare as every 10–20 years at Winnall Down, though this seems unduly restricted.[11] There is no possibility of providing a detailed consideration of all the different issues that Hill raised in this very important study, as it provides a serious methodological challenge to the way every archaeologist working in later prehistory should interpret their data. However, his analysis does examine the significance of human remains on settlements and the relationship between human remains and deposits of animals and material culture.

Hill builds up his analysis through a detailed consideration of individual contexts, the structured infilling of pits, and the organization of settlement space. The analysis of individual contexts reveals a pattern of exclusion between different categories of material above a base level of small quantities of badly preserved bone and pot, which has a universal presence in most contexts. Special deposits of human remains, animal bone concentrations or articulated bone groups, and small finds are seldom found in the same contexts. The analysis of the animal bones defined four categories: A, complete/partial skeleton; B, skulls; C, complete/partial articulated limbs; D, portions of vertebral columns. This structure is similar to that used for categorizing human remains but relates to the manner in which animal bones are butchered rather than how the carcass decays. A significant difference between human and animal deposits is the small quantity of complete animal burials and the large numbers of articulated limbs. There

---

[10] Hill did not consider post holes or quarry fills, though he recognized that special deposits were present in these features.

[11] I find these estimates problematic and believe the long intervals between depositions reflect the importance of surface deposits that have been completely destroyed by systematic cultivation.

are certain associations between species but these vary considerab[ly?]
different sites. However, a general point was that dog and horse
portionately represented in the articulated/associated bone grou[p]
They are not more common but if these species are present they :
be found in ABGs. If wild animals are present they were also placed as special
deposits.

Hill's analysis of the pits immediately highlighted associations between
different types of deposits. Human remains are found in close association
with large groups of both pot and bone, ABGs, and small finds, especially if
they are present in large numbers. In general it was normal in the Iron Age to
place an ABG in the basal deposits of a pit, whereas human bones would be
later deposits, placed after the pit had received exceptional deposits of bone,
pot and small finds, though Danebury is an exception and unusually had
basal deposits of complete humans. These patterns indicate that placing a
special deposit was part of a sequence of activities that was probably completed in a relatively constrained time period. The associations are remarkably
inconsistent, varying from site to site and within site from period to period.
However 'three groups of finds seem to have been particularly put in the same
pits as human remains on all sites: quern stones, iron objects, worked bone/
antler' (Hill 1995b: 55). The variability of the record may well highlight
conflicting views on how these activities should take place between residential
groups within the region.

The final stage of the analysis examined how these special deposits were
used to structure settlement space and concentrated on the analysis of
Winnall Down. During the occupation in the Early Iron Age, distinctions
between the front and back of the enclosure, and between the centre and the
periphery, were important. The front had an impressive ditch which had
placed deposits of bone, fine wares, small finds, and adult human remains.
At the back the ditch was a relatively slight feature, and the fill included
some coarse ware pot and complete child burials. Inside the enclosure the
centre was kept free of structures and the few pits present contained only
small quantities of bones but lots of fine ware sherds. In the north corner
was an impressive porched house, the best-preserved ABGs and a hoard of
loom weights. Adjacent to the south side were ancillary buildings and pits
containing one ABG and pottery that was characterized by various unusual
fabrics. At the back of the enclosure a group of two ancillary buildings
was associated with shallow scoops containing small badly-preserved assemblages of bone, high densities of ceramics with unusual fabrics, and two
infant burials.

In the Middle Iron Age the site of the enclosure was reoccupied and though
the enclosure ditch was infilled it was still visible and used as a symbolic

boundary.[12] The settlement was organized into three zones with a formal entrance from the south-east. At the front, facing south-east, was a zone of pits, split in two by the entrance path. Behind this was a band of ancillary buildings and at the back, the north-west, were the inhabited houses. Densities of animal bone rise from south-east to north-west and less well preserved ABGs were close to the houses, particularly cattle and dog, but not sheep. Pot densities are high around the domestic houses and in the pits, and daub was deposited in the pit area. The highest densities of all material are found to the south of the entrance path. Deposits of adult human remains are separated from the settlement by the old enclosure ditch and there was a cluster of burials in the quarry hollows to the north and another cluster in the pits to the south. One burial was placed in a pit that cut the infilled enclosure ditch on the line of the access path, effectively providing a threshold burial. The only human remains found inside the enclosure ditch are children or adolescents. It seems the inhabitants used acts of deposition to structure activity within the settlement and to reinvigorate the abandoned boundary of the settlement area.

These patterns were replicated at other sites and provide a more detailed analysis of the distribution of human remains than that provided by Wilson (1981) and Wait (1985). The important points appear to be:

- a distinction between inside and outside;
- a concern with the cardinal points;
- an emphasis on the threshold;
- a distinction between front and back.

Hill argues that the special deposits present on later prehistoric sites are unconnected with the importance of human remains and cannot be a fertility ritual concerned with the productivity of grain storage pits. Instead, he suggests these sacrificed objects are a means of mediating between the sacred and profane world that provides an insight into how the world was categorized by Iron Age people. The use of animals in particular suggests an important distinction is being made between domesticated species, such as cattle and sheep, and wild species, such as red deer. The principal concern appears to be with animals that are only partially domesticated and have a certain amount of freedom, horse and dog, though the status of pigs and certain species of birds is also important. The close similarity between the treatment of these

---

[12] This might be a slightly misleading statement as I would argue that the shape of the enclosure is designed to fit into the field system established in the Middle Bronze Age (see Figure 4.15) and that this was probably marked by hedges. It may have been the field system that survived to structure the later settlement, rather than the Early Iron Age enclosure.

animals and human remains suggests to Hill that humans are also placed ambiguously between culture and nature: 'The human body was used, amongst other items, as part of a complex strategy of representation, as metonyms for different types of humanity particularly related to age and completeness of the body/subject/agent' (Hill 1995b: 106). The classification of the animal world is argued to be analogous to the classification of the human world. Similarly, the objects preferentially selected for deposition in these special deposits may be incorporated within these systems of classification. Querns in particular might have a complex ritual significance that results from their distribution as specialist products (see Chapter 3). Animal bone and antler tools would also be implicated in the classification of animals. These symbolic classifications are used to partition and differentiate the landscapes that surround settlements and to embellish prohibitions on movement within the settlement context.

Analysing the Record

Most of the surveys discussed above were undertaken some time ago and though many of the most important large assemblages were available to these authors, there has been a steady accumulation of sites producing human remains in the last twenty years that now have to be considered.[13] There have been several particularly important discoveries dating to the first half of the first millennium BC, including an additional set of deposits from Danebury and the Danebury Environs projects. A dataset collected by the author contains 37 sites and almost 700 deposits of human bone. The largest assemblage comes from Danebury and consists of over 300 deposits (Walker in Cunliffe 1984a; Cunliffe and Poole 1991; Cunliffe 1995) that cover the period from the Early Iron Age to the Late Iron Age.[14] However, an important assemblage of 139 disarticulated fragments came from the Late Bronze Age/Early Iron Age midden at Potterne, Wiltshire (McKinley in Lawson 2000), and the extensive excavations at Winnall Down/Easton Lane, Hampshire (Fasham 1985; Fasham *et al.* 1989), and Gussage All Saints, Dorset (Wainwright 1979a)

---

[13] It is also important to note that many sites outside Wessex were included in these studies which are not relevant to the present study.

[14] The number of deposits varied, depending on how mixed bone assemblages are counted. Two bones together could be counted as one but if they are obviously from two different individuals they should be counted as two. In the first volume on Danebury (Cunliffe 1984a), any evidence for age differences led to the bones being given different deposit numbers, but this was not consistently done in the second volume. In the catalogue created to undertake this examination, deposits have been split if there are obvious indications that different individuals are present.

produced 71 and 67 deposits respectively. There is also an important assemblage from Glastonbury, Somerset (Bulleid and Gray 1917) that provides an example from the end of the first millennium BC. These large assemblages dominate the overall picture and essentially provide the basic patterns. It seems sensible, therefore, to describe these sites and some other important assemblages before summarizing the overall patterns.

Potterne, Battlesbury and New Buildings
(Late Bronze Age/Early Iron Age)

Our understanding of the disposal of the dead at the beginning of the first millennium BC is best realized through a consideration of the large assemblage from Potterne, Wiltshire (McKinley in Lawson 2000), and two smaller assemblages from the settlements at Battlesbury, Wiltshire (McKinley in Ellis and Powell 2008) and New Buildings, Hampshire (Cunliffe and Poole 2000c).

The excavations at the midden of Potterne, in the Vale of Pewsey, recovered an assemblage of approximately 139 bones, which came from a very small sample of the midden deposits (McKinley in Lawson 2000). All the remains were isolated fragments except for an articulated foetus, which was not found in the archaeological excavations but during recent grave digging. Skull fragments were the most common bone present, comprising 52.3% of the deposits. Apart from one phalanx and a metatarsal, the rest of the assemblage was largely limb bone; 28.9% were lower limbs, mostly femur, and 19.6% upper limbs. This disparity in the representation of the human skeleton was not the result of differential survival rates. There was no evidence for butchery or gnawing of the human bone but it was more abraded than the animal bone, with only a small quantity (4%) described as fresh (McKinley in Lawson 2000: 97). It seems clear that the bones present in the midden were carefully selected and brought to Potterne for deposition from somewhere else.[15] The bulk of the remains date to the beginning of midden deposition on the site (stratigraphic zones 11 and 10), and were associated with the transition from Post Deverel Rimbury plain wares to Post Deverel Rimbury decorated wares which suggests a date around 800 BC (Morris in Lawson 2000). This assemblage of human bones is comparable to that recovered from similar midden sites at All Cannings Cross (Cunnington 1923) and East Chisenbury (McOmish 1996).

---

[15] The report does not identify any deliberate modification of the human bone but a recent re-examination of the material has argued that most of the skull fragments have been shaped by human action (Waddington 2009).

Recent excavation close to the hillfort of Battlesbury, Wiltshire, recovered an assemblage of human bones from an apparently unenclosed settlement comprised of pit clusters and timber buildings (McKinley in Ellis and Powell 2008). Activity took place from the eighth to seventh centuries through to the fourth to third centuries BC, but the evidence for settlement in the later part of this period is very limited. Thirty-three deposits of human bone were recovered, and though overall the assemblage is characterized by disarticulated long bones (44%) and skull fragments (29%), six crouched inhumations were found in circular grain storage pits (two pits contained two bodies laid one on top of the other). Amongst the disarticulated remains, bone from the pelvis and vertebrae were almost completely absent, but there was an articulated foot, which is a rare discovery. A large proportion (60%) of the long bones were from the right side of the body. Most of the other remains came from pits but they were also found in the ditch of an adjacent field boundary, and several came from post holes. The bones were not as heavily weathered as the bones at Potterne but they appear to have been fractured when the bone was still relatively fresh. Animal gnawing is much more common than at Potterne, but it is even more common on the animal bones. The complete burials appear to be a late feature of the settlement occupation, occurring probably as late as the Middle Iron Age.

Early first millennium deposits have also been recovered from the enclosure and boundary at New Buildings in Hampshire (Cunliffe and Poole 2000c). These excavations produced only a small assemblage of bones (13 deposits) but included amongst them were four complete inhumations placed in an area of quarry hollows dug around the north-east corner of the enclosure. One of these burials was accompanied by a copper alloy pin of Late Bronze Age type. Contemporary with these deposits was an articulated foot, and in the Early Iron Age the recut enclosure ditch produced a collection of disarticulated human bones.[16]

Danebury (Early to Middle Iron Age)

In the original report, the Danebury human bone assemblage was broken down into six categories of deposit, with one category divided into three sub-categories (Walker in Cunliffe 1984a). In this analysis I have reduced the

---

[16] Two badly decayed crouched inhumations were also discovered in a pit at the Late Bronze Age settlement at Reading Business Park (Boyle in Moore and Jennings 1992: 98).

assemblage to four categories and divided each category into different sub-categories:[17]

A. Complete bodies:
    i. neonatal,[18]
    ii. juvenile/adult,
    iii. juveniles/adults in multiple burials.

B. Articulated deposits:[19]
    i. fragmentary torsos without skulls and arms,
    ii. fragmentary torsos with disarticulated limbs,
    iii. assemblages comprising a mixture of bones from the same individual,
    iv. small groups of articulated or potentially articulated bones.

C. Not used (multiple partially articulated skeletons in charnel pits).[20]

D. Heads:[21]
    i. largely complete skulls,
    ii. skull fragments,
    iii. mandible/maxilla fragments,
    iv. individual teeth.

E. Not used (pelvic girdles).[22]

F. Isolated bones:[23]
    i. long bones,
    ii. trunk bones,
    iii. extremities.

---

[17] To avoid confusion, the original letter codes have been used even though two of the original categories are not used here. Furthermore, additional sub-categories have been added and many of the bones have been reassigned to completely different categories.

[18] This includes partial skeletons where the bones were not recorded *in situ* and where it is assumed they were lost during excavation.

[19] This category includes many more deposits than are recorded in the original report. These include partial skeletons from category C, the charnel pits, and many bones in category Biii and Biv, that were classified as category F, isolated bones, but which the fiche description indicates were two or more bones which were potentially articulated. Some of the category E deposits, pelvic girdles, were reclassified into this category.

[20] This category was split up between the other categories. The deposits were identified as individuals in the initial catalogue, and these have been allocated to the appropriate categories depending on whether complete bodies, partial bodies, skulls, or isolated bones were present.

[21] This category has been considerably increased from the original report by the inclusion of the heads found in the charnel pits and the fragmentary remains previously categorized as isolated bones (F).

[22] The bones in this category were either articulated sections (Biv) or isolated trunk bones (Fii).

[23] Examination of the catalogue in the fiche revealed that many of these isolated bones comprise more than one bone. Where these could be articulated, they have been assumed to be articulated (Biv); where they could not be articulated, they have been split into separate entities.

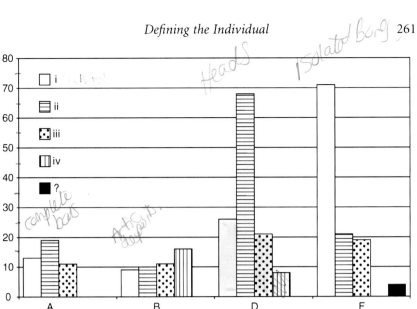

Figure 5.3 The quantities of different burial types at Danebury: A. Complete bodies: i) neonatal; ii) juvenile/adult; iii) juvenile adults in multiple burials. B. Articulated deposits: i) fragmentary torsos without skulls and arms; ii) fragmentary torsos with disarticulated limbs; iii) assemblages comprising a mixture of bones from the same individual; iv) small groups of articulated or potentially articulated bones. D. Heads: i) largely complete skulls; ii) skull fragments; iii) mandible/maxilla fragments; iv) individual teeth; F. Isolated bones: i) long bones; ii) trunk bones; iii) extremities.

The relative proportions of the different categories of deposit are depicted in Figure 5.3. The largest group of deposits are skulls, or fragments from the skull (123 deposits), but isolated bones (115 deposits) are only slightly less frequent. There is then a substantial drop to the group of fragmentary torsos and articulated bones (46 deposits) and this is only slightly more common than the complete bodies (43 deposits). It is clear, therefore, that the burial of complete humans was an irregular and occasional event; an estimated 83 complete juvenile and adult burials are probably present in the hillfort, which would indicate a rate of roughly 0.18 burials per year (using the ratio discussed by Cunliffe 1995: 75). Clearly this does not represent the normal manner of disposing of the dead. A large number of the deposits in categories A, B, and D could be sexed; males dominated in all three categories and there were more than double the number of male to female complete burials.

The Danebury assemblage is particularly important because it is possible to estimate the number of burial events made by year, as the estimated life of each is known and a reasonable estimate of the number of deposits is possible. Human bone deposits, in general, were much more frequent in the early years

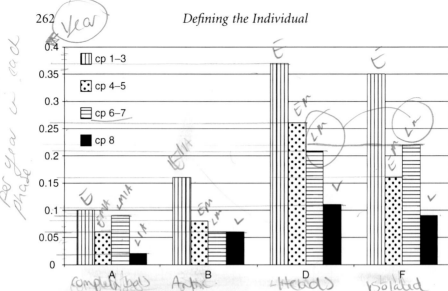

Figure 5.4 The rate of deposition for the four different categories of human remains at Danebury. The y-axis indicates the number of deposits per year in each phase.

of the occupation of the hillfort (0.9 bones/year), were fairly stable in the middle phases (0.56 and 0.54 bones/year respectively) and declined in the final phase (0.25 bones/year), when the occupation of the hillfort appears to be relatively ephemeral. All categories are deposited most frequently in the Early Iron Age (Figure 5.4). There is then a marked decline in all categories in the earlier Middle Iron Age. Partially articulated groups and skulls continue to decline in the later Middle Iron Age but complete burials and isolated bones increase their deposition rate in this period. All categories, apart from partially articulated remains, are deposited much less frequently in the final phase.

Figure 5.5 shows the composition of the assemblage present in each of the four different phases. Isolated long bones and fragmented skulls are the most common human remains present in almost all the phases, but in the Early Iron Age largely complete skulls are also an important feature of the archaeological record. In the early Middle Iron Age skulls comprise almost 50% of the record and there were no neonatal or multiple burials. The much larger assemblage of the later Middle Iron Age had a higher proportion of isolated bones. In the Late Iron Age complete burials and isolated bones became less important and partial burials and skull fragments become relatively more significant.

Most of the complete adult and juvenile bodies were found at the base, or near the bottom (18 out of 28), of grain storage pits.[24] The complete bodies

---

[24] Two burials came from features that were not grain storage pits.

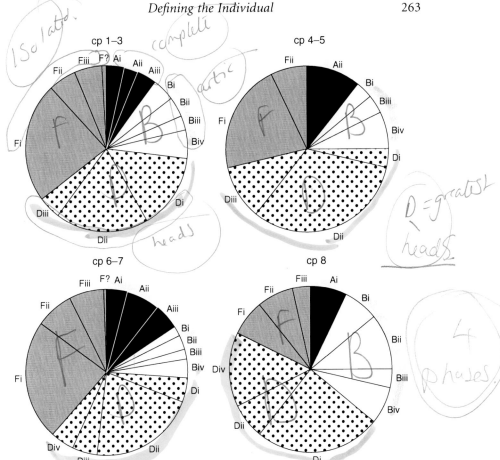

Figure 5.5 The composition of the assemblage of human remains in four phases of the occupation at Danebury.

were normally either tightly contracted or loosely flexed but there are two extended burials (one in a grave apparently specifically dug to receive the body). The very tightly contracted nature of seven of the 13 contracted bodies led to the suggestion (Cunliffe 1995: 75) that they may have been deliberately and carefully bound prior to burial, and one individual clearly had her hands tied behind her back.[25] There is also a suggestion that some of the bodies were deliberately covered by rubble and possibly even had slingstones thrown at them after

[25] These burials are very similar to the skeletons discovered at the Late Bronze Age settlement of Cladh Hallan in the Western Isles (Parker Pearson *et al.* 2005) and at this site it was argued that the burials represented mummified corpses. One of the Cladh Hallan skeletons was composed of at least three different individuals and was probably deposited between

they had been laid out in the pit.[26] Some of the bodies (notably 44 and 46) were clearly exposed after they were placed in the pit and this was a distinctive feature of the multiple burials and those found in the 'charnel pits' (Walker in Cunliffe 1984a: 448). All these activities suggest the complete burials were problematic and regarded as potentially threatening to the occupants of the hillfort.

The complete bodies could be laid on their sides (right and left), front and back. The most common position was on the back (nine) but this was only slightly more popular than laying them on the right-hand side (seven) or on the left-hand side (six). There seems to be little significance to these positions at Danebury and a comparison of position, orientation, age, and sex shows little obvious patterning. Walker (in Cunliffe 1984a: 448–50) had cautiously noted some possible patterns in the original analysis of the remains, most notably that bodies in the early phases of the hillfort were lying on the left-hand side and those in the later phases were on their right-hand side, and although these patterns were slightly undermined by later discoveries, it is still most likely that a complete inhumation lying on its right-hand side dates to the later phases of the hillfort's occupation. Furthermore, if an individual is lying on his or her back, they will almost certainly date to the later phases of the occupation.

The number of incomplete bodies and partially articulated remains has been considerably enhanced by an examination of the fiche catalogue. Cunliffe suggested that these articulated remains were collected from a location away from the settlement where the bodies had been exposed, 'the completeness of the body reflecting the duration of the exposure, the hands and limbs being the first to pull away as the connecting tissue rotted' (Cunliffe 1995: 76). The largest sub-group (Biv) consists of bones from osteologically adjacent limbs, most of which were not observed to be articulated in the ground, but this group also includes an articulated foot and a pelvic girdle with accompanying chopped leg bones. There are 19 large groups of articulated bone that represent the substantial remains of

---

200 and 400 years after the death of the different individuals. It is impossible to make similar statements about the Danebury remains without re-examining the skeletal material, but it is difficult to explain the very tightly contracted positions of many of the skeletons if the skeleton was still fleshed and it suggests these were at least partially decayed. However, this does not necessarily indicate that the bodies were mummies—they could simply be individuals who died and were kept for a period of time sufficient for some wastage of bodily tissue. Pauses between death and burial would be necessary if the burials were specifically related to seasonal rituals and would be very different from the situation at Cladh Hallan.

[26] This is reminiscent of the deliberate spearing of some burials in the Yorkshire inhumation cemeteries (Stead 1991a).

individuals (with or without the skull), and these were clearly regarded as a significant element in the ritual activity within the hillfort.

An examination of the sex and age of the complete juvenile/adult burials and the partial remains indicates a significant difference in the two populations. The partial burials include a much larger number of adolescents and do not include any individuals over 50, whereas the complete burials were dominated by adults.[27] There is a relatively even distribution of sex in the partial burials but the complete burials have more than double the number of males to females. These factors led Cunliffe to suggest that there were different criteria for selecting these two groups (A and B) and that they indicate two different living populations. The partial bodies represent ancestors derived from the community occupying the hillfort, whereas the complete bodies represent sacrificial victims derived from communities in conflict with the Danebury community. This may be the case, but alternative explanations are possible. The form of deposition may reflect a different ritual purpose and necessitate the use of individuals or remains that were categorized in quite different ways.

The charnel pits represent a discrete depositional context separated out by the original analysis, but the identified deposits were not a particularly coherent group. Only three of the contexts (923, 1078, and 2496) appeared to represent deposits where many different individuals were present. These three deposits were clearly the result of complex ceremonies that involved the deposition of complete and almost complete burials of various ages and sexes, plus skull collections and isolated bones.[28] The remains were accompanied by animal bones, grain and ash, and other cultural debris, and they may also have

---

[27] These figures are slightly different from those used by Cunliffe but essentially corroborate his observations (Cunliffe 1995: 76: tbl 13).

[28] These deposits have been interpreted as the result of warfare and indicating an attack on the hillfort (Craig *et al.* 2005) but this interpretation does not really help to explain the nature of the remains (Lally 2008). Whilst there seems to be no doubt that violence was endemic in Iron Age society (Sharples 1991b), the composition, location, and character of these deposits cannot be explained simply as the result of a violent encounter. Why did the deposits comprise skulls and complete individuals? The former are normally interpreted as trophies collected from warriors killed in battle and yet they accompany complete bodies argued to result from a specific act of violence. The age and sex ranges of the deposits vary, including young and old, male and female, and if one applies the warfare hypothesis this should represent the slaughter of a resident population (Bishop and Knüsel 2005). Most of the remains are fragmented and had been lying around for a long period of time. They could represent the tidying up of the settlement some time after a battle, long enough for decomposition. Does this indicate that the site was abandoned? It seems strange that the site would be abandoned after an assault in which only a handful of people died. There is no evidence for the deliberate dismemberment of the bodies and very little evidence for trauma on the skeletons (Walker in Cunliffe 1984a: 451). Re-analysis of this material (Craig *et al.* 2005) suggested a high degree of fresh breakage amongst the bones from the charnel pits, and marks indicating decapitation on jaw bones from a pit (2509) containing a collection of skulls. However, neither of these observations could be taken to

been deliberately stoned. Pit 1078 was backfilled fairly quickly with debris; but pit 923 appears to have lain open for some time and to have been allowed to fill naturally.

Skull fragments are the largest single category of deposit present.[29] The numbers in this group have been considerably expanded by the inclusion of any part of the head, including isolated mandibles, frontal bones, and teeth. It seems likely that all these fragments, with the possible exception of the teeth, would have been regarded as having an association with the head that gave them a special significance. Some of the skulls were found with a mandible, which suggests either the soft tissue survived to hold these remains together or that they were held together by an organic binding. Complete skulls and skull fragments are often grouped together and this led to many of these deposits being categorized as charnel pits in the original analysis. Pit 923 had eight largely complete skulls and some fragments, and is the principal reason that skulls predominate in the Early Iron Age tables. The remains were heavily biased towards older individuals, to an even greater extent than the complete burials.

The assemblage of isolated bones can be divided into long bones (71), bones from the body (21), and bones from hands and feet (19). The assemblage of long bones is dominated by remains of the femur (43.6 %) with tibia and humerus fragments providing the next most common bones; there is also a preference for bones from the right-hand side of the body. The bones from the trunk were divided between vertebra, scapula, clavicle, rib (rare), sternum, and pelvis, but there was no evidence that the pelvis was particularly important. Many of these bones show evidence of breakage when the bone was still fresh; this is also a feature of the skull fragments and probably indicates a deliberate desire to fragment complete bones. The importance of long bones, and the infrequent presence of bones from the trunk and the small bones of the hand is significant. It supports the argument that bodies were not exposed in the interior of the hillfort; if this had happened there would be larger quantities of small bones.[30] The presence of long bones and skulls was

support the claim that the charnel pits indicate endemic warfare. The breakage patterns indicate the manner in which dead bodies were treated during burial and have been noted at other sites (e.g. Battlesbury). The decapitation marks are an indication of how a head was removed from a body but do not indicate a violent act of warfare and are not unexpected, given the evidence for an Iron Age interest in the head.

[29] The category could be classed within the category of isolated bones but the size of both categories encouraged separation into two different groups. This was how they were categorized in the original report.

[30] Danebury would have been the perfect site to discover concentrations of bones around four-posters if these had been used for excarnation, as several four-posters were found in the quarry hollow behind the rampart, where deposits were very well preserved by the rapid in-wash of silts.

therefore a cultural choice; these bones were specifically selected, to be brought from the place where the bodies were originally deposited, to the hillfort.

Winnall Down and Gussage All Saints (Early to Late Iron Age)

The Iron Age assemblage from Winnall Down/Easton Lane produced about 22 complete and eight partially complete skeletons, plus 51 deposits of isolated human bone (Fasham 1985; Fasham *et al.* 1989). The complete burials included eight females and four males. The Early Iron Age assemblage is dominated by isolated bones with only one young infant burial present. In the early Middle Iron Age, complete burials become important, and only two isolated bones were identified. Most of the human remains came from the late Middle Iron Age phase and included a large assemblage of complete burials, partial burials, and isolated bones; young infants (<1 year old) become very important in this phase. In the Late Iron Age and Early Roman phase isolated bones were almost completely absent.

The complete skeletons were mostly crouched or flexed, though some of the infants were extended. Two bodies were very tightly crouched, suggesting they were bound, and one example (174) appears to have had his hands and feet tied together. The bodies were placed on both their right- (5) and left-hand (4) side and one lay on his back. There seemed to be little difference between the sexes except that males were oriented with their heads to the north and north-west, whereas females had their heads between south-south-west and east. The age and sex distinctions were quantified separately for the complete/ partial skeletons and the isolated bones (Bayley, Fasham, and Powell in Fasham 1985: tbl. 28) and demonstrate that there was a significant difference between the assemblages. The isolated bones contained a much higher proportion of adult material than the complete and partial burials, which had a much higher proportion of children.

The Gussage All Saints assemblage is quite different (Wainwright 1979a): it comprises 37 complete and 13 partial burials, compared with only 17 isolated bones (ten of which are skulls). It is difficult to know if this is an accurate reflection of the depositional choice of the inhabitants or the recovery strategy of the excavation. It was possible to identify seven females and three males in the complete burials: an unusually high proportion of females compared with the assemblage from Danebury, but similar to the 8/4 ratio at Winnall Down/ Easton Lane. The chronological distribution of the assemblage was very biased and only one deposit was associated with the Early Iron Age activity. There was a more substantial collection in the Middle Iron Age, with seven complete/partial burials and 13 isolated bones. The bulk of the assemblage came from the Late Iron Age and this was dominated by complete burials, with only four isolated bones present.

Most of the complete burials were crouched, but five were in an extended position and there were a few tightly contracted individuals who appeared to have been bound (Figure 5.6). The number of extended individuals resulted in the most common position being on the back (six) but this was only slightly more common than being placed on the right- or left-hand side (five each). The burials on the right were evenly split between males and females, but females formed a higher proportion of burials on the left, and the only sexed skeletons on their front and back were female. The three male skeletons were oriented with their heads to the north and north-east, whereas the bulk of the female skeletons were oriented between east-south-east and south-east.[31]

Conclusion

The evidence from the sites discussed above provides a large proportion of the database of human remains recovered from the first millennium BC in Wessex, and thus provides a representative picture of the complexity of the material. It is clear that there are basically two forms of burial that are associated with settlements: the deposition of complete burials and the deposition and manipulation of isolated and partially articulated human remains. Analysis by age of the remains from Danebury and Winnall Down indicates that these involve populations with quite different age structures, though the sites do not show a consistent pattern.

There is considerable chronological and spatial variation in the relative significance of the two forms of burial. The patterns at Potterne, Gussage, and Winnall suggest that disarticulated remains were a feature of the earlier part of the Iron Age and that complete or largely complete bodies are a dominant feature of the later parts of the Iron Age, supporting the patterns observed by Wait (1985) and Wilson (1981). However, new discoveries at Battlesbury and New Buildings suggest that complete burials were also present in the Early Iron Age, and both Wait and Wilson ignored the assemblage from the Middle to Late Iron Age settlement of Glastonbury, which comprised skulls or skull fragments (23 of the 43 deposits) and neonatal infants (Coles, J. and Minnitt 1995: 170–4), but not complete adults. The Danebury evidence is also slightly

---

[31] Two female skeletons were oriented north-north-east and north-west, but it is difficult to know what this signifies. Sex discrimination is not exact, so these could be males; alternatively these may be females who assumed a male social identity.

Figure 5.6 A selection of the complete human burials in grain storage pits at Gussage All Saints, Dorset (after Wainwright 1979a: figs. 25–27; © Crown copyright).

more complex. Complete burials become increasingly frequent in the later Middle Iron Age and skulls decline in importance after the Early Iron Age. In the Late Iron Age complete burials are rare and the assemblage is dominated by isolated bones, a complete contrast to the pattern at Gussage. However, it is possible that the Late Iron Age assemblage simply represents residual deposition of little significance on this complicated and long-lived settlement. There are also significant differences in the number of isolated bones at Gussage All Saints and Winnall Down and this might suggest that the manipulation of isolated human bones was much less important in Dorset. This is not contradicted by the other sites in the analysis, and may reflect the development of a formal burial rite in Late Iron Age Dorset (see below).

The complete burials have formally distinct properties. They are normally crouched and placed in circular grain storage pits. The large assemblages of burials normally include a few individuals that are extended, and purpose-dug graves are also known, but these simply highlight the norm. Several of the skeletons were bound and this is a feature of both hillfort and non-hillfort settlements. The burials are normally placed on the right- or left-hand side but there are examples placed on their back and very rarely on their front. There seems to be little difference between the preference for either side and it does not clearly differentiate age, sex, or period. Burials on the back are particularly prevalent in the Late Iron Age at Gussage All Saints and Danebury, though they are also known from earlier periods at Winnall Down/Easton Lane and New Buildings. An important difference between males and females is visible in the orientation of the body (Figure 5.7).

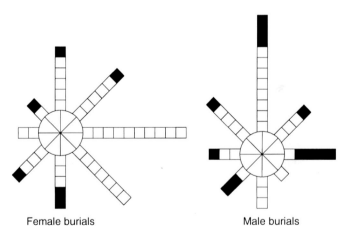

Female burials   Male burials

Figure 5.7 A diagram showing the orientation of male and female burials from all the Wessex pit burials (the Danebury burials are marked in black).

Males are predominantly oriented with their heads to the north whereas females have their heads in a more general orientation to the east (the opposite direction seems to be specifically avoided by both sexes). This pattern was not particularly visible in the analysis of the individual sites, but it is a trend in all of the large assemblages that becomes clear when they are combined. The data is not good enough to look at complex changes in the different age groups, but children do seem to be more common as complete burials in the later part of the Iron Age.

Partially articulated deposits are found on both hillforts and settlements and there seems no great difference in the percentages in either group. The significance of these remains is ambiguous; some of them clearly represent bones brought to the site from other locations and are therefore similar in significance to the isolated bones. However, largely complete bodies may represent complete inhumations exposed *in situ* from which bones have been removed. These are therefore more equivalent to the complete bodies. The situation is clearly complex and the idea that these are two separate populations may have been over-emphasized.

The isolated bones present on the site are dominated by two sets of bones: skulls (and skull fragments) and long bones. The femur is the most common long bone chosen and the right side is favoured over the left side. Skulls are more common at Danebury, Glastonbury, and Potterne, but long bones are more favoured at Battlesbury. However, it is difficult to be certain about the relative proportions of bones from the body and skull as it is quite possible that earlier excavations would not have consistently identified human long bone fragments; the bulk of the animal bones were often discarded without specialist examination and this probably resulted in the discard of many human bones. There is no evidence that hillforts have more skulls than non-hillfort settlements.

Many archaeologists have argued that the bulk of the Iron Age population of Wessex was disposed of by excarnation (Carr and Knüsel 1997; Cunliffe 1995: 72; Ellison and Drewett 1971; Lally 2008) and the principal concern appears to be to identify locations where human remains were exposed. One of the most common suggestions is that the bodies were placed on the four-post structures that are such a ubiquitous feature of the settlement record (Ellison and Drewett 1971), but they could also be exposed inside houses, or in trees, and there are ethnographic parallels for all of these methods. If these practices were commonplace then one might expect weathering and gnawing to be a feature of the assemblages and it would also be expected that bone fragments and small bones would be concentrated around the exposure platforms. However, a consistent feature of the record is the small numbers of bones from the hands and feet. It seems likely, therefore, that the dead must have been taken away from the settlement, allowed to decay and then returned. The lack of evidence for extensive gnawing and weathering of the bones also undermines the belief that the body was exposed to the elements. Recent analysis of a sample of animal and human bones from Winnall Down and Danebury (Madgwick 2008) has demonstrated that the human bones are considerably less gnawed and weathered than the animal bones, and that this must indicate they are not exposed for a lengthy period. Similar differences have also been noted at Battlesbury (McKinley in Ellis and Powell 2008). I will return to discuss these patterns after an examination of other forms of burial practice.

River Deposition

The idea that the bulk of the population was being deposited in rivers has achieved a certain degree of support because of the large quantities of Bronze Age and Iron Age metalwork found in rivers, particularly the Thames (Barrett and Needham 1988; Fitzpatrick 1984). Most of this material was recovered by dredging in the nineteenth and early twentieth centuries when the practice of paying rewards encouraged recovery. Large quantities of human remains were also found at the same time, and though these were less well recorded and are less well known, a couple of collections, with reasonably accurate contextual descriptions, have been examined by Bradley and Gordon (1988). Nine radiocarbon dates were obtained from bones from the River Thames and its tributary the River Walbrook. The dates range from the Neolithic to the Saxon period, but the Thames dates were clustered in a period from the Middle to Late Bronze Age, and the Walbrook dates, from a discrete cluster of skulls, indicated a date between the Late Iron Age and the Late Roman period. The collections are dominated by skulls of individuals aged between 25 and 35 years of age and there is also a slight preference for males over females. Bradley and Gordon argue that this was not due to taphonomic bias and indicate that these are the remnants of exposed or excarnated bodies; but others (e.g. Knüsel and Carr 1995) have been more cautious. It seems highly likely that the dredgers would recognize and select skulls more than any other bones, and male adults in the prime of life would have the most robust skulls.

It is difficult to judge the importance of riverine deposition in Wessex as all the documented cases come from eastern England. There are significant regional differences in the deposition of bronze artefacts in Britain, and in Wessex riverine deposits are not an important context (Fitzpatrick 1984; Hingley 1990b) so it seems best to assume that river burials were not common in Wessex. However, the use of rivers as a funeral area may explain the strange

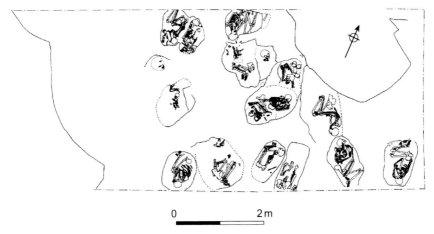

0   2 m

Figure 5.8 The burials in the quarry at Suddern Farm, Hampshire (after Cunliffe and Poole 2000d: fig. 3.93; reproduced with the permission of Professor B. W. Cunliffe).

reluctance of the inhabitants of Britain, including those in Wessex, to eat fish prior to the Roman conquest (Dobney and Ervynck 2007). This would be a rational taboo if fish were consuming human flesh, and might suggest fish played a role in the funerary process, perhaps symbolically carrying or guiding the dead to another world.

Inhumation Cemeteries

Formal inhumation cemeteries were thought to be a feature of only the last 100 years of the first millennium BC, when they appear in Dorset at the same time as cremation cemeteries appear in Hampshire and Sussex. However, recent discoveries indicate that cemeteries were a significant feature earlier in the millennium, and in this section we will consider the evidence for Middle Iron Age and Late Iron Age cemeteries.

The most important recent discovery occurred at Suddern Farm, Hampshire (Cunliffe and Poole 2000b), where a cemetery, in a large quarry, was found at the south-west corner of a large triple-ditched enclosure (Figure 5.8).[32] The west side of the enclosure appears to have been laid out in relation to a long-lived linear boundary represented by three ditches running roughly north–south. The full chronological relationship of these linear boundaries

[32] The enclosure could be classified as a large settlement or a small hillfort and highlights the flexible nature of the classification.

and the enclosure boundaries was complex, and not completely established by the excavations, but the shape of the Early Iron Age enclosure suggests it was constructed to abut an existing boundary. The quarry containing the burials was created on the east side of the main linear ditch and cut through an adjacent parallel ditch. The outer ditch of the enclosure, which appears to be Late Iron Age, then cut the quarry. It is assumed that the quarry was created after the original enclosure was laid out, but there is no physical relationship between the two. The burials contained only two iron artefacts, a fibula and an object that may be a finger ring, and there are no radiocarbon dates. However, the relationship with the enclosure and the fibula suggest the burials were deposited in the Early to Middle Iron Age (500–250 BC).

Thirty-four formal inhumations were excavated and a further 300 adults, 80 children, and 180 infant burials are estimated to be present in the quarry (Cunliffe and Poole 2000b: 201). The burials were crouched inhumations lying in shallow graves cut into the infilled quarry. Many graves cut earlier graves and many other graves contained loose human bone unconnected with the articulated skeleton present in the grave. The excavator is unclear whether this disturbance was accidental, because the individual graves were not marked, or whether it was a deliberate attempt to place related individuals together. The total collection of formal burials and isolated bones indicates the presence of approximately 31 adults, nine children, and 20 infants (six of whom were probably foetal) (Hooper in Cunliffe and Poole 2000b). Approximately 11 males (including five probable) and five females (including four probable) could be identified in the formal graves. The average age at death for both males and females was 28–29. The male burials were placed on both their right- (five) and left-hand (five) sides but included one on his front and two on their backs. Two females were placed on their left-hand side and one was found on her back. The orientation of the bodies heavily favoured the north or north-west, but there was a subsidiary group oriented to the south, which included two of the four oriented females. The heads faced west or north and some trouble seems to have gone into obtaining this orientation as a couple of individuals had their heads twisted in relation to the body orientation.

The context of this cemetery is comparable with the burials found at several other settlements. A group of eight burials was found in a large quarry hollow on the northern corner of the enclosure at Winnall Down (Figure 5.9; Fasham 1985).[33] The quarry has a distinctive linear southern

---

[33] Chalk quarries are a common feature of Iron Age settlements in Wessex; there were large quarries in the centre of Little Woodbury and Winklebury, though neither of these quarries appears to have been used for burial. The function of the quarries is unclear and they seldom

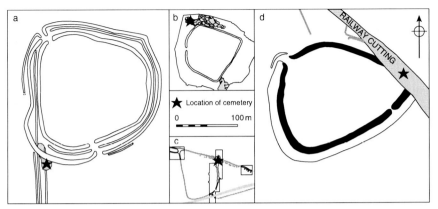

Figure 5.9 The location of the cemeteries at a) Suddern Farm, b) Winnall Down, c) New Buildings and d) Spettisbury (after Cunliffe and Poole 2000d; Fasham 1985; Cunliffe and Poole 2000e; RCHME 1970).

edge that coincides with, but is chronologically earlier and more extensive than, the northern ditch of the enclosure. This suggests that the quarries and the enclosure were created in relation to an invisible linear boundary, such as a hedge. This boundary would have been an integral part of the ditched Middle Bronze Age field system that was identified to the west of the enclosure. The burials in the quarry were dated to the late Middle Iron Age, but it is unclear why, as there is no associated material culture and they were not radiocarbon dated. Some of the quarries in this area were truncated by the Early Iron Age enclosure and a Middle Iron Age house, but the burials were some distance from these features and could have been deposited any time in the Iron Age or after.

Four of the Late Bronze Age burials at New Buildings, Hampshire (see page 259), came from a similar location in a quarry adjacent to an enclosure ditch (Figure 5.9). The enclosure ditch also appears to have been laid out in relation to an existing boundary though the formalization of this boundary, by a ditch, was a later act (Cunliffe and Poole 2000c: 91–3).

The numbers of burials present at these three sites seem to be directly proportional to the density of settlement in the adjacent enclosure. New Buildings is a very sparsely occupied site with only a small number of pits, whereas Winnall Down is a long-lived small farmstead and Suddern Farm is a densely occupied enclosure surrounded by substantial boundaries. All the

produce much in the way of material culture. As a result of this relative sterility they are frequently left unexcavated, particularly when they are located on the periphery of a site. It is therefore possible that some of these unexcavated quarries conceal substantial cemeteries and they could have been routinely used for the disposal of the dead.

cemetery quarries are located at the corner of distinctively angular enclosures and seem to be related to boundaries that pre-date the enclosure. They are not close to an entrance and they can be found on both the north and the south side of the enclosure.

A large number of burials (two groups: one of between 80–90 individuals, and one of over 40 individuals) were recovered from the hillfort at Spettisbury in Dorset (Gresham 1939). They were reported to have come from 'a pit about 35 ft long, by 15 ft wide, and from 4 to 9 or 10 feet deep' (Durden, quoted by Gresham 1939: 129), which was discovered in a railway cutting that truncated the eastern corner of the enclosure ditch (Figure 5.9). This corner is some distance from the entrance to the hillfort, and the burial pit is located at the end of a straight section of the enclosure ditch, a location comparable to that at Suddern Farm. The Spettisbury burials are not described in great detail but they were associated with an assemblage of weapons including scabbard fragments and spearheads, one of which was still embedded in a skull, and this has led people to assume that this was a massacre deposit. However, as Gresham noted, the objects present include items of Middle Iron Age and Roman date, which undermines the idea that this deposit derived from a single event. It is possible that a long-lived cemetery could have included individuals who had met a violent death (e.g. Maiden Castle), and isolated grave goods have been found at Suddern Farm and scabbard fragments at Owslebury. It is therefore possible that the deposits at Spettisbury represent a cemetery closely comparable to that at Suddern Farm.

A different form of cemetery was found adjacent to the enclosure at Cookey Down in Wiltshire (Lovell 1999). A group of seven inhumations in five graves was identified approximately 60 m south of an Early/Middle Iron Age enclosure.[34] There is a suggestion that the graves were arranged in rows. None of the graves has any associated material culture, but three radiocarbon dates indicate they belong to the Middle to Late Iron Age.[35] Other graves were noted in earlier excavations and suggest this is a fairly extensive cemetery.

---

[34] The enclosure was later the location for a Late Iron Age/Romano-British settlement that extended beyond the boundary.

[35] This cemetery is very similar to a more thoroughly explored cemetery on the river gravels at Yarnton, Oxfordshire (Hey *et al.* 1999) that lies outside the study area of this volume. Extensive excavations identified 46 inhumations and six cremations to the east of an unenclosed settlement. Two clusters appeared to define separate cemeteries of fifteen and ten individuals and a further ten individuals were dispersed across the area between the settlement and the cemetery. The burials were crouched, on both the right- and left-hand side, and were oriented north–south. Some eleven males and six females were identified and there were nineteen adults, six adolescents (12–20), six sub-adults (below 12). All the neonates were buried in the settlement. The demography suggests a normal population. Nine radiocarbon dates were obtained, which are argued to represent a cemetery occupied for approximately two generations in the third to fourth centuries cal BC.

An important feature of the graves is the evidence for repeated use. Two of the graves contained two burials, and one of these double burials and one of the single burials contained isolated fragments of other individuals; between ten and 11 people were present in total. There were five immature (one possible male), one sub-adult or young adult and four adults (three males and a female) and the ages ranged from neonatal to mature adults (McKinley 1997b). Jacqueline McKinley suggests that one of the double burials was a simultaneous event, but that the other burials were placed separately after a gap of some time. She also argues that when the second internment took place 'the skull and right lower leg bones were removed' (McKinley 1997b: 3). The isolated bones in the other graves could indicate burials that had been placed in graves but were subsequently almost completely removed. This is similar to the situation at Suddern Farm where burials were clearly being dug into, and bones removed. However, whereas at Suddern Farm the assumption was that this was accidental, at Cookey Down the isolated nature of the graves suggests that individual graves were specifically reopened. The removal of human bones suggests that the reuse of old burials may provide a source for the isolated and partially articulated remains found in pits in enclosures and hillforts.

Prior to the discovery of the Suddern Farm cemetery, the only inhumation cemeteries noted in Wessex were the Durotrigian cemeteries of south Dorset. This is a well-known tradition that has been discussed in detail by numerous authors (Sharples 1990a; Whimster 1981; Woodward in Farwell and Molleson 1993). Cemeteries are particularly common around Dorchester and Portland but they extend as far as the Bride valley in west Dorset and Purbeck in the east (Figure 5.10). Typical cemeteries are not common in north Dorset, though a few isolated burials have been classified as Durotrigian. The tradition probably developed near the end of the first century BC and continued into the Roman period as late as the first quarter of the second century AD at Alington Avenue (Davies *et al.* 2002: 125).

Durotrigian burials are normally found in shallow rectangular or oval graves in small cemeteries close to settlements.[36] The body is placed in a crouched position lying predominantly on the right side with the head to the east. Males and females are found in roughly even numbers and children/ infants are much less common. The most common grave goods are pots and animal bones, but ornaments worn on the body are sometimes present and weapons and other equipment are found occasionally (Woodward in Farwell and Molleson 1993). Males generally have more grave goods than females; females never have weapons or equipment and tend to have a higher proportion

---

[36] Poundbury is the best example of the relationship between cemetery and settlement (Farwell and Molleson 1993; Green, C. S. 1987).

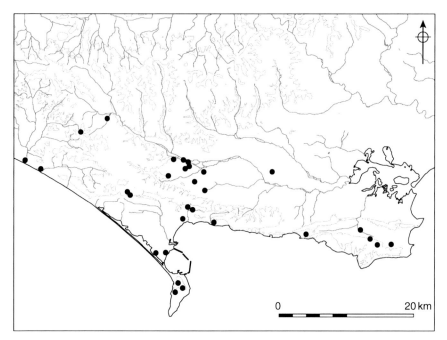

Figure 5.10 The distribution of Durotrigian cemeteries in Dorset (after Fitzpatrick 1996: fig. 1).

of ornaments. However, these are general trends and there are exceptions. For example, the most frequent grave goods in the cemetery at Litton Cheney were ornaments. Recent work at Alington Avenue (Davies *et al.* 2002) and Portesham (Valentin 2003) suggests that burials can be quite widely dispersed and may occur in pairs. There is also a suggestion that the alignments in the west are slightly different from those in the core areas. One of the Poundbury cemeteries (in Farwell and Molleson 1993) consisted almost exclusively of children and the Maiden Castle 'war cemetery' (Wheeler 1943) has a much higher proportion of males. Many of the burials in the 'war cemetery' are placed in an extended position and there are several unusual double graves.

Exceptionally rich burials are known from Whitcombe and Portesham (Figure 5.11). At Whitcombe (Aitken and Aitken 1990) a 25–30 year old male was buried in a crouched position, with a brooch holding his clothing in place on his shoulder; a hammer and file; a spindle whorl; a spear; and a sword in a scabbard with associated fittings. He was not accompanied by a pot and there was no bone to suggest a joint of meat in the grave. At Portesham (Fitzpatrick 1996) a typical crouched inhumation of a mature woman was

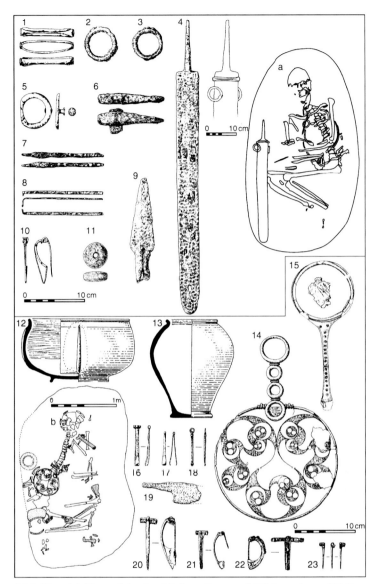

Figure 5.11 Two rich Durotrigian burials from Dorset: a) Whitcombe and b) Portesham. They were accompanied by a wide range of grave goods: 1) copper alloy scabbard mount; 2, 3) iron suspension rings; 4) iron sword (note scale is different); 5) copper alloy ring; 6) iron hammer head; 7) iron file; 8) copper alloy strip; 9) iron spear; 10) copper alloy brooch; 11) chalk spindle whorl; 12, 13) pots; 14) copper alloy mirror; 15) copper alloy vessel; 16, 17) copper alloy tweezers; 18) copper alloy ear scoop; 19) iron knife; 20–23) copper alloy brooches (after Aitken and Aitken 1990: figs. 9, 10 and pl. 10; Fitzpatrick 1996: figs. 2–5; reproduced with the permission of the Dorset Natural History and Archaeological Society at the Dorset County Museum).

discovered, accompanied by a shoulder of mutton and the almost complete carcass of a young pig; a complete bowl and a high-shouldered jar were placed behind the body; and she was accompanied by an iron knife; a handled copper alloy vessel (possibly a strainer); a toilet set, consisting of two pairs of tweezers and an ear scoop; three elaborate copper alloy brooches, two at the shoulders, presumably attached to a dress, and one attached to the handle of an elaborately decorated copper alloy mirror.

Both these burials can be dated to the middle of the first century AD. The mirror burial from Portesham probably occurred after the Roman conquest, whereas the sword burial from Whitcombe possibly occurred before the conquest. The presence of a mirror and sword link these burials to traditions that are spread across southern England.[37] Mirrors comparable to that from Portesham come from Desborough in Northamptonshire, Birdlip in Gloucestershire, and Holcombe in Devon. Sword burials comparable to that from Whitcombe come from Deal in Kent, Owslebury in Hampshire, and North Grimston in Yorkshire, and a burial from Bryher in the Isles of Scilly has both a mirror and a sword.

The identification of an Early to Middle Iron Age tradition of communal burial in quarry hollows is an important discovery. These cemeteries clearly suggest a corporate sense of identity, which is closely associated with a sense of place expressed through enclosure, and the intimate and complex relationship with boundary ditches is clearly important (Figure 5.9). It has taken some time to identify this tradition because the burials are placed in features, quarries, and in locations to the rear of enclosures, which are not normally targeted for excavation. These burials are also likely to be the source for the partially articulated and disarticulated human remains that are found on settlements, which I have already argued are not from excarnation burials (see above). The bones are recovered by the deliberate re-excavation of the burials some time after they have been buried. The re-excavation could be associated with the placement of new burials, but there may be occasions when this was not the case.

Formal cemeteries might evolve from the communal burial tradition, and it may be significant that Durotrigian burials are found on the periphery of settlements. However, it is also possible that more formally organized cemeteries glimpsed in the excavations at Cookey Down were an influential feature of the archaeological record in western Wessex. In either circumstance there is clearly a change from the fragmented partible people of the Middle Iron Age to those circumscribed and sacrosanct individuals of the Late Iron Age.

---

[37] Mirrors have recently been discussed in detail by Joy (2008) and swords by Stead (2006).

Cremation

Cremation was the most common form of burial in the latter part of the second millennium BC, but there is very little evidence that it was an important rite for most of the first millennium BC. It only re-emerges in the first century BC, when a small number of formal cemeteries are identified in Hampshire and Sussex (Fitzpatrick 1997). These later cemeteries indicate close contacts between this area and the emerging Romanized polities of north-west France and south-east England, where cremation cemeteries are relatively common.

The Middle Bronze Age is characterized by cremation cemeteries (Figure 5.12).[38] These vary considerably in size; it is not unusual to find a couple of cremations placed around the edge of an Early Bronze Age barrow (e.g. Coburg Road, Dorset: Smith, R. J. C. *et al.* 1992) but large cemeteries are also known (up to 138 individuals at Simons Ground, Dorset: White 1982). Burials can be placed underneath barrows constructed in the Middle Bronze Age, adjacent to barrows constructed either in the Early or Middle Bronze Age, or as cemeteries unmarked by any prominent mound. The burials can be placed in pots (inverted or upright), or adjacent to pots, but there is seldom more than one pot in the grave. The quantity of cremated bone present in the grave varied considerably, but there is some suggestion that burials placed central to a mound had more bone than burials in peripheral locations (McKinley 1997a). There were generally few grave goods other than the pot that contained the dead. The occasional find of metalwork is often an indicator of the death of the individual present rather than a 'grave good'; at South Lodge, Wiltshire, the distorted tip of a spearhead was found amongst the cremated bones of a burial placed in the ditch fill of a small barrow (Barrett *et al.* 1991: 174).

There is clearly considerable variability, but in general the Middle Bronze Age was characterized by relatively small cemeteries, possibly representing close family (Ellison 1980b). Little effort went into monumentalizing the dead and there were few grave goods deposited with the deceased; pottery is relatively plain and probably represents vessels previously used in domestic contexts (possibly even the deceased's possessions). All members of the community were given similar treatment and there were no great disparities in wealth comparable to those visible in the Early Bronze Age. The burial sites were close to the settlement locations, but in slightly more prominent locations. The larger cemeteries appear to occur in the sand and gravel regions of

---

[38] It should be noted that an increasing number of these cemeteries are being found to include contemporary inhumations and these are particularly common at the cemetery of Twyford Down, Hampshire (Figure 5.12).

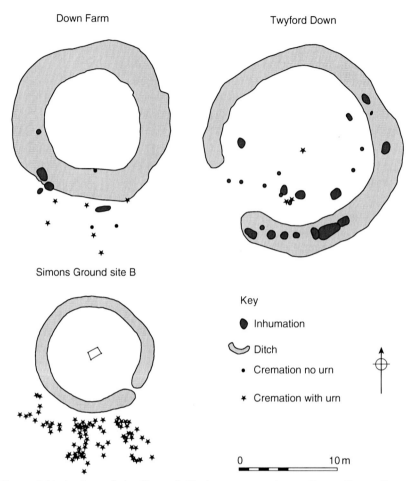

Figure 5.12 A plan of the Deverel Rimbury cemeteries at Down Farm, Dorset; Twyford Down, Hampshire; Simons Ground, Dorset (after Barrett *et al.* 1991: fig. 5.44; Walker and Farwell 2000: fig. 8; White 1982: fig. 2).

the Dorset Heaths. These areas do not seem to have the historical depth of settlement that existed on the chalk downlands, and the ephemeral evidence for Middle Bronze Age settlement suggests activity was less substantial and permanent in these areas. The relatively large cemeteries may therefore represent locations where relatively dispersed and mobile communities regularly met in an otherwise open and undifferentiated landscape.

Some archaeologists have argued for the continued importance of cremation in the early centuries of the first millennium BC (Cunliffe 1995: fig. 36). However, this argument is based on late radiocarbon dates from Deverel

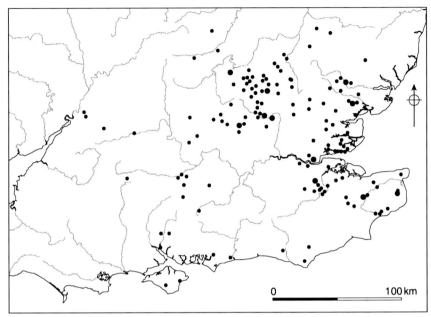

Figure 5.13 The distribution of Aylesford Swarling cemeteries in south-east England (after Fitzpatrick 1997: fig. 115).

Rimbury cremation cemeteries such as Simons Ground, Dorset (White 1982), and these dates have been demonstrated to be due to laboratory error (Needham 1996). Cremations were occasionally deposited on Late Bronze Age settlement sites[39] but, in a recent survey, Brück (1995) convincingly argues that this was largely abandoned as a formal burial rite at this time everywhere except East Anglia (Brück 1995: 247).

In the first century BC cremation reappears as a formal burial rite (the Aylesford Swarling tradition) in south-east England (Whimster 1981). The distribution is concentrated in Kent, Essex, and Hertfordshire, but it extends north to Cambridgeshire, and west along the south coast to Hampshire (Figure 5.13). The distribution is not continuous and there is a significant gap in the Weald, East Sussex, and Greater London. Cemeteries are normally quite small, most containing fewer than five burials (Fitzpatrick 1997).

---

[39] Two cremations were found in settlement contexts associated with Late Bronze Age pottery at Green Park (Reading Business Park), Berkshire, and a further five cremations came from settlement contexts that were less securely dated to the Late Bronze Age (Boyle in Moore and Jennings 1992: 98; Boyle in Brossler *et al.* 2004: 106). A cremation was also noted at the nearby settlement of Knights Farm, Berkshire (Bradley *et al.* 1980).

The size and significance of the burials are variable, but most are placed in pits in unmarked graves. Pottery is the most common accompaniment, and vessels could be used either to contain the cremated remains or as an offering adjacent to the cremation; these vessels probably contained food and drink that has disappeared. Other grave goods include brooches, but a significant feature of the burial record is the rarity of weapons and offerings of food, such as joints of meat.

A fairly typical small cremation cemetery was excavated at Owslebury in Hampshire, adjacent to a small settlement that was occupied from the third century BC through to the fourth century AD (Collis 1977b). Middle Iron Age burial traditions were represented by isolated human bones in settlement contexts, but in the middle of the first century BC, a well-defined cemetery was established in the loop of a linear boundary. Two other less clearly defined burial areas are known, and there is a scatter of burials within the settlement boundaries. The primary burial in the main cemetery area is an extended inhumation of a 40–50-year-old male accompanied by a shield, a spear, and a sword with its accompanying belt fittings. This burial is the only inhumation of this date and lay at the centre of a small rectangular enclosure within which are another two Late Iron Age cremations and one Roman cremation. The adjacent enclosure had 13 burials, five of which were thought to be Iron Age. The most richly equipped of these burials again lies at the centre of the enclosure, but in this case it is a cremation.

The Aylesford Swarling tradition includes two groups of rich burials, the Welwyn Type dating from c.70 to 20 BC, and the Lexden Type, which continues from 20 BC up to and beyond the Roman conquest. However, neither of these types has been found south of the Thames in the area we are concerned with, though they may be found there in the future. Unusually large cemeteries have been identified at two sites: King Harry Lane, St Albans (Stead and Rigby 1989) and Westhampnett near Chichester (Fitzpatrick 1997). Both the rich burials and the large cemeteries are located close to *oppida*.[40]

Westhampnett is an important cemetery that lies within our research area and deserves detailed comment (Fitzpatrick 1997). Some 161 graves were found, and these were deposited between 90 and 50 BC, making this one of the earliest cemeteries of this type in southern Britain. The cemetery is characterized by pit burials, pyre sites, and structures of presumed ritual significance (Figures 5.14, 5.15). The burials comprised: cremated bones, normally placed

---

[40] After writing this chapter a new discovery was made at North Bersted in West Sussex of a male about 30 years old. He was accompanied by three large jars, a knife, a helmet, and a shield, and placed in an iron-bound coffin. It is interesting to note that this burial was found close to the large cemetery of Westhampnett and the putative *oppidum* of Chichester (Thames Valley Archaeological Services website 2009).

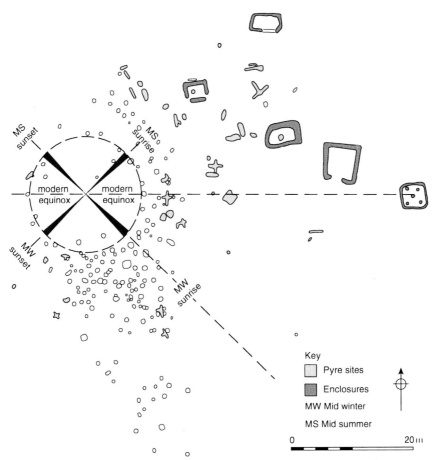

Figure 5.14 A plan of the cemetery at Westhampnett, Sussex, showing the cremation pits and mortuary structures. The major cardinal alignments are imagined for a primary circular mound or structure that no longer survives (after Fitzpatrick 1997: fig. 137).

in the pit rather than in a pot; grave goods, almost exclusively pots that were placed in the grave; and pyre offerings that were taken to the grave with other pyre debris, mostly animal bone and brooches. The quantity of cremated bone deposited was variable; small quantities were quite common and seem to bear no relationship to age or sex, the number of pots present, or the shape and location of the grave (Figure 5.15). It appears, therefore, that the physical remains of the deceased were only a token presence in the final ritual of closure. A range of ages and both sexes were present. Sex did not appear to have a great deal of influence on the burial practice, but age was significant;

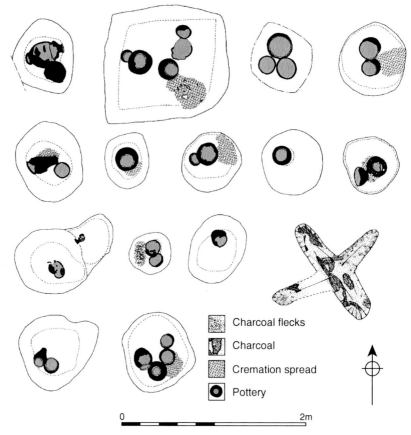

Figure 5.15 A selection of plans for the Westhampnett graves and one of the distinct-ive pyre features (after Fitzpatrick 1997; reproduced with the permission of Wessex Archaeology).

children and young adults appear in association with a more restricted range of ceramic vessels, and the presence of pyre offerings was also much less common.

The burials appear to be arranged around a circle of open space and it was argued that this 'echoes the shape of the contemporaneous roundhouse' (Figure 5.14; Fitzpatrick 1997: 238), and provided a cosmological structure and orientation for the placing of the burials, which were concentrated to the south-east of the centre of the open space (see Chapter 4 for a discussion of house cosmologies). It is also noted that a group of large square burial pits appear to indicate important individuals with larger than normal assemblages of grave goods. These burials also tended to have more space around them than other burials and, in some cases, it was clear that smaller burials were arranged around the large burials. A similar pattern was observed at King Harry Lane (Stead and Rigby 1989: 80–1) where ditched compounds had large rich central burials surrounded by rings of smaller burials. Hill (2007) has suggested that these arrangements indicate family groups comprising an elder, surrounded by his family, and though the details of this interpretation can be questioned (Millett 1993), the presence of separate groups within the cemetery does seem significant.

In general, the cremation cemeteries of eastern Wessex represent small cemeteries associated with family units living in small farmsteads. They are not conspicuously positioned and are not normally associated with elaborate consumption rituals. The presence of a large cemetery at Westhampnett indicates the bringing together of several of these communities, and the development of the Chichester region as an important centre for the Sussex coastal plain at the beginning of the first century BC. However, there is no evidence that a substantial permanent settlement existed in this area and it is also unclear if the dyke systems and other characteristic *oppida* features were present at this early date. The rite of cremation does not appear to be connected with earlier Bronze Age burial rites and is much more likely to indicate the influence of Continental practice. It was routinely believed that the appearance of the Aylesford Swarling culture in the first century BC indicated an invasion from the Continent; the only Iron Age invasion recorded in history and referenced by Caesar in his text on the Gallic Wars. Whilst the nature of contact with the Continent has been much debated, there can be no doubt that the appearance of these burials indicates a dramatic change in first century BC practices. This creation of formal cemeteries with identifiable burials would suggest an increasing concern with the definition and integrity of the Iron Age individual that contrasts significantly with the situation in the preceding 1,000 years.

RECONSIDERING INDIVIDUALITY IN THE FIRST MILLENNIUM BC

The detailed analysis of the human bones from Iron Age Wessex helps us to understand the nature of individual personhood in the first millennium BC. There clearly are significant differences in the Late Iron Age concepts of the individual in the west (south Dorset) and the east (Hampshire and West Sussex), and with the individuals from the previous 900 years of the first millennium BC. The most important distinctions are between the individual graves arranged in cemeteries in the Late Iron Age, and the much more complex processes that are visible in the previous nine centuries. I will start with the patterns that immediately precede the Roman conquest, since these have the benefit of being clearly defined, at least in two areas within the region.

It might seem that the presence of individual burials in clearly defined cemeteries implies similar developments in both south Dorset and Hampshire and West Sussex. In both areas the body was contained and proscribed: in the west, the body was confined by the sides of the individual grave in which it was placed; in the east, the body was defined by the sides of the pit and possibly by an organic container or fabric wrap.[41] In both areas the burial pit/grave was inviolate and was not disturbed by later burials, which assumes some form of marker exists. However, there are significant differences between the complete inhumations in the west and the cremated remains in the east. The cremations were transformed by fire from flesh to ash: from person to ancestor (Fitzpatrick 1997: 241). The act of cremation gave the living control over the transition process and enabled them to carry out this transition much quicker than if the body were left to normal decay processes. Furthermore, only a token, a small representative fragment of the individual, was transferred to the grave, the bulk of the ashes remaining at the pyre site to be dispersed by the elements.[42] In contrast, in the west, inhumations retained their integrity throughout the process of burial. Their transformation to ancestors, the decay and disappearance of flesh, did not require any intervention by human action and took place slowly, out of sight of the descendants. The orientation and layout of the body were carefully controlled, and represent an attempt to place the individual in a cosmological space; the deceased were oriented so that when they emerged in the next world they could quickly locate themselves.

The deceased is normally accompanied by grave goods in both regions. In the east, understanding is limited by the possibility that material placed in the grave pit has decayed; nevertheless, it is clear that offerings of food were placed on the pyre and that the deceased were clothed, as burnt and fragmented animal bones and brooches are found with the ashes. The only unburnt items placed in the grave were pots, jars and bowls, presumably connected with the display and consumption of food. In the west, there are offerings of joints of sheep, cattle and pig, and pottery, which again emphasize

---

[41] This cemetery is distinguished from later Aylesford Swarling burial practices, particularly those to the north of the Thames where the ashes are placed in a ceramic container.

[42] It is also possible that some of the ash was collected to be taken away from the site by the mourners, and if this was the case this might make these practices similar to those of the preceding Iron Age.

the consumption of food and drink in a culturally acceptable fashion. However, there are grave goods such as brooches and other body ornaments that delineate the individuality of the person buried. There are some very high-status objects, including a sword and a mirror, which link individuals into a wider network of exchange relationships. Sex and status are distinguished in these burials and clearly represent criteria for differentiating individuals in the communities of south Dorset.

The arrangement of the burials in cemeteries gives some indication of the nature of the communities these individuals belonged to; in both areas the cemeteries are normally small and it has been argued that they indicate family groups living in immediately adjacent farms (Collis 1977b). However, both areas also have large cemeteries; in the west, the largest is found in the entrance to the hillfort at Maiden Castle (Sharples 1991c: 116–24). This was, by then, an ancient monument whose population had shrunk dramatically, as independent farmers moved out into the surrounding countryside. However, it was still occupied, unlike most of the hillforts to the east, and it was an ancestral symbol that probably drew people together for important ceremonies. In contrast, the large cemetery in the east was located at a new site, one that was in the process of becoming. Westhampnett lies to the east of Chichester within the area defined by the Late Iron Age dykes (Figure 2.24) and in a locality producing large quantities of coins (Bean 2000). This area was clearly a focus for Late Iron Age activity (Hamilton 2007), and the establishment of the Roman town, and the important early Roman palace at Fishbourne, demonstrated its significance. People were gathering here to establish social relationships, and the exceptional nature of the place was marked by the creation of the largest cemetery in the region. The structure of the cemetery at Westhampnett suggests small family groups subsumed within a larger overarching structure, which might well reflect the changing nature of the emerging community.

The burial traditions that characterize the first millennium BC prior to the last century BC are significantly different from these individual burials noted above. If the Middle Iron Age cemetery at Suddern Farm is representative, then the individual identity of the deceased is not nearly as highly valued. The body, though arguably interred in a grave, had no bounded space around it that separated it from other bodies. Rather, it was placed within an ill-defined quarry, which acted as a communal grave for the people living in the immediately adjacent enclosure. The pit, in which the individual was placed, was simply a conduit that accessed this communal space. The situation at Cookey Down and Suddern Farm suggests that old burials were deliberately sought out to provide bones that could be removed, taken to settlements and subsequently deposited in grain storage pits. The act of interment therefore provided access to the ancestors and encouraged the recovery of the ancestors' remains.[43]

The disturbance of existing burials was not random but involved the deliberate selection of skulls and long bones. The former is clearly the most distinctive part of the body and may be assumed to have represented a particular aspect of humanity: the soul or the intellect. The choice of the long bone is more difficult to understand, but it seems clear that the right femur was the favoured bone in Wessex for a long period of time.[44] The thigh bone (femur) is a symbolically significant part of the human anatomy, appearing notably in the skull and cross bones, and this at least partially reflects its size and solidity, as one of the largest and strongest bones in the human skeleton. Once removed, the handling and fragmenting of the bones may have been significant; many of the isolated bones found in settlement contexts have green fractures (Bishop and Knüsel 2005; McKinley in Ellis and Powell 2008). This might indicate deliberate fragmentation to enable these selected bones to be distributed more widely within the community. These ancestral remains could have circulated for a long period of time or they could have been interred very soon after they were exhumed, but in either case the act of deposition would have been a moment of considerable significance.

It would appear, therefore, that for the bulk of the population, and for most of the first millennium BC, being human involved a subversion of personal identity into the community. This was physically expressed in death by the incorporation of the body into a communal grave. The individual was no more than a fragment of that community and on death this partibility was clearly expressed by the breakdown of the body and the movement of token elements amongst the living. These skeletal elements, skulls and femurs, again must have represented the community but perhaps this was the community of the ancestors, and the bones were a means by which the ancestors were represented and influenced the activities of the living.

The fragmented or partible individuals that make up the bulk of the population throughout the first millennium BC contrast with the complete burials found in the settlements. As has been noted above, the age and sex of complete burials differ from the partial and disarticulated remains, and suggest that there is a process of selection involved that differentiates the two groups. The treatment of complete individual burials is clearly very different from the normative burial rite identified above. Instead of being

---

[43] The burials at New Buildings and the large quantities of fragmented bone at Potterne and Battlesbury suggest that the recovery of ancestral bone was a tradition that developed at the beginning of the first millennium BC and is little affected by the transition from bronze to iron.

[44] Perhaps the side is not a specific choice but simply reflects the predominance of burials placed on the left-hand side which would expose the right side to the excavators.

placed together as a group, they are isolated from the community of ancestors. Analysis by Wait (1985) demonstrated the peripheral position of complete burials in the earlier phases of the Iron Age. This spatial significance is most clearly demonstrated by the distribution of these human remains at Winnall Down. Hill (1995b: 87–91) has shown that these burials mark out the northern and southern extent of the settlement area in the Middle Iron Age. It is probably significant that human remains were found just outside or cutting into the infilled ditch of the Early Iron Age enclosure. It seems reasonable to suggest that the boundary of the site was marked by human burials because the inhabitants were not allowed to have an enclosure ditch (see Chapter 3). Complete human remains are often found on the edge of settlements and these include some incorporated into hillfort ramparts. There are several from Maiden Castle (e.g. Wheeler 1943: 123) but unfortunately very little of the boundary at Danebury was excavated. In the Late Iron Age, the boundaries of the settlement appear to become less clearly defined and burials are more commonly located in the interior (Wait 1985).

The circumstances of the deposition of these burials are also very distinctive. Many of the burials are very tightly crouched, and to achieve this position they must have been bound. Some individuals have been noted with hands tied together, several were covered with large blocks of stone that appear to deliberately conceal them, and some of the Danebury burials appear to have been pelted with slingstones. These characteristics have led some to suggest that they are sacrifices, people deliberately punished and excluded from the community.[45]

The role of these individual burials cannot be clarified without a detailed consideration of social relationships in these small tightly bounded communities. We have to broaden our discussion of individuality and partibility by examining a broader range of the archaeological evidence for the importance of community, but first we need to provide a theoretical framework for this analysis. I will do this by considering the ideas of Mary Douglas.

---

[45] The temporal nature of these acts of deposition is more difficult to ascertain, as it is very difficult to estimate how frequently these deposits occur. Hill (1995b: 75) suggests that these deposits may take place once every 10–20 years at a site such as Winnall Down but may be much more common at hillforts such as Danebury. Cunliffe's (1995: 76–7) figures suggest that a complete body was deposited every 5.8 years whereas body segments and the isolated bones could be deposited roughly every four years. If we combine these two figures it is likely that human burials occurred roughly every 2.4 years at Danebury. However, these estimations are fraught with difficulty as they assume we have recovered evidence for all the people buried, which is very unlikely.

Mary Douglas

Mary Douglas is an author all too often overlooked by archaeologists. Very few archaeologists have referenced her substantial work on social analysis, *Natural Symbols* (Douglas 1970), which forms the theoretical basis for an analysis of risk, goods and exchange, and social institutions. The ideas presented in *Natural Symbols* created a field of sociological research known as Cultural Theory (Thompson *et al.* 1990), which provides a comparative framework for understanding how individuals respond to problems and opportunities to create a particular form of society. *Natural Symbols* is also important in providing a general explanation for the development of the pollution taboos discussed in Douglas's earlier book, *Purity and Danger* (Douglas 1966); which is a study much more frequently referenced by archaeologists.

Using the ideas of Basil Bernstein (1971), and with reference to ethnographic examples from colonial Africa and 1960s Britain, Douglas (1970) constructed a system of classification that is based on the importance of relationships that bind individuals to both grid and group. The group, in its extreme form, is a tight-knit closed social unit and has obvious symbols to indicate inclusion and exclusion. These groups can be kin-based, but this is not essential. The behaviour of individuals within these societies is influenced by factors of 'grid'; relationships based on the coming together of ego-centred networks, focused on age, sex, status, and practical or ritual knowledge (Douglas 1970: 57). The principal differences are between group relations of solidarity and grid relations of position. The relative strength of the relationship to grid or group creates a fourfold division of societies (Figure 5.16). In section B, individuals are tied to neither grid nor group and all relationships are between individuals. In section A, there are no defined groups, but individuals are constrained by roles that are ascribed to them. In section C, individuals belong to closed groups that are clearly structured, normally in a hierarchical fashion. In section D, belonging to a defined group is crucial, but the internal structure of the group is undifferentiated.

In her original analysis, Douglas (1970) was prepared to categorize complete African societies on the basis of the strengths of grid and group relationships, but in recent years she, and others, applied these ideas to localized groups operating within contemporary Western societies (Delamont 1992; Douglas 2005; Hendry 1999). They also further developed the ideas behind the model, and this resulted in significant alterations to the structure of the grid, and the beliefs and attitudes ascribed to

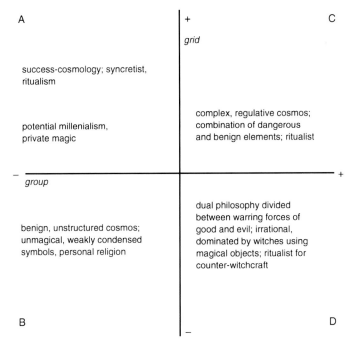

Figure 5.16 The Grid and Group matrix (after Douglas 1970: diag. 9).

the different groups.[46] In recent work, Douglas was at pains to stress that every society was composed of groups that could be placed in all four corners of her matrix; people in these groups define themselves in relation to each other and these relationships are critical and competitive (Douglas 2005). Nevertheless, Douglas was still prepared to accept that these groups could be more or less dominant in any society, and therefore that societies could be classed by certain tendencies in relation to grid and group. This change in emphasis reflects Douglas's shift in interest from the

---

[46] Grid and group have been discussed by Douglas in several publications since the original idea was proposed in 1970 and in the process the idea has changed its emphasis quite considerably. These changes have been discussed by Fardon (1999) and Hendry (1999). The most significant is that concerning the relative position of the ego-centred individualist which resulted in the reversal of the grid axis, and positions A and B swap places between Douglas 1970 and Douglas 1982a. The textual history of *Natural Symbols* is also problematic as the most readily available British version of this book (Douglas 1973) is the second edition, which Fardon (1999: 221) has argued is an inferior presentation of the theory. This author prefers the first edition and owns a copy of the New York reprint (Douglas 1982c), which provides the basis for most of the discussion in this chapter.

anthropological study of relatively small-scale societies, which feature in the original text, to the analysis of contemporary social groups belonging to complex twentieth-century society. Although the earlier analysis may provide a more appropriate understanding of the later prehistoric societies of Britain, the realization that society comprises groups with the full range of relationships to grid and group could explain change during the Iron Age. Furthermore, the interpretation of sub-groups in contemporary society is relevant to the discussion of Iron Age studies (Sharples forthcoming).

To Douglas (1970: 103–4) the increasing importance of grid relationships creates a series of cosmological beliefs that are predictable and standardized. In these societies:

- individuals relate to others in categories equivalent to themselves;
- group boundaries are ephemeral;
- the cosmos is manipulative but not regulative;
- leaders are characterized by courage, determination, and cunning;
- the external manifestation of life is valued;
- wealth and material possessions are perceived in a positive light as good for society and for the individual.

In a society where group relations are of fundamental significance:

- roles are ambiguous and undefined;
- leadership is precarious;
- boundaries are the main definers of roles—you are either a member or a stranger;
- there is a complex cosmos;
- magical danger is associated with the boundary;
- society is 'preoccupied with rituals of cleansing, expulsion and re-drawing of boundaries';
- the individual is self-subordinated to the group.

Small-scale Bounded Societies

The emphasis placed on bounded and unbounded societies is clearly significant to this study since the most visually characteristic feature of Iron Age societies in Wessex is bounded settlements. To a certain extent, Douglas is speaking of metaphorical boundaries, but in places she quite explicitly states that she 'would expect the small closed group to use a recursive patterning of external boundaries at all levels: village boundaries will be clearly demarcated'

(Douglas 1982a: 214). Her concern with the sociological implications of boundedness coincides with recent archaeological interpretations that emphasize how physical boundaries indicate a conceptual concern with group definition (Bowden and McOmish 1987; Hingley 1984). It is therefore important to reconsider the analysis of earlier chapters in this book as they certainly help to substantiate many of the generalizations that Douglas makes about bounded societies.

In Chapter 3, I discussed how the act of creating a hillfort boundary provided a mechanism for competitive display in the Early to Middle Iron Age, but I stressed that these boundaries had many roles, including a desire to create a viable community that is clearly and emphatically distinguished from other neighbouring communities. The boundary does this in a number of different ways:

- it encloses a group of people who would previously have been living in individual farmsteads;
- the residential stability provided by the creation of the boundary creates a temporal connection to a location which the previously shifting farmsteads did not have;
- the boundaries themselves symbolize the landscape of the various groups in the hillfort;
- the construction process restructures daily routines away from the family towards the community.

The settlement record for Later Bronze Age societies on the chalk downlands was explored in Chapter 2 and it was demonstrated that people were living in small isolated farmsteads, which were the location for single family units, as at Easton Lane/Winnall Down, Hampshire, and Coburg Road, Dorset. In contrast the Early Iron Age enclosures generally contained much larger and more densely packed settlements. This is certainly the case with hillforts such as Danebury, which was densely occupied, but even the smallest of the Iron Age enclosures, such as Winnall Down, arguably contained three households and were closely connected to groups living in adjacent enclosures.

The relatively large numbers of houses in the Middle Bronze Age landscape are likely to be due to the relatively short lifespan of the houses constructed at this time (see Chapter 4). In the Late Bronze Age, houses appear still to have relatively short lifespans but they are now being rebuilt on the same spot. In the Early Iron Age the construction of permanently occupied hillforts clearly demonstrates a long-term commitment to a location, and implies the residential stability of the community. Houses still have short lives but they are often rebuilt on the same spot again and again, possibly indicating the inheritance of certain plots by specific families.

The boundaries around these settlements (discussed in Chapter 3) were argued to symbolize the landscape occupied by the communities, by actually incorporating readily identifiable aspects of the landscape into the construction: limestone at Maiden Castle and substantial quantities of timber at Segsbury. The source for both these very visual materials would be well known to the community, and to any visitor to the hillfort it would be a clear indication of the extent of the community's territory.

The construction process involved the organization of large numbers of people and even the small hillforts of the Early Iron Age would require the gathering together of a substantial labour force. These construction events are not just a necessary stage in the building of the enclosure but actually define the social relationships of the community created by the hillfort. The organization of the work would require the breaking down of individual family units into much larger work units that were assigned specific jobs during the construction process, and these work units could be maintained beyond the period of the construction. This organizational mechanism effectively deconstructs family units and creates a larger community that operated at a wider, but probably still notionally kin-based, level.

The continued construction and reconstruction of the hillfort boundary became the major mechanism for the expansion of certain communities, and for the development of asymmetrical power relationships between communities in the Middle Iron Age. Successful communities, such as the group occupying Maiden Castle, were able to expand and absorb previously autonomous bounded communities. Coercion was clearly part of this process, and I have no doubt that warfare was endemic in these societies. However, the main means of integrating and restructuring these communities continued to be through the construction of the rampart, which in the Middle Iron Age appears to be a regular, possibly annual process of heightening, expansion, and redesign. Communities in competition with successful hillforts were forced to abandon their bounded settlements, or to destroy the boundaries that surrounded them. They may even have been forced to attend the rampart construction events by the removal of a substantial portion of their crop after harvest. By summer the supplies in smaller settlements would have been running low, which would have required the movement of at least some of the people, probably the males if the skeletal evidence is representative, to the hillfort where their grain was stored.

The hillforts, and the other bounded settlements, that emerge at the beginning of the Iron Age indicate what Douglas would call 'small bounded units', and even the larger examples of the Middle Iron Age would be labelled small in her social categorization. According to Douglas, these societies are characterized by the subordination of the individual to the group, roles are ambiguous and undefined, and leadership is unstable. In other words, individuality is not encouraged; indeed, it is regarded as counter to the stability of the group and potentially threatening.

The clearest archaeological indication of self-expression is the variability of material culture and one of the characteristic features of the Bronze Age/ Iron Age transition in Wessex is the disappearance of the wide range of bronze tools, ornaments, and weapons that were such an important feature of the early first millennium BC (see Chapter 3). These objects are not replaced by iron examples, and after the Llyn Fawr period there is nothing remotely comparable in scale or technological complexity for at least 300 years. The most common ornamental objects in the Early and Middle Iron Age are fibulae, but these are not comparable in scale to the ornaments that were circulating in the Late Bronze Age, and they are not present in large numbers.

A finds assemblage recovered from a Middle Iron Age settlement would normally consist of tools such as whetstones, knives, bone gouges/points, hammerstones and textile equipment such as weights, spindle whorls, needles, and weaving combs. The craftsmanship on most of these artefacts is simple, and there is very little evidence for an investment of social capital in the production of these objects.[47]

For a short period, at the end of the Bronze Age and the beginning of the Iron Age, the ceramic record becomes diverse and includes a variety of forms, sizes, and qualities (Figure 3.4). There are some particularly fine vessels, such as 'scratch cordoned bowls', that are elaborately decorated and provided with a shiny red surface that makes them visually attractive and possibly reminiscent of metal vessels. The variety of forms and the presence of high-quality vessels contrast with the limited range of the assemblages in the Late Bronze Age and with contemporary ceramic assemblages from areas outside southern England. These fine ware vessels are almost certainly used for serving food and probably indicate the increasing social importance of food consumption. They might also indicate a concern with household relationships, perhaps stressing household meals compensated for the lost spatial independence of people who had moved into hillforts.

---

[47] In his recent catalogue Stead (2006) lists 37 objects in Wessex that might have come from swords or scabbards. These included only five largely complete artefacts, and where dating evidence was available these items appear to belong to the last three, if not the last two, centuries BC. The only weapon that is commonly found in the Early to Middle Iron Age is the slingstone, and this may have a more prosaic function in a society of shepherds.

As we move into the Middle Iron Age the quantity, quality, and technical sophistication of the pottery assemblages become more restricted. The fine wares disappear and there seem to be very few small vessels that would be appropriate to the individual serving of food—communal cooking vessels appear also to have been used for serving food (Figure 3.10). Decoration is almost completely non-existent. We are left with a range of very simple forms, all of roughly the same size, which had multiple functions for storage, cooking, and consumption. This could be interpreted as the increasing social control over food consumption. It may well have become a more communal activity where the complex symbolism of the family meals would be inappropriate.

Another archaeological indication of internal social variability within these communities is domestic architecture. As was noted in Chapter 4, during the transition from the Bronze Age to the Iron Age, there was considerable variability in architectural form, and large houses were constructed at sites such as Pimperne and Longbridge Deverill Cow Down. These could well indicate the presence of high-status families conspicuously displaying their importance within the community. However, these houses are short lived and the sites on which they are constructed are normally abandoned by the end of the Early Iron Age. In the Middle Iron Age, houses are small and surprisingly uniform, particularly in hillforts such as Danebury.[48]

Pollution in Bounded Societies

The archaeological characteristics of Early to Middle Iron Age societies in Wessex therefore conform remarkably accurately to the social characteristics of bounded societies described by Douglas. The settlements are emphatically bounded and appear to lack any archaeological evidence for hierarchies, based on the individual or the household. There are also no obvious indications of clearly separate craftsmen, or any form of specialization, within these relatively self-sufficient communities. The evidence from the burial record of large communal burial pits, and the re-excavation and partibility of the dead, also clearly indicate a society where individuality is subordinate to the identity of the group.

---

[48] The organization of these structures at Danebury is reminiscent of terraced housing in the industrial cities of northern England where it arguably represents an attempt to create a dehumanized and compliant workforce in the class-based society of nineteenth-century Britain.

Table 5.1 The characteristics of societies with weak grid and strong group relations (after Douglas 1982a: 205–6).

	Ethnographic characteristic	Archaeological corollary
1.	All social experience is constrained by the external boundary	The enclosure is the locus for all socially significant activity
2.	The group will impose tight constraints on all external contacts and these will be prescribed by ritual activity	Exchange relationships are limited and the material derived from these features strongly in ritual deposits
3.	Individual behaviour will be tightly prescribed by the group	Material culture associated with decorating the body is limited
4.	Internal divisions, such as segregating, delegating and specializing roles, will be absent	There is no evidence for the development of craft specialists, ritual specialists or leaders. Enclosures are not subdivided into separate compounds
5.	As a result of 4, relationships between individuals will always be difficult as all adjudicating rights are implicit	
6.	Because of 4 and 5, internal conflicts are difficult to resolve; only expulsion or fission of the group is possible	Settlement patterns are unstable, with enclosures abandoned and reconfigured on a regular basis
7.	Because of 4 and 2, disagreement is suppressed and ill-will flourishes below the surface and encourages plots to expel awkward members	
8.	Because of 7, covert factions will exist	
9.	Consequent on 6 and 7, controls on admission and efforts to strengthen the boundary will be desired by members who wish to avoid disintegration	The amount of effort involved in developing and elaborating the ramparts of hillforts and the entrances to enclosures becomes substantial
10.	Because of weakness in organization and problems in controlling individuals these groups tend to be small and long-term persistence is unlikely	There is very little evidence for the development of centralized polities with extensive territorial control on the hillfort-dominated areas of the chalk downland

In a later work, Douglas (1982a: 205–6) lays out very explicitly how societies with weak grid and strong group relations will behave, and her conclusions are laid out in Table 5.1 which also shows how they may be related to archaeologically observed phenomenon.

The key aspect of ritual activity in all these societies is the concern with social boundaries, and it is with this in mind that we should reconsider the individual burials that characterize the Middle Iron Age societies of Wessex. One of the themes that Douglas returns to again and again is the importance of witchcraft in these societies (Douglas 1970). The closed and idealistic nature of the communities makes it difficult to explain illness, both personal and social, and the normal explanatory framework is to assume that the body, or the body politic, has been penetrated by outside forces or polluted by poisonous substances. These substances and forces need to be controlled by renewed and intensified ritual activity that is designed to fortify the boundary. Identifying and expelling a traitor within the group, who has enabled the external polluter to penetrate the boundary, can cure the problem; and these traitors are what we term witches. Witchcraft accusations are a result of weak authority structures and an overriding concern with conformity, and they will result in the expulsion of any individuals who challenge the social norms.

The nature of the expulsion is important; individuals could be cast out of the group to join another group, or to live an isolated existence in the interstices of society, but historically witchcraft accusations are likely to lead to a more terminal form of expulsion. It is therefore possible that many of the isolated individual burials found in settlement contexts were the result of witchcraft accusations. These people were being excluded from normal society so they clearly cannot be given the normative burial rite. Their crime is to have undermined the boundaries that define the community and therefore it seems appropriate that many of these burials are placed on the boundaries. Their execution, and the ceremonies that accompany this act of socially approved violence, can be used to reinvigorate the boundary and to strengthen the social inclusion of the group.

Douglas also believed that the emphasis on boundary control would dictate approaches to nature (Douglas 1982a: 209). Nature is likely to be seen as analogous to human society in having groups that are akin to the groups humans belong to, and as such, these will include groups of animals that are classified as dangerous or polluting (possible examples include deer and fish). These comments support Hill's observation that humans and animals are classified together and have complex layers of equivalence (Hill 1995b: 107). However, they do not agree with his suggestion that the human species was classified as lying between dog/horse and wild animals. Hill makes the assumption that the isolated human burials represent the norm, which I have argued is not the case. These burials represent people who have been extracted from society because they have transgressed important boundaries. It is therefore significant that their position in Hill's classification is close to dog and horse, as both these animals transcend the boundary between wild and domesticated. These animals live relatively uncontrolled lives that contrast markedly with the cattle, sheep, and pig that dominate the domestic food assemblages (Maltby 1996). They are, however, consumed, unlike uncontrolled wild animals such as deer and fish. This transitional social position, which allows them to transgress the boundary of the community, would make them problematic and even ritually dangerous: not unlike the boundary-transgressing humans who are also found in these deposits.

A similar conceptual approach could be taken to explain the treatment of material culture in a manner akin to the sacrifice of humans and animals. The objects singled out for breakage and special deposition could be objects that have transgressed social boundaries. In a general sense this would emphasize objects that derived from specialist sources outside the society defined by the hillfort. This is clearly an appropriate interpretation of the querns, which are very often smashed and placed in association with other special deposits. Querns are normally made from exotic stones that have been imported from special quarries outside the control of the community (see Chapter 3). Copper alloy, and, in the later Middle Iron Age, iron objects, are likewise acquired from outside and it is no surprise that these are routinely found in special deposits. However, other less obvious objects could also transgress. Gift exchange relationships between local communities need not necessarily involve objects that were made from unusual natural sources. They could be made from material that was available throughout the landscape and in forms that were identical to those used in both communities. The significance of difference is not necessarily an immutable criterion for all gifts; pottery, domestic animals, and bone tools could all be moving between communities in a manner that is normally regarded as unproblematic. However, if these objects become involved in socially trans- gressive behaviour, or were associated with communities and individuals who became enemies, their status could quickly change to a potentially threatening pollutant that required sacrifice. Indeed, anything has the potential to become polluted, which may explain why a wide range of objects and materials were placed in special deposits. The prevalence of certain objects reflects the likelihood that they would be involved in a socially transgressive act.

TRANSITIONS: MIDDLE TO LATE IRON AGE

Having discussed in detail the bounded societies of the Middle Iron Age, it is now important to consider how these societies were transformed to become the distinctively different Late Iron Age societies where individuals are clearly identifiable in burial practices and by the use of elaborate personal jewellery. This transition should not be seen as a sudden flip to another area of the grid/group matrix produced by Douglas (Figure 5.16). Instead, we should see the transformation as a gradual shift in the import- ance of existing groups who already occupied a different ideological pos- ition in the grid/group matrix. A key to understanding how this transformation occurred is to remember that there is considerable variation in the position taken up by the individuals within any society. All societies are composed of individuals with ideologies appropriate to all four sectors of the diagram. Locating the Early to Middle Iron Age in the sector of low grid and high group is simply stating that most people in this society adopted this ideology.

The presence of contrasting perspectives in this period is amply illustrated by reconsidering the significance of the objects from Maiden Castle discussed at the beginning of this chapter. The bone comb (Figure 5.17), placed at the bottom of the pit, is one of the most attractive objects found during the recent excavations and illustrates the characteristics of many Middle Iron Age objects. The comb was carved from a cattle leg bone and was clearly designed to undertake a specific function.[49] It had been heavily used; the teeth are worn and repeated handling has polished the surface of the bone. The surface was decorated with two double-lined crosses that were carefully and evenly incised. This was clearly an object that meant something to the owner and could possibly even have expressed the character of its creator; a precise person who took pride in their work. These combs are relatively commonplace objects, and there is no reason not to assume that it was made by the person who used it.[50] The form and decoration was probably a personal preference rather than the deliberate expression of ethnic or status affiliations (Hodder and Hedges 1977; Tuohy 1999); it reflects personality rather than individuality. This object may have been exchanged between family members or neighbours, but it is unlikely to have been regarded as having a significant role in complex gift exchange networks. Nevertheless, it was chosen to be sacrificed as part of the rituals associated with the infilling of this pit.

The brooch is quite different (Figure 5.18). This object was undoubtedly meant to be worn, and though it probably functioned to hold a garment in place, it also served to identify the individual who wore it as somewhat special. These objects were produced in a standardized form that changed at regular intervals to reflect, but not mimic, Continental changes (Haselgrove 1997). They were almost certainly produced by specialist craftsmen who had a much wider knowledge of the outside world than the people belonging to

---

[49] The precise function of these objects is the subject of some debate. It was assumed for a long period that they were associated with weaving and the most recent reconsideration has accepted that they are 'used for making the starting borders for the warp, for making braids and webbing, or decorative panels for garments all of which are forms of specialist weaving' (Tuohy 1999: 97).

[50] Tuohy (1999: 97–8) has argued that making these combs is difficult and that there may have been specialist craftsmen, but I am not convinced.

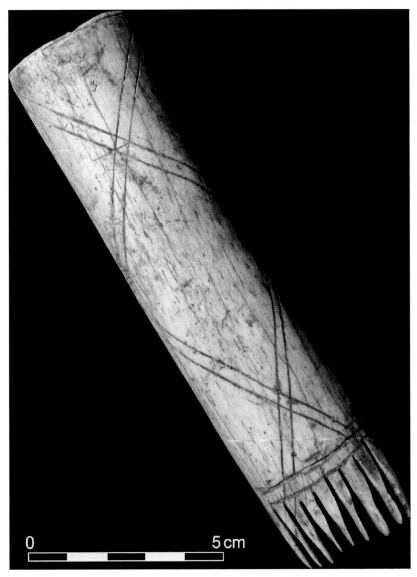

0   5 cm

Figure 5.17 A bone weaving comb found during the excavations at Maiden Castle.

the hillfort community. These individuals were skilled craftsmen and had access to raw materials, such as metals, that were imported from distant lands. The brooch was clearly an item that indicated, and indeed created, the positions that were highlighted by the grid axis of Douglas's

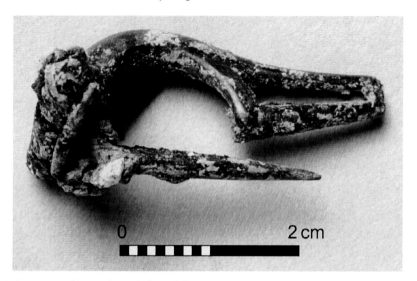

Figure 5.18 A bronze brooch found during the excavations at Maiden Castle.

matrix. Brooches were used to create ego-centred relationships that cut across local groups. The individuals who supplied these objects were located within gift exchange networks that connected them with individuals who were not part of this community, and they themselves might not have been regarded as belonging to a hillfort community because of these connections.

The point of this digression is to emphasize that in every society, even the extremely bounded societies of Middle Iron Age Dorset, there was scope for individual expression. Societies always contained people whose role it was to transgress boundaries to acquire key resources. These boundary transgressions, and aspects of individual expression, could be more or less tolerated, and it is instructive to contrast the material evidence of individuality in west and east Wessex. There appear to be more brooches and other items of personal adornment in Dorset than Hampshire throughout the Iron Age (Sharples 1991a: 249), which suggests an increased openness to potentially polluting exchange relationships in the west. The difference between the individual burials at Cookey Down and the communal burial pit at Suddern Farm, and the difference between the identical houses at Danebury and the much more variable domestic architecture at Maiden Castle, also suggest that personal and household identity is less controlled in the west.

The flexibility visible in Middle Iron Age Dorset might well have been a positive strength to these societies as it would reduce the tensions inherent in

Figure 5.19 A view of the substantial earthworks that protect the west entrance to Maiden Castle (reproduced with the permission of the Society of Antiquaries of London).

these 'bounded societies' that encourage fission and extreme instability (Douglas 1982a). It is noticeable that Dorset has two hillforts, Maiden Castle (Figure 5.19) and Hod Hill, that are substantially larger than the hillforts in other areas of Wessex. It has been argued that the size and complexity of a hillfort was an indication of the strength of the community involved in its construction, and the size of Maiden Castle probably indicates that it controlled a much larger territory than hillforts such as Danebury and Segsbury.

The ability to control large areas of the landscape implies a political complexity that is beyond the capacity of the introverted hillfort societies located in the bottom corner of Douglas's matrix. It is difficult to envisage all the male inhabitants of south Dorset moving to Maiden Castle to help refurbish the rampart every summer, and it would be almost impossible to police boundaries, and control social pollution, in the large polities of later Middle Iron Age Dorset. It seems much more likely that the growing importance of specialist craft activities, such as pottery production in the second century BC, indicates the increasing use of gift exchange to create alliances that bound people to the larger hillfort communities.

The size of the Dorset hillforts might therefore be an indication of the flexibility of Middle Iron Age society in Dorset, and contrasts with the much more rigid and inflexible societies in Hampshire. This in turn might explain the different evolution of these societies in the Late Iron Age. In Dorset, large hillforts continue to be occupied up to, and beyond, the Roman conquest. However, it is clear that their occupation and significance became less and less important. The growth of craft specialization provided an opportunity for individuals to manipulate exchange relationships and to gradually establish their personal relationships with other members of that society; or, as Douglas would put it, individuals began to regard the grid axis as more important than the group axis. By the end of the Iron Age, gender, hierarchy, and household distinctions are visible in the burial and settlement record of Dorset, and the importance of exchange is emphasized by the widespread use of coinage. However, the region has no evidence for dynastic kingship and the hillforts seem to have retained a central symbolic significance for the community, and were important focal points in the response to the Roman invasion.

The evidence from Hampshire is very different. In the Middle Iron Age these societies appear to be much more extreme examples of the bounded societies discussed by Douglas and they have a much more abrupt and disrupted transition to the Late Iron Age. A striking feature of the landscape explored by the Danebury Environs Project (Cunliffe 2000) is the abandonment and reoccupation of enclosures in the first century BC. Danebury appears to suffer a dramatic and possibly violent end to its occupation at the beginning of the first century BC, at the same time as a new and substantial enclosure is built at Bury Hill. This new enclosure has only a short life before it is abandoned in the middle of the first century BC, and this coincides with the construction of a massive double-ditched enclosure at Suddern Farm. These dramatic changes might reflect the extreme instability of small bounded groups that was predicted by Douglas. Furthermore, when change comes it is not driven internally, by the gradual adoption of new ideas and new modes of expression, but it comes from outside. The Late Iron Age power centres are established in regions such as the coastal plain and the Kennet valley hinterland that were external to the hillfort-dominated societies of the chalk downlands. The developments in these regions may indicate the introduction of 'foreigners' from exotic places, such as the Continent, but this is not necessarily so. They could be generated by people escaping the increasingly oppressive, and unstable, societies occupying the Hampshire hillforts.

The relatively unstructured and unoccupied landscapes of the periphery would encourage the development of relationships based on exchange and craft specialization. They provide opportunities to develop individual status that was a total contrast with the earlier hillfort communities and which resulted in the abandonment of the Hampshire hillforts in the first century AD. These societies inevitably developed strong hierarchies, and by the middle of the first century BC in east Wessex leaders are identified by the use of names, the title Rex on coinage, the presence of elite regalia, such as the objects found in the Winchester hoard, and the creation of religious centres.

TRANSITIONS: LATE BRONZE AGE TO EARLY IRON AGE

When I originally conceptualized the transition from the Late Bronze Age to Early Iron Age in terms of Douglas's grid/group structure I envisaged it as a radical transformation from a hierarchical big man society at the extreme corner of the grid/group matrix. However, my ideas have been changed by this re-examination of the evidence, and these changes have been driven by the reappraisal of the evidence of the Late Bronze Age. There is a tendency to assume that the Late Bronze Age is a homogeneous entity, which is essentially the same across the whole of south Britain; but this is not the case. There are significant differences in the nature of the settlements, in the quantities of metalwork that are present, and in the types of artefacts that were used.

In the archetypical Late Bronze Age society there are strong indications of hierarchy denoted by the presence of elaborate weaponry, notably swords, and there is also some evidence that shields and armour were available, though not in the quantities found in Continental Europe. There are also less presti-gious weapons, such as spears, which occasionally achieve dimensions that make them impractical for anything other than symbolic use. Bracelets, pins, and other decorative metalwork are also known, and emphasize the import-ance of bodily ornamentation, though again these are noticeably rare in comparison with the Continental material. Clearly, these societies conform to Douglas's concept of an ego-focused grid-based system where 'questions about the identity and value of the self are hardly soluble except by the manifestations of success' (Douglas 1982a: 136). In the Late Bronze Age, success is perceived as the acquisition and symbolic destruction of material culture. The destruction could be perceived as a deliberate attempt to ma-nipulate the cosmos and to enhance the position of the individual in control of the ceremony. In these excessively competitive societies, boundaries of family, kin, and ethnicity are there to be manipulated and overcome and thus are not a significant feature of the archaeological record of houses, settlements, or landscapes.

This description might be applicable to some Late Bronze Age societies but it is not applicable to all. Areas such as the Thames valley and the Fens have produced large quantities of metalwork and large numbers of swords, but these contrast with the Wessex region, which is very different (Needham and Burgess 1980; Taylor 1993). After a period when large quantities of metalwork were being deposited in the Taunton phase of the Middle Bronze Age, Wessex is characterized by low levels of relatively prosaic tools, weapons, and orna-ments until the end of the Bronze Age when the metalwork of the Llyn Fawr period is particularly well represented (Thomas, R. 1989). It is also important to recognize that the Late Bronze Age landscape of Wessex was partitioned by large boundaries (see Chapter 2). These linear earthworks clearly indicate a concern with the definition of territory and boundedness, which anticipates the hillfort communities of the Early Iron Age. Nevertheless, the linear earthworks are noticeably never completed systems. They stop and start seemingly at random, and in places, such as south of Sidbury hillfort, they appear to have been realigned several times. These are very permeable boundaries, which may even have acted as channels for communication, and they failed to clearly define or protect the communities of the Late Bronze Age.

It would seem, therefore, that during the Late Bronze Age there was a much less extreme form of ego-based competitiveness in Wessex. Nevertheless, the presence of metalwork and the manner in which it is accumulated in hoards and ritually deposited in the landscape clearly indicates that competitive gift exchange networks were operating. Bounded settlements are almost unknown and material culture was not being used to define ethnic groups. This society should be located within the high grid low group-based societies that Mary Douglas characterized in *Natural Symbols* (1970), but it is not an extreme version of this type.

In the transition period between the Bronze Age and Iron Age (*c.*800–600 BC) there appear to be a wide range of responses within the communities of Wessex which testify to the 'weakening of classification systems' (Hendry 1999: 564), and an increasing opportunity for individuals and communities to choose an alternative cosmological view of their society. These strategies are represented by widely varying archaeological phenomena that indicate quite different responses to the collapse of the gift exchange networks that had dominated society for over 1,000 years.

The strategies include an attempt to continue with the Late Bronze Age practice of accumulation and ritual deposition. The availability of plentiful supplies of debased Continental bronze in the Llyn Fawr period seems to have encouraged an increasing interest in hoarding in Wessex. The appearance of the large middens at Potterne, All Cannings Cross, and East Chisenbury might represent a development of this practice, peculiar to certain areas of Wessex distant from coastal connections. These middens may well be intimately connected with the production and circulation of metalwork (Waddington and Sharples 2007), but they incorporate a much wider range of materials, including vast quantities of high-quality ceramics and animal bones, which are probably connected with extensive feasting, plus materials such as bone tools, human remains, and animal dung, which would have been more productively spread on the fields.

Other groups, who might have been relatively disenfranchised in the traditional gift-giving exchanges of the Late Bronze Age, began to separate themselves into relatively self-sufficient communities. These are characterized by the creation of bounded enclosures, which include early hilltop enclosures and possibly hillforts. There was also a proportion of the community that invested a considerable amount of resources in the construction of very large houses. It is difficult to see how all these different manifestations of identity integrate, but this may well represent the fractured and complex nature of the response to the collapse of the bronze exchange networks. The movement of bronze objects had been the most important means of defining people and communities for over 1,000 years, and what appears to be happening in the transition period is that people are experimenting with the cultural media that are available to them, in an attempt to find an alternative process for bringing people together and differentiating them. In Wessex, hillforts emerge as the basic cultural differentiator, and the atomized societies indicated by their construction clearly indicate the disruptive significance of the Late Bronze Age/Early Iron Age transition.

6

Wessex in Context

In this book I have attempted to create a new agenda for the study of Britain in the last millennium BC. The book consciously sets out, in its structure and content, to direct attention away from the nature of the archaeological record towards the nature of past human societies. This does not mean I am not interested in the archaeological record, and readers will have noted there is a considerable amount of detail in the text, perhaps too much for some people; but the data has to be examined in relation to the people who lived in a particular place at a particular time: 'the archaeologist is digging up, not things, but people' (Wheeler 1954b: v).[1]

The objective has been to outline the overall constraints of place and time (Chapter 2) and to see how these created a distinctive archaeological record that differed not only from other areas of Britain, but which varied significantly within the region. I examine how people created communities (Chapter 3) and explore how the mechanisms used to organize human relationships, within that society, changed through time. These changes were partly brought about through events outside their control, but always in a way that was affected by their own particular circumstances. I consider how the most ubiquitous architectural form in later prehistory, the house, was used to structure social relationships on a daily basis in relation to the family, and how this provided a template for thinking about the world (Chapter 4). The analysis concludes with an examination of how these societies considered individual freedom and connectedness, and how the complex variability of individual agency provides an internal dynamic to social change that was influenced by external events, but not led by them (Chapter 5).

When I originally conceived of this book the structure was reversed: I started with the individual and worked up to the organization of the larger landscapes. At first sight this may sound a more sensible way of presenting the evidence, moving from small-scale structures to large-scale processes, but during the writing of the book I found this did not seem to work. My

---

[1] Wheeler unfortunately did not follow this dictum, and most of his writing consists of technical descriptions of archaeological practice rather than a committed attempt to understand the past.

interpretation of how past society was structured seemed to arise through the discussion of the individual rather than the discussion of the landscape. The latter provided an important context, which constrained or provided the resources for the story, but it was the people who gave it the texture and individuality that make this a unique and informative narrative.

As I stated in the Introduction, Wessex is just one of many regions of Britain, and this examination is specific to this particular place at this particular time. At the beginning of the first millennium BC, the region was well connected with other areas of Britain and Ireland, and the Continent. The movement of bronze (copper, tin, and lead) and gold was central to this society and to all the other societies of Western Europe. This common theme created a society in Wessex that was comparable to societies throughout Britain and the near Continent. This is not to say that these societies were identical. The amount of metal available in Wessex appears to be significantly smaller than in other areas. The Thames and the Fens seem to have been able to dispose of vast quantities of Bronze objects, including complex and sophisticated weaponry that must indicate a privileged access to Continental sources. In Ireland, the availability of natural deposits of gold (as well as copper) enabled the development of a spectacular gold industry, and the production of an amazing variety of body ornaments. Clearly, these differences reflect important social differences in these societies. The emphasis on bodily ornamentation and weaponry suggests societies where social hierarchies based on the individual were much more pronounced than in the relatively impoverished landscape of Wessex. However, these differences should not be overstated and should not detract from the essential similarities of the period; people were using the same materials, bronze and gold, but some had access to more of it than others.

In contrast, the Iron Age appears to be a very different period; the societies of Wessex had little in common with the societies of south-east England, northern England, or Scotland, and even less in common with their neighbours across the Channel. These differences were not superficial but are indicative of fundamentally different views of the basic building blocks of society. As I have discussed above, the key component of society in Wessex was the community, a group that combines individuals and households, and acts together in agricultural production, warfare, and religious observance. The archaeological evidence indicates a suppression of the cultural expression of prestige and independence, and by the third century BC most people appeared to be living in large self-sufficient communities: hillforts. The importance placed on the boundaries of these settlements and the ubiquitous presence of human skeletal material in most settlements suggest a society riven by brutal internal and external violence, and anthropological analogy suggests contact with external communities would be restricted and shrouded in taboo.

This society was very different to the societies of northern England and in particular to the Middle Iron Age society occupying the East Riding of Yorkshire (Bevan 1999b; Stead 1991a). The archaeological record of this region is dominated by cemeteries containing individual graves covered by small individual mounds. These burials are furnished with food offerings and small brooches but some also have elaborate weapons, spears mostly, and a few have swords and scabbards decorated with carefully inscribed designs of the highest artistic quality (Giles 2008). This society has a lot in common with the societies of the Continental Iron Age (see below), as do many of the groups in eastern England. The evidence here suggests a society concerned with the role and status of individuals, investing resources in the acquisition of rare and precious materials that can only be manipulated by specialist craftsmen and which can only be used by individuals set apart from the community. This society contrasts with areas immediately to the west and north which are materially impoverished for most of the Iron Age, and because of this they are under-explored archaeologically (Chadwick 2008).

Further north on the Atlantic fringes of Britain there is another fundamentally different Iron Age society. In this area, the archaeological record is dominated by large stone-built roundhouses, or brochs (Sharples 2004; Sharples and Parker Pearson 1997). These structures are monumental in size and indicate an enormous investment of resources for the isolated communities of these agriculturally marginal landscapes. Detailed examination of these structures suggests that buildings were designed to be occupied by extended families and they indicate an investment, presumably by the wider community, in households and families. These families appear to have provided leadership for the local community, and there is certainly evidence that they controlled their agricultural surplus (Dockrill 2002) and places of sanctity and spirituality (Sharples 2006).

The emphasis on these different social phenomena and the development of distinctive regional traditions coincides with the end of the Bronze Age and must in some way be connected with the widespread changes that swept across Europe at this time. It is a little easier to explain how catastrophic the end of the Bronze Age was, given the collapse of the financial markets that devastated national economies in 2008. In the Bronze Age, bronze was as important as money is today; it connected people and created a system whereby people relied on others to provide materials that were not locally available, animals when they were needed for consumption and sexual partners necessary for the continuity of human communities. In times of crisis, the credit built up through the long-term exchange of gifts would enable people to acquire the essentials to rebuild their lives. It also provided a way of classifying and contrasting people and communities by status and identity. This complex system of exchange relationships, and indebtedness, which had been operating for over 1,000 years, was completely undermined and abandoned at the end of the Bronze Age.

Can we imagine what would happen if the banking system that supports the cash economies and capitalist system of the twenty-first century had collapsed in September 2008? If the bank could not guarantee the value of the cash in your pocket, how would you purchase food? How would you be paid? This is normally all done through bank transfers; would shopkeepers accept only precious metals for their purchases? How would our gas, electric, and water supplies be paid for? This situation is unimaginable, but we are assured by politicians that many banks came dangerously close to being insolvent, and would have collapsed if the government had not acted.

The very distinctive regional phenomena found in Wessex, Yorkshire, and Atlantic Scotland resulted from this period of trauma, the Llyn Fawr period, when people experimented with new ways of organizing social relationships: middens, enclosures, large houses. These phenomena took elements of existing practice and enhanced and elaborated them to make them the focus for personal and communal expression and competition. Many of these responses were firmly rooted in the settlement landscapes of the local region and emphasized the importance of economic intensification and reproductive autonomy. The developments in Wessex were probably the most extreme version of this, and people in this region seem to have become particularly concerned with restricting social expression and controlling relationships between communities. It took over 400 years to re-establish networks of trust that would enable long-distance exchange, but even in the Late Iron Age, these appear to be tightly controlled and surrounded by ritual.

The significance of this economic collapse leads to the obvious question of what caused it. This has been the subject of considerable debate and no satisfactory answer has been given. Arguments are polarized around two opposing positions based on whether one believes in indigenous or external agency as a motor for social change. Was the collapse in the British Bronze Age inevitable once Continental Europe stopped mining copper and ceased using it for exchange relationships? Almost certainly. However, did this mean that the Wessex Iron Age would take the form that it did? Obviously not. As we have seen, there are many quite different responses to the end of the Bronze Age, all of which presumably derive from much less significant differences in the Late Bronze Age societies, such as the nature of the environment in each area and the individual circumstances of the people involved. If we briefly consider the Continental evidence for this period of transformation it is possible to identify societies where the transformation from bronze to iron was much less disruptive.

In the southern Netherlands (Fontijn and Fokkens 2007) the transition to iron occurs within the Hallstatt C period (British Llyn Fawr period), and though this does involve a dramatic change in social relations, these are almost the opposite of the situation in Wessex. Elaborate burial mounds associated with complex high-status metalwork, including swords, bronze vessels for food and drink, and cart fittings, make an appearance in this phase. In the previous period of the Late Bronze Age, graves were fairly homogeneous, relatively unmarked and materially poor; metalwork was available but it was deposited in watery contexts. The latter pattern is similar to contemporary patterns in eastern England. David Fontijn and Harry Fokkens associate this change in depositional practice with a decision made by the elite to move from death rituals that expressed their allegiance to the local community, to death rituals that expressed a supranational allegiance to elite peer groups in Continental Europe. The changes also indicate a shift in certain ways of behaving, such as feasting, and the development of elite gift exchange networks. There is a move away from previous exchange networks which link this region with Atlantic Europe towards Central European networks. These political changes may be linked to fundamental changes in the structure of society. Large communal houses, so characteristic of the Bronze Age, are replaced by smaller single family longhouses that are occupied throughout the Iron Age. This suggests a breakdown in local community relationships and an increasing emphasis on individualism, which contrasts with the growing importance of local communities and the suppression of individualism in Wessex.

The development of highly visible elites is even more evident further south in the Hallstatt D period. In southern Germany and western France, this period is characterized by the development of some of the most impressive burials found in Europe (Diepeveen-Jansen 2001, 2007; Wells 1980). Large barrow mounds cover elaborate timber burial chambers, containing complex four-wheeled wagons, and an elaborate material record which seems primarily concerned with the correct way to eat and drink. These burials appear to be closely related to important enclosed hilltop centres which are densely occupied and have access to a rich material culture. A significant feature of these societies is their contact with the Mediterranean, and this is represented by imported pottery and some extremely elaborate metalwork, including the large cauldron placed in the burial at Vix in western France. The interpretation placed on these burials varies considerably. It was suggested that the appearance of these complex societies is based on the prestige gained by controlling inter-regional exchange relationships (Frankenstein and Rowlands 1978), but recently the limited nature of contact with the Mediterranean has been emphasized and it is instead argued that complexity developed from the manipulation of indigenous exchange networks and agricultural production (Diepeveen-Jansen 2007). The nature of display in these Hallstatt D societies, the quantity and quality of the elaborate metalwork, and the conspicuous consumption of that metalwork in burial ceremonies, reflect 1,000 years of Bronze Age practice in central Europe. This pattern continues into the La Tène A period when again, despite significant changes, notably in the geographic area where concentrations of rich graves are found, and in the nature of the objects deposited, burial rites and elaborate metalwork continue to define the existence of an elite. The principal change in material culture is the increasing use of iron weapons, including the development of distinctive long swords and the use of two-wheeled 'chariots' as opposed to four-wheeled 'carts'.

These changes indicate that elaborate craftsmanship and access to good-quality sources of metal, copper, tin, gold, and iron continued to be central to the organization of social relationships. Exchange, probably gift exchange, continued to be supported by, and indeed was essential to the definition and maintenance of, the elite. There is some indication that the beginning of the Iron Age in central Europe was not characterized by the widespread exploitation of local poor-quality iron sources as it was in Britain, but instead, good-quality sources were accessed and the production of surplus for exchange was quickly developed. There seems to be much less disruption in the fundamental principles, though the particularities of exchange relationships and the nature of the material produced and circulated did change.

In Wessex, the changes instigated at the beginning of the Iron Age only seem to be reversed in the last two centuries of the millennium. In this period the traditional emphasis of archaeological texts is on the nature of the contact with Rome. I have again tried to argue in this book that the development of Iron Age Wessex in these centuries does not simply reflect the agency of the Roman empire as it moved inexorably across Europe. The problems of organizing the increasingly extensive territories that developed around the more successful Middle Iron Age hillforts drove change and encouraged a renewed interest in the role of material culture and the development of exchange relationships. A range of materials, including iron and ceramics, was being produced by specialist craftsmen and circulated across southern Britain by the second century BC, and associated with these developments was the introduction of coinage (not by the Romans but by the indigenous groups of northern France). The exchange relationships that these objects testify to developed in the first century BC, and by the time of Caesar's invasion in the middle of this century, which occurred only after a rapid expansion of the western empire in the preceding three years, they were already well established and associated with tribal leadership and political centres in many different areas. These leaders and centres could be targeted by Caesar's invasion and it is very unlikely that Caesar would have made his foray across the Channel if an indigenous leadership had not existed, since the costs of attacking a decentralized polity had been demonstrated by the campaigns in Armorica and Germania. In the following century it is clear that Rome strongly influenced, indeed manipulated, the societies of south-east England, but in this period the indigenous inhabitants of Britain were still able to express their own personality. Some areas, most notably Dorset, developed a distinctive identity that appears to consciously reject Roman culture, whilst developing an economy that was surprisingly effective when the region was eventually incorporated into the Roman empire.

In writing this book I have deliberately avoided using the term Celt or Celtic to refer to the people or the material culture discussed. This term is regarded as deliberately provocative by some archaeologists and there is considerable debate about its validity (Collis 2003; James 1993, 1999). However, I regard this reticence as simply a reflection of the archaeological nature of my training and career. I am interested in developing an understanding of the people inhabiting southern Britain through the archaeological record. I do not believe that this understanding requires the addition of a historical gloss from other vaguely connected regions or periods, and my preference is to use anthropological generalizations about the nature of society to illuminate the archaeology. I feel these have more theoretical complexity than most of the models derived from analysing Celtic society. I have no doubt that the people I have been talking about spoke a Celtic language and were to all intents and purposes Celtic; I am also convinced by linguists (John Koch pers. comm.) that the recent argument for Germanic-speaking populations living in south-east England (Oppenheimer 2006) is erroneous. However, I am not sure that this statement has the significance some people might place on it. The considerable variations in social organization that I believe to have existed in 'Celtic' Britain suggest that a linguistic relationship need not imply any cultural similarities. Nor do the differences that exist between linguistic groups need to be as great as those within the linguistic units. For example, it may be that the similarities that existed between Britain and some areas of Germanic speaking northern Europe were more important than the similarities that existed within Celtic speaking areas of central and Western Europe. These similarities would arise, not because there were connections and communication between the two areas, but because the two areas happened to resolve problems of social organization in similar ways. The archaeological record is now sufficiently detailed to enable the creation of a complex story that is independent of other disciplines but sufficiently convincing to be of interest to not only archaeologists, but also historians, linguists, anthropologists, geneticists, and anyone else who has an enquiring mind.

Appendix

THE CHRONOLOGICAL BASIS

The principal means of dividing and understanding the later prehistory of Wessex depend on the existence of changing styles of metalwork and pottery. Radiocarbon dating has been used only infrequently for dating sites belonging to this period.[1]

The chronology of the Bronze Age metalwork has been refined since the 1990s (Needham 1996; Needham *et al.* 1997; Needham 2007; O'Connor 2007) and is closely related to other well-dated sequences on the Continent. In his paper of 1996, Needham divided the Bronze Age into seven periods that encompass the whole of the Bronze Age, but for the purpose of this book it is sufficient to outline the final three periods. Period 5 extends from 1500 to 1150 BC and encompasses three successive phases of metalwork known as Acton Park 2, Taunton and Penard, which essentially comprise the Middle Bronze Age. Period 6 spans the period from 1150 to 1020 BC, is defined by Wilburton metalwork and represents the first part of the Late Bronze Age. This is followed by period 7, which is characterized by Ewart Park metalwork. It begins about 1020 BC and lasts until around 800 BC (Needham 2007), and is the main period of the Late Bronze Age.

The end of the Bronze Age is characterized by Llyn Fawr metalwork, which dates to between 800 and 600 BC (Needham 2007; O'Connor 2007). This appears to be a transitional stage when the role of bronze metalwork is changing and iron is becoming increasingly important. In some areas, such as the Thames valley, bronze metalwork is increasingly rare during this period and none of the metalwork hoards that are so characteristic of the Bronze Age proper are found here. However, in other areas, such as Wessex, hoards are as important as they were in earlier periods. As a consequence, the term used to describe this period varies. Needham refers to it as the Early Iron Age (Needham 1996: 137) or the Earliest Iron Age (Needham 2007: 40), whilst others refer

---

[1] The only large-scale dating programme undertaken was carried out in the early years of the Danebury project (Cunliffe and Orton in Cunliffe 1984: 190–8) and relied on bulk samples rather than single entities. The taphonomy of the materials dated is therefore problematic. Nevertheless, the dates were re-analysed and modelled using a Bayesian methodology (Buck *et al.* 1992; Buck and Litton in Cunliffe 1995: 131–6) and this analysis forms the basis for creating an absolute chronology for the settlement. The Bayesian analysis also suggested that the ceramic phases had significant periods of overlap and do not appear to be a sequence of successive but separate phases as the excavator had suggested.

to the Ultimate or Latest Bronze Age. In this book the period is referred to as the Late Bronze Age/Early Iron Age transition.

The generally low quantities and undistinguished nature of metalwork at the beginning of the Iron Age, particularly in Wessex, mean that this can no longer be used to define chronological periods. The most useful chronological markers are bow brooches, or fibula that resemble safety pins (Hull and Hawkes 1987). The form of these brooches undergoes regular and systematic changes throughout the Iron Age which correspond to changes taking place on the Continent. They can therefore be related to the European periodization of Hallstatt and La Tène with their increasingly refined subdivisions (Haselgrove 1997) and can be particularly accurately dated in the Late Iron Age when rapid changes of form occur.[2] The increasing importance of coinage at the end of the second century BC is also extremely important in refining the chronology of the end of the Iron Age: this is discussed in detail in Chapter 3.

In southern Britain a considerable amount of effort has been expended on resolving the chronological changes in pottery form, decoration, and fabric that occur during the first millennium BC. It is now possible to be confident of the chronological position of any archaeological site that produces an assemblage containing a reasonable quantity of ceramics. However, the significance of some of the assemblage variation visible is still open to debate, and whereas some have chosen to emphasize fine chronological changes (Davis 1995; Brown 2000), others might argue for a more general process of change, with regions or communities adopting different styles at different times. For instance, there is still some debate over the existence of a separate phase of undecorated saucepan pots in the early Middle Iron Age (Brown 1995: 247; Hawkes 1989: 94).

The later prehistoric pottery sequence begins with the development of Deverel Rimbury traditions in the Middle Bronze Age (Ellison 1975). The pottery characteristically consists of bucket and barrel-shaped urns that are mostly fairly crudely made and sparsely decorated with finger (tip and nail) impressed cordons. A distinct class of fine globular urns exists in the south, and these often have more complex grooved decoration. The characteristics of the Late Bronze Age assemblages of the first part of the first millennium BC are most comprehensively described by Barrett (1980), but a number of assemblages have been published since this synthetic statement, notably Reading Business Park (Moore and Jennings 1992; Brossler *et al.* 2004), and Potterne (Lawson 2000), which have confirmed the chronological patterns and refined the absolute dating of the changes. In the Iron Age the sequence outlined by Cunliffe in the first volume of *Iron Age Communities* (1974) has been refined by the excavations at Danebury (Cunliffe 1984a; Cunliffe and Poole 1991; Cunliffe 1996) and the Danebury

---

[2] The Continental terms Hallstatt and La Tène were used in the initial discussion of the Iron Age (Smith 1925) but were replaced by a systematic reconsideration of the Iron Age by Hawkes (1931) when it was divided into three periods labelled A, B, C. Since then these terms have never been popular with British prehistorians as they are associated with European developments that are not common in England. Several archaeologists have made futile attempts to re-establish the significance of these terms in Britain, notably Harding (1974), but these have been studiously ignored.

Environs programme (Brown in Cunliffe 2000). This now provides a detailed picture of change during the Iron Age for central Wessex. Regional distinctions are more important in this period. The distinctive characteristics of the Sussex assemblages have been examined by Hamilton (1993, 2002) and Seager Thomas (2008), and the sequence in Dorset has been clarified by the excavations at Hengistbury Head (Cunliffe 1987) and Maiden Castle (Sharples 1991a). The latter two sites also provide substantial Late Iron Age assemblages which clarify the changes that occur at the end of the first millennium BC. These changes are much more significant further east and the assemblages from Silchester (Fulford and Timby 2000) and Chichester (Manley and Rudkin 2005) are very different from the assemblages from central Wessex, due to the influence of Continental ceramics.

THE LATE BRONZE AGE (1140–800 BC)

The assemblages of the first part of the millennium are dominated by distinctive shouldered jars, bowls, and cups, though cups are not common (Figure 3.4). The jars and bowls can both be split into coarse and fine ware versions. The former have relatively coarse fabrics and are roughly finished with decoration restricted to applied cordon or finger impressions, whereas the latter are often carefully finished by burnishing or with an applied haematite coated slip, and can have complex incised decoration. The bulk of the jars and bowls have a very distinctive shouldered form, and an open or flaring rim is common. These forms sharply contrast with the straight-sided or biconical forms of the preceding period. Very large jars are known, but these are much less frequent than the very large bucket urns present in the Deverel Rimbury tradition. The quality of the vessels is not related to size, and therefore the distinction between heavy-duty and everyday wares identified by Ellison in the Deverel Rimbury tradition is difficult to determine.[3] The fine ware element is largely restricted to the bowl form.

THE LATE BRONZE AGE/EARLY IRON AGE TRANSITION (800–600/500 BC)

In his original paper Barrett (1980: 314) argues that in the Thames valley the transition from Deverel Rimbury to Late Bronze Age 'Plain Wares' occurred around 1000 BC. These wares became increasingly elaborately decorated as time progresses, and after

---

[3] Woodward has suggested that Barrett identified 'five functional size categories' (1995/7: 197) but this is misleading. Barrett argued that there were essentially two important classes of material, coarse ware jars and fine ware bowls (Barrett 1980: 302–3). These forms are equivalent to the everyday and fine wares identified by Ellison (1975) but the heavy-duty wares are no longer present. Fine jars, coarse bowls, and cups exist but are very rare and by blurring the functional distinctions they appear to make the picture more complex than it really is.

about 800 BC a distinctive 'decorated tradition' existed. In his assessment of the chronology of the Bronze Age, Needham (1996: 134) has argued that the 'Plain Wares' probably begin about 1150 BC but he accepts the date of 800 BC for the development of the 'Decorated Wares'. This dating is based on the large radiocarbon dated assemblages from the Thames valley, and in particular the material from Runnymede Bridge (Needham and Spence 1997b) and the adjacent site of Petters Field (O'Connell 1986).[4]

The decorated tradition is much better represented in Wessex, and large assemblages are known from several sites (Potterne: Lawson 2000; All Cannings Cross: Cunnington 1923; East Chisenbury: McOmish 1996). Cunliffe (1993: 64–5) divided this material into two regional traditions; the All Cannings Cross group and the Kimmeridge-Caburn group.[5] The latter is found in the coastal areas of Dorset and Sussex, the former in the inland areas of Hampshire and Wiltshire. The inland group is characterized by 'red finished bowls with furrowed decoration, large jars with zones of incised geometric or impressed decoration, and a coarse ware component of shouldered jars with finger nail/tip or stabbed decoration on the rim and shoulder' (Figure 3.4; Brown in Cunliffe 2000: 120). The Kimmeridge-Caburn group is similar but the amount of decoration is much less and the distinctive furrowed bowls are uncommon.

Analysis of the material from Potterne (Morris in Lawson 2000) suggests that the midden deposits span the eighth and seventh centuries. During this period bowls become an increasingly important feature of the assemblage; initially biconical bowls are the most frequent type but these are replaced by long-necked bowls as the most common type. There is an increasing range of jars present in the later period, and these are more elaborately decorated.

Dating the end of the decorated tradition is problematic as there is a good deal of continuity with the succeeding phase of the Early Iron Age. The principal distinction

---

[1] In his original paper Barrett suggested that Deverel Rimbury ceramic traditions continue for a much longer period on the Wessex chalk and that Plain Ware traditions were never fully developed in this region. Needham (1996: 135) has convincingly argued that there are problems with the late dates for Deverel Rimbury assemblages in this area and would expect the chronological sequence to be similar (see also Raymond in Bradley *et al.* 1994: 69). The number of Plain Ware assemblages from the Wessex chalk is still very limited. The principal assemblages available to Barrett were from Eldon's Seat and several settlements on the Marlborough Downs (Cleal in Gingell 1992: 100–3) and the contextual information from these sites was not good enough to distinguish the relationship between Deverel Rimbury and Plain Ware traditions. Since then Plain Ware assemblages were recovered at Coburg Road, Dorchester, Dorset (Cleal in Smith *et al.* 1992); and Balksbury, Hampshire (Rees in Wainwright and Davies 1995); and several discrete Plain Ware assemblages have been recovered during fieldwalking on Salisbury Plain (Raymond in Bradley *et al.* 1994). These clearly demonstrate the existence of this tradition in the Wessex heartlands but suggest settlements are more ephemeral and susceptible to plough damage (Healy in Smith *et al.* 1997). Both factors have made identification difficult.

[5] Cunliffe would split the All Cannings Cross group into an early and a later phase based on an increase in the number of furrowed bowls present and the relative percentage of vessels with haematite coating but this division has yet to be identified on any well-preserved site and is not used by other specialists.

is the appearance of the 'scratch-cordoned bowls' described below. These are closely associated with the hillfort at Danebury whose construction is best dated to the beginning of the fifth century BC. This is a century after the accepted end of the Llyn Fawr phase so it appears that the decorated tradition continued across the metalwork-defined boundary between the Late Bronze Age/Early Iron Age transition and the Early Iron Age. The continuation of Decorated Wares/Early All Cannings Cross Wares into the sixth century BC appears to be supported by recent radiocarbon dating of the midden at East Chissenbury.

THE EARLY IRON AGE (600/500–400/300 BC)

Early Iron Age ceramics are well represented in Wessex and the period is characterized by the assemblage from the hillfort at Danebury (Brown 2000), which indicates a continuation of the traditions established at the beginning of the first millennium. A relatively wide range of jar and bowl forms is present (Figure 3.4) but these are generally not as well finished or as highly decorated as the earlier traditions, with the exception of 'scratch-cordoned bowls'. These are very distinctive: they have a rounded body, a high flaring rim, and a foot ring on the base. The upper part of the body is divided by horizontal cordons into zones that are infilled with a geometric decoration created by grooves incised into the body after firing, which are then infilled with a white paste. This bowl form is probably imported from a specialist production centre in the Avon valley in Wiltshire (Brown in Cunliffe 2000: 121) and they are not found in the coastal areas of Dorset, or in Somerset. In the former region small carinated bowls with vertical or slightly flaring upper bodies appear to be the dominant fine ware form. These are again haematite coated.

THE MIDDLE IRON AGE (400/300–100/50 BC)

At the beginning of this period (the early Middle Iron Age) there is a dramatic decline in the quality and variety of forms available. The fine ware bowls disappear and the coarse ware jars are represented by a relatively formless and undecorated group of jars and a new type of plain 'vertical-sided vessel best described as proto-saucepan pots' (Figure 3.10; Brown in Cunliffe 2000: 122). Ceramics from this period are most clearly visible at Easton Lane (Hawkes in Fasham *et al.* 1989: 94) where the Early Middle Iron Age settlement is spatially separated from the preceding and succeeding phases, but the period can also be recognized at Danebury and Old Down Farm. A similar simplification of the range of forms can be seen in the Maiden Castle sequence (Brown in Sharples 1991a).

After about a century, new forms of pottery develop with more clearly defined traits; and Wessex, and the rest of southern Britain, appear to be divided into regional ceramic traditions (Cunliffe 1991: 79–85). The most dominant tradition extends from the south coast of Sussex, through Hampshire and Wiltshire, into south Wales and Herefordshire and is characterized by a distinctive tub-shaped vessel, the 'saucepan pot', and associated round shouldered jars (Figure 3.10). The county of Dorset is distinguished by a very different tradition, known as the Maiden Castle–Marnhull style. This contains 'bead rim bowls and jars, some with counter-sunk lugs, frequently decorated with scrolls, waves, "eyebrows", dimples and other motifs' (Brown in Sharples 1991a: 189).

On the periphery of the area covered by this book are two other ceramic traditions. To the west is a region (Devon, Cornwall, and part of Somerset) identified with Glastonbury Wares (or the South West Decorated Wares). This style is characterized by neckedbowls and jars that are sometimes elaborately decorated with complex incised decoration and curvilinear designs; these are frequently infilled by fine incised hatching. To the north, in Oxfordshire, is the Stanton Harcourt–Cassington style. This starts off rather plain but in the second century some fine bowls with incised swags and arcs appear.

Saucepan pots are very distinctive vessels, normally well fired and at least partially decorated. The form is unknown in the Early Iron Age. However, in the following 300 years, the form comes to dominate across a wide sweep of the countryside. The nature of the decoration on these vessels is significant in identifying seven different regionally specific traditions within the overall area of 'saucepan pot' use (Table A.1).

The regional patterning is crude and it is still unclear what percentage of each assemblage contains regionally specific decorative traits, and the basic premise on

Table A.1 The regional styles of saucepan pot identified by Cunliffe (1991: 80–1)

Name	Location	Common decorative traits
Caburn–Cissbury	Sussex	Simple regular and asymmetrical curvilinear designs
St Catherine's Hill–Worthy Down	Hampshire	Shallow-tooled oblique and vertical lines, in a band below the rim, often defined by horizontal lines or rows of dots
Yarnbury–Highfield	Wiltshire	Swags, arcs, or waves springing from shallow depressions, stab marks, and infilled blocks
Southcote–Blewburton Hill	Berkshire	Varied decoration including arcs, diagonal lines, and cross-hatching
Croft Ambrey–Bredon Hill	Herefordshire & Cotswolds	'Duck-stamped' impressions or linear tooling in a restricted band immediately below rim
Lydney–Llanmelin	South Wales	Chevrons and oval-shaped stab marks are the distinctive features
Glastonbury–Blaise Castle Hill	Somerset & Avon	Curvilinear decoration with large areas infilled with hatching and cross-hatching

which the regional structures have been defined has been challenged (Collis 1994). Recent work on the sites around Danebury (Brown in Cunliffe 2000) has emphasized how complex the relationship between these different styles can be.

THE LATE IRON AGE (100/50 BC–AD 43)

In the Late Iron Age, Dorset continues to develop the traditions established in the previous period: bead rim and upright rimmed jars dominate, and counter-sunk handles continue to be important (Brailsford 1958). New forms include distinctive straight-sided, footed bowls and tankards, and decoration becomes increasingly common. During this period production is monopolized by the industries of Poole Harbour and the geographical distribution expands into areas previously characterized by different ceramic traditions (Brown in Cunliffe 2000: 124). These industries are developed by the Roman Army and Dorset Black-Burnished Wares are their direct successors.

There are more drastic changes in the rest of Wessex where wheel-turned forms become increasingly common and reflect the growing importance of Continental contacts. The forms are dominated by high-shouldered and necked jars with pedestal bases (Figure 3.11) and fine wares copy Continental forms such as bowls, platters, dishes, beakers, and lids. Distinctive grog-tempered fabrics dominate to the north and east but these vary in importance over the period. Saucepan pots remained important for an unknown period of the first century BC, and there are some indications that contemporary settlements could have different assemblages (Timby in Fulford and Timby 2000), but whether this reflects preference or access is unknown.

Bibliography

Aitken, G. M. and Aitken, N. 1990. Excavations at Whitcombe, 1965–1967. *Proceedings of the Dorset Natural History and Archaeological Society* 112, 59–94.

Alcock, L. 1962. Settlement patterns in Celtic Britain. *Antiquity* 36, 51–4.

—— 1972. *'By South Cadbury, is that Camelot....' Excavations at Cadbury Castle 1966–70.* London: Thames and Hudson.

—— 1980. The Cadbury Castle Sequence in the first millennium BC. *Bulletin of the Board of Celtic Studies* 28, 656–718.

Allen, D. F. 1960. The origins of coinage in Britain: a reappraisal. In S. S. Frere (ed.), 97–128.

—— 1967. Iron Age currency bars in Britain. *Proceedings of the Prehistoric Society* 33, 307–35.

—— 1980. *The Coins of the Ancient Celts.* Edinburgh: Edinburgh University Press.

Allen, M. J. 2005. Beaker settlement and environment on the Chalk Downs of Southern England. *Proceedings of the Prehistoric Society* 71, 219–46.

—— and Gardiner, J. 2000. *Our Changing Coast: A Survey of the Intertidal Archaeology of Langstone Harbour, Hampshire.* York: Council for British Archaeology (Research Report 124).

—— and Scaife, R. G. 1991. The exploitation of the flora and fauna and its impact on the natural and derived landscape. In P. W. Cox and C. M. Hearne, 216–20.

Allen, T. G. and Robinson, M. A. 1993. *The Prehistoric Landscape and Iron Age Enclosed Settlement at Mingies Ditch, Hardwick-with-Yelford, Oxon.* Oxford: Oxford University Committee for Archaeology.

Andrews, P. 2006. A Middle to Late Bronze Age settlement at Dunch Hill, Tidworth. *Wiltshire Archaeological and Natural History Magazine* 99, 51–78.

—— and Laidlaw, M. 1996. Metallurgical debris. In C. A. Butterworth and A. Hutcheson (eds) Excavations at Rooksdown Hospital, Hampshire, 1989 and 1995. Salisbury: Wessex Archaeology unpublished draft.

Appadurai, A. 1986. *The Social Life of Things: Commodities in Cultural Perspective.* Cambridge: Cambridge University Press.

Armit, I., Murphy, E., Nelis, E., and Simpson, D. 2003. *Neolithic Settlement in Ireland and Western Britain.* Oxford: Oxbow Books.

Ashbee, P. 1960. *The Bronze Age Round Barrow in Britain: An Introduction to the Study of the Funerary Practice and Culture of the British and Irish Single-grave People of the Second Millennium BC.* London: Phoenix.

—— Smith, I. F., and Evans, J. G. 1979. Excavations of three long barrows near Avebury, Wiltshire. *Proceedings of the Prehistoric Society* 45, 207–300.

Audouze, F. and Büchsenshütz, O. 1991. *Towns, Villages and Countryside of Celtic Europe: From the Beginning of the Second Millennium to the End of the First Century BC.* London: Batsford.

Avery, M. and Close-Brooks, J. 1969. Shearplace Hill, Sydling St Nicholas, Dorset, House A: a suggested re-interpretation. *Proceedings of the Prehistoric Society* 35, 345–51.

Baillie, M. G. L. 1989. Do Irish bog oaks date the Shang dynasty? *Current Archaeology* 117, 310–13.

Barber, M. 2003. *Bronze and the Bronze Age: Metalwork and Society in Britain c.2500–800 BC.* Stroud: Tempus.

—— 2005. 'There wur a bit of ould brass': Bronze Age metalwork and the Marlborough Downs landscape. In G. Brown *et al.* (eds), 137–48.

—— Field, D., and Topping, P. 1999. *The Neolithic Flint Mines of England.* Swindon: English Heritage.

Barclay, G. J., Brophy, K., and MacGregor, G. 2002. Claish, Stirling: an early Neolithic structure in its context. *Proceedings of the Society of Antiquaries of Scotland* 135, 65–137.

Barnett, J. 1989. *Stone Circles in Britain: Taxonomic and Distributional Analyses and a Catalogue of Sites in England, Scotland and Wales.* Oxford: British Archaeological Report (British Series) 215.

Barnes, I., Boismier, W. A., Cleal, R. M. J., Fitzpatrick, A. P., and Roberts, M. R. 1995. *Early Settlement in Berkshire: Mesolithic-Roman Occupation in the Thames and Kennet Valleys.* Salisbury: Wessex Archaeology.

—— Butterworth, C. A., Hawkes, J. W., and Smith, L. 1997. *Excavations at Thames Valley Park, Reading, 1986–8: Prehistoric and Romano-British Occupation of the Floodplain and a Terrace of the River Thames.* Salisbury: Wessex Archaeology.

Barraud, C., de Coppet, D., Iteanu, A., and Jamous, R. 1994. *Of Relations and the Dead: Four Societies Viewed from the Angle of their Exchanges.* Oxford: Berg.

Barrett, J. C. 1980. The pottery of the Later Bronze Age in Lowland England. *Proceedings of the Prehistoric Society* 46, 297–320.

—— 1985. Hoards and related metalwork. In D. V. Clarke *et al.* (eds), 95–106.

—— 1987. The Glastonbury Lake Village: models and source criticism. *Archaeological Journal* 144, 409–23.

—— 1989. Food, gender and metal: questions of social reproduction. In M. L. S. Sørenson and R. Thomas (eds), 304–20.

—— 1994a. *Fragments from Antiquity: An Archaeology of Social Life in Britain, 2900–1200 BC.* Oxford: Blackwell.

—— 1994b. The Bronze Age. In B. Vyner (ed.) *Building the Past: Papers Celebrating 150 Years of the Royal Archaeological Institute.* London: Royal Archaeological Institute, 123–48.

—— and Bradley, R. 1980. (eds) *The British Later Bronze Age.* Oxford: British Archaeological Report (British Series 83).

—— and Needham, S. 1988. Production, circulation and exchange: problems in the interpretation of Bronze Age bronzework. In J. C. Barrett and I. A. Kinnes (eds) *The Archaeology of Context in the Neolithic and Bronze Age: Recent Trends.* Sheffield: Dept of Prehistory and Archaeology, 127–40.

—— Bradley, R., and Green, M. 1991. *Landscape, Monuments and Society: The Prehistory of Cranborne Chase.* Cambridge: Cambridge University Press.

Barrett, J. C. Freeman, P. W. M., and Woodward, A. 2000. *Cadbury Castle Somerset: The Later Prehistory and Early Historic Archaeology.* London: English Heritage.

Bazelmans, J. 1991. *By Weapons Made Worthy: Lords, Retainers and their Relationship in Beowulf.* Amsterdam: Amsterdam University Press.

Bean, S. C. 2000. *The Coinage of the Atrebates and the Regni.* Oxford: Oxford University School of Archaeology (Monograph 50).

Bedwin, O. 1978. Excavations inside Harting Beacon hillfort, 1976. *Sussex Archaeological Collections* 116, 225–40.

——1979. Excavations at Harting Beacon, West Sussex; second season 1977. *Sussex Archaeological Collections* 117, 21–36.

——1981. Excavations at Lancing Down, West Sussex 1980. *Sussex Archaeological Collections* 119, 37–55.

——1983. The development of prehistoric settlement on the West Sussex coastal plain. *Sussex Archaeological Collections* 121, 31–44.

——and Holgate, R. 1985. Excavations at Copse Farm, Oving, West Sussex. *Proceedings of the Prehistoric Society* 51, 215–45.

——and Pitts, M. W. 1978. The excavations of an Iron Age settlement at North Bersted, Bognor Regis, West Sussex 1975–76. *Sussex Archaeological Collections* 116, 293–346.

——and Place, C. 1995. Late Iron Age and Romano-British occupation at Ounces Barn, Boxgrove, West Sussex; Excavations 1982–83. *Sussex Archaeological Collections* 133, 45–101.

Bell, M. 1977. Excavations at Bishopstone. *Sussex Archaeological Collections* 115, 1–299.

——1990. *Brean Down: Excavations 1983–1987.* London: English Heritage (Archaeological Report 15).

Bell, T. and Lock, G. 2000. Topographic and cultural influences on walking the Ridgeway in later prehistoric times. In G. Lock (ed.) *Beyond the Map: Archaeology and Spatial Technologies.* Amsterdam: IOS Press, 85–100.

Bellamy, P. 1991. The investigation of the prehistoric landscape along the route of the A303 road improvement between Andover, Hampshire and Amesbury, Wiltshire 1984–1987. *Proceedings of the Hampshire Field Club and Archaeological Society* 47, 5–81.

Bender, B. 1998. *Stonehenge: Making Space.* Oxford: Berg.

Bernstein, B. 1971. *Class, Codes and Control.* Vol.1: *Theoretical Studies towards a Sociology of Language.* London: Routledge.

Bersu, G. 1940. Excavations at Little Woodbury, Wiltshire, Part 1: The settlement revealed by excavation. *Proceedings of the Prehistoric Society* 6, 30–111.

Bevan, B. (ed.) 1999a. *Northern Exposure: Interpretive Devolution and the Iron Ages in Britain.* Leicester: Leicester University Press.

——1999b. Land–life–death–regeneration: interpreting a Middle Iron Age landscape in eastern Yorkshire. In B. Bevan (ed.), 123–48.

Birbeck, V. 2002. Excavations on Iron Age and Romano British settlements at Cannards Grave, Shepton Mallet. *Somerset Archaeology and Natural History* 144, 41–116.

Birbeck, V. 2006. Excavations on the Old Ditch Linear Earthwork, Breach Hill, Tilshead. *Wiltshire Archaeological and Natural History Magazine* 99, 79–103.

Birchall, A. 1965. The Aylesford Swarling culture: the problem of the Belgae reconsidered. *Proceedings of the Prehistoric Society* 31, 241–367.

Birdwell-Pheasant, D. and Lawrence-Zúñiga, D. 1999. *House Life: Space, Place and Family in Europe.* Oxford: Berg.

Bishop, N. A. and Knüsel, C. J. 2005. A paleodemographic investigation of warfare in prehistory. In M. Parker Pearson and I. J. N. Thorpe (eds) *Warfare, Violence and Slavery in Prehistory.* Oxford: British Archaeological Report (International Series 1374), 201–16.

Bloch, M. 1995a. People into places: Zafimaniry concepts of clarity. In E. Hirsch. and M. O'Hanlon (eds) *The Anthropology of Landscape: Perspectives on Place and Space.* Oxford: Oxford University Press, 63–77.

—— 1995b. The resurrection of the house amongst the Zafimaniry of Madagascar. In J. Carsten and S. Hugh-Jones (eds), 69–83.

Boas, F. 1966. *Kwakiutl Ethnography.* Chicago: University of Chicago Press.

Bond, D. 1988. *Excavation at the North Ring, Mucking, Essex: A Late Bronze Age Enclosure.* Norwich: East Anglian Archaeology (Monograph 43).

Bourdieu, P. 1977. *Outline of a Theory of Practice.* Cambridge: Cambridge University Press.

Bowden, M. 1998. *Barbury Castle: Archaeological Survey Report.* Swindon: RCHME.

—— 2001. *Liddington Castle: Archaeological Earthwork Survey.* Swindon: English Heritage.

—— 2004. *Oldbury Castle Hillfort, Wiltshire.* Swindon: English Heritage.

—— and McOmish, D. 1987. The Required Barrier. *Scottish Archaeological Review* 4, 76–84.

—— Ford, S., and Mees, G. 1993. The date of the ancient fields on the Berkshire Downs. *Berkshire Archaeological Journal* 74 (1991–3), 109–33.

Bowen, H. C. 1990. *The Archaeology of Bokerley Dyke.* London: HMSO.

Bowman, S., Ambers, J., and Leese, M. N. 1990. Re-evaluation of British Museum radiocarbon dates issued between 1980 and 1984. *Radiocarbon* 32.1, 59–79.

Bradley, R. 1971. Stock raising and the origins of hillforts on the South Downs. *Antiquaries Journal* 51, 8–29.

—— 1978. Prehistoric field systems in Britain and north-west Europe: a review of some recent work. *World Archaeology* 9, 265–80.

—— 1990. *The Passage of Arms: An Archaeological Analysis of Prehistoric Hoards and Votive Deposits.* Cambridge: Cambridge University Press.

—— 1998a. *The Significance of Monuments: On the Shaping of the Human Experience in Neolithic and Bronze Age Europe.* London: Routledge.

—— 1998b. Rereading *The Passage of Arms.* In R. Bradley 1998 *The Passage of Arms: An Archaeological Analysis of Prehistoric Hoards and Votive Deposits.* Oxford: Oxbow Books.

—— 2000. *An Archaeology of Natural Places.* London: Routledge.

—— 2007. *The Prehistory of Britain and Ireland.* Cambridge: Cambridge University Press.

Bradley, R. and Ellison, A. 1975. *Rams Hill: A Bronze Age Defended Enclosure and its Landscape.* Oxford: British Archaeological Report (British Series 19).

—— and Gordon, K. 1988. Human skulls from the River Thames, their dating and significance. *Antiquity* 62, 503–9.

—— Entwhistle, R., and Raymond, F. 1994. *Prehistoric Land Divisions on Salisbury Plain: The work of the Wessex Linear Ditches Project.* London: English Heritage (Archaeological Report 2).

—— Lobb, S., Richards, J., and Robinson, M. 1980. Two Late Bronze Age settlements on the Kennet Gravels: excavations at Aldermaston Wharf and Knights Farm, Burghfield, Berkshire. *Proceedings of the Prehistoric Society* 46, 217–95.

Brailsford, J. 1958. Early Iron Age 'C' in Wessex. *Proceedings of the Prehistoric Society* 24, 101–19.

—— and Jackson, J. W. 1948. Excavations at Little Woodbury, Wiltshire (1938–39): Part II The Pottery and Part III The Animal Bone. *Proceedings of the Prehistoric Society* 14, 1–23.

Brewster, T. C. M. 1963. *The Excavation of Staple Howe.* Scarborough.

Britnell, W. 1982. The excavation of two round barrows at Trelystan, Powys. *Proceedings of the Prehistoric Society* 48, 133–202.

Brossler, A., Early, R., and Allen, C. 2004. *Green Park (Reading Business Park): Phase 2 Excavations 1995: Neolithic and Bronze Age Sites.* Oxford: Oxford Archaeological Unit.

Brown, G., Field, D., and McOmish, D. 2005. *The Avebury Landscape: Aspects of the Field Archaeology of the Marlborough Downs.* Oxford: Oxbow Books.

Brown, L. 1997. Marketing and commerce in Late Iron Age Dorset: the Wareham/Poole Harbour pottery industry. In A. Gwilt and C. Haselgrove (eds), 40–5.

Brück, J. 1995. A place for the dead: the role of human remains in Late Bronze Age Britain. *Proceedings of the Prehistoric Society* 61, 245–77.

—— 1999. Houses, lifecycles and deposition on Middle Bronze Age settlements in southern England. *Proceedings of the Prehistoric Society* 65, 145–66.

—— 2000. Settlement, landscape and social identity: the Early/Middle Bronze Age transition in Wessex, Sussex and the Thames Valley. *Oxford Journal of Archaeology* 19.3, 273–300.

—— 2001. (ed.) *Bronze Age Landscapes: Tradition and Transformation.* Oxford: Oxbow Books.

—— 2006. Fragmentation, personhood and the social construction of technology in Middle and Late Bronze Age Britain. *Cambridge Archaeological Journal* 16.3, 297–315.

Buck, C. E., Litton, C. D., and Smith, A. F. M. 1992. Calibration of radiocarbon results pertaining to related archaeological events. *Journal of Archaeological Science* 19, 497–512.

Buckley, D. G. and Hedges, J. G. 1987. *The Bronze Age and Saxon Settlements at Springfield Lyons, Essex: An Interim Report.* Chelmsford: Essex County Council (Occasional Paper 5).

Buckley, V. 1990. *Burnt Offerings: International Contributions to Burnt Mound Archaeology.* Dublin: Wordwell.

Budd, P., Gale, D., Pollard, A. M., Thomas, R. G., and Williams, P. A. 1992. Early mines in Wales: a reconsideration. *Archaeology in Wales* 32, 36–8.

Bulleid, A. and Gray, H. St. G. 1911. *The Glastonbury Lake Village*, vol. 1. Glastonbury: Glastonbury Antiquarian Society.

———— 1917. *The Glastonbury Lake Village*, vol. 2. Glastonbury: Glastonbury Antiquarian Society.

Burgess, C. 1969. The Later Bronze Age in the British Isles and North-Western France. *Archaeological Journal* 125, 1–45.

—— 1974. The Bronze Age. In C. Renfrew (ed.) *British Prehistory: A New Outline*. London: Duckworth, 223–32.

—— 1980. *The Age of Stonehenge*. London: Dent.

—— 1985. Population, climate and upland settlement. In C. Burgess (ed.) *Upland Settlement in Northern Britain*. Oxford: British Archaeological Report (British Series 143), 195–229.

—— 1986. Britain at the time of the Rhine-Swiss group. In P. Brun and C. Mordant (eds) *Le Groupe Rhin-Suisse-France Orientale et la Notion de Civilisation des Champs d'Urnes*. Nemours: Mémoires du Musée de Préhistoire d'Ile-de-France, 559–73.

—— 1989. Volcanoes, catastrophe and the global crisis of the late second millennium BC. *Current Archaeology* 117, 325–29.

—— 1991. The East and the West: Mediterranean influence in the Atlantic World in the Later Bronze Age, *c*.1500–700 BC. In C. Chevillot and A. Coffyn (eds) *L'Age du Bronze Atlantique: ses facies, de l'Ecosse à l'Andalousie et leurs relations avec le Bronze Continental et la Méditerranée*. Beynac: Association des Musées du Sarlardais, 25–45.

—— Coombs, D., and Davies, D. G. 1972. The Broadward Complex and barbed spearheads. In F. Lynch and C. Burgess (eds) *Prehistoric Man in Wales and the West*. Bath: Adams and Dart, 211–83.

Burnett, A. M. 1989. Review of Van Arsdell (1989). *British Numismatic Journal* 59, 235–7.

—— 1992. A new Iron Age issue from near Chichester. *Spink Numismatic Circular* 100, 340–2.

Burstow, G. P. and Holleyman, G. A. 1957. Late Bronze Age settlement on Itford Hill, Sussex. *Proceedings of the Prehistoric Society* 23, 167–212.

Busby, C. 1997. Permeable and partible persons: a comparative analysis of gender and the body in south India and Melanesia. *Journal of the Royal Anthropological Institute* 7, 649–78.

Bushe-Fox, J. P. 1915. *Excavations at Hengistbury Head, Hampshire, in 1911–12*. Oxford: Society of Antiquaries of London (Research Report 3).

Bushnell, D. I. 1927. *Burials of the Algonquian, Siouan and Caddoan Tribes West of the Mississippi*. Washington: Government Printing Office (Bulletin of the Bureau of American Ethnology 83).

Butterworth, C. A. 1994. Rooksdown Hospital, Basingstoke, Hampshire. In A. Fitzpatrick and E. Morris (eds), 76–8.

Butterworth, C. A. and Gibson, C. 2005. Neolithic pits and a Bronze Age field system at Middle Farm, Dorchester. *Proceedings of the Dorset Natural History and Archaeological Society* 126, 15–26.

—— and Lobb, S. J. 1992. *Excavations in the Burghfield Area, Berkshire: Developments in the Bronze Age and Saxon Landscapes*. Salisbury: Wessex Archaeology.

Calkin, J. B. 1949. The Isle of Purbeck in the Iron Age. *Proceedings of the Dorset Natural History and Archaeological Society* 70, 28–59.

—— 1962. The Bournemouth area in the Middle and Late Bronze Age, with the 'Deverel-Rimbury' problem reconsidered. *Archaeological Journal* 119, 1–65.

Carr, G. and Knüsel, C. 1997. The ritual framework of excarnation by exposure as the mortuary practice of the early and middle Iron Ages of central southern Britain. In A. Gwilt and C. Haselgrove (eds), 167–73.

Carsten, J. and Hugh-Jones, S. 1995. *About the House: Levi-Strauss and Beyond*. Cambridge: Cambridge University Press.

Catherall, P. D., Barnett, M. and McClean, H. 1984. *The Southern Feeder: The Archaeology of a Gas Pipeline*. London: The British Gas Corporation.

Chadwick, A. M. 2008. Fields for discourse. Landscape materialities of being in south and west Yorkshire and Nottinghamshire during the Iron Age and Romano-British periods. A study of people and place. Unpublished PhD, University of Wales, Newport.

Champion, T. C. 1985. Written sources and the study of the European Iron Age. In T. C. Champion and J. V. S. Megaw (eds) *Settlement and Society: Aspects of West European Prehistory in the First Millennium bc*. Leicester: Leicester University Press, 9–22.

—— 1989. From Bronze Age to Iron Age in Ireland. In M. L. S. Sørenson and R. Thomas (eds), 287–303.

—— 1990. Review of Bradley 1990. *Antiquaries Journal* 70, 479–81.

—— 1994. Socio-economic development in Eastern England in the first millenium bc. In K. Kristiansen and J. Jensen (eds) *Europe in the First Millennium bc*. Sheffield: Sheffield Archaeological Monograph 6, 125–44.

—— 2001. The beginnings of the Iron Age archaeology in Wessex. In J. R. Collis (ed.) *Society and Settlement in Iron Age Europe*. Sheffield: J. R. Collis Publications, 9–22.

—— and Collis, J. R. 1996. *The Iron Age in Britain and Ireland: Recent Trends*. Sheffield: J. R. Collis Publications.

Chapman, A. 2006. An Iron Age enclosure at site A, Kennel Farm, Basingstoke, Hampshire. *Proceedings of the Hampshire Field Club and Archaeological Society* 61, 16–62.

Childe, V. G. 1956. *Piecing Together the Past: The Interpretation of Archaeological Data*. London: Routledge & Kegan Paul.

Clarke, D. L. 1979. A provisional model of an Iron Age society and its settlement system. In D. L. Clarke (ed.) *Analytical Archaeologist: Collected Papers of David L. Clarke*. London: Academic Press, 363–434.

Clarke, D. V. and Kemp, M. M. B. 1984. A hoard of late Bronze Age gold objects from Heights of Brae, Ross and Cromarty District, Highland Region. *Proceedings of the Society of Antiquaries of Scotland* 114, 189–98.

—— Cowie, T., and Foxon, A. (eds) 1985. *Symbols of Power at the Age of Stonehenge.* Edinburgh: HMSO.

Clay, R. C. C. 1925. An inhabited site of La Tène I date, on Swallowcliffe Down. *Wiltshire Archaeological Magazine* 43, 59–93.

Cleal, R. M. J., Walker, K. E., and Montague, R. 1995. *Stonehenge in its Landscape: The Twentieth-century Excavations.* London: English Heritage (Archaeological Report 10).

Clough, R. E. 1985. The iron industry in the Iron Age and Romano-British period. In P. T. Craddock and M. J. Hughes (eds) *Furnaces and Smelting Technology in Antiquity.* London: British Museum (Occasional Paper 48), 179–87.

Coe, D. and Newham, R. 1993. Excavations of an Early Iron Age building and Romano-British enclosure at Brighton Hill South, Hampshire. *Proceedings of the Hampshire Field Club and Archaeological Society* 48, 5–26.

Coles, J. 1961. Scottish Late Bronze Age metalwork: typology, distribution and chronology. *Proceedings of the Society of Antiquaries of Scotland* 93, 16–134.

—— 1987. *Meare Village East. The Excavations of Arthur Bulleid and H. St. George Gray 1932–1956.* Exeter: Somerset Levels Project.

—— and Minnitt, S. 1995. '*Industrious and Fairly Civilized': The Glastonbury Lake Village.* Taunton: Somerset County Council Museum Service.

Coles, S. 2004. Three Bronze Age barrows at Mockbegger Lane, Ibsley, Hampshire. *Proceedings of the Hampshire Field Club and Archaeological* Society 59, 31–64.

Collard, M., Darvill, T., and Watts, M. 2006. Ironworking in the Bronze Age: evidence from a 10th century BC settlement at Hartshill Copse, Upper Bucklebury, West Berkshire. *Proceedings of the Prehistoric Society* 72, 367–421.

Collis, J. R. 1971. Markets and Money. In M. Jesson and D. Hill (eds) *The Iron Age and its Hill-forts: Papers Presented to Sir Mortimer Wheeler.* Southampton: University of Southampton, 97–104.

—— 1977a. *The Iron Age in Britain: A Review.* Sheffield: Department of Prehistory and Archaeology.

—— 1977b. Owslebury (Hants) and the problem of burials on rural settlements. In R. Reece (ed.) *Burial in the Roman World.* London: Council for British Archaeology (Research Report 22), 26–35.

—— 1984a. *Oppida. Earliest Towns North of the Alps.* Sheffield: Department of Prehistory and Archaeology, University of Sheffield.

—— 1984b. *The European Iron Age.* London: Batsford.

—— 1994. The Iron Age. In B. Vyner (ed.) *Building the Past: Papers Celebrating 150 Years of the Royal Archaeological Institute.* London: Royal Archaeological Institute, 123–48.

—— 2003. *The Celts: Origins, Myths and Inventions.* Stroud: Tempus.

Colquhoun, I. A. 1979. The late Bronze Age hoard from Blackmoor, Hampshire. In C. Burgess and D. Coombs (eds) *Bronze Age Hoards: Some Finds Old and New.* Oxford: British Archaeological Reports (British Series 67), 9–116.

Cook, A. M. and Dacre, M. W. 1985. *Excavations at Portway, Andover*. Oxford: Oxford University Committee for Archaeology (Monograph 4).

Cooney, G. and Grogan, E. 1994. *Irish Prehistory: A Social Perspective*. Dublin: Wordwell.

Corney, M. 1989. Multiple ditch systems and Late Iron Age settlement in central Wessex. In M. Bowden, D. Mackay, and P. Topping (eds) *From Cornwall to Caithness: Some Aspects of British Field Archaeology. Papers Presented to Norman V. Quinnell*. Oxford: British Archaeological Report (British Series) 209, 111–28.

Countryside Agency and Scottish Natural Heritage 2002. *Landscape Character Assessment: Guidance for England and Scotland*. Countryside Agency and Scottish Natural Heritage.

Countryside Commission 1996. *Views from the Past: Historic Landscape Character in English Countryside*. Cheltenham: Countryside Commission.

—— and English Nature 1996. *The Character of England: Landscape, Wildlife and Natural Features*. Cheltenham and Peterborough: Countryside Commission and English Nature.

Cowell, M. 1992. An analytical survey of the British Celtic gold coinage. In M. Mays (ed.), 207–34.

Cox, P. W. and Hearne, C. M. 1991. *Redeemed from the Heath: The Archaeology of the Wytch Farm Oilfield (1987–90)*. Dorchester: Dorset Natural History and Archaeology Society (Monograph 9).

Craig, R., Knüsel, C. J. and Carr, G. 2005. Fragmentation, mutilation and dismemberment: an interpretation of human remains on Iron Age sites. In M. Parker Pearson and I. J. N. Thorpe (eds) *Warfare, Violence and Slavery in Prehistory*. Oxford: British Archaeological Report (International Series 1374), 165–80.

Crawford, I. 1953. *Archaeology in the Field*. London: Phoenix House.

Creighton, J. 2000. *Coins and Power in Late Iron Age Britain*. Cambridge: Cambridge University Press.

—— 2001. The Iron Age–Roman transition. In S. James and M. Millett (eds) *Britons and Romans: Advancing an Archaeological Agenda*. York: Council for British Archaeology (Research Report 125), 4–11.

—— 2005. Gold, ritual and kingship. In C. Haselgrove and D. Wigg-Wolf (eds), 69–84.

Crew, P. 1994. Currency bars in Britain—typology and function. In M. Mangin (ed.) *La Sidérurgie ancienne de l'Est de la France dans son contexte européen*. Besançon: Université de Besançon, 345–50.

—— 1995. Aspects of the iron supply. In B. W. Cunliffe (ed.), 276–84.

—— and Crew, S. 1990. *Early Mining in the British Isles*. Plas Tan y Bwlch, Snowdonia.

Cromarty, A. M., Barclay, A., Lambrick, G., and Robinson, M. 2006. *Late Bronze Age Ritual and Habitation on a Thames Eyot at Whitecross Farm, Wallingford: the Archaeology of the Wallingford Bypass, 1986–92*. Oxford: Oxford Archaeological Unit.

Cumberpatch, C. G. 1995. Production and society in the Later Iron Age of Bohemia and Moravia. In J. D. Hill and C. G. Cumberpatch (eds) *Different Iron Ages: Studies on the Iron Age in Temperate Europe*. Oxford: British Archaeological Report (International Series 602), 67–94.

Cunliffe, B. W. 1968. Early pre-Roman Iron Age communities in eastern England. *Antiquaries Journal* 48, 175–91.

—— 1970. A Bronze Age settlement at Chalton, Hants (site 78). *Antiquaries Journal* 50, 1–13.

—— 1971. Some aspects of hill-forts and their cultural environments. In M. Jesson and D. Hill (eds) *The Iron Age and its Hill-forts: Papers Presented to Sir Mortimer Wheeler*. Southampton: University of Southampton, 53–70.

—— 1974. The Iron Age. In C. Renfrew (ed.) *British Prehistory: A New Outline*. London: Duckworth, 258–62.

—— 1982. Iron Age settlements and pottery 650 BC–60 AD. In M. Aston and I. Burrows (eds) *The Archaeology of Somerset*. Taunton: Somerset County Council, 53–61.

—— 1983. *Danebury: Anatomy of an Iron Age Hillfort*. London: Batsford.

—— 1984a. *Danebury: An Iron Age Hillfort in Hampshire*. London: Council for British Archaeology (Research Report 52).

—— 1984b. Gloucestershire and the Iron Age of southern Britain. *Transactions of the Bristol and Gloucestershire Archaeological Society* 102, 5–15.

—— 1987. *Hengistbury Head*. Vol. 1: *Prehistoric and Roman Settlement, 3500 BC–AD 500*. Oxford: Oxford University Committee for Archaeology (Monograph 13).

—— 1988a. *Greeks, Romans and Barbarians: Spheres of Interaction*. London: Batsford.

—— 1988b. *Mount Batten, Devon. An Iron Age and Roman Port*. Oxford: Oxford University Committee for Archaeology (Monograph 26).

—— 1990. Social and economic contacts between western France and Britain in the Early and Middle La Tène period. *Revue Archéologique de l'Ouest* (*Supplement* 2), 245–51.

—— 1991. *Iron Age Communities in Britain*. (3rd edn) London: Routledge.

—— 1992. Pits, preconceptions and propitiation in the British Iron Age. *Oxford Journal of Archaeology* 11.1, 69–83.

—— 1995. *Danebury: An Iron Age Hillfort in Hampshire. Volume 6. A Hillfort Community in Perspective*. York: Council for British Archaeology (Research Report 102).

—— 1997. *The Ancient Celts*. Oxford: Oxford University Press.

—— 2000. *The Danebury Environs Programme, the Prehistory of a Wessex Landscape*. Vol. 1: *Introduction*. Oxford: Oxford University Committee for Archaeology (Monograph 49).

—— 2003. *The Celts: A Very Short Introduction*. Oxford: Oxford University Press.

—— 2005. *Iron Age Communities in Britain*. (4th edn) London: Routledge.

—— and De Jersey, P. 1997. *Armorica and Britain: Cross-Channel Relationships in the Late First Millennium BC*. Oxford: Oxford University Committee for Archaeology (Studies in Celtic Coinage 3).

Cunliffe, B. W. and Miles, D. 1984. (eds) *Aspects of the Iron Age in Central Southern Britain*. Oxford: Oxford University Committee for Archaeology (Monograph 2).

—— and Orton, C. 1984. Radiocarbon age assessment. In Cunliffe, B. W. 1984a, 190–8.

—— and Phillipson, D. W. 1969. Excavation at Eldon's Seat, Encombe, Dorset. *Proceedings of the Prehistoric Society* 34, 91–237.

—— and Poole, C. 1991. *Danebury an Iron Age Hillfort in Hampshire*. Vols 4 and 5. London: Council for British Archaeology (Research Report 73).

———— 2000a. *Bury Hill, Upper Clatford, Hants, 1990*. Oxford: Oxford University Committee for Archaeology (Danebury Environs Programme 2.2).

———— 2000b. *Suddern Farm, Middle Wallop, Hants, 1991 and 1996*. Oxford: Oxford University Committee for Archaeology (Danebury Environs Programme 2.3).

———— 2000c. *New Buildings, Longstock, Hants 1992 and Fiveways, Longstock, Hants, 1996*. Oxford: Oxford University Committee for Archaeology (Danebury Environs Programme 2.4).

———— 2000d. *Nettlebank Copse, Wherwell, Hants, 1993*. Oxford: Oxford University Committee for Archaeology (Danebury Environs Programme 2.5).

———— 2000e. *Houghton Down, Stockbridge, Hants, 1994*. Oxford: Oxford University Committee for Archaeology (Danebury Environs Programme 2.6).

———— 2000f. *Windy Dido, Cholderton, Hants, 1995*. Oxford: Oxford University Committee for Archaeology (Danebury Environs Programme 2.7).

———— 2008. *The Danebury Environs Roman Programme: A Wessex Landscape during the Roman Era*. Oxford: Oxford University School of Archaeology.

—— Down, A., and Rudkin, D. 1996. *Excavations at Fishbourne 1969–1988*. Chichester: Chichester District Council.

Cunnington, M. E. 1923. *The Early Iron Age Inhabited Site at All Cannings Cross, Wiltshire*. Devizes: George Simpson.

—— 1933. Excavations at Yarnbury Castle Camp, 1932. *Wiltshire Archaeological Magazine* 46, 198–213.

Curwen, E. C. 1939. The Iron Age in Sussex. *Sussex Archaeological Collections* 80, 214–16.

—— 1951. Cross-Ridge dykes in Sussex. In W. F. Grimes (ed.) *Aspects of Archaeology in Britain and Beyond*. London: H.W. Edwards, 93–107.

—— 1954. *The Archaeology of Sussex*. (2nd edn) London: Methuen.

Darvill, T. and Thomas, J. 1996. *Neolithic Houses in Northwest Europe and Beyond*. Oxford: Oxbow Books.

Davenport, C. 2003. The Late pre-Roman Iron Age of the West Sussex coastal plain: continuity or change? In D. Rudling (ed.) *The Archaeology of Sussex to AD 2000*. Brighton: University of Sussex, 101–9.

David, A. and Payne, A. 1997. Geophysical surveys within the Stonehenge landscape: a review of past endeavour and future potential. In B. W. Cunliffe and C. Renfrew (eds) *Science and Stonehenge*. Oxford: Oxford University Press, 73–114.

Davies, S. M. 1981. Excavations at Old Down Farm, Andover. Part II: Prehistoric and Roman. *Proceedings of the Hampshire Field Club and Archaeological Society* 37, 81–164.

—— Bellamy, P. S., Heaton, M. J., and Woodward, P. J. 2002. *Excavations at Alington Avenue, Fordington, Dorchester, Dorset, 1984–87*. Dorchester: Dorset Natural History and Archaeological Society (Monograph 15).

Davis, O. 2002. Localities, localities, localities: a reinterpretation of the Danebury evidence. Cardiff University: Unpublished Master's Dissertation.

—— 2007. *Winnall Down II*. Cardiff: Cardiff Studies in Archaeology.

—— 2008. Twin freaks? Paired enclosures in the Early Iron Age of Wessex. In O. Davis, N. Sharples, and K. Waddington (eds) *Changing Perspectives on the First Millennium BC*. Oxford: Oxbow Books, 31–42.

De Jersey, P. 2006. (ed.) *Celtic Coinage: New Discoveries, New Discussion*. Oxford: British Archaeological Reports (International Series 1532).

Delamont, S. 1992. Old Fogies and Intellectual Women: an episode in academic history. *Women's History Review* 1.1, 39–61.

Dent, J. S. 1982. Cemeteries and settlement patterns of the Iron Age on the Yorkshire Wolds. *Proceedings of the Prehistoric Society* 48, 437–57.

—— 1984. Weapons, wounds and war in the Iron Age. *Archaeological Journal* 140, 120–8.

—— 1985. Three chariot burials from Wetwang, Yorkshire. *Antiquity* 59, 85–92.

DeRoche, C. D 1997. Studying Iron Age Production. In A. Gwilt and C. Haselgrove (eds) 19–25.

Diepeveen-Jansen, M. 2001. *People, Ideas and Goods*. Amsterdam: Amsterdam University Press.

—— 2007. Early La Tène burial practices and social (re)constructions in the Marne-Moselle region. In C. Haselgrove and R. Pope (eds), 374–89.

Dixon, P. 1976. Crickley Hill 1969–72. In D. W. Harding (ed.) *Hillforts. Later Prehistoric Earthworks in Britain and Ireland*. London: Academic Press.

Dobney, K. and Ervynck, A. 2007. To fish or not to fish? Evidence for the possible avoidance of fish consumption during the Iron Age around the North Sea. In C. Haselgrove and T. Moore (eds), 403–18.

Dockrill, S. J. 2002. Brochs, economy and power. In B. Ballin Smith and I. Banks (eds) *In the Shadow of the Brochs: The Iron Age of Scotland*. Stroud: Tempus, 153–62.

Donachie, J. D. and Field, D. J. 1994. *Cissbury Ring, Worthing, West Sussex*. Salisbury: RCHME.

Douglas, M. 1966. *Purity and Danger: An Analysis of Concepts of Pollution and Taboo*. London: Routledge and Kegan Paul.

—— 1970. *Natural Symbols: Explorations in Cosmology*. London: Cresset Press.

—— 1973. *Natural Symbols: Explorations in Cosmology*. (2nd edn) Harmondsworth: Penguin.

—— 1982a. *In the Active Voice*. London: Routledge and Kegan Paul.

—— 1982b. *Essays in the Sociology of Perception*. London: Routledge and Kegan Paul.

Douglas, M. 1982c. *Natural Symbols: Explorations in Cosmology.* (1st edn reprint) New York: Pantheon Books.

—— 1986. *How Institutions Think.* Syracuse: Syracuse University Press.

—— 2005. *Grid and Group, New Developments.* Paper presented to a Workshop on Complexity and Cultural Theory in honour of Michael Thompson. London: London School of Economics.

Down, A. 1989. *Chichester Excavations VI.* Chichester: Chichester District Council.

Downes J. 1993. Distribution and significance of Bronze Age metalwork in the North Level. In C. A. I. French and F. M. M. Pryor (eds) *The South-West Fen Dyke Survey Project 1982–86.* Norwich: East Anglian Archaeology Report 59, 21–30.

—— 1999. Cremation a spectacle and a journey. In J. Downes and T. Pollard (eds) *The Loved Body's Corruption: Archaeological Contributions to the Study of Human Mortality.* Glasgow: Cruithne Press, 19–29.

Drewett, P. 1982. Later Bronze Age downland economy and excavations at Blackpatch, East Sussex. *Proceedings of the Prehistoric Society* 48, 321–400.

—— and Hamilton, S. 1999. Marking time and making space: excavations and landscape studies at the Caburn Hillfort, East Sussex, 1996–98. *Sussex Archaeological Collections* 137, 7–38.

Driver, O. 1961. *Indians of North America.* Chicago: University of Chicago Press.

Dungworth, D. B. 1996. The production of copper alloys in Iron Age Britain. *Proceedings of the Prehistoric Society* 62, 399–421.

Dutton, A. and Fasham, P. J. 1994. Prehistoric copper mining on the Great Orme, Llandudno, Gwynedd. *Proceedings of the Prehistoric Society* 60, 245–86.

Eagles, B. N. 1989. Woolbury Fields, Stockbridge Down, Hampshire. In M. Bowden, D. Mackay and P. Topping (eds) *From Cornwall to Caithness: Some Aspects of British Field Archaeology. Papers Presented to Norman V. Quinnell.* Oxford: British Archaeological Report (British Series 209), 93–8.

—— 1991. A new survey of the Hillfort on Beacon Hill, Burghclere, Hampshire. *Archaeological Journal* 148, 98–103.

Edmonds, M. 1999. *Ancestral Geographies: Landscape Monuments and Memory.* London: Routledge.

Ehrenreich, R. M. 1985. *Trade, Technology and the Ironworking Community of Southern Britain in the Iron Age.* Oxford: British Archaeological Report (British Series 144).

—— 1991. Metalworking in Iron Age Britain: hierarchy or hetrarchy? In R. M. Ehrenreich (ed.) *Metals in Society: Theory Beyond Analysis.* Philadelphia: MASCA Research papers in science and archaeology 8.2, 69–80.

Ellis, C. J. and Powell, A. B. 2008. *An Iron Age Settlement outside Battlesbury Hillfort, Warminster and Sites along the Southern Range Road.* Salisbury: Wessex Archaeology.

—— and Rawlings, M. 2001. Excavations at Balksbury Camp, Andover 1995–97. *Proceedings of the Hampshire Field Club and Archaeological Society* 56, 21–94.

Ellison, A. 1975. Pottery and settlements of the Later Bronze Age in Southern England. University of Cambridge: Unpublished PhD thesis.

—— 1978. The Bronze Age. In P. L. Drewett (ed.) *The Archaeology of Sussex to 1500 AD.* London: Council for British Archaeology (Research Report 29), 30–7.

Ellison, A. 1980a. Settlements and regional exchange: a case study. In J. Barrett and R. Bradley (eds), 127–40.

—— 1980b. Deverel-Rimbury urn cemeteries: the evidence for social organisation. In J. Barrett and R. Bradley (eds), 115–26.

—— 1981. Towards a socio economic model for the Middle Bronze Age in southern England. In I. Hodder, G. L. Isaacs, and N. Hammond (eds) *Pattern of the Past: Studies in Honour of David Clarke.* Cambridge: Cambridge University Press, 413–38.

—— and Drewett, P. L. 1971. Pits and post holes in the British Early Iron Age. *Proceedings of the Prehistoric Society* 37, 183–94.

—— and Rahtz, P. 1987. Excavations at Whitsbury Castle Ditches, Hampshire, 1960. *Proceedings of the Hampshire Field Club and Archaeological Society* 43, 63–81.

Eogan, G. 1964. The Later Bronze Age in Ireland in the light of recent research. *Proceedings of the Prehistoric Society* 30, 268–351.

—— 1983. *The Hoards of the Irish Later Bronze Age.* Dublin: University College.

—— 1994. *The Accomplished Art: Gold and Gold Working in Britain and Ireland during the Bronze Age (c.2300–650 BC).* Oxford: Oxbow Books.

Evans, C. 1989. Archaeology and modern times: Bersu's Woodbury 1938 & 1939. *Antiquity* 63, 436–60.

—— 1999. Christopher Hawkes (1905–1992). In T. Murray (ed.) *Encyclopedia of Archaeology: The Great Archaeologists,* vol. 2. Oxford: ABC–CLIO, 461–80.

—— and Knight, M. 2000. A fenland delta: later prehistoric land use in the lower Ouse reaches. In M. Dawson (ed.) *Prehistoric, Roman and Post-Roman Landscapes in the Great Ouse Valley.* York: Council for British Archaeology (Research Report 119), 87–106.

Evans, J. G. 1972. *Land Snails in Archaeology.* London: Seminar Press.

—— 1999. *Land and Archaeology: Histories of Human Environment in the British Isles.* Stroud: Tempus.

—— 2005. *Environmental Archaeology and the Social Order.* London: Routledge.

—— and Vaughan, M. P. 1985. An investigation into the environment and archaeology of the Wessex linear ditch system. *Antiquaries Journal* 65, 11–38.

—— Limbrey, S., Máté, I., and Mount, R. 1993. An environmental history of the Upper Kennet valley, Wiltshire, for the last 10,000 years. *Proceedings of the Prehistoric Society* 59, 139–95.

Fabech, C. and Ringtved, J. 1999. *Settlement and Landscape.* Moesgard: Jutland Archaeological Society.

Fagan, B. 2001. *Grahame Clark: An Intellectual Life of an Archaeologist.* Oxford: Westview Press.

Fairbairn, A. S. 2000. *Plants in Neolithic Britain and Beyond.* Oxford: Oxbow Books.

Fairclough, G. 1999. *Historic Landscape Characterisation—'The State of the Art'.* London: English Heritage.

Fairclough, G. J., Lambrick, G., and McNab, A. 1999. *Yesterday's World, Tomorrow's Landscape (The English Heritage Historic Landscape Project 1992–94).* London: English Heritage.

Fardon, R. 1999. *Mary Douglas: An Intellectual Biography.* London: Routledge.

Farwell, D. E. and Molleson, T. I. 1993. *Excavations at Poundbury 1966–80.* Vol. 2: *The Cemeteries.* Dorchester: Dorset Natural History and Archaeological Society (Monograph 11).

Fasham, P. J. 1985. *The Prehistoric Settlement at Winnall Down, Winchester.* Gloucester: Hampshire Field Club (Monograph 2).

—— 1987. *A Banjo Enclosure in Micheldever Wood, Hampshire.* Gloucester: Hampshire Field Club (Monograph 5).

—— and Whinney, R. J. (eds) 1991. *Archaeology and the M3.* Gloucester: Hampshire Field Club (Monograph 7).

—— Farwell, D. E., and Whinney, R. J. B. 1989. *The Archaeological Site at Easton Lane, Winchester.* Gloucester: Hampshire Field Club (Monograph 6).

—— Keevil, G., and Coe, D. 1995. *Brighton Hill South (Hatch Warren): An Iron Age Farmstead and Deserted Medieval Village in Hampshire.* Salisbury: Trust for Wessex Archaeology.

Ferrell, G. 1995. Space and society: new perspectives on the Iron Age of North East England. In J. D. Hill and C. Cumberpatch (eds) *Different Iron Ages: Studies on the Iron Age in Temperate Europe.* Oxford: British Archaeological Report (International series 602), 129–48.

Fitzpatrick, A. P. 1984. The deposition of La Tène Iron Age metalwork in watery contexts in Southern England. In B. W. Cunliffe and D. Miles (eds), 178–90.

—— 1985. The distribution of Dressal A amphorae in north-west Europe. *Oxford Journal of Archaeology* 4.3, 305–40.

—— 1989. Celtic (Iron Age) religion: traditional and timeless. *Scottish Archaeology Review* 8, 123–9.

—— 1994. Outside in: the structure of an Early Iron Age house at Dunstan Park, Thatcham, Berkshire. In A. Fitzpatrick and E. Morris (eds), 68–72.

—— 1995. Appendix: an Early Iron Age (7th century BC) pit with ironworking debris from Cooper's Farm, Dunstan Park. In I. Barnes *et al.* (eds), 89–92.

—— 1996. A 1st-century AD 'Durotrigian' inhumation burial with a decorated Iron Age mirror from Portesham, Dorset. *Proceedings of the Dorset Natural History and Archaeological Society* 118, 51–70.

—— 1997. *Archaeological Excavations on the Route of the A27 Westhampnett Bypass, West Sussex.* Vol. 2: *The Cemeteries.* Salisbury: Wessex Archaeology (Report 12).

—— and Morris, E. (eds) 1994. *The Iron Age in Wessex: Recent Work.* Salisbury: Trust for Wessex Archaeology.

—— Barnes, I., and Cleal, R. 1995. An Early Iron Age settlement at Dunston Park, Thatcham. In I. Barnes *et al.* (eds), 65–92.

Fleming, A. 1988. *The Dartmoor Reaves: Investigating Prehistoric Land Divisions.* London: Batsford.

—— 1989. Coaxial field systems in later British prehistory. In H. A. Nordstrum and A. Knape (eds) *Bronze Age Studies.* Stockholm: Statens Historiska Museum (Stockholm Studies 6), 151–62.

Fokkens, H. 2003. The longhouse as a central element in Bronze Age daily life. In J. Bourgeois, I. Bourgeois, and B. Charette (eds) *Bronze Age and Iron Age Communities in North-western Europe*. Brussels: Koninklijke Vlaamse Academie van België, 9–38.

Fontijn, D. R. 2003. *Sacrificial Landscapes: The Cultural Biographies of Persons, Objects and Natural Places in the Bronze Age of the Southern Netherlands, c.2300– 600 BC*. Leiden: Analecta Praehistorica Leidensia 33/34.

—— and Fokkens, H. 2007. The emergence of early Iron Age 'chieftains' graves' in the southern Netherlands: reconsidering transformations in burial and depositional practices. In C. Haselgrove and R. Pope (eds), 354–73.

Ford, S. 1982a. Fieldwork and excavation on the Berkshire Grims Ditch. *Oxoniensia* 47, 13–36.

—— 1982b. Linear earthworks on the Berkshire Downs. *Berkshire Archaeological Journal* 71, 1–20.

Foster, J. 1980. *The Iron Age Moulds from Gussage All Saints*. London: British Museum (Occasional Paper 12).

Foucault, M. 1977. *Discipline and Punish: The Birth of the Prison*. London: Allen Lane.

Fowler, C. 2003. Rates of (ex)change: decay and growth, memory and transformation of the dead in early Neolithic southern Britain. In H. Williams (ed.) *Archaeologies of Remembrance: Death and Memory in Past Societies*. New York: Kluwer Academic/ Plenum Press, 45–63.

—— 2004. *The Archaeology of Personhood*. London: Routledge.

Fowler, P. J. 1964. Cross-ridge dykes on the Ebble-Nadder Ridge. *Wiltshire Archaeological Magazine* 59, 46–57.

—— 2000. *Landscape Plotted and Pieced: Landscape History and Local Archaeology in Fyfield and Overton, Wiltshire*. London: Society of Antiquaries of London.

—— (n.d.). Excavation within a later prehistoric field system on Overton Down, West Overton, Wiltshire. York: Archaeological Data Service. (FYFOD Working paper FWP 63.)

—— and Blackwell, I. 1998. *The Land of Lettice Sweetapple: An English Countryside Explored*. Stroud: Tempus.

Fox, C. F. 1946. *A find of the Early Iron Age from Llyn Cerrig Bach, Angelsey*. Cardiff: National Museum of Wales.

Frankenstein, S. and Rowlands, M. J. 1978. The internal structure and regional context of Early Iron Age society in south-western Germany. *Bulletin of the London Institute of Archaeology* 15, 73–112.

Frere, S. S. (ed.) 1960. *Problems of the Iron Age in Southern Britain*. London: Institute of Archaeology (Occasional Paper 11).

Frow, J. 1997. *Time and Commodity Culture: Essays in Cultural Theory and Postmodernity*. Oxford: Clarendon Press.

Fulford, M. G. 1984. *Silchester: Excavations on the Defences 1974–80*. London: Society for the Promotion of Roman Studies (Britannia Monograph 5).

—— and Timby, J. 2000. *Late Iron Age and Roman Silchester: Excavations on the Site of the Forum Basilica 1977, 1980–86*. London: Society for the Promotion of Roman Studies (Britannia Monograph 15).

Fulford, M., Powell, A. B., Entwhistle, R., and Raymound, F. 2006. *Iron Age and Romano-British Settlements and Landscape of Salisbury Plain.* Salisbury: Wessex Archaeology and the University of Reading.

Gardiner, J. 1987. Hengistbury Head and its region: Neolithic and Bronze Age. In Cunliffe 1987: 329–35.

Gelling, P. 1977. Excavations on Pilsden Pen, Dorset, 1964–71. *Proceedings of the Prehistoric Society* 43, 263–86.

Gent, H. 1983. Centralised Storage in Later Prehistoric Britain. *Proceedings of the Prehistoric Society* 49, 243–67.

Gerritsen, F. 1999. To build and to abandon. *Archaeological Dialogues* 6.2, 78–97.

—— 2003. *Local Identities: Landscape and Community in Late Prehistoric Meuse-Damer-Scheldt Region.* Amsterdam: Amsterdam University Press.

Gibson, A. 1998. *Stonehenge and the Timber Circles of Britain and Europe.* Stroud: Tempus.

Gibson, C. 2004. The Iron Age and Roman site of Viables two (Jays Close), Basingstoke. *Proceedings of the Hampshire Field Club and Archaeological Society* 59, 1–30.

Giles, M. 2008. Seeing red: the aesthetics of martial objects in the British and Irish Iron Age. In D. Garrow, C. Gosden, and J. D. Hill (eds) *Rethinking Celtic Art.* Oxford: Oxbow Books, 59–77.

—— and Parker Pearson, M. 1999. Learning to live in the Iron Age: dwelling and praxis. In B. Bevan (ed.), 217–32.

Gingell, C. 1979. The bronze and iron hoard from Melksham and another Wiltshire find. In C. Burgess and D. Coombs (eds) *Bronze Age Hoards: Some Finds Old and New.* Oxford: British Archaeological Reports (British Series 67), 245–52.

—— 1982. Excavation of an Iron Age enclosure at Groundwell Farm, Blunsdon St. Andrew, 1976–7. *Wiltshire Archaeology and Natural History Magazine* 76, 33–75.

—— 1992. *The Marlborough Downs: A Later Bronze Age Landscape and its Origins.* Devizes: Wiltshire Archaeology and Natural History Society (Monograph 1).

—— and Harding, P. 1983. A fieldwalking survey in the Vale of Wardour. *Wiltshire Archaeology and Natural History Magazine* 77, 11–25.

—— and Lawson, A. J. 1985. Excavations at Potterne 1984. *Wiltshire Archaeological and Natural History Magazine* 79, 101–8.

Godelier, M. 1999. *The Enigma of the Gift.* Cambridge: Polity Press.

González-Ruibal, A. 2006. House societies vs. kinship-based societies: an archaeological case from Iron Age Europe. *Journal of Anthropological Archaeology* 25, 144–73.

Goody, J. 1966. The fission of domestic groups among the Lo Dagaba. In J. Goody (ed.) *The Development Cycle in Domestic Groups.* Cambridge: Cambridge University Press, 53–91.

Gosden, C. 1994. *Social Being and Time.* Oxford: Basil Blackwell.

—— and Lock, G. 2001. Hillforts of the Ridgeway Project: excavations at Alfred's Castle 2000. *South Midlands Archaeology* 31, 80–9.

—— and Lock, G. 2003. Becoming Roman on the Berkshire Downs: the evidence from Alfred's Castle. *Britannia* 34, 65–80.

Gosden, C. and Lock, G. 2007. The aesthetics of landscape on the Berkshire Downs. In C. Haselgrove and R. Pope (eds), 279–92.

Graham, A. H., Hinton, D. A., and Peacock, D. P. S. 2002. The excavation of an Iron Age and Romano-British settlement in Quarry Field, south of Compact Farm, Worth Matravers, Dorset. In D. A. Hinton (ed.) *Purbeck Papers.* Oxford: Oxbow Books, 1–83.

Grant, A. 1984. Animal husbandry in Wessex and the Thames Valley. In B. W. Cunliffe and D. Miles (eds) 102–19.

—— 1991. Economic or symbolic? Animals and ritual behaviour. In P. Garwood, D. Jennings, R. Skeates, and J. Toms (eds) *Sacred and Profane.* Oxford: Oxford University Committee for Archaeology (Monograph 32), 109–14.

Green, C. S. 1987. *Excavations at Poundbury, Dorchester, Dorset 1966–1982.* Vol. 1: *The Settlements.* Dorchester: Dorset Natural History and Archaeological Society (Monograph 7).

Green, F. J. 1994. Early Iron Age stream deposits at La Sagesse, Romsey, Hampshire. In A. Fitzpatrick and E. Morris (eds), 49–51.

Green, M. 1992. Excavation of a prehistoric ceremonial complex at Ogden Down, Gussage St Michael. *Proceedings of the Dorset Natural History and Archaeology Society* 114, 240–44.

—— 2000. *A Landscape Revealed: 10,000 Years on a Chalkland Farm.* Stroud: Tempus.

Gregory, C. A. 1982. *Gifts and Commodities.* London: Academic Press.

Greig, I. M. 1997. Excavation of a Bronze Age settlement at Varley Halls, Coldean Lane, Brighton, East Sussex. *Sussex Archaeological Collections* 135, 7–58.

Gresham, C. A. 1939. Spettisbury Rings, Dorset. *Archaeological Journal* 96, 114–31.

Guilbert, G. C. 1975. Planned hillfort interiors. *Proceedings of the Prehistoric Society* 41, 203–21.

—— 1981. Double-ring roundhouses probable and possible. *Proceedings of the Prehistoric Society* 47, 299–317.

—— 1982. Post-ring symmetry in roundhouses at Moel y Gaer and some other sites in prehistoric Britain. In P. J. Drury (ed.) *Approaches to the Interpretation of the Excavated Remains of Buildings.* Oxford: British Archaeological Report (British Series 110), 67–86.

Gwilt, A. 1997. Popular practices from material culture: a case study of the Iron Age settlement at Wakerley, Northamptonshire. In Gwilt and Haselgrove (eds), 153–66.

—— and Haselgrove, C. 1997. *Reconstructing Iron Age Societies.* Oxford: Oxbow Books (Monograph 71).

Hambleton, E. 1999. *Animal Husbandry Regimes in Iron Age Britain: A Comparative Study of Faunal Assemblages from British Iron Age Sites.* Oxford: British Archaeological Report (British Series 282).

Hamilton, S. 1993. First millennium BC pottery traditions in Southern Britain. University of London: Unpublished PhD thesis.

—— 2001. A review of early first millennium BC pottery from Chanctonbury Ring: a contribution to the study of Sussex hillforts of the Late Bronze Age/Early Iron Age transition. *Sussex Archaeological Collections* 139, 89–100.

Hamilton, S. 2002. Between ritual and routine: interpreting British prehistoric pottery production and distribution. In A. Woodward and J. D. Hill (eds), 38–53.

—— 2003. Sussex not Wessex: a regional perspective on southern Britain 1200–50 BC. In D. Rudling (ed.) *The Archaeology of Sussex to AD 2000*. Brighton: University of Sussex, 2–20.

—— 2007. Cultural choices in the 'British Eastern Channel Area' in the Late Pre-Roman Iron Age. In C. Haselgrove and T. Moore (eds), 81–105.

—— and Gregory, K. 2000. Updating the Sussex Iron Age. *Sussex Archaeological Collections* 138, 57–74.

—— and Manley, J. 1997. Points of View: Prominent enclosures in 1st millennium Sussex. *Sussex Archaeological Collections* 135, 93–112.

—— —— 2001. Hillforts, monumentality and place: a chronological and topographic review of first millennium BC hillforts of Southeast England. *European Journal of Archaeology* 4.1, 7–42.

Harding, D. W. 1973. Round and rectangular: Iron Age houses, British and foreign. In C. F. C. Hawkes and S. C. Hawkes (eds) *Archaeology into History, 1. Greeks, Celts and Romans*. London: J. M. Dent & Sons Ltd, 43–62.

—— 1974. *The Iron Age in Lowland Britain*. London: Routledge.

—— (ed.) 1982. *Later Prehistoric Settlement in South East Scotland*. Edinburgh: University of Edinburgh (Occasional Paper 8).

—— Blake, I. M., and Reynolds, P. J. 1993. *An Iron Age Settlement in Dorset: Excavations and Reconstruction*. Edinburgh: Department of Archaeology, University of Edinburgh (Monograph Series 1).

Harding, J. 2003. *The Henge Monuments of the British Isles*. Stroud: Tempus Books.

Haselgrove, C. 1982. Wealth, prestige and power: the dynamics of late Iron Age political centralisation in south-east England. In A. C. Renfrew and S. Shennan (eds) *Ranking, Resource and Exchange*. Cambridge: Cambridge University Press, 79–88.

—— 1986. An Iron Age community and its hillfort: the excavations at Danebury, Hampshire, 1969–79, a review. *Archaeological Journal*, 143, 363–69.

—— 1987. *Iron Age coinage in south-east England: The Archaeological Context*. Oxford: British Archaeological Report (British Series 174).

—— 1989. The later Iron Age in southern Britain and beyond. In M. Todd (ed.) *Research on Roman Britain 1960–89*. London: Society for the Promotion of Roman Studies (Britannia Monograph 11), 1–18.

—— 1990. After Mack: Van Arsdell's insular Celtic coins. *Antiquity* 64, 416–18.

—— 1993. The development of British Iron Age coinage. *Numismatic Chronicle* 153, 48–51.

—— 1996. Iron Age coinage: recent work. In T. Champion and J. Collis (eds), 67–86.

—— 1997. Iron Age brooch deposition and chronology. In A. Gwilt and C. Haselgrove (eds), 51–72.

Haselgrove, C. 2005. A trio of temples: a reassessment of Iron Age coin deposition at Hayling Island, Harlow and Wanborough. In C. Haselgrove and D. Wigg-Wolf (eds), 381–418.

—— 2006. Early potin coinage in Britain: an update. In P. De Jersey (ed.), 17–27.

—— and Millett, M. 1997. Verlamion reconsidered. In A. Gwilt and C. Haselgrove (eds), 282–96.

—— and Moore, T. (eds) 2007. *The Later Iron Age in Britain and Beyond.* Oxford: Oxbow Books.

—— and Pope, R. (eds) 2007. *The Earlier Iron Age in Britain and the Near Continent.* Oxford: Oxbow Books.

—— and Wigg-Wolf, D. (eds) 2005. *Iron Age Coinage and Ritual Practices.* Mainz: Philipp von Zabern.

—— Armit, I., Champion, T., Creighton, J., Gwilt, A., Hill, J. D., Hunter, F., and Woodward, A. 2001. *Understanding the British Iron Age: An Agenda for Action.* Salisbury: Wessex Archaeology.

Hawkes, C. F. C. 1931. Hillforts. *Antiquity* 5, 60–97.

—— 1939. Excavations at Quarley Hill, 1938. *Proceedings of the Hampshire Field Club and Archaeological Society* 14, 136–94.

—— 1940. The excavations at Bury Hill, 1939. *Proceedings of the Hampshire Field Club and Archaeological Society* 14, 291–337.

—— 1951. Bronze workers, cauldrons and bucket-animals in Iron Age and Roman Britain. In W. F. Grimes (ed.) *Aspects of Archaeology in Britain and Beyond.* London: H. W. Edwards, 172–99.

—— 1959. The ABC of the British Iron Age. *Antiquity* 33, 170–82.

—— 1989. Christopher Hawkes. In G. Daniel and C. Chippendale (eds) *The Pastmasters: Eleven Modern Pioneers of Archaeology.* London: Thames and Hudson, 46–60.

—— and Crummy, P. 1995. *Camulodonum 2.* Colchester: Colchester Archaeological Trust (Report 11).

—— and Hull, M. R. 1947. *Camulodonum.* London: Society of Antiquaries of London.

—— Myres, J. N. L., and Stevens C. G. 1930. St Catherine's Hill, Winchester. Part 1: The Early Iron Age. *Proceedings of the Hampshire Field Club and Archaeological Society* 11, 1–187.

Hawkes, J. 1982. *Mortimer Wheeler: Adventurer in Archaeology.* London: Weidenfeld and Nicolson Ltd.

Hawkes, S. C. 1994. Longbridge Deverill Cow Down, Wiltshire, House 3: a major round house of the Early Iron Age. *Oxford Journal of Archaeology* 13.1, 49–69.

Hearne, C. M. and Adam, N. 1999. Excavation of an extensive Late Bronze Age settlement at Shorncote Quarry, near Cirencester, 1995–6. *Transactions of the Bristol and Gloucestershire Archaeological Society* 117, 35–73.

Hearne, C. M., Adam, N., and Birbeck, V. 1999. *A35 Tolpuddle to Puddleton Bypass DBFO, Dorset, 1996–8.* Salisbury: Wessex Archaeology.

Hedges, J. W. 1983. *Isbister: A Chambered Tomb in Orkney.* Oxford: British Archaeological Report (British Series 115).

Henderson, J. 1989. The scientific analysis of ancient glass and its archaeological interpretation. In J. Henderson (ed.) *Scientific Analysis in Archaeology and its Interpretation.* Oxford: Oxford University Committee for Archaeology (Monograph 19), 30–62.

—— 1991. Industrial specialisation in Late Iron Age Britain and Europe. *Archaeological Journal* 148, 104–48.

Hendry, J. 1999. Cultural theory and contemporary management organization. *Human Relations* 52.5, 557–77.

Herbert, E. W. 1984. *Red Gold of Africa: Copper in Pre-colonial History and Culture.* Madison: University of Wisconsin Press.

—— 1993. *Iron, Gender, and Power: Rituals of Transformation in African Societies.* Bloomington: Indiana University Press.

Herman, G. 1987. *Ritualised Friendship and the Greek City State.* Cambridge: Cambridge University Press.

Hey, G., Bayliss, A., and Boyle, A. 1999. Iron Age inhumation burials at Yarnton, Oxfordshire. *Antiquity* 73, 551–62.

Hill, J. D. 1989. Rethinking the Iron Age. *Scottish Archaeological Review* 6, 16–24.

—— 1993. Can we conceive of a different Europe in the past? A contrastive archaeology of Later Prehistoric Settlement in Southern England. *Journal of European Archaeology* 1, 57–76.

—— 1995a. How should we understand Iron Age societies and hillforts? A contextual study from southern Britain. In J. D. Hill and C. Cumberpatch (eds) *Different Iron Ages: Studies on the Iron Age in Temperate Europe.* Oxford: British Archaeological Report (International Series 602), 45–66.

—— 1995b. *Ritual and Rubbish in the Iron Age of Wessex: A Study in the Formation of a Specific Archaeological Record.* Oxford: British Archaeological Report (British Series 242).

—— 1996. Hill-forts and the Iron Age of Wessex. In T. C. Champion and J. R. Collis (eds), 67–86.

—— 2007. The dynamics of social change in Later Iron Age eastern and south-eastern England c.300 BC–AD 43. In C. Haselgrove and T. Moore (eds), 16–40.

—— Spence, A. J., La Neice, S., and Worrell, S. 2004. The Winchester Hoard: a find of unique Iron Age gold jewellery from southern England. *Antiquaries Journal* 84, 1–22.

Hingley, R. 1984. Towards social analysis in archaeology: Celtic society in the Iron Age of the Upper Thames Valley. In Cunliffe and Miles (eds), 72–88.

—— 1990a. Domestic organisation and gender relations in Iron Age and Romano-British households. In R. Samson (ed.) *The Social Archaeology of Houses.* Edinburgh: Edinburgh University Press, 125–49.

Hingley, R. 1990b. Iron Age 'currency bars': the archaeological and social context. *Archaeological Journal* 147, 91–117.

—— 1997. Iron, ironworking and regeneration: a study of the symbolic meaning of metalworking in Iron Age Britain. In A. Gwilt and C. Haselgrove (eds), 9–15.

—— 1999. The creation of the later prehistoric landscape and the context of the reuse of Neolithic and earlier Bronze Age monuments in Britain and Ireland. In B. Bevan (ed.), 233–52.

—— 2005. Iron Age 'currency bars' in Britain: items of exchange in liminal contexts? In C. Haselgrove and D. Wigg-Wolf (eds), 183–206.

—— 2006. The deposition of iron objects in Britain during the later prehistoric and Roman periods: contextual analysis and the significance of iron. *Britannia* 37, 213–58.

—— and Haselgrove, C. 2006. Iron deposition and its significance in pre-Roman Britain. In G. Bataille and J.-P. Guillaumet (eds) *Les dépôts métalliques au second âge du Fer en Europe tempérée*. Glux-en-Glenne: Centre Archéologique Européen, 147–63.

Hirst, S. and Rahtz, P. 1996. Liddington Castle and the Battle of Badon: excavation and research 1976. *Archaeological Journal* 153, 1–59.

Hodder, I. 1982. *Symbolic and Structural Archaeology*. Cambridge: Cambridge University Press.

—— 1991. *The Domestication of Europe: Structure and Contingency in Neolithic Studies*. London: Blackwell.

—— and Hedges, J. W. 1977. 'Weaving combs': their typology and distribution, with some introductory remarks on date and function. In J. Collis (ed.), 17–28.

Holden, E. W. 1972. A Bronze Age cemetery barrow on Itford Hill, Beddingham. *Sussex Archaeological Collections* 113, 83–103.

Howell, L. and Durden, T. 2005. Further excavation of an Iron Age enclosure at Danebury Road, Hatch Warren, Basingstoke, Hampshire, 1995. *Proceedings of the Hampshire Field Club and Archaeological Society* 60, 39–61.

Hull, M. R. and Hawkes, C. F. C. 1987. *Corpus of Ancient Brooches in Britain: Pre-Roman Bow Brooches*. Oxford: British Archaeological Report (British Series 168).

Hunter, F. 1997. Iron Age hoarding in Scotland and northern England. In A. Gwilt and C. Haselgrove (eds), 108–33.

—— 2006. Art in Later Iron Age society. In C. Haselgrove (ed.) *Celtes et Gaulois, l'archéologie face à l'histoire: Les mutations de la fin de l'âge du fer*. Glux-en-Glenne: Centre Archéologique Européen, 93–115.

Ingold, T. 2000. *The Perception of the Environment: Essays on Livelihood, Dwelling and Skill*. London: Routledge.

James, S. 1993. *Exploring the World of the Celts*. London: Thames and Hudson.

—— 1999. *The Atlantic Celts: Ancient People or Modern Invention?* London: British Museum Press.

Johnston, S. A. and Wailes, B. 2007. *Dun Ailinne: Excavations at an Irish Royal Site, 1968–1975*. Philadelphia: University of Pennsylvania Museum of Archaeology and Anthropology.

Jones, A. 2005. Lives in fragments? Personhood and the European Neolithic. *Journal of Social Archaeology* 5.2, 193–224.

Jones, M. 1984. Regional patterns in crop production. In B. W. Cunliffe and D. Miles (eds), 120–25.

—— 1985. Archaeobotany beyond subsistence reconstruction. In G. Barker and C. Gamble (eds) *Beyond Domestication in Prehistoric Europe*. London and New York: Academic Press, 107–28.

—— 1996. Plant exploitation. In T. Champion and J. Collis (eds), 29–40.

Jones, M. U. and Bond, D. 1980. Later Bronze Age settlement at Mucking, Essex. In J. Barrett and R. Bradley (eds), 471–82.

Jope, E. M. 1961. Daggers of the Early Iron Age in Britain. *Proceedings of the Prehistoric Society* 13, 307–43.

—— 1995. The social implications of Celtic art. In M. J. Green (ed.) *The Celtic World*. London: Routledge, 376–410.

—— 2000. *Early Celtic Art in the British Isles*. Oxford: Clarendon Press.

Joy, J. 2008. Reflections on Celtic art: a re-examination of mirror decoration. In D. Garrow, C. Gosden, and J. D. Hill (eds) *Rethinking Celtic Art*. Oxford: Oxbow Books, 78–99.

Jundi, S. and Hill, J. D. 1998. Brooches and identities in first century AD Britain: more than meets the eye? In C. Forcey, J. Hawthorne, and R. Witcher (eds) *TRAC 97. Proceedings of the Seventh Annual Theoretical Roman Archaeology Conference, Nottingham 1997*. Oxford: Oxbow Books, 125–37.

Karl, R. 2008. Random coincidences—Or: the return of the Celtic to Iron Age Britain. *Proceedings of the Prehistoric Society* 74, 69–78.

Keef, P. A. M. 1953. Two gold penannular ornaments from Harting Beacon. *Antiquaries Journal* 33, 204–6.

Keefe, L. 2005. *Earth Building, Methods and Materials, Repair and Conservation*. London: Taylor and Francis.

Kendrick, T. D. and Hawkes, C. F. C. 1932. *Archaeology in England and Wales 1914–1931*. London: Methuen.

Kent, J. P. C. 1990. Review of Van Arsdell (1989). *Numismatic Chronicle* 150, 266–8.

Kenyon, K. M. 1952. A survey of the evidence concerning the chronology and origins of Iron Age A in southern and midland Britain. *London Institute of Archaeology Annual Report* 8, 29–78.

King, A. and Soffe, G. 2001. Internal organisation and deposition at the Iron Age temple on Hayling Island, Hampshire. In J. R. Collis (ed.) *Society and Settlement in Iron Age Europe*. Sheffield: J. R. Collis Publications, 111–24.

Kirkham, G. 2005. Prehistoric linear ditches on the Marlborough Downs. In G. Brown, D. Field, and D. McOmish (eds) 149–55.

Knüsel, C. and Carr, G. 1995. On the significance of the crania from the River Thames. *Antiquity* 63, 162–9.

Ladle, L. and Woodward, A. 2003. A middle Bronze Age house and burnt mound at Bestwall, Wareham, Dorset: an interim report. *Proceedings of the Prehistoric Society* 69, 265–78.

Lally, M. 2008. Bodies of difference in Iron Age southern England. In O. Davis, N. Sharples, and K. Waddington (eds) *Changing Perspectives on the First Millennium BC.* Oxford: Oxbow Books, 119–38.

Lambrick, G. and Allen, T. 2005. *Gravelly Guy, Stanton Harcourt, Oxfordshire: the development of a prehistoric and Romano-British community.* Oxford: Oxford University School of Archaeology and Oxford Archaeology.

Last, J. 2008. *Beyond the Grave: New Perspectives on Barrows.* Oxford: Oxbow Books.

Lawson, A. J. 1999. The Bronze Age hoards of Hampshire. In A. F. Harding (ed.) *Experiment and Design: Archaeological Studies in Honour of John Coles.* Oxford: Oxbow Books.

—— 2000. *Potterne 1982–1985: Animal Husbandry in Later Prehistoric Wiltshire.* Salisbury: Wessex Archaeology.

Lees, D. 1999. The sanctuary, Avebury: an architectural re-assessment. *Wiltshire Archaeology and Natural History Magazine* 92, 1–6.

Lewis-Williams, D. J. and Dowson, T. A. 1988. The signs of all times: entoptic phenomena in Upper Palaeolithic art. *Current Anthropology* 29, 201–45.

—— —— 1993. On vision and power in the Neolithic: evidence from the decorated monuments. *Current Anthropology* 34, 5–65.

Liddell, D. M. 1933. Excavations at Meon Hill. *Proceedings of the Hampshire Field Club and Archaeological Society* 12, 127–62.

—— 1935. Report on the Hampshire Field Club's excavation at Meon Hill. *Proceedings of the Hampshire Field Club and Archaeological Society* 13, 7–54.

Lobb, S. J. and Rose, P. G. 1996. *Archaeological Survey of the Lower Kennet Valley, Berkshire.* Salisbury: Wessex Archaeology.

Lock, G., Gosden, C. and Daly, P. 2005. *Segsbury Camp: Excavations in 1996 and 1997 at an Iron Age Hillfort on the Oxfordshire Ridgeway.* Oxford: University of Oxford School of Archaeology (Monograph 61).

Longley, D. 1980. *Runnymede Bridge 1976: Excavations on the Site of a Late Bronze Age Settlement.* Guildford: Surrey Archaeological Society (Research Volume 6).

Lovell, J. 1999. Further investigation of an Iron Age and Romano-British farmstead on Cookey Down, near Salisbury. *Wiltshire Archaeological and Natural History Magazine* 92, 33–8.

McKinley, J. I. 1997a. Bronze Age 'barrows' and funerary rites and rituals of cremation. *Proceedings of the Prehistoric Society* 63, 129–45.

—— 1997b. The human remains from Cookey Down. Wessex Archaeology unpublished report.

McOmish, D. 1989. Non-hillfort settlement and its implications. In M. Bowden, D. Mackay, and P. Topping (eds) *From Cornwall to Caithness: Some Aspects of British Field Archaeology. Papers Presented to Norman V. Quinnell.* Oxford: British Archaeological Report (British Series 209), 99–110.

—— 1996. East Chissenbury: ritual and rubbish at the British Bronze Age–Iron Age transition. *Antiquity* 70, 68–76.

—— Field, D. and Brown, G. 2002. *The Field Archaeology of Salisbury Plain Training Area.* Swindon: English Heritage.

Macready, S. and Thompson, F. H. (eds) 1984. *Cross-channel Trade between Gaul and Britain in the Pre-Roman Iron Age.* London: Society of Antiquaries of London (Occasional Paper 4).

Madgwick, R. 2008. Patterns in the modification of animal and human bones in Iron Age Wessex: revisiting the excarnation debate. In O. Davis, N. Sharples, and K. Waddington (eds) *Changing Perspectives on the First Millennium BC.* Oxford: Oxbow Books, 99–118.

Maltby, M. 1985. Patterns in faunal assemblage variability. In G. Barker and C. Gamble (eds) *Beyond Domestication in Prehistoric Europe.* London/New York: Academic Press, 33–74.

—— 1994. Animal exploitation in Iron Age Wessex. In A. P. Fitzpatrick and E. Morris (eds), 9–11.

—— 1996. The exploitation of animals in the Iron Age: the archaeozoological evidence. In T. Champion and J. Collis (eds), 17–28.

—— and Coy, J. P. 1991. The animal bone analysis on the M3 project. A review. In P. J. Fasham and R. J. B. Whinney (eds), 97–104.

Manley, J. 2003. Facing the palace: Excavations in front of the Roman Palace at Fishbourne. *Sussex Archaeological Collections* 141, 1–160.

—— and Rudkin, D. 2005. A pre-AD 43 ditch at Fishbourne Roman Palace, Chichester. *Britannia* 36, 55–95.

Manning, W. G. 1995. Ritual or refuse: the Harrow Hill enclosure reconsidered. In B. Raftery, V. Megaw, and V. Rigby (eds) *Sites and Sights of the Iron Age.* Oxford: Oxbow Books (Monograph 56), 133–8.

Marchant, T. 1989. The evidence for textile production in the Iron Age. *Scottish Archaeological Review* 6, 5–12.

Mare, E. and Le Goff, I. 2006. Malleville-sur-le-Bec/Bonneville-Aptot (Eure), organisation et chronologie de l'habitat du Bronze final. *Bulletin de l'association pour la promotion des recherches sur l'âge du Bronze* 3, 37–42.

Marriot, M. 1976. Hindu transactions: diversity without dualism. In B. Kapferer (ed.) *Transactions and Meaning: Directions in the Anthropology of Exchange and Symbolic Behaviour.* Philadelphia: Institute for the Study of Human Issues, 109–37.

Martin, D. P. 1996. On the cultural ecology of sky burial on the Himalayan Plateau. *East and West* 46 (3–4), 353–70.

Mattingly, D. 2006. *An Imperial Possession: Britain in the Roman Empire.* London: Allen Lane.

Mauss, M. 1990. [1925] *The Gift: The Form and Reason for Exchange in Archaic Societies.* New York: W. W. Norton.

Mays, M. (ed.) 1992. *Celtic Coinage: Britain and Beyond.* Oxford: British Archaeological Reports (British Series 222).

Megaw, J. V. S. and Megaw, M. R. 1989. *Celtic Art: From its Beginning to the Book of Kells.* London: Thames and Hudson.

—— and Simpson, D. D. A. 1979. *Introduction to British Prehistory.* Leicester: Leicester University Press.

Menez, Y., Daire, M.-Y., Hyvert, J., Langouet, L., LeBihan, J.-P., and Tanguy, D. 1990. Les bâtiments de l'Age du Fer en Armorique. In A. Duval, J.-P. LeBihan, and Y. Menez (eds) *Les Gaulois d'Armorique: La fin de l'Age du Fer en Europe Tempérée.* Rennes: Revue archéologique de l'Ouest (no. 3), 121–38.

Mepham, L. N. 1997. Pottery. In A. P. Fitzpatrick (ed.), 114–38.

Mercer, R. and Healy, F. 2008. *Hambledon Hill, Dorset, England. Excavation and Survey of a Neolithic Monument Complex and its Surrounding Landscape.* London: English Heritage.

Miles, D., Palmer, S., Lock, G., Gosden, C. and Cromarty, A. M. 2003. *Uffington White Horse: Investigations at White Horse Hill, Uffington, 1989–95, and Tower Hill, Ashbury, 1993–4.* Oxford: Oxford Archaeology.

Millett, M. 1983. Excavation at Cowdrey's Down, Basingstoke, Hampshire 1978–81. *Archaeological Journal* 140, 151–279.

—— 1993. A cemetery in an age of transition: King Harry Lane reconsidered. In M. Strück (ed.) *Römerzeitlicher Gräber als Quellen zu Religion, Bevölkersungsstruktur und Sozialgeschichte.* Mainz: Archäologische Schriften des Instituts für Vor- und Frühgeschichte der Johannes Gutenberg Universität Mainz 3, 255–82.

—— and Russell, D. 1982. An Iron Age burial from Viables Farm, Basingstoke. *Archaeological Journal* 139, 69–90.

Mitford, J. 1963. *The American Way of Death.* London: Hutchinson.

Moore, J. and Jennings, D. 1992. *Reading Business Park: a Bronze Age Landscape. Thames Valley Landscapes: the Kennet Valley,* vol. 1. Oxford: Oxford Archaeological Unit.

Moore, T. 2003. Rectangular houses in the British Iron Age: squaring the circle. In J. Humphrey (ed.) *Researching the Iron Age.* Leicester: University of Leicester (Monograph 11), 47–58.

—— 2006. *Iron Age Societies in the Severn–Cotswolds: Developing Narratives of Social and Landscape Change.* Oxford: British Archaeological Report (British Series 421).

Morris, B. 1994. *Anthropology of the Self: The Individual in Cultural Perspective.* London: Pluto Press.

Morris, E. L. 1994. Production and distribution of pottery and salt in Iron Age Britain: a review. *Proceedings of the Prehistoric Society* 60, 371–93.

—— 1996. Artefact production and exchange in the British Iron Age. In T. Champion and J. Collis (eds), 41–66.

—— 1997. Where is the Danebury Ware? In A. Gwilt and C. Haselgrove (eds), 36–9.

Muckelroy, K. 1981. Middle Bronze Age trade between Britain and Europe: a maritime perspective. *Proceedings of the Prehistoric Society* 47, 275–98.

Musson, C. R. 1970. House-plans and prehistory. *Current Archaeology* 2.10, 267–75.

Nash, D. 1984. The basis of contact between Britain and Gaul in the Late Pre-Roman Iron Age. In S. Macready and F. H. Thompson (eds), 92–107.

Neal, D. S. 1980. Bronze Age, Iron Age and Roman settlement sites at Little Sombourne and Ashley, Hampshire. *Proceedings of the Hampshire Field Club and Archaeological Society* 36, 91–113.

Neal, D. S., Wardle, A., and Hunn, J. 1990. *Excavation of the Iron Age, Roman and Medieval Settlement at Gorhambury, St Albans.* London: English Heritage (Archaeological Report 14).

Needham, S. P. 1990. *The Petters Late Bronze Age Metalwork: An Analytical Study of Thames Valley Metalworking in its Settlement Context.* London: British Museum (Occasional Paper No 70).

—— 1991. *Excavation and Salvage at Runnymede Bridge 1978: The Late Bronze Age Waterfront Site.* London: British Museum Press.

—— 1993. The structure of settlement and ritual in the Late Bronze Age of south-east Britain. In C. Mordant and A. Richard (eds) *L'habitat et l'occupation du sol à l'Age du Bronze en Europe.* Paris: Editions du Comité des travaux historiques et scientifiques (Documents Préhistoriques 4), 46–69.

—— 1996. Chronology and periodisation in the British Bronze Age. *Acta Archaeologica* 67, 121–40.

—— 2007. 800 BC, The great divide. In C. Haselgrove and R. Pope (eds), 39–63.

—— and Ambers, J. 1994. Redating Rams Hill. *Proceedings of the Prehistoric Society* 60, 225–43.

—— and Burgess, C. 1980. The Later Bronze Age in the Lower Thames Valley: the metalwork evidence. In J. C. Barrett and R. Bradley (eds), 437–70.

—— and Dean, M. 1987. La cargaison de Langdon Bay à Douvres (Grande Bretagne): la signification pour les échanges à travers la Manche. In J.-C. Blanchet (ed.) *Les relations entre le Continent et les Iles Britanniques à l'Age du Bronze: actes du colloque de Bronze de Lille, 1984.* Amiens: Supplément à la Revue archéologique de Picardie, 119–24.

—— and Spence, T. 1997a. *Refuse and Disposal at Area 16 East Runnymede.* London: British Museum Press.

——— 1997b. Refuse and the formation of middens. *Antiquity* 71, 77–90.

—— Bronk Ramsey, C., Coombs, D., Cartwright, C., and Petit, P. 1997. An independent chronology for British Bronze Age metalwork: the results of the Oxford radiocarbon accelerator programme. *Archaeological Journal* 154, 55–107.

Niblett, R. 1999. *The Excavation of a Ceremonial Site at Folly Lane, Verulamium.* London: Society for the Promotion of Roman Studies (Britannia Monograph 14).

Northover, P. 1982. The exploration and long distance movement of bronze in Bronze Age and Early Iron Age Europe. *Bulletin of the Institute of Archaeology* 19, 45–72.

—— 1992. Materials issues in the Celtic coinage. In M. Mays (ed.) 235–300.

Nowakowski, J. A. 1991. Trethellan Farm, Newquay: the excavation of a lowland Bronze Age settlement and Iron Age cemetery. *Cornish Archaeology* 30, 5–242.

O'Brien, W. 1994. *Mount Gabriel: Bronze Age Mining in Ireland.* Galway: Galway University Press.

O'Connell, M. 1986. *Petters Sports Field, Egham: Excavation of a Late Bronze Age/Early Iron Age Site.* Guildford: Surrey Archaeological Society (Research Volume 10).

O'Connor, B. 1980. *Cross Channel Relations in the Later Bronze Age.* Oxford: British Archaeology Report (International Series 91).

O'Connor, B. 2007. Llyn Fawr metalwork in Britain: a review. In C. Haselgrove and R. Pope (eds), 64–79.

Oppenheimer, S. 2006. *The Origins of the British: A Genetic Detective Story.* London: Constable and Robinson.

Oswald, A. 1997. A doorway on the past: practical and mystic concerns in the orientation of roundhouse doorways. In A. Gwilt and C. Haselgrove (eds), 87–95.

—— Dyer, C. and Barber, M. 2001. *The Creation of Monuments: Neolithic Causewayed Enclosures in the British Isles.* Swindon: English Heritage.

Palmer, R. 1984. *Danebury: An Iron Age Hillfort in Hampshire. An Aerial Photographic Interpretation of its Environs.* London: RCHME (Supplementary Series 6).

Parfitt, K. 1995. *Iron Age Burials from Mill Hill, Deal.* London: British Museum.

Parker Pearson, M. 1993. *English Heritage Book of Bronze Age Britain.* London: Batsford and English Heritage.

—— 1996. Food, fertility and front doors in the first millennium BC. In T. Champion and J. Collis (eds), 117–32.

—— 1999. Food, sex and death: cosmologies in the British Iron Age with particular reference to East Yorkshire. *Cambridge Archaeological Journal* 9.1, 43–69.

—— and Ramilisonina 1998. Stonehenge for the ancestors: the stones pass on the message. *Antiquity* 72, 308–26.

—— and Richards, C. 1994. Architecture and order: spatial representation and archaeology. In M. Parker Pearson and C. Richards (eds) *Architecture and Order: Approaches to Social Space.* London: Routledge, 38–72.

—— and Sharples, N. M. 1999. *Between Land and Sea: Excavations at Dun Vulan, South Uist.* Sheffield: Sheffield Academic Press.

—— Chamberlain, A., Craig, O., Marshall, P., Mulville, J., Smith, H., Chenery, C., Collins, M., Cook, G., Craig, G., Evans, J., Hiller, J., Montgomery, J., Schwenninger, J.-L., Taylor, G., and Weiss, T. 2005. Evidence for mummification in Bronze Age Britain. *Antiquity* 79, 529–46.

—— Pollard, J., Richards, C., Thomas, J., Tilley, C., Welham, K., and Albarella, U. 2006. Materializing Stonehenge: the Stonehenge Riverside Project and new discoveries. *Journal of Material Culture* 11, 227–61.

Parkes, P. 2006. Celtic fosterage: adoptive kinship and clientage in northwest Europe. *Comparative Studies in Society and History* 48, 359–95.

Pasmore, A. and Pallister, J. 1967. Boiling mounds in the New Forest. *Proceedings of the Hampshire Field Club and Archaeological Society* 24, 14–19.

Payne, A., Corney, M., and Cunliffe, B. 2006. *The Wessex Hillforts Project: Extensive Survey of Hillfort Interiors in Central Southern England.* London: English Heritage.

Peacock, D. P. S. 1987. Iron Age and Roman quern production at Lodsworth, West Sussex. *Antiquaries Journal* 67, 61–85.

Pearce, S. M. 1983. *The Bronze Age Metalwork of South Western Britain.* Oxford: British Archaeological Report (British Series 120).

Petersen, F. 1981. *The Excavation of a Bronze Age Cemetery on Knighton Heath, Dorset.* Oxford: British Archaeological Report (British Series 98).

Piggott, C. M. 1942. Five Late Bronze Age enclosures in north Wiltshire. *Proceedings of the Prehistoric Society* 8, 48–61.

—— 1944. The Grim's Ditch complex in Cranborne Chase. *Antiquity* 18, 65–71.

Piggott, S. 1930. Butser Hill. *Antiquity* 3, 187–200.

—— 1940. Timber circles: a re-examination. *Archaeological Journal* 96, 193–222.

—— 1959. The carnyx in Early Iron Age Britain. *Antiquaries Journal* 39, 19–32.

Pitt Rivers, A. H. L. F. 1881. Excavations at Mount Caburn camp, near Lewis. *Archaeologia* 46, 423–95.

—— 1888. *Excavations in Cranborne Chase*, vol. 2. London: Privately printed.

Pollard, J. and Reynolds, A. 2002. *Avebury: The Biography of a Landscape*. London: Tempus.

Pope, R. E. 2007. Ritual and the roundhouse: a critique of recent ideas on domestic space in later British prehistory. In C. Haselgrove and R. Pope (eds), 204–28.

Potter, T. W. and Trow, S. D. 1988. Puckeridge–Braughing, Herts: the Ermine Street excavations, 1971–1972. *Hertfordshire Archaeology* 10, 1–189.

Pryor, F. 1980. *Excavations at Fengate, Peterborough, England: The Third Report*. Northamptonshire: Northamptonshire Archaeological Society (Monograph 1).

—— 1984. *Excavations at Fengate, Peterborough, England: The Fourth Report*. Northamptonshire: Northamptonshire Archaeological Society (Monograph 2).

—— (ed.) 1992a. Current research at Flag Fen, Peterborough. *Antiquity* 66, 439–531.

—— 1992b. *The English Heritage Book of Flag Fen*. London: Batsford.

—— 1996. Sheep stockyards and field systems. *Antiquity* 70, 313–24.

—— 2001. *The Flag Fen Basin: Archaeology and Environment of a Fenland Landscape*. London: English Heritage.

Qualman, K. E., Rees, H., Scobie, G. D., and Whinney, R. 2004. *Oram's Arbour: The Iron Age Enclosure at Winchester*. Vol. 1: *Investigations 1950–1999*. Winchester: Winchester Museums Service.

Radcliffe, F. M. 1995. Archaeology and historical landscape in Wessex from the air. *Proceedings of the Dorset Natural History and Archaeological Society* 117, 51–66.

Raftery, B. 1994. *Pagan Celtic Ireland*. London: Thames and Hudson.

Rahtz, P. A. 1961. An excavation on Bokerley Dyke, 1958. *Archaeological Journal* 118, 65–99.

Rankin, D. 1987. *Celts and the Classical World*. London: Routledge.

Rawlings, M., Allen, M. J., and Healy, F. 2004. Investigation of the Whitesheet Down environs 1989–90: Neolithic causewayed enclosure and Iron Age settlement. *Wiltshire Studies* 97, 144–96.

RCHME 1970. *An Inventory of the Historical monuments in the County of Dorset*. Vol. 2: *South-East*. London: HMSO.

—— 1972. *An Inventory of the Historical Monuments in the County of Dorset*. Vol. 4: *North Dorset*. London: HMSO.

—— 1975. *An Inventory of the Historical Monuments in the County of Dorset*. Vol. 5: *East Dorset*. London: HMSO.

RCHME 1979. *Stonehenge and its Environs: Monuments and Land-use.* Edinburgh: HMSO.
—— 1994. A new earthwork survey of Old Winchester Hill, Hampshire. Cambridge: RCHME (Archaeological Field Survey Report).
—— 1995. A causewayed enclosure and the Trundle hillfort on St Roche's hill, Singleton, West Sussex. Cambridge: RCHME (Archaeological Field Survey Report).
—— 1996. *Hambledon Hill, Child Okeford, Hanford and Iwerne Coutney or Shroton, Dorset.* Cambridge: RCHME (Archaeological Field Survey Report).
—— 1999. South Wiltshire Project. Draft text.
Redon, S. von 1995. *Exchange in Ancient Greece.* London: Duckworth.
Renfrew, C. 1979. *Investigations in Orkney.* London: Society of Antiquaries of London.
—— and Bahn, P. 1991. *Archaeology: Theories, Methods and Practice.* London: Thames and Hudson.
Reynolds, P. J. 1979. *Iron-Age Farm: The Butser Experiment.* London: British Museum Publications.
Richards, C. 2005. *Dwelling among the Monuments: The Neolithic Village of Barnhouse, Maeshowe Passage Grave and Surrounding Monuments at Stenness, Orkney.* Cambridge: MacDonald Institute for Archaeological Research.
Richards, J. 1978. *The Archaeology of the Berkshire Downs: An Introductory Survey.* Reading: Berkshire Archaeology Committee (Publication 3).
—— 1990. *The Stonehenge Environs Project.* London: English Heritage (Archaeological Report 16).
Richardson, K. M. 1940. Excavations at Poundbury, Dorchester, Dorset, 1939. *Antiquaries Journal* 20, 429–48.
—— 1951. The excavation of Iron Age villages on Boscombe Down West. *Wiltshire Archaeology and Natural History Magazine* 54, 123–68.
Richmond, I. 1968. *Hod Hill. Vol. 2: Excavations Carried Out between 1951 and 1958 for the Trustees of the British Museum.* London: British Museum.
Robertson-Mackay, M. E. 1977. The defences of the Iron Age hillfort at Winklebury, Basingstoke, Hampshire. *Proceedings of the Prehistoric Society* 43, 131–54.
—— 1980. A 'head and hooves' burial beneath a round barrow, with other Neolithic and Bronze Age sites, on Hemp Knoll, near Avebury, Wiltshire. *Proceedings of the Prehistoric Society* 46, 123–76.
Rodwell, W. J. 1976. Coinage, oppida and the rise of Belgic power in South Eastern Britain. In B. W. Cunliffe and R. T. Rowley (eds) *Oppida: The Beginnings of Urbanisation in Barbarian Europe.* Oxford: British Archaeological Report (International Series 11), 184–367.
Rohl, B. and Needham, S. P. 1998. *The Circulation of Metal in the British Bronze Age.* London: British Museum (Occasional Paper 69).
Rohner, R. P. and Rohner, E. C. 1970. *The Kwakiutl Indians of British Columbia.* New York: Holt, Rinehart and Winston.
Rowlands, M. J. 1976. *The Production and Distribution of Metalwork in the Middle Bronze Age in Southern Britain.* Oxford: British Archaeological Report (British Series 31).

Rowlands, M. J. 1980. Kinship, alliance and exchange in the European Bronze Age. In J. Barrett and R. Bradley (eds), 15–56.

—— Larsen, M. T., and Kristiansen, K. 1987. *Centre and Periphery in the Ancient World*. Cambridge: Cambridge University Press.

Roymans, N. 1990. *Tribal Societies in Northern Gaul: An Anthropological Perspective*. Amsterdam: Cingula 12.

Rudd, C. 2006. The Belgae and Regini. In P. De Jersey (ed.), 145–81.

Rudling, D. 1987. The excavation of a Late Bronze Age site at Yapton, West Sussex, 1984. *Sussex Archaeological Collections* 125, 51–67.

—— 1990. Archaeological finds at Rustington, West Sussex, 1986–88. *Sussex Archaeological Collections* 128, 1–20.

—— (ed.) 2002. *Downland Settlement and Land-use: The Archaeology of the Brighton Bypass*. London: Archetype.

—— and Gilkes, G. 2000. Important discoveries made during the construction of the A259 Rustington Bypass, 1990. *Sussex Archaeological Collections* 138, 15–28.

Russell, M. 1996a. Problems of phasing: a reconsideration of the Black Patch Middle Bronze Age 'Nucleated Village'. *Oxford Journal of Archaeology* 15, 33–8.

—— 1996b. *A Reassessment of the Bronze Age Cemetery-barrow on Itford Hill, East Sussex*. Bournemouth: School of Conservation Sciences (Research Report 2).

Sahlins, M. 1972. *Stone Age Economics*. Chicago: Aldine.

Salter, C. J. 1989. The scientific examination of the iron industry in Iron Age Britain. In J. Henderson (ed.) *Scientific Analysis in Archaeology and its Interpretation*. Oxford: Oxford University Committee for Archaeology (Monograph 19), 250–73.

—— and Ehrenreich, R. 1984. Iron Age metallurgy in Central Southern England. In B. W. Cunliffe and D. Miles (eds), 146–61.

Savoury, H. N. 1976. *Guide Catalogue of the Early Iron Age Collections*. Cardiff: National Museum of Wales.

Seager Thomas, M. 1998. New evidence for a Late Bronze Age occupation of Selsey Bill. *Sussex Archaeological Collections* 136, 7 22.

—— 2001. Two early first millennium BC wells at Selsey, West Sussex and their wider significance. *Antiquaries Journal* 81, 15–50.

—— 2008. From potsherds to people: Sussex prehistoric pottery. Collared urns to post Deverel Rimbury, *c*.2000–500 BC. *Sussex Archaeological Collections* 146, 19–52.

Sellwood, L. 1984. Tribal boundaries viewed from the perspective of numismatic evidence. In B. W. Cunliffe and D. Miles (eds), 191–204.

Sharples, N. M. 1990a. Discussion. In G. Aitken and N. Aitken (eds), 57–94.

—— 1990b. Late Iron Age society and continental trade in Dorset. In A. Duval, J.-P. LeBihan, and Y. Menez (eds) *Les Gaulois d'Armorique, La fin de l'Age du Fer en Europe Tempérée*. Rennes: Revue archéologique de l'Ouest (Supplément 3), 299–304.

—— 1991a. *Maiden Castle: Excavations and Field Survey 1985–86*. London: English Heritage (Archaeological Report 19).

Sharples, N. M. 1991b. Warfare in the Iron Age of Wessex. *Scottish Archaeological Review* 9, 79–89.

—— 1991c. *English Heritage Book of Maiden Castle.* London: Batsford.

—— 1996. Nationalism or internationalism: the problematic Scottish experience. In J. Atkinson, I. Banks, and J. O'Sullivan (eds) *Nationalism and Archaeology; Scottish Archaeological Forum, Conference Proceedings Spring 1994.* Glasgow: Cruithne Press, 77–88.

—— 1999. Stuart Piggott (1910–1996). In T. Murray (ed.) *Encyclopaedia of Archaeology: The Great Archaeologists,* vol. 2. Oxford: ABC–CLIO, 615–34.

—— 2004. From brochs to brooches: changing social relationships in the first millennium AD. In J. Downes and A. Ritchie (eds) *Sea Change: Orkney and Northern Europe in the Later Iron Age and after, 300–800 AD.* Balgavies: Pinkfoot Press, 151–65.

—— 2006. The first (permanent) houses: an interpretation of the monumental domestic architecture of Iron Age Orkney. In V. O. Jorge (ed.) *Approaching 'Prehistoric and Protohistoric Architectures' of Europe from a 'Dwelling Perspective'.* Porto: ADECAP (Journal of Iberian Archaeology 8), 281–305.

—— 2007. Building communities and creating identities in the first millennium BC. In C. Haselgrove and R. Pope (eds), 174–84.

—— 2009. Aspiring to greatness: the recent excavations at Maiden Castle. In J. Schofield (ed.) *Great Excavations: Shaping the Archaeological Profession.* Oxford: Oxbow Books.

—— forthcoming. Boundaries, status and conflict: an exploration of Iron Age research in the 20th century. In T. Moore and L. Armada (eds) *Atlantic Europe in the First Millennium BC: Crossing the Divide.* Oxford: Oxford University Press.

—— and Pearson, M. P. 1997. Why were brochs built? Recent studies in the Iron Age of Atlantic Scotland. In A. Gwilt and C. Haselgrove (eds), 254–65.

Sherratt, A. 1996. Why Wessex? The Avon route and river transport in later British Prehistory. *Oxford Journal of Archaeology* 1.2, 211–34.

Sloan, K. 2007. *A New World: England's First View of America.* London: British Museum Press.

Smith, I. F. 1965. *Windmill Hill and Avebury: Excavations by Alexander Keiller 1925–1939.* Oxford: Clarendon Press.

Smith, K. 1977. The excavation of Winklebury Camp, Basingstoke, Hampshire. *Proceedings of the Prehistoric Society* 43, 31–130.

—— Coppen, J., Wainwright, G.J., and Beckett, S. 1981. The Shaugh Moor Project Third Report—Settlement and environmental investigations. *Proceedings of the Prehistoric Society* 47, 205–73.

Smith, M. A. 1959. Some Somerset hoards and their place in the Bronze Age of southern Britain. *Proceedings of the Prehistoric Society* 25, 144–87.

Smith, N. 1999a. Burnt mounds of the New Forest. *Northern Archaeology* 17/18, 41–8.

—— 1999b. The earthwork remains of enclosure in the New Forest. *Proceedings of the Hampshire Field Club and Archaeological Society* 54, 1–56.

Smith, P. J. 1999. The coup: How did the Prehistoric Society of East Anglia become the Prehistoric Society? *Proceedings of the Prehistoric Society* 65, 465–70.

Smith, R. J. C., Rawlings, M. N., and Barnes, I. 1992. Excavations at Coburg Road and Weymouth Road, Dorchester, Dorset, 1988–9. *Proceedings of the Dorset Natural History and Archaeological Society* 114, 19–46.

——Healy, F., Allen, M. J., Morris, E. L., Barnes, I., and Woodward, P. J. 1997. *Excavations Along the Route of the Dorchester Bypass, Dorset, 1986–8.* Salisbury: Wessex Archaeology.

Sørenson, M. L. S. 1997. Reading dress: the construction of social categories and identities in Bronze Age Europe. *Journal of European Archaeology* 5.1, 93–114.

——and Thomas, R. (eds) 1989. *The Bronze Age–Iron Age Transition in Europe.* Oxford: British Archaeological Report (International Series 483).

Stanford, S. C. 1974. *Croft Ambrey.* Hereford: Adams and Sons.

Stansbie, D. and Laws, G. 2004. Prehistoric settlement and medieval to post medieval field systems at Latton Lands. *Wiltshire Archaeology and Natural History Magazine* 97, 106–43.

Stead, I. M. 1979. *The Arras Culture.* York: Yorkshire Philosophical Society.

——1984. Some notes on imported metalwork in Iron Age Britain. In S. Macready and F. H. Thompson (eds), 43–66.

——1985. *The Battersea Shield.* London: British Museum.

——1991a. *Iron Age Cemeteries in East Yorkshire.* London: English Heritage (Archaeological Report 22).

——1991b. The Snettisham Treasure: excavations in 1990. *Antiquity* 65, 447–65.

——1998. *The Salisbury Hoard.* Stroud: Tempus.

——2006. *British Iron Age: Swords and Scabbards.* London: British Museum Press.

——and Rigby, V. 1989. *Verulamium: The King Harry Lane Site.* London: English Heritage (Archaeological Report 12).

——and Turner, R. C. 1985. Lindow Man. *Antiquity* 59, 25–9.

——Bourke, J. B., and Brothwell, D. 1986. *Lindow Man: The Body in the Bog,* London: British Museum.

Stevens, C. J. 2003. An investigation of consumption and production models for prehistoric and Roman Britain. *Environmental Archaeology* 8, 61–76.

Stevens, S. 1997. Excavations at Potlands Farm, Patching, West Sussex. *Sussex Archaeological Collections* 135, 59–70.

Stewart, D. A. 2008. Hod Hill: 'Too much wasted by cultivation for definite survey'. *Proceedings of the Dorset Natural History and Archaeological Society* 129, 97–103.

Stone, J. F. S. 1936. An enclosure on Boscombe Down East. *Wiltshire Archaeological and Natural History Magazine* 47, 466–89.

——1937. A Late Bronze Age habitation site on Thorney Down, Winterbourne Gunner, S. Wilts. *Wiltshire Archaeological and Natural History Magazine* 57, 640–60.

Stone, J. F. S., Piggott, S., and Booth, A. 1954. Durrington Walls, Wiltshire: recent excavations at a ceremonial site of the early second millennium BC. *Antiquaries Journal* 34, 155–77.

Stopford, J. 1987. Danebury: an alternative view. *Scottish Archaeological Review* 4, 70–75.

Strathern, M. 1988. *The Gender of the Gift: Problems with Women and Problems with Society in Melanesia*. Berkeley: University of California Press.

Sunter, N. J. and Woodward, P. J. (eds) 1987. *Romano-British Industries in Purbeck*. Dorchester: Dorset Natural History and Archaeological Society (Monograph 6).

Taylor, R. 1993. *Hoards of the Bronze Age in Southern Britain: Analysis and Interpretation*. Oxford: British Archaeological Report (British Series 228).

—— 1991. Celtic art. *Scottish Archaeological Review* 8, 129–32.

Thomas, J. 1999. *Understanding the Neolithic*. London: Routledge.

—— 2001. Death, Identity and the Body in Neolithic Britain. *Journal of the Royal Anthropological Institute* 6, 653–68.

Thomas, N. 2005. *Snail Down, Wiltshire: The Bronze Age Cemetery and Related Earthworks, in the Parishes of Collingbourne Ducis and Collingbourne Kingston. Excavations 1953, 1955 and 1957*. Devizes: Wiltshire Archaeology and Natural History Society (Monograph 3).

Thomas, R. 1989. The bronze-iron transition in southern England. In Sørensen and Thomas (eds), 287–303.

—— 1997. Land, kinship relations and the rise of enclosed settlement in first millennium BC Britain. *Oxford Journal of Archaeology* 16.2, 211–18.

—— 1998. When land first became private property. *British Archaeology* 34, 8–9.

Thompson, M., Ellis, R., and Wildavsky, A. 1990. *Cultural Theory*. Boulder, CO: Westview Press.

Tilley, C. 2004. Round barrows and dykes as landscape metaphors. *Cambridge Archaeological Journal* 14.2, 185–203.

—— Hamilton, S., Harrison, S., and Anderson, E. 2000. Nature, culture, clitter: distinguishing between cultural and geomorphological landscapes: the case of Hilltop Tors in south-west England. *Journal of Material Culture* 5.2, 197–224.

Timberlake, S. 2003. *Excavations on Copa Hill, Cwmystwyth (1986–1999): An Early Bronze Age Copper Mine within the Uplands of Central Wales*. Oxford: British Archaeological Report (British Series 348).

Tingle, M. 1991. *The Vale of the White Horse Survey: The Study of a Changing Landscape in the Clay Lowlands of Southern England from Prehistory to the Present*. Oxford: British Archaeological Report (British Series 218).

Treherne, P. 1995. The warrior's beauty: the masculine body and self-identity in Bronze Age Europe. *Journal of European Archaeology* 3.1, 105–44.

Trigger, B. G. 1989. *A History of Archaeological Thought*. Cambridge: Cambridge University Press.

Tringham, R. 2005. Weaving house life and death into places: a blueprint for a hypermedia narrative. In D. Bailey, A. Whittle, and V. Cummings (eds) *(Un)Settling the Neolithic*. Oxford: Oxbow Books, 98–111.

Tullett, A. 2008. Black earth, bone and bits of old pot: the Pewsey middens. Recent work by the University of Sheffield. In O. Davis, N. Sharples, and K. Waddington (eds) *Changing Perspectives on the First Millennium BC*. Oxford: Oxbow Books, 11–20.

Tuohy, T. 1999. *Prehistoric Combs of Antler and Bone*. Oxford: British Archaeological Report (British Series 285).

Tylecote, R. F. 1986. *The Prehistory of Metallurgy in the British Isles*. London: Institute of Metals.

Valentin, J. 2003. Manor Farm, Portesham, Dorset: excavation on a multi-period religious and settlement site. *Proceedings of the Dorset Natural History and Archaeological Society* 125, 23–70.

van Arsdell, R. D. 1989. *Celtic Coinage of Britain*. London: Spink.

van der Veen, M. 1992. *Crop Husbandry Regimes: An Archaeobotanical Study of Farming in Northern England 1000 BC–AD 500*. Sheffield: J. R. Collis Publications.

van Gennep, A. 1909. *The Rites of Passage*. London: Routledge and Keegan Paul.

Verdon, M. 1998. *Rethinking Households: An Atomistic Perspective on European Living Arrangements*. London: Routledge.

Vince, A. 2003. Characterisation studies of Iron Age flint-tempered pottery in Hampshire. Unpublished: AVAC report 2003/68.

Waddell, J. and Shee Twohig, E. 1995. *Ireland in the Bronze Age*. Dublin: Stationery Office.

Waddington, K. 2009. Reassembling the Bronze Age: Exploring the Southern British Midden Sites. University of Cardiff: Unpublished PhD thesis.

—— and Sharples, N. M. 2007. Pins, pixies and thick dark earth. *British Archaeology* 95, 28–33.

Wainwright, G. J. 1968. The excavation of a Durotrigian farmstead near Tollard Royal in Cranborne, Southern England. *Proceedings of the Prehistoric Society* 34, 102–47.

—— 1969. The excavation of Balksbury Camp, Andover, Hampshire. *Proceedings of the Hampshire Field Club and Archaeological Society* 26, 21–56.

—— 1979a. *Gussage All Saints: An Iron Age settlement in Dorset*. London: Department of the Environment.

—— 1979b. *Mount Pleasant, Dorset: Excavations 1970–1971*. London: Society of Antiquaries of London.

—— 1989. *The Henge Monuments: Ceremony and Society in Prehistoric Britain*. London: Thames and Hudson.

—— and Davies, S. M. 1995. *Balksbury Camp, Hampshire: Excavations 1973 and 1981*. London: English Heritage (Archaeological Report 4).

—— and Longworth, I. H. 1971. *Durrington Walls: Excavations 1966–1968*. London: Society of Antiquaries of London.

—— and Smith, K. 1980. The Shaugh Moor Project: Second Report. *Proceedings of the Prehistoric Society* 46, 65–122.

—— Donaldson, P., Longworth, I., and Swan, V. 1971. The excavation of prehistoric and Romano-British settlements near Durrington Walls, Wiltshire, 1970. *Wiltshire Archaeology and Natural History Magazine* 66, 78–128.

Wainwright, G. J., Fleming, A., and Smith, K. 1979. The Shaugh Moor Project: First Report. *Proceedings of the Prehistoric Society* 45, 1–33.

Wait, G. 1985. *Ritual and Religion in Iron Age Britain.* Oxford: British Archaeological Report (British Series 149).

Walker, K. E. and Farwell, D. E. 2000. *Twyford Down, Hampshire Archaeological Investigations on the M3 Motorway from Bar End to Compton, 1990–93.* Gloucester: Hampshire Field Club (Monograph 9).

Warner, R. B. 2000. Keeping out the Otherworld: the internal ditch at Navan and other Iron Age 'Hengiform' enclosures. *Emania* 18, 39–44.

Waterman, D. M. 1997. *Excavations at Navan Fort 1961–71.* Belfast: Stationery Office.

Waterson, R. 1990. *The Living House.* Oxford: Oxford University Press.

Weaver, S. D. G. 2002. The excavation of Iron Age and Early Roman features at Viking Way, Andover, Hampshire, 1996. *Proceedings of the Hampshire Field Club and Archaeological Society* 57, 1–19.

Webley, L. 2007. Using and abandoning roundhouses: a reinterpretation of the evidence from Late Bronze Age–Early Iron Age southern England. *Oxford Journal of Archaeology* 26, 127–44.

Webster, D. B. 1991. *Hawkeseye: The Early Life of Christopher Hawkes.* Stroud: Alan Sutton.

Webster, J. and Cooper, N. 1996. (eds) *Roman Imperialism: Post-colonial Perspectives.* Leicester: Leicester University Press.

Weiner, A. B. 1992. *Inalienable Possessions: The Paradox of Keeping–While–Giving.* Berkeley: University of California Press.

Wellington, I. 2001. Iron Age coinage on the Isle of Wight. *Oxford Journal of Archaeology* 20, 39–57.

Wells, P. 1980. *Culture Contact and Culture Change: Early Iron Age Central Europe and the Mediterranean World.* Cambridge: Cambridge University Press.

Wells, P. S. 1995. Settlement and social systems at the end of the Iron Age. In B. Arnold and D. B. Gibson (eds) *Celtic Chiefdom, Celtic State: The Evolution of Complex Social Systems in Prehistoric Europe.* Cambridge: Cambridge University Press, 88–96.

Wessex Archaeology 2008. *The Putlake Adventure Farm, Dorset, Late Bronze Age Hoards: Archaeological Excavation of the Findspot.* Salisbury: Wessex Archaeology (Report 67990.02).

Wheeler, R. E. M. 1943. *Maiden Castle.* London: Society of Antiquaries of London.

—— 1949. Earthwork since Hadrian Allcroft. *Archaeological Journal* 106, 62–82.

—— 1953. An Early Iron Age 'beach-head' at Lulworth, Dorset. *Antiquaries Journal* 33, 1–13.

—— 1954a. *The Stanwick Fortifications.* London: Society of Antiquaries of London.

—— 1954b. *Archaeology from the Earth.* Oxford: Clarendon Press.

—— 1956. *Still Digging: Interleaves from an Antiquary's Notebook.* London: Readers Union.

—— and Richardson, K. M. 1957. *Hillforts of Northern France.* London: Society of Antiquaries of London.

Whimster, R. 1981. *Burial Practices in Iron Age Britain.* Oxford: British Archaeological Report (British Series 90).

White, D. A. 1982. *The Bronze Age Cremation Cemeteries at Simons Ground, Dorset.* Dorchester: Dorset Natural History and Archaeological Society (Monograph 3).

Whitley, M. 1943. Excavations at Chalbury Camp, Dorset, 1939. *Antiquaries Journal* 23, 98–121.

Whittle, A. 2003. *The Archaeology of People: Dimensions of Neolithic Life.* London: Routledge.

Wilkinson, K., Barber, L., and Bennell, M. 2002. The excavation of six dry valleys in the Brighton area: the changing environment. In D. Rudling (ed.), 203–38.

Williams, D. and Evans, J. G. 2000. Past environments in river valley bottoms around Danebury. In B. W. Cunliffe 2000, 39–43.

Williams, J. H. C. 2001. Coin inscriptions and the origin of writing in pre-Roman Britain. *British Numismatic Journal* 71, 1–17.

Williams, M. and Creighton, J. 2006. Shamanic practices and trance imagery in the Iron Age. In P. De Jersey (ed.), 49–59.

Williams, R. J. 1993. *Pennylands and Hartigans: Two Iron Age and Saxon Sites in Milton Keynes.* Aylesbury: Buckinghamshire Archaeological Society (Monograph 4).

—— and Zeepvat, R. J. 1994. *Bancroft: A Late Bronze Age/Iron Age Settlement, Roman Villa and Temple–Mausoleum.* Aylesbury: Buckinghamshire Archaeological Society (Monograph 7).

Williams-Freeman, J. P. 1915. *An Introduction to Field Archaeology as Illustrated by Hampshire.* London: Macmillan.

Wilson, A. 1940. Report on the excavations on Highdown Hill, Sussex, August 1939. *Sussex Archaeological Collections* 81, 173–203.

—— 1950. Excavations on Highdown Hill, 1947. *Sussex Archaeological Collections* 89, 163–78.

Wilson, B. 1992. Considerations for the identification of ritual deposits of animal bones in Iron Age pits. *International Journal of Osteoarchaeology* 2, 341–9.

—— 1999. Symbolic and ritual activity in depositing Iron Age animal bones. *Oxford Journal of Archaeology* 18, 297–305.

Wilson, C. 1981. Burials within settlements in Southern Britain during the Pre-Roman Iron Age. *Bulletin of the Institute of Archaeology at the University of London* 18, 127–69.

Winton, H. 2004. Possible Iron Age 'banjo' enclosures on the Lambourn Downs. *Oxoniensia* 67, 15–26.

Woodward, A. 1995. Vessel size and social identity in the Bronze Age of southern Britain. In I. Kinnes and G. Varndell (eds) *The Unbaked Urns of Rudely Shape. Essays on British and Irish Pottery for Ian Longworth.* Oxford: Oxbow Books, 195–202.

—— 1997. Size and style: an alternative study of some Iron Age pottery in southern England. In A. Gwilt and C. Haselgrove (eds), 26–35.

—— and Gardiner, J. (eds) 1998. *Wessex before Words: Some New Directions for Prehistoric Wessex.* Salisbury: Wessex Archaeology.

Woodward, A. and Hill, J. D. (eds) 2002. *Prehistoric Britain: The Ceramic Basis.* Oxford: Oxbow Books.

Woodward, P. J. 1987a. The excavation of a Late Iron Age settlement and Romano-British industrial site at Ower, Dorset. In N. J. Sunter and P. J. Woodward (eds), 44–124.

—— 1987b. The excavation of an Iron Age and Romano-British settlement at Rope Lake Hole, Corfe Castle, Dorset. In N. J. Sunter and P. J. Woodward (eds), 125–84.

—— 1991. *The South Dorset Ridgeway: Survey and Excavations 1977–84.* Dorchester: Dorset Natural History and Archaeological Society (Monograph 8).

—— 2002. A Late Neolithic/Early Bronze Age triple ring monument and a Late Bronze Age house near Chickerell. *Proceedings of the Dorset Natural History and Archaeological Society* 124, 109–10.

Woolf, G. 1993. Rethinking the Oppida. *Oxford Journal of Archaeology* 12.2, 223–34.

—— 2000. *Becoming Roman: The Origins of Provincial Roman Civilisation in Gaul.* Cambridge: Cambridge University Press.

Worrell, S. 2007. Detecting the Later Iron Age: a view from the Portable Antiquities Scheme. In C. Haselgrove and T. Moore (eds), 371–88.

Wylie, T. V. 1965. Mortuary customs at Sa-Skya, Tibet. *Harvard Journal of Asiatic Studies* 25, 229–42.

Yates, D. 1999. Bronze Age field systems in the Thames Valley. *Oxford Journal of Archaeology* 18, 157–70.

—— 2001. Bronze Age agricultural intensification in the Thames valley and estuary. In Brück (ed.), 65–82.

—— 2007. *Land, Power and Prestige: Bronze Age Field Systems in Southern England.* Oxford: Oxbow Books.

Index

Bold page numbers refer to illustrations